KOREAN STUDIES OF THE HENRY M. JACKSON
SCHOOL OF INTERNATIONAL STUDIES

Clark W. Sorensen, *Editor*

KOREAN STUDIES OF THE HENRY M. JACKSON
SCHOOL OF INTERNATIONAL STUDIES

Over the Mountains are Mountains: Korean Peasant Households and Their Adaptations to Rapid Industrialization by Clark W. Sorensen

Cultural Nationalism in Colonial Korea, 1920–1925 by Michael Edson Robinson

Offspring of Empire: The Koch'ang Kims and the Colonial Origins of Korean Capitalism, 1876–1945 by Carter J. Eckert

Confucian Statecraft and Korean Institutions: Yu Hyŏngwŏn and the Late Chosŏn Dynasty by James B. Palais

Peasant Protest and Social Change in Colonial Korea by Gi-Wook Shin

The Origins of the Chosŏn Dynasty by John B. Duncan

Protestantism and Politics in Korea by Chung-shin Park

Marginality and Subversion in Korea: The Hong Kyŏngnae Rebellion of 1812 by Sun Joo Kim

Building Ships, Building a Nation: Korea's Democratic Unionism under Park Chung Hee by Hwasook Nam

Japanese Assimilation Policies in Colonial Korea, 1910–1945 by Mark E. Caprio

JAPANESE ASSIMILATION POLICIES IN COLONIAL KOREA, 1910–1945

MARK E. CAPRIO

UNIVERSITY OF WASHINGTON PRESS   *Seattle & London*

This publication was supported in part by the Korea Studies Program of the University of Washington, in cooperation with the Henry M. Jackson School of International Studies.

UNIVERSITY OF WASHINGTON PRESS
P.O. Box 50096, Seattle, WA 98145 U.S.A.
www.washington.edu/uwpress

LIBRARY OF CONGRESS CATALOGING-IN-PUBLICATION DATA
Caprio, Mark E.
Japanese assimilation policies in colonial Korea, 1910–1945 / Mark E. Caprio. — 1st ed.
    p. cm. — (Korean studies of the Henry M. Jackson School of International Studies)
  Includes bibliographical references and index.
  ISBN 978-0-295-98900-6 (hardback : alk. paper)
  ISBN 978-0-295-98901-3 (pbk. : alk. paper)
  1. Japan—Foreign relations—Korea. 2. Korea—Foreign relations—Japan.
3. Japan—Colonies—Korea—History—20th century. 4. Korea—History—Japanese occupation, 1910–1945. 5. Koreans—Cultural assimilation—Korea—History—20th century. I. Title.
DS849.K6C37 2009   325'.3520519—dc22   2008056042

Unless otherwise noted, illustrations appeared in newspapers and magazines published during Japan's colonial rule over Korea.

CONTENTS

ACKNOWLEDGMENTS

I BEGAN RESEARCH FOR THIS PROJECT IN 1994, AS A DOCTORAL STUDENT at the University of Washington under the guidance of James Palais, who was always generous with his time, advice, and criticism. His influence is evident on every page of this manuscript. My biggest regret is not completing the book before he passed away in 2006. His legacy remains in the values of dedicated and honest scholarship that he instilled in his students through instruction and example. I humbly dedicate this volume to his memory.

I am also indebted to Clark Sorensen, who introduced me to important books that influenced the direction of this project and who offered invaluable comments in its later stages. I also thank Wilton Fowler, Kent Guy, and Kenneth Pyle for their helpful instruction and guidance. Lectures offered during my time at the University of Washington by George Beckman, Herbert Bix, Susan Hanley, Laurie Sears, and Kozo Yamamura helped formulate my ideas on Japanese and colonial history. Auditing a seminar conducted by Orlando Patterson at Harvard University introduced me to various issues of race relations in the United States.

I am grateful for assistance of various kinds from scholars in both Japan and South Korea, including Igarashi Akio, Aoki Atsuko, Frank Baldwin, Lim Chol, Kobayashi Hideo, Unno Fukuju, Kimura Kenji, Gotō Ken'ichi, Mizuno Naoki, Lee Jong-Chan, Kim Joong-Seop, Park Tae-Gyun, Yamada Shōji, Suh Sung, Arano Yasunori, Kono Yasunori, Sugita Yoneyuki, Ha Yong-Chool, and Koshiro Yukiko. Elsewhere, input from Lionel Babicz, Kristine Dennehy, Carter Eckert, Hyung Gu Lynn, Ann Heylan, Christine Kim, Reo Matsuzaki, Hyung Il Pai, Igor Saveliev, Jun Uchida, Dong Wonmo, and many others helped smooth the long and often bumpy path that this research project assumed over its duration. Mrs. Namhi Kim Wagner's recollections over lunch of her years in Japan in the early 1940s were especially enlightening. I am particularly indebted to Alexis Dudden, Sun Joo Kim, Mark Lincicome, Harry Wray, and two anonymous reviewers for comments on all or parts of the manuscript. It goes without saying that I take unqualified responsibility for any shortcomings in the final book.

My research was greatly enriched by the year I spent as a postgraduate fellow at Harvard University, with the generous support of the Korea Foundation. Librarians at the University of Washington, Harvard University, Rikkyo University, the Japanese National Diet Library, and the Arirang Center for Korean History and Culture were particularly helpful in directing me to useful sources. Feedback from participants who heard my presentations at the Korean History Research Group (Chōsenshi kenkyūkai) and the Japan Colonial Studies Group (Nihon shokuminchi kenkyūkai) in Tokyo, and the Korean Society for the History of Medicine (Taehan ŭisa hakhoe) in Seoul, the University of Washington's Institute for Korean Studies, Harvard University's Korea Institute, the University of Hawai'i's Center for Korean Studies, and the University of Wales-Aberystwyth often challenged my thinking on Japan's colonial experience in Korea in a positive way.

Throughout my studies, I have also benefited in more ways than I can possibly acknowledge from the friendship and companionship of friends and fellow students: Linda Angst, Barbara Brooks, Erin Chung, Patti Goedde, Hong Hang-gu, Yi Hyangjin, Han Jung-sun, Haruki Kazuhiro and his wife Ikumi, Mark McIntyre, Stephen Miles, Li Narangoa, John Sagers, David Satterwhite, Donald Smith, Dick Stegewerns, Julia Thomas, and Igarashi Yoshikuni. Family support on both sides of the Pacific Ocean has provided an indispensable inspiration that both encouraged the project's advancement and reminded me of its minor position within the broader picture of world phenomena. I am indebted to Michael Duckworth and Marilyn Trueblood at the University of Washington Press and to copyeditor Stacey Lynn for their assistance in bringing this project to fruition.

Lastly, it would be disingenuous for me to ignore the contribution that experiences gained at Northfield–Mt. Hermon School in north-central Massachusetts would eventually have on this research. It was here, while rooming with Daryl Floyd, that I was immersed in the kind of experience that I found lacking in Japanese-Korean relations during the period addressed in this study. I am forever indebted to the astute administrator who placed as roommates this future white historian and future black physical therapist. Since commencing this study, I have learned much from Daryl's thoughtful insight and input to my endless inquiries and half-baked thoughts regarding the assimilation of peoples of different background and culture.

JAPANESE ASSIMILATION POLICIES IN COLONIAL KOREA, 1910–1945

INTRODUCTION

COLONIAL ADMINISTRATION DECISIONS

A PROUD KOREAN FATHER BEGAN HIS BRIEF THREE-PAGE CONTRIBUTION to the March 1940 issue of *Chōsen* (Korea), a monthly journal published by the government-general, with the words "My eldest son has become a volunteer soldier."[1] His pride stemmed from more than just his son's enlistment. For he saw embedded within his son's success the success of his fellow Koreans, their imperial status having risen two years earlier when the Japanese government initiated legislation that allowed Korean boys the privilege of serving the empire as volunteer soldiers. To some Koreans, this reform demonstrated that the Japanese were finally taking a pivotal step toward matching their colonial policy rhetoric to assimilate Koreans with an appropriate action.[2]

Cho Pyŏngsang, who headed the Chongno civil defense bureau (*keibō-dan*) in Keijō (Kor. Kyŏngsŏng or Seoul) and sat on the government general's central advisory committee (*chūsūin sangi*), repeatedly emphasized two points in his essay. First he emphasized that he had offered (*susumeta*) his eldest son to the Japanese military. By his sacrifice Cho demonstrated his liberation from Korea's traditional lineage-centered society. It was unnecessary to explain the significance of this act in detail: the Confucian heritage that his Japanese and Korean readers shared allowed both peoples to grasp the magnitude of this sacrifice simply by his repeating the words "eldest son." From the time of annexation, Japanese had used this shared heritage to argue the ease with which they could assimilate Koreans.

Cho also believed that by publicizing his son's accomplishment, Japanese readers would understand this sacrifice as part of a wider trend among the Korean people: their acceptance of the modern (national/imperial) over the traditional (familial/lineage). Rather than as the exception, he hoped that the Japanese would recognize his sacrifice as increasingly the rule among Koreans. Changes in this direction, Cho explained, began at the time of annexation. Although not recognized by all Koreans at the time, Japan's incorporation of the Korean Peninsula in 1910 rescued the country from the "lonely" (*sabishii*) direction in which it was heading. Annexation had also divided the Korean people into three groups: pro-Japanese (*shin-Nichiha*) Koreans, who trusted the Japanese pledge to make them "real Japanese" (*hontō no Nihonjin*); anti-Japanese (*hai-Nichiha*) Koreans, who believed that Korea's salvation could be realized only by seeking independence through ethnic self-determination (*minzoku jiketsu*); and Koreans who waffled in a gray zone (*haiiro sonzai*) between these extreme views.[3] Since the September 1931 Manchurian Incident, Cho claimed, public sentiment had shifted in Japan's favor. Many anti-Japanese Koreans had joined the middle, neutral, group; and members of this neutral contingent had shifted their sentiment toward the pro-Japanese group. The July 1937 Marco Polo Bridge Incident further accelerated this trend. Clearly evident in these developments, Cho emphasized, was a greater willingness by the Korean people to marry their national sentiments with Japan's imperial mission.

This conclusion led to Cho's second point—the need for Japanese to acknowledge Korean support for this mission. The Korean people's "real aspiration" (*shin no yōkyū*), he revealed, was to become true Japanese. That is, they anticipated that eventually the peninsular people (*hantōmin*) and the heartland people (*Naichijin*) would form equal subsets of a greater Japanese people (*Nihonjin*). Again, Cho believed that his aspiration was more than simply that of an individual Korean, but rather was one that reflected the "voice of the entire Korean people" (*hantōmin zenbu no koe*). The Japanese government, by permitting Korea's youth to protect the empire, had taken one important step toward the "embodiment of *Naisen ittai*" (literally, Japan-Korea, one body). Cho's challenge to the Japanese was subtle but clear: the Korean people were doing their part, but were the Japanese ready to recognize Koreans as their equal? This conclusion also suggested Cho's support for Korean assimilation to be contingent on the policy's application over a broader context than simply Japanese absorbing Koreans. Rather, he envisioned the assimilation of both peoples into a larger Korea-Japan union. Japan's Korea administration, he reminded his readers, aimed to realize coexistence and co-prosperity for both peoples, to "fulfill the potential for Japan and Korea becoming one body."[4]

Other Korean supporters of Japan's assimilation policy explored a similar concern. Like Cho, they welcomed the Japanese decision to accept Koreans into their military as a positive sign. Yun Ch'iho, a leader in Korea's late
nineteenth-century reform movements, actively worked to engage Koreans
in Japan's wartime policies. He recruited Korean boys for the Japanese military; he participated in their send-off ceremonies; and he welcomed home
those who survived the battlefront.[5] Sŏ Ch'un, who had helped organize the
February 1919 Korean independence demonstration in Tokyo before joining
the staff of the Japan-owned newspaper *Maeil sinbo* (Daily Times), was also
encouraged by Japan's decision to enlist Koreans into its military. In 1942,
he wrote of the "emotional inspiration" (*kangeki*) that Koreans felt upon
hearing of Japan's plans to finally include Korea's youth in the empire's universal military conscription.[6]

Both men echoed Cho's concern over whether the Japanese shared this
enthusiasm. Did the colonizers recognize the sacrifices and gains that the
Korean people had made since annexation? Yun Ch'iho addressed this concern at the plush Chōsen Hotel, where in July 1939 he participated in a
roundtable discussion on the topic of *Naisen ittai*. His July 3, 1939, diary
entry summarized his advice to the colonizers: Japan must end its discrimination policy but Koreans must work to earn the privilege of Japanese
respect. His advice hinted that the Japanese might prove incapable of
rewarding deserving Koreans with positions of responsibility: Though Koreans as a whole do not have a "high sense of responsibility and of public
morality . . . when [an individual] Korean is found who comes up to the standard of efficiency of the Japanese no discrimination should be shown in his
treatment."[7] Sŏ Ch'un, who believed that all Koreans—to varying degrees—
were "soldiers of the emperor," urged Koreans to prove themselves to be
elite troops (*seihei*) indistinguishable from their Japanese counterparts in
their "divine work" (*seigyō*), the formation of the Great East Asian Co-
Prosperity Sphere.[8]

This challenge to the Japanese—to back their lofty promises to assimilate
Koreans with appropriate policy—represented a minority, but for this study
a critical, response to Japanese rule. The majority of Koreans did not share
Cho's "voice," nor did they consider themselves to be imperial soldiers in
any shape or form. While the Manchurian Incident clearly had a positive
impact on the Japanese-Korean relationship, many continued to answer
Japan's calls to assimilate with passive or active resistance to its policies and
its presence. As objects of the policy, the Korean voice—both the critical and

the supportive—provides an important dimension to our understanding and evaluation of Japanese assimilation policy in Korea.

This study examines assimilation in a broad historical context to ascertain the position that Japanese envisioned Koreans assuming in their empire. It first examines Western colonial examples to understand the global political situation of these times, and to determine the extent that these examples influenced Japan's colonial decisions. In this latter context it considers the following: how Japanese thinking toward assimilation evolved over its three decades of rule in Korea; what measures the Japanese took to instruct the people of the merits of accepting Japanese language, culture, and society; how the Japanese measured success; and finally, how the objects of this policy, the Korean people, reacted to Japanese assimilation overtures. Cho, Yun, and Sŏ all pointed to Korean military participation as a sign of Japan's willingness to match its assimilation rhetoric with appropriate practice. Did the Japanese administration offer any other hope or reason—besides dispatching Korean boys to fight in a reckless war—to encourage their confidence?

INTERNAL, PERIPHERAL, AND EXTERNAL COLONIAL EXPANSION

One of the most important choices that Japan had to make upon annexing new territory was the administration under which it would govern its new subjects. At this time colonial scholars and officials generally summarized a colonial power's choice as one between French-style direct rule (assimilation) and British-style indirect rule (association). This distinction suggests the decision as a national preference. More accurately, it was based on the colonizer-colonized relationship. Colonizers, including the French and British, based their administrative decisions on their geographical and racial proximity to the people they colonized.

In question here is our image of "colonized." Specifically, what constitutes "colonized" territory? Which people were "colonized"? A scan of colonial historiography suggests answers to these questions are very much determined by contemporary geopolitics: liberated states were colonized; incorporated regions were not. Territories that remain a part of another state are generally excluded from this discussion. In the context of British historiography, liberated India and Burma were colonized; Wales and Scotland were not.[9] In Japan's case, Korea and Taiwan were colonized; Okinawa and Hokkaido were not. Another factor concerns our traditional images of "colonized" as peoples of different races and cultures from their subjugators. Bruce Cumings, for example, noted Japan's colonization of Korea as unique in its subjugation of a racially and culturally similar people.[10] The Japanese repeatedly listed their similarities with Koreans as the primary reason why they could integrate (rather than colonize) Koreans.

The rhetoric employed by assimilation practitioners suggests a need for a more nuanced definition of "colonized." In theory, assimilation advanced the idea that the colonizer and the colonized would, in time, stand shoulder-to-shoulder as members of equal standing in an extended nation-state. The French were exceptional in imagining black representatives of its African empire joining white representatives from French provinces in its national assembly. Their practices drew criticism from social Darwinists who argued that "inferior" races could not be uplifted to civilization. Most other practitioners limited their employment of assimilation to territories of racially similar peoples adjacent to the colonial center. Their rhetoric informed the colonized of their potential to assume a status equal to that of the colonizer should they adopt his customs, language, and polity. In this sense the purpose driving assimilation policy resembled that of nation building: the dissemination of common cultural and political systems among the state's constituents. We shall argue the distinction between these two as one of degree and practice, rather than of kind.

A number of studies have identified colonialism at multiple levels to distinguish expansion across contiguous, or near contiguous, lands. This breaks from the more traditional impression of colonialism as overseas land grabbing, and offers an expanded concept of "colonized." Hannah Arendt introduced "continental imperialism"—a "cohesive expansion [that] does not allow for any geographic distance between the methods and institutions of colony and of nation"—to distinguish "pan-movements" from the more traditional "overseas imperialism."[11] Michael Hechter, examining Celtic assimilation into the United Kingdom, similarly uses "internal" and "external" colonialism to question why the internally colonized Welsh, Scots, and Irish retained a separate identity from the Anglican English.[12] Harold Wolpe's "internal" (versus "normal") colonialism considers cases "internal to a particular society," including those of Arab-Israelis, black Americans, and black South Africans.[13]

Wolpe's "internal" colonization further extends our definition by considering as colonized culturally subjugated minorities residing within state borders. Foreign residence thus is not prerequisite for a people to be considered "colonized." Others have advanced this definition to consider nation building itself as colonial. Partha Chatterjee suggested this similarity when he questioned whether it served "any useful analytical purpose to make a distinction between the colonial state and the forms of the modern state."[14] Ernest Geller's definition of nationalism as the subjugation of "low" cultures by the hegemonic "high" culture suggests colonial activity.

> Nationalism is, essentially, the general imposition of a high culture on society, whose previously low cultures had taken up the lives of the majority, and in some cases of the totality, of the population. It means that generalized diffusion of a school-mediated, academy-supervised idiom, codified for the requirements of reasonably precise bureaucratic and technological communication. It is the establishment of an anonymous, impersonal society, with mutually substitutable atomized individuals, held together above all by a shared culture of this kind, in place of a previous complex structure of local groups, sustained by folk cultures reproduced locally and idiosyncratically by the micro-groups themselves. That is what *really* happens.[15]

"Nationalism" quickly became "colonialism" when this "imposition" was forced upon a foreign people. There is a distinction to be made between the two concepts, but it is not one of kind. The process of, in Benedict Anderson's words, "inventing nations" involved determining the ethnic groups that would be admitted to the "image of [the nation's] communion."[16] New imperial acquisitions thus required renewed considerations as to how this territory fit into the empire. The most basic decision involved whether the territory would be governed under indirect association or direct assimilation. Peoples residing at the nation-state's peripheries—those either physically separated or socially marginalized—were prevented from immediately entering the internal community; they were conditionally offered membership contingent upon their advancement in civilization. This distinction points to a major consideration of this study—the factors that determined a people's place in the empire. Through assimilation, could a foreign people become nationalized citizens? If so, what factors influenced their status change? To what extent could the object of this policy, the colonized, influence their imperial status?[17]

The decision to colonize, as well as the administration to administer the colonized, was based primarily on the needs and interests of the colonizer subject; those of the colonized object received minimal consideration. Colonizers generally chose among three broad levels of administration that ranged from the rather relaxed external colonization to the exhaustive internal colonization; peripheral colonialism occupied a middle position. Colonizers introduced external colonization, which corresponded with Arendt's overseas imperialism and Hechter's external colonialism, in distant territories where their indirect policy exerted minimal effort to forge political, social, or cultural bonds with the peoples under their jurisdiction.[18] Employed to administer a population geographically and racially different from the homeland, the colonizers claimed few (if any) cultural affiliations with these peoples. Rather than change them, the colonizers "grew to love their absurd . . . ways."[19] Their "mission" to civilize these peoples fortified their myths of superiority that justified their colonial subjugation over the people. The colonizers exploited the land for its resources and the people for their labor with minimal human or capital investment. External colonialism's primary ambition was economic; security concerns arose when the colony's location contributed to the security of the colonial power's other territorial possessions.[20]

External colonization's antithesis—internal colonization: the intense assimilation of the people as nationals, in other words nation building—provided colonizers with a second option.[21] With a primary goal of securing a people's political allegiance, the core colonial agent assumed control over the mechanisms required to disseminate a hegemonic culture among its constituents. It determined the dialect that would function as the nation's national language; it guided nation-building institutions such as education, the media, and the military to instruct the people of their membership, and to guide their participation, in the nation; and it established national events and icons (holidays, flags, currency, and songs) to remind its constituents of their new allegiance. Successful internal colonization was contingent on the newly formed state's ability to dismantle local political, social, and cultural barriers that political bodies had traditionally maintained. Administrative caretakers who failed to assimilate its people as national subjects faced charges of incompetence and accusations of "inept government," a shortcoming that colonial powers exploited to justify their intervention in the territory.

The high level of integration that internal colonization required, and the strong geographical and historical ties it assumed among its constituents, rendered the approach inappropriate for peoples residing at the periphery of the internal colony. Yet, the close proximity of these peoples required that bonds be established to secure their allegiance and loyalty. The images established to justify the people's colonization— cultural difference rather than geographical or historical affinity—assumed a vertical relationship that precluded their incorporation as internal subjects. Peripheral colonization— Arendt's continental imperialism and Hechter's internal colonialism—thus served as an intermediate stage that dangled before the colonized the promise of their assimilation as internal citizens, but invariably introduced policy that compromised this vision.[22] Assimilation thus served as a rhetorical goal rather than a political assumption. The heavy intrusion into the people's lives reflected the peripheral territory's most important responsibility: as a strategic buffer to protect the colonial center from regional rivals.

A number of factors influenced the expansionists' choice of administration policy. Their perceptions of the colonized people(s) played an important role in their decision. These perceptions determined the degree to which the colonized peoples would be integrated as full members in the state's nation-building institutions. The geographic proximity of the territory to the homeland was an important, but inconclusive, factor. Many of the examples cited as "internal" in the colonial literature are considered as "peripheral" or even "external" in this framework. Black and Native American residents in the United States, for example, were institutionally excluded from institutions that welcomed white U.S. citizens unconditionally. In contrast, colonizing agents in external colonies generally co-opted a selection of indigenous elite by offering them an education equal to (and often exceeding) that of the colonizers' children, ostensibly to train them to act as intermediaries between colonized and colonizers.

One important distinction between the internal and the peripheral colonizer was the syntactical position in which its rhetoric placed its colonized object. Internal colonial administrations persuaded their constituents to accept their roles as national subjects by socializing them in the behavioral and ideological tenets of the hegemonic polity and culture: as national subjects they were expected to act in determined ways. Peripheral colonial administrations, on the other hand, defined the colonized as the object to be changed: as inferior peoples they had to be prepared for their acceptance as national subjects. Assimilation was the civilizing process in both cases, but it was more strongly articulated in the peripheral case than in the internal case. Assimilation assumed an inferior people being integrated into a more civilized cultural body, rather than, as in the case of the internal subject, into a body to which they theoretically already belonged. The articulated goal to assimilate Koreans as Japanese made rhetorical sense; one aiming to assimilate Japanese as Japanese was nonsensical.

This distinction manifested in practice, particularly in the different education policies that colonizing powers advanced to internal, peripheral, and external subjects. Education policy is an appropriate example for two reasons. The conditions under which the colonizers accepted the colonized into their schools reveal the images they held of the people at the time, as well as the vision they held of the people's future. Limiting a people to an inferior education (or no formal education at all) dramatically increased the probability that they would occupy an inferior social position in the future. Internal colonizing powers defined their education goal as universal and compulsory: all citizens would be admitted to schools just as soon as the state constructed the schoolhouses to educate children and extended the infrastructure needed to transport them there. Colonizers at the peripheral level encouraged education participation but generally did not make school attendance compulsory. They generally offered the colonized people—who were deemed unfit to join the internal subject in the classroom—a noncompulsory education inferior in duration and resources and available to fewer people. The operative word here is *intention*. Both situations initially lacked the required resources to extend to the entire population a modern education. Yet, internal colonizers declared their intention to extend compulsory education to the entire population. Peripheral colonizers may have vowed to increase education facilities but stopped short of declaring their intention to make attendance mandatory.

In addition to segregated educational systems, the colonizers devised other ways to maintain distinctions between internal and peripheral subjects. The status of the territory in relation to the homeland determined the legal codes under which it was to be governed. It also determined the form and extent to which the subjects could participate in political institutions. Peripheral and external colonial cities mirrored the colonial relationship, as internal subjects occupied their particular section of the city to protect themselves from the disturbing textures and smells of native districts. Both colonizers and colonized who passed through each other's zones described these excursions as foreign adventures, as if they were crossing a national border or entering a living museum. Descriptions left by colonizers of the filth and smell contributed to the mosaic of images arranged to advertise the colonized peoples as incapable of managing their immediate surroundings, much less their sovereignty.

The images that the colonizers drew of their colonized peoples contained stereotypes that displayed remarkable resilience across space and time. These images, as Edward Said notes, formed a "style of thought based upon an ontological and epistemological distinction"[23] to separate colonizer from colonized. The subjugating agent painted the colonized as victims of inept government that failed to disseminate to them the customs and mannerisms required of a civilized people. Their antiquated living environment reflected their inferior "habitus," in Pierre Bourdieu's thinking "a set of schemas or dispositions, acquired through the process of socialization."[24] In the minds of colonizers, the inferior habitus of the colonized was reflected in the inferiority of their clothing, their cuisine, their social and work ethics, and even their language. The first task of the colonizing agents was to determine how to deal with these differences: internal colonial policy dismantled cultural barriers to create a unified culture across a diverse array of peoples; external administrations sustained colonizer-colonized distinctions by encouraging the colonized to maintain their traditional institutions; and peripheral colonial agents strengthened walls of division while preaching colonizer-colonized integration.

To this point we have focused attention on decisions made by the colonizers, and devoted little attention to the colonized. This unfortunately reflects the reality of the colonial situation: colonizers made decisions regarding colonial administrations with little, if any, direct input from the colonized people, whose most important contribution came in their responses to these decisions. Responses by the colonized were complex and are worthy of independent inquiry. Many accepted their assimilation as inevitable and, in the words of Franz Fanon, "married white culture, white beauty, white whiteness."[25] Others challenged the subjugation of their homeland with nationalist rhetoric and physical rebellion. Both reactions gripped the population simultaneously, prompting the people to reconsider their identity in larger national terms. Colonizers exploited the diversity of responses to their rule that divided and weakened the colonized people's social fabric and thus their ability to formulate a unified challenge to colonial rule. The potential sway that these factions held over the noncommitted both encouraged and discouraged policy decisions that colonial administrators made.

JAPANESE EXPANSION AND ASSIMILATION

Japanese historiography generally dates Japan's baptism into colonial expansion with its 1895 acquisition of Taiwan, as part of Japan's peace settlement to conclude the Sino-Japanese War. Defining Japan as a latecomer to colonial expansion strengthens images of Tokugawa-era "isolation" (*sakoku*) and the Meiji rise to power in 1868 as a "restoration" (*ishin*). The Tokugawa era (1603–1868) is most often depicted as a regime that enforced a strict isolation policy to protect the islands from a global community embarking on colonial expansion. It would follow that Japan at this time would have little interest in expanding its borders. Thus, Japanese expansion is generally seen as a late Meiji initiative, one that the government embarked upon after it had advanced its domestic nationalizing agenda. This interpretation also draws from the narrow vision of "colonized" discussed above.

Arano Yasunori and Ronald Toby independently have challenged the image of an isolated Tokugawa Japan. They argue, first, that the Tokugawa *bakufu* never initiated an "isolation policy" (*sakoku seisaku*), but actively participated in a rather extensive network of foreign trade and diplomacy.[26] On a number of occasions the Tokugawa, or individual domains, reached beyond its internal control to exert its influence on peripheral territories, namely northern Ryukyu and Ezo.[27] The Tokugawa never incorporated these territories as formal colonies; they better served its interests as sovereign territories, even if but as a fiction. In this sense the Tokugawa administration is more accurately rendered as a cautious and xenophobic polity that often demonstrated knowledge of colonial expansion, and occasionally interest in foreign intervention, to protect its local interests. Meiji Japan continued this process by officially incorporating these peripheral territories into Japan proper.

That Meiji Japan (1868–1912) may have continued Tokugawa practices challenges the idea of the 1868 "coup" as a "restoration" of ancient practices. Some have argued this process as a revolutionary advancement.[28] At the domestic level it adopted institutions built upon a new social, political, and economic foundation to forge within its internal subjects a sense of membership in a new (Japanese) ethos.[29] At the diplomatic level it immediately sought to expand Japan's borders to strengthen its security. The imperial institution served as the Meiji Restoration's symbolic center; colonial expansion—both internal and peripheral—propelled this process. By the end of this period Japan had completed the initial phase of this process, and was prepared to embark on further expansion.[30] The majority of its children had been enrolled in schools; its military had defeated two formidable enemies; and it had surrounded the archipelago with peripheral acquisitions now firmly under its control—Okinawa and Taiwan to the south and Korea,

Hokkaido and southern Karafuto (Sakhalin). Its greatest threats lay beyond these annexed territories, threats that trained a vigilant eye upon Japan lest it encroach upon their Asian interests. Japanese leaders confirmed assimilation as their colonial administrative policy soon after Japan annexed Taiwan in 1895. However, Japan had been practicing various forms of assimilation since the Tokugawa *bakufu* briefly took control of Ezo in the late eighteenth century. It practiced a more intrusive form of internal assimilation from the start of the Meiji period by spreading a unified Japanese dialect and culture to the corners of the Japanese archipelago. Meiji officials adapted these practices to integrate the peoples of the Ryukyu Islands and Ezo, but with less intensity.

Korean scholars, who have long argued Japanese expansion as a major platform of Japan's Meiji Restoration, will welcome this interpretation.[31] The Meiji government began showing an aggressive posture toward Korea soon after its inception. In 1875–76, Japan mimicked the United States' "gunboat diplomacy" to force the Korean government to sign the Kanghwa Treaty, the first of a series of treaties that over the next few decades increasingly compromised Korea's sovereignty. Koreans who participated in the 1881 "gentry-officials touring group" (*sinsa yuramdan*) recognized Japan's efforts in Okinawa and Hokkaido as colonial expansion and raised the concern that Japanese expansionists might eventually turn to Korea.[32] Japanese continued to press an important ambition of the Kanghwa Treaty—freeing Korea from Chinese influence by "protecting" Korean independence. Fukuzawa Yukichi, who dubbed Japan Korea's "teacher of civilization" (*bunmei no kyōshi*), explained that as Korea's doctor, Japan must inquire over every aspect of the patient's life and prescribe the proper medicine to strengthen Korea's independence.[33] Ōi Kentarō, of Japan's Liberal Party (*jiyūtō*), on trial for trying to raise funds and enlist men to aid Kim Okkyun's failed 1884 Kapsin coup ("Osaka incident" [*Osaka jiken*]), summarized Japan's responsibility to maintain Korean independence through pan-Asianism that the Liberal Party pushed: it must preserve Korea's "national independence" at the expense of its "state independence," which was a concern "to the whole Orient."[34]

Reform efforts initiated by different parties in Korea from the 1880s showed promise until squelched by either the Korean government or foreign elements. From the early 1880s the Korean government negotiated treaties with several Western governments, sponsored overseas study tours, and dispatched Koreans abroad for overseas studies. These efforts were interrupted by a Chinese initiative to reestablish its traditional ties with Korea under a modern guise. Kim and Kim write that the Chinese Resident, Yüan Shih-k'ai, arrived in 1885 to assume a role that more accurately resembled a "Chinese viceroy." His presence stifled efforts to, in Young Ick Lew's words, "put the 'hermit kingdom' on the road to full-fledged membership in the family of nations while enriching and strengthening the country sufficiently to maintain her independence."[35] More recently, Kirk W. Larsen, considering the Chinese role in connecting Korea to modern institutions, has argued their efforts in Korea at this time to have been "more ambiguous and complex" than previously acknowledged.[36]

China's defeat in the Sino-Japanese War encouraged a second series of modernizing efforts by reform groups and the central government. Foreign observers gave Korea mixed appraisals for its advances. The journalist Angus Hamilton, noting Seoul's infrastructural improvements, wrote in 1904 "the old order is given way to the new. So quickly has the population learned to appreciate the results of foreign intercourse that, in a few more years, it will be difficult to find in Seoul any remaining link with the capital of yore."[37] That same year, however, U.S. representative Horace Allen wrote to William Rockhill, President Theodore Roosevelt's "unofficial East Asian advisor," as follows: "These people . . . cannot govern themselves. They must have an over-lord as they have had for all time. When it was not China, it was Russia or Japan, and as soon as they [come] out from one they make such an awful mess of things as to oblige someone else to take charge of them. . . . Let Japan have Korea outright."[38] The more important question thus became not whether Korea could reform, but whether the international community would recognize its efforts to do so. Comments from foreign observers do not, of course, tell us the complete story of Korea's pre-annexation conditions. However, their impressions cannot be ignored given the considerable influence that global powers exercised over Japan at this time. When Japan, citing "Korea [as] the source of all dangers in the Extreme East,"[39] moved to annex the peninsula it encountered few foreign voices of dissent.

Scholars of late Chosŏn Korea history remain equally undecided in their evaluation of this period. A number of studies focus on the weaknesses in Korea's reform efforts. James B. Palais, whose research focuses on the contribution of the Taewŏngun (1866–73), maintains that Korea's "traditional system was incapable of allowing a major shift . . . toward strong central and monarchical leadership."[40] Martina Deuchler, examining reform efforts following the 1876 Kanghwa Treaty that Japan forced upon Korea, criticizes the reformers' reluctance to break from the traditional Confucian system.[41]

Shin Yong-ha and Vipan Chandra, examining the Independence Club reform movement (1896–98), both argue that the club's success required revolutionary action. Chandra suggests that the movement's leaders were ill equipped to succeed at such an effort.[42] Yi T'aejin, however, focuses on the regime's strengths in portraying Kojong as a capable monarch whose efforts to reform Korean institutions were blocked by foreign intervention, first by the Chinese and later by the Japanese. Yi claims that Korea's capacity to modernize, rather than its stagnation, motivated Japan's efforts to annex the peninsula.[43]

This study stops short of arguing that Meiji Japan followed a blueprint to absorb the Korean Peninsula. Yet, Japanese were well aware of the important role that colonial expansion occupied in their quest to develop a "rich country strong military" (*fukkoku kyōhei*).[44] Korea's location was to Japan both strategically critical and tantalizingly convenient. This in and of itself does not justify Japan's annexation of the peninsula. However, the foreign threats felt by both Korea and Japan, the support that Japan received from other foreign powers for its actions in Korea (mainly to protect their own Asian interests), and the strategically critical location of the Korean Peninsula completed an equation that made Japan's annexation of Korea the most predictable scenario.

Japanese discussion on assimilation, often incorrectly associated with Japan's wartime imperialization (*kōminka*) policies, preceded Korean annexation. Japanese debated the policy's merits and demerits in 1895 after Taiwan was absorbed into the empire; discussion in 1910 considered the pace and direction to which the colonial administration would push Korean assimilation. Japan's "uniqueness" as a colonial power was in its attempts to assimilate an ethnically similar people amid the unbridled land grabbing that characterized the period that Eric Hobsbawm famously dubbed the "Age of Empire" (1875–1914).[45] Yet, Japanese were inspired by British, Prussian, and French efforts in their peripheral territories, rather than these states' efforts in their external possessions. A survey of Meiji-era discourse on assimilation policy reveals Japan's views of "colonized" to consist of a rather broad set of examples, with the English formation of the United Kingdom, the French annexation of Algeria, and the Prussian incorporation of Alsace and Lorraine serving as the most popular examples. The Japanese recognized assimilation to be the governing policy in territories such as Scotland and Wales, territories generally not treated in the contemporary literature as "colonies." They revised pre-annexation images that saw Koreans as foreign to argue that the similarities shared by the two peoples made assimilation more appropriate in Korea than in other European situations.[46] Such discussions were required to address the more difficult question of whether assimilation was indeed the most appropriate policy for the Korean situation. Japanese assumed that their culture was superior, but did this justify their security needs requiring Koreans to undergo such drastic cultural revision? Did viable alternatives exist to total assimilation?

The components of Japan's administration in Korea have received substantial consideration in colonial historiography.[47] Yet, little research has been conducted to analyze and evaluate Japanese assimilation as a policy in Korea. This study seeks to fill this gap in a number of ways. It first considers the question of assimilation's place in modern colonial history by examining European and American examples.[48] The Japanese used these examples as models, as well as to legitimize their own decision to adopt this policy. They also used these examples as benchmarks to measure their own success. Considering other assimilation examples provides criteria by which we can evaluate Japan's application of this policy. By defining Japanese colonialism in global terms we can see this history as a complex instance of multiple narratives, rather than the simple narrative of Japanese aggressors and Korean victims.[49]

This study also traces the process of Japan choosing assimilation as its colonial policy, and the lessons it learned from its earlier acquisitions.[50] The precarious position that Japan held in the global community through much of its prewar history greatly influenced its Korean policy. Japan expanded with one aggressive eye fixed on the desired territory, but another cautious eye focused on Western reactions.[51] But Japan was a rather experienced colonizer by the time it prepared to annex Korea. The lessons it learned from its previous colonial experiments in internal and peripheral settings potentially influenced its policy decisions in Korea and thus are worth reviewing.

A third dimension of this study traces policy evolution in Korea—how Japan's assimilation policy developed over its thirty-six-year occupation of the Korean Peninsula.[52] Japanese envisioned their policy as a gradual process. They argued that Koreans would require decades, and possibly as long as a century, of guidance before they could shed their traditional culture to absorb Japanese culture. This attitude continued into the 1930s, when the urgency of the wartime situation on the Asian continent forced the government-general to radically accelerate this process. Throughout the duration, the Japanese government used education and the media to instruct Koreans on their new status as Japanese subjects. Beyond this rhetoric,

Japan's most important task was to dismantle the walls that separated colo-nized from colonizer to encourage Japanese to accept Koreans as their fellow imperial subjects.

Success here required that both peoples shed the disparaging images they traditionally held toward each other. These images, evident during Japan's Tokugawa era, intensified in concert with Japan's intrusion upon Korean sovereignty.[53] Annexation forced Japanese to soften these images to accom-modate their assimilation rhetoric. The images remained negative, but Japa-nese interjected the hope that with good (Japanese) administration, the people could be guided to a higher level of civilization. They saw Koreans as in need of help, but not helpless. Could the Japanese imagine the Korean people one day assuming a partnership role in Japan's imagined Asian com-munity? Or did they believe the Koreans would always remain the inferior people? Many Korean supporters of Japanese policy assumed the former to be the goal of assimilation. Japanese rhetoric suggested as much. But its pol-icy suggested the latter. Japan's success depended on whether it could square its rhetorical goals with its policy decisions.

The important critics of Japanese assimilation were the Korean people. Until recently, most research from the Korean perspective has trumpeted their heroic and determined resistance to Japan's harsh colonial administra-tion. Korean patriotic resistance was noble; it is also a well-documented com-ponent of this history. It does not, however, add to our understanding of Korean views of assimilation beyond the predictable fact that many Koreans vehemently opposed this policy. Groups that believed Koreans unprepared to accept national sovereignty—Japan's Korean supporters and Koreans who favored gradual self-strengthening reforms—at this time provided more insightful critiques of Japanese ambitions in their discussions on Korea's future. Many of these Koreans believed that Japan's modernizing experi-ences could prove useful.[54] The question that separated them was Korean identity: would their learning from Japan assist in their self-strengthening as Koreans or their integration as assimilated Japanese? Both groups criticized Japanese arrogance toward Koreans. They agreed that no advancement could be made unless Japanese recognized Koreans as their equals. Japan's most ardent Korean supporters advised the Japanese to offer a policy that matched Japan's assimilation rhetoric. Statements by Koreans such as Cho Pyŏngsang argued that Japan had made progress, and suggested their confidence that this progress would continue. Our inquiry examines Japanese assimilation policy in a search for evidence that justifies their confidence.

1

WESTERN ASSIMILATION PRACTICES

THE FOUR DECADES LEADING UP TO WORLD WAR I REPRESENT A NEW FORM of colonial expansion that saw a small number of global powers partition and claim "most of the world outside Europe and the Americas." Eric Hobsbawm calls this partition

> the most spectacular expression of that growing division of the globe into the strong and the weak, the "advanced" and the "backward.". . . It was also strikingly new. Between 1876 and 1915 about one-quarter of the globe's land surface was distributed or redistributed as colonies among a half-dozen states. Britain increased its territories by some 4 million square miles, France by some 3.5 millions, Germany acquired more than 1 million, Belgium and Italy just under 1 million each. The USA acquired some 100,000. . . . Japan something like the same amount.[1]

Japanese participants on the Iwakura Mission that left Japan in late 1871 on a world tour were well aware of the extent of European expansion at the time. The tour's official historian, Kume Kunitake, noted in his introduction to Great Britain that the British Empire, at 8.7 million square miles, was "seventy-five or six times bigger than Japan," and that it subjugated 243 million people.[2] By contrast, the French Empire at the time totaled only 350,000 square miles and 3.6 million people.[3] By the time Japan acquired Taiwan in 1895, the British Empire would assume control over 23 percent of the earth's land surface, an empire that dwarfed its French rival, which claimed but 9.3 percent.[4]

This sudden increase in colonial expansion is directly related to the increase in nation-building activity at the time. Hobsbawm calculates that over this period, the number of heads of state who considered themselves to be "emperors" peaked, as well.[5] This reflects the rather high degree of internal colonial expansion that encouraged the (primarily) external expansion of this period. It is rather difficult to imagine the emergence of an "Age of Empire" of this proportion without the emergence of new colonial powers. Rival states, primarily Germany but also the United States, Italy, Belgium, and Japan, encouraged the traditional expansion states (particularly England and France) to expand their empires. Territorial acquisition came to be seen, in Friedrich List's words, as a "means of protecting . . . markets and sources of raw materials from possible retaliation by foreign competitors."[6] Expansion also strengthened global status. French expansion, as Joseph Chailley-Bert explained at the 1908 North African Congress, was an "event or effort through which [France] should later seek to recover [its] position as a first-class power" following defeat to Prussia in 1871.[7]

Reactions by the Japanese and the Korean governments to these developments were very different: Japan joined the colonial expansion bandwagon while Korea attempted to preserve its sovereignty though diplomatic maneuvering. The Korean Peninsula, like Siam, was caught between competing states—Russia, China, and Japan—and attempted to remain sovereign by exploiting the competition. This no longer remained a viable option after Japan defeated China and Russia in war; soon after, Korea succumbed to Japanese expansion. Japan's interest in expansion in general, and the Korean Peninsula in particular, was greatly encouraged by the expansion of this period. The nascent Meiji state quickly learned that its fundamental goal—to create a rich state and a strong military—depended on its demonstrating the capacity to extend its influence internally, but also peripherally and (eventually) externally.

ASSIMILATION AS A COLONIAL POLICY

The Iwakura Mission represents one of the most important fact-finding endeavors undertaken by the Meiji government. This mission failed in its most urgent ambition—to convince the Western powers to rescind the unequal treaties imposed upon the previous Tokugawa regime (1603–1868). It succeeded, however, in completing an equally important pledge: to "busily, without rest, brave the cold and hot to investigate the near and far."[8] The mission's agenda did not specifically list Western expansion as a point to be investigated. However, it would be inconceivable for the participants not to have entertained this issue given its paramount importance at the time. Indeed, the records kept by Kume Kunitake suggest this to be the case.

En route, the mission's participants were exposed to colonialism from a number of dimensions. They directly witnessed internal colonialism as they passed through Germany, France, and Italy, and peripheral expansion when they visited Wales and Scotland. Their discussions with government officials and tours of government institutions also reminded participants of the institution's importance and clearly influenced their thinking. The travelers would identify closely with the efforts being made to create nation-states in Europe, particularly in Germany. Indeed, through Kume's official tour history we learn that the majority of the participants' time abroad was spent examining the components of nation building. Their realization of the magnitude of the task that Japan faced internally convinced participants of the need to limit their peripheral colonial activities, at least until the more pressing internal (domain integration) and relatively safer peripheral (Ryukyu and Ezo) expansion realized success.

The Japanese mission encountered peripheral colonialism soon after it crossed the Pacific Ocean, in the United States. The country, having concluded a bloody civil war just six years earlier, was busily engaged in efforts to reconstruct the union. One part of this process included assimilating recently emancipated blacks and Native Americans into mainstream American society. The mission then crossed the Atlantic Ocean, where it was exposed to assimilation at different levels of advancement: from the more developed efforts by the English to amalgamate the Welsh, Scots, and Irish, to the embryonic German ambition to incorporate the peoples of its newly annexed territories—Alsace and Lorraine. Upon arriving in France the Japanese travelers witnessed the inauguration of the French government's intense campaign to integrate its southern provinces, and the revision of its Algerian administrative policies to secure direct bureaucratic (rather than military) control over this colony. Japanese officials writing on colonial policy when Japan acquired Taiwan and Korea exploited all of these examples in their discussions regarding the administrative policy their country should adopt in its expanding empire.

By the end of the nineteenth century, assimilation as a theoretical construct for colonial policy had come to be associated with French colonial policy. Direct rule rhetoric promised its recipients benefits reserved for those colonized as internal citizens, yet in practice the policy treated these peoples as marginalized subjects. Indirect rule, favored by the English, advanced separate colonized-colonizer existences, and its practitioners generally governed their charges in this spirit. Contrary to this distinction, close examination of these colonial histories reveals that while the French philosophized on assimilation and invited a small, but diverse, number of colonized to their parliament, their assimilation practices hardly approached the ambitious inclusive goals trumpeted by Enlightenment thinkers. The English, on the other hand, practiced indirect rule in most of their colonies but also introduced assimilation practices in others. While the French trumpeted assimilation as a universal right to all peoples, the English quietly introduced the practice in a more practical way, as one applicable to a selection of its peripheral possessions. While the French demanded cultural rebirth as a prerequisite to assimilation, the English incorporated assimilated peoples as political subjects, without requiring (but occasionally prodding) them to adopt English culture.

Forms of assimilation could be found as early as the colonial policies of the Roman Empire, which encouraged the absorption of peoples throughout the empire as citizens. The policy gained philosophical support from Age of Reason thinkers such as Claude Adrien Helvétius, Thomas Hobbes, and John Locke, who preached the universality of human reason. Helvétius, for example, saw education as a "possible means of correcting discrepancies between classes and other social classes." Supporters of the policy were encouraged by ideas such as Jean-le-Rond D'Alembert's "universal enlightenment," Jean Marie de Condorcet's theory of the perfectibility of humankind, and Jean-Jacques Rousseau's belief that people "who may be unequal in strength or intelligence, become every one equal by convention and legal right."[9] This idea of universal affinity manifested in French views on citizenship—a right (rather than a privilege) that was open to all human beings provided they demonstrate their capacity to perform three basic requirements: an ability to speak the French language, a desire to faithfully follow a "civilized" religion, and a willingness to drop their barbarous customs and mannerisms.

The French government's advancement of assimilation was hardly consistent. It embraced the idea in its 1791 French Constitution, which declared its colonies to be an "integral part of the Republic and subject to the same constitutional law." However, subsequent constitutions rejected and re-embraced it over the nineteenth century.[10] At the turn of this century, the policy faced a severe challenge by promoters of social Darwinist thought. In Paris, Gustave Le Bon, a man described by Raymond Betts as "one of the first and most ardent opponents of the Enlightenment idea of human equality," attacked the idea with vigor. In his *Les Lois psychologiques de l'évolution des peuples* (The Laws of the Psychology and Evolution of Peoples), Le Bon advanced a scientific approach that classified members of the human race into four racial categories: primitive races, inferior races, intermediate races, and superior races. The "mental gap" that separated these groups, he argued, rendered cross-group integration impossible. Educating an inferior people in the hope of changing their national habits would bear feeble results. This assimilation was "one of the most harmful illusions that the theorists of pure reason have ever engendered."[11] These racist ideas were supported by biological experimental frameworks that sought to scientifically prove racial division.[12]

Those out in the colonial field voiced similar criticisms. Joseph Gallieni, who served in both Tonkin and Madagascar, warned of the dangers wrought by exporting European ideas to colonial lands: "Nothing is more damaging . . . in colonial affairs than preconceived formulas, imported principles, which based most often on European ideas, do not apply to the environments, situations, or occasions for which one has wanted to adopt them."[13]

The French declaration that all peoples regardless of race could become French no doubt invited these racist challenges and criticism. Yet, French success at assimilating colonized peoples was pitifully poor. First, the French limited the implementation of the policy to but a selection of the colony's urban centers. In Senegal, for example, they designated St. Louis, Goree, Rufisque, and Dakar as *communes* whose residents were eligible for citizenship. Here the colonizers divided the Senegalan people into native "subjects" and native "citizens." To advance to native citizenship the Senegalese had to serve in a French public or private office for a minimum of ten years, be literate in French, possess a means of existence, and be of good character (i.e., non-Muslim).[14] Even still, the French qualified their status as "native," rather than "French," citizen. In Vietnam, the French bestowed French citizenship on a small minority of the native population.[15] As we shall see, this honor did not protect the recipients from French harassment.

Even in Algeria, the territory often cited as the exemplar of French assimilation policy, stringent conditions for inclusion severely limited the number of indigenous people who actually gained French citizenship.[16] After World War I, the French government enacted legislation to increase the number of people assimilated, particularly to reward those who contributed to France's war effort as either a soldier or a laborer. This provoked counter efforts to block its implementation by French expatriates and European residents, who rejected efforts made by the colonized to meet French standards of civilization. Rather than the indigenous Algerian, it was the European immigrant from the former French territories of Alsace and Lorraine, and from Malta and Italy, that benefited from French assimilation policy. This affected an ethnic hierarchy that placed the French at the top; the Jews, Arabs, and Berbers at the bottom; and other European migrants in between.[17]

The most telling example of the discrepancy between French rhetoric and practice in Algeria was in the colonizer's dealings with the Jeunes Algérians (Young Algerians), a group that made efforts to move linguistically, culturally, and politically toward France. The government-general responded by charging the group with "anti-French and nationalist" behavior.[18] The list of reform demands that this group presented to the colonial government in June 1912, when faced with military conscription, demonstrates the extent of French discrimination toward Algerians: abolishment of the *code de l'indigénat*, equality in taxes and public expenditure, representation in Algerian local assemblies, representation of Muslims in the French government, and automatic French citizenship for each conscript who returned with a good record.

The Algerian who favored assimilation found the *code de l'indigénat* particularly disturbing, as it codified the indigenous people's inferior status in the colony. Instituted by the French Parliament in the early 1870s, soon after French bureaucratic rule replaced military rule, the code listed thirty-three infractions of humiliation that curtailed Algerian, but not French, activity: it prohibited them from traveling without a permit, speaking disrespectfully to a French official, begging outside their *commune*, or protesting *corvée* duty. Penalties for violations of this code were set at a maximum prison sentence of five days and a maximum fine of fifteen francs.[19]

Efforts by the French government to strengthen its assimilation policy, and by the expatriate to weaken it, were most evident when in February 1919 the parliament attempted to pass the Jonnart Laws designed to allow Algerians easier access to French citizenship. Named after Charles Jonnart, the governor general who initiated the effort, the legislation initially aimed to provide Algerians with greater representation and voting rights even if they retained their religious beliefs. Predictably, European residents believed the reforms to be excessive while the Muslim population argued their shortcomings. The French retaining the religious conversion requirement in the legislation's final draft limited the number of Algerians who benefited from the relaxed provisions. Through this legislation, about 425,000 Muslims gained suffrage rights upon being certified with "intermediate native citizenship" status.[20] However, between the years 1919 and 1924, just 359 Algerians were awarded full French citizenship.[21] Frustration mounted with French inaction. In 1922, on the occasion of a visit to Algeria by French president Alexandre Millerand, leader Emir Khaled, who had signed the Young Algerians' demand list after serving as an officer in the French army, declared

> the people of Algeria are all, without distinction as to religion or
> race, equally children of France and have an equal right to her
> home. . . . The desire we have to create within the bosom of France
> a status worthy of us and worthy of France is the best proof that we
> are good Frenchmen and wish only to strengthen the bonds that
> attach us to the mother country.[22]

This declaration earned Khaled the reputation among the French as the "principle troublemaker" among the Young Algerians. His forced exile to Egypt two years later gained him the (perhaps exaggerated) reputation as the "first Algerian nationalist."[23] In 1946, perhaps out of desperation, the French allowed Muslim Algerians citizenship.[24]

French assimilation policy in Vietnam resembled this trend. The French granted a small minority of Vietnamese, mostly among the bourgeoisie class, French citizenship,[25] a status that gained recipients voting rights and widened their employment opportunities. Bui Quang Chieu's case is perhaps exemplary. Born in 1872, just as the French were consolidating their control over southern Vietnam, Bui received a "thoroughly French education," both in France and Algeria, before returning to accept a position in the colonial bureaucracy. Later he was selected to edit the *Tribune Indigéne*, a newspaper that targeted Vietnam's French-educated population. Bui proved to be more elitist than populist. His newspaper often advertised the elite status that assimilated Vietnamese enjoyed, while preaching against the French "admitting [Vietnamese] undesirables, those he defined as people without means of livelihood or without culture,"[26] into the great French family. The colonial government felt the zealousness that he showed in French assimilation, however, to be a "thorn in the side of the colonial regime." In 1919 Governor General Georges Maspéro funded a rival newspaper to neutralize Bui. Bui's protests over the governor general of Cochinchina's decision to grant a French consortium monopoly rights to develop port facilities in Saigon (now Ho Chi Minh City) led the French colonial administration to exile the editor to Phnom Penh, the capital of present-day Cambodia. His newspaper folded soon thereafter.[27]

The Vietnamese example, along with that of Algerian assimilation, suggests the French efforts to be rather similar to those of the British in their external colonies. The British also targeted a sample of the colonized population to receive a privileged education with the aspiration that they would return to assist them in the running of the colony after completing their studies. Those like Bui Quang Chieu and Emir Khaled, who in the colonizers' plan did not cooperate, were easily neutralized and replaced by other collaborators. The French preached assimilation in Vietnam as they did in Algeria. Bui, who was allowed to return to Vietnam in March 1925, reiterated his support for total assimilation, which dangled promises of equal rights and equal opportunity for those who cooperated. However, as Hue-Tam Ho Tai reflects, the "majority of Vietnamese had no wish to become French; many were running out of patience with [the French administration's] unfulfilled promises."[28]

A more successful application of French assimilation occurred closer to home, in its southern provinces. This colonizing activity differed from the above examples in that the people, although regarded by the Parisian French as "savage," resided within the traditional borders of the French state. Following the French defeat in 1871 by the Prussian army, the French government undertook an intensive effort to "make French" the language, beliefs, and mannerisms of this region's residents. The French drew images of these peoples that resembled those that colonizers generally drew of their peripheral colonial peoples—the French, as one Parisian put it, did not "need to go to America to see savages . . . [in the Burgundian countryside] are the Redskins of Fennimore Cooper."[29] Their treatment, however, reflected the French government's image of these peoples as internal citizens. As French citizens, they were expected to participate in the state's political, social, educational, and cultural institutions.

Colonial powers that emerged at the end of the nineteenth century believed the English and French to differ in their approaches to colonial administration. They found their indirect rule to be more applicable to colonial efforts in external territory. A survey of British colonial history reveals, however, that earlier in the century the English, too, debated whether to implement an assimilation policy in what became the "jewel" of its overseas empire—the Indian subcontinent. It took a bloody revolt by Indian soldiers in the employment of the British military to convince assimilation supporters of the policy's inappropriateness, at least toward peoples imagined as harboring radically different social and cultural practices and beliefs.

Ideas voiced during the 1830s "Great Indian Education Debate" reflected arguments both for and against assimilation that would constitute critical parts of the debates that took place toward the latter part of the century. Historian Thomas Macaulay, for example, advised in 1833 that all teaching across India be conducted in the English language and rely on texts used in England. He was among those who believed that Great Britain had the ability, and the obligation, to remake India into a British mold. For this purpose, he argued, two of India's more contemptible customs—Hinduism and the caste system—must be purged from Indian society.[30] In 1835, Macaulay, who chaired an education reform committee, articulated the goal of Indian education reform as forming "a class of persons Indian in blood and color, but English in tastes, in opinions, in morals, and in intellect."[31] Charles Trevelyan, a missionary and reformist, offered a similar message in 1838 by listing the "spread of knowledge" as one of Great Britain's "most sacred duties."

> What we have to do is, not to dispute, but to teach—not to prepossess the minds of the natives with false systems, and to keep our good instruction till it is too late to be of use, but to get the start of their prejudice by educating them, from the beginning, according to our own views. We ought to cherish European learning, which has already taken deep root and begun to throw out vigorous shoots, leaving the trunk of the old system to a natural and undisturbed decay. The rising generation will become the whole nation in the course of a few years. They are all craving for instruction, and we may mould their unoccupied and supple minds in any way we please.[32]

Opposition to these optimistic opinions predated by decades counterarguments offered by social Darwinists and members of the German "scientific colonialism" school later in the century: human beings were a product of their environment; it was futile to attempt to civilize these otherwise "unoccupied and supple minds." H. H. Wilson characterized the Indians as possessors of "gross ignorance and inveterate superstition," a people like the Bengali *sircar* or *kerani* employed to copy letters and keep accounts, who understood the English language well enough to comprehend everything he is told to do by his British employer, but "is as genuine and unenlightened a Hindu as if he had never known or spoken any other mother tongue."[33]

The Indian Mutiny of 1857 ended any serious discussion regarding the acculturation of the Indian people with English values. The uprising began after 85 Muslim Indian soldiers were court-martialed for refusing to use newly greased cartridges—rumored to be treated in pig fat—issued to them by the British military. Other members of the regiment revolted upon seeing their comrades paraded in shackles in humiliation. The mutineers took their anger out on the British civilian population, slaughtering 125 women and children. The extent of this brutality led the colonizers to conclude that the character flaws of Indians as a people rendered impossible their salvation by exposure to European religion and knowledge. It was more productive to segregate the colonized indigenous from the colonizing "civilized"; Britain's mission should guide the natives' self-government but allow them to retain their traditional institutions.[34]

Association emerged as the favored administrative policy. Here the colonizers would guide the colonized "by influence and advice [rather] than to rule [them] by direct command."[35] A strong central British administration oversaw a network of local traditional governing entities that exerted little effort to change those peoples under its jurisdiction. Any reform of the natives would come about "slowly and gently," and within the context of their own traditional institutions and rulers.[36] As indicated above, this policy became known as the British approach by those colonial powers that emerged in the latter half of the nineteenth century. As we shall see later, the British also advertised it as such.

The debate on Indian assimilation ended too quickly to ascertain the extent to which the English were willing to incorporate a "civilized" Indian into British political and social systems. It would perhaps be overstating its proponents' intentions, for example, to interpret Indian Anglicization as a movement that would eventually have placed Indian representatives in the British Parliament. Other examples closer to home, however, demonstrate more successful applications of assimilation by England. These emphasized among their constituents political participation rather than cultural submission. Indeed, the English assimilation of the Celtic peoples who bordered English territory represents the longest sustained effort to assimilate a peripheral people in recent history. Like French efforts in its southern provinces, English incorporation of the Welsh, Scots, and Irish peoples generally receives scant mention in colonial histories. One exception is Michael Hechter's research that questions why the English failed to integrate these peoples into their nation-state to the extent that it had its residents of other shires.[37] We see the experiment's success in the support and loyalty that these peoples demonstrated during centuries of diplomatic turbulence.

A unique feature of this peripheral colonial activity was that Celtic "unions" with the English were to an extent negotiated. In the Welsh and Scottish cases, negotiations toward union benefited greatly from the English throne being occupied by a native of the incorporated territory, the Welshman Edward VI and the Scotsman James III. These unions allowed the people to retain a number of their institutions in return for agreeing to dissolve their local parliaments and send representatives to the English (later British) national assembly at Westminster. The Welsh, for example, retained the use of their language, while the Scots preserved many of their institutions, including their education and legal systems.[38] In this sense, their assimilation was primarily political. The English may have criticized these peoples' languages and cultures, but did not impose their own upon them. The value of these relationships was in Wales, Scotland, and Ireland remaining loyal to England throughout the centuries of wars it fought with France and Germany. Indeed, England's success in war and empire building contributed to their remaining a part of the United Kingdom.

Other "latecomers" to expansion, including Germany and the United States, also employed assimilation practices in peripheral colonial activity. The Prussian administrations in Alsace and Lorraine from 1871, following the state's acquisition of these territories at the conclusion of the Franco-Prussian War, centered on assimilating its "long lost brothers" into the emerging German state. This represents a good example of internal and peripheral expansion working alongside each other. In contrast to the self-governing rights enjoyed by the other German states, the two acquired territories were governed by a *statthalter*, a governor general figure who reported directly to the Kaiser. The central government gradually allowed the peoples of these two regions admission to its institutions, albeit at a slower and unequal pace. From 1872 they became subject to military conscription; in 1874 they were granted a constitution that permitted them to send fifteen representatives to the Reichstag, the German lower house, but none to the more powerful Bundesrath.[39] Before they were to take their seats in the national assembly, however, the German government enacted peace preservation legislation that empowered the governing authorities to curb any action that, by their interpretation, constituted a threat to public safety and order.[40]

The United States' use of assimilation differed from the situations mentioned above in that it was directed at marginalized minority groups within its territory either directly or indirectly under its jurisdiction. Blacks and Native Americans had historically been ostracized from mainstream American society. Yet, post-Civil War governments during Reconstruction (1865–1877) established policies to culturally, socially, and even politically incorporate these groups. General Richard H. Pratt formulated his opinions on Native American assimilation from his experience at commanding an all-black regiment during the Civil War:

> the end to be gained . . . is the complete civilization of the Indian
> and his absorption into our national life, with all the rights and
> privileges guaranteed to every other individual, the Indian to lose
> his identity as such, to give up his tribal relations and to be made
> to feel that he is an American citizen.[41]

The period of Reconstruction that followed the bloody Civil War realized an increase in the number of learning institutions for both blacks and Native Americans. Blacks gaining suffrage rights helped elect many southern blacks to political office.

The message delivered to justify these efforts preached the need to incorporate blacks and Native Americans as internal members of American society. On the other hand, the voice calling for the integration of these peoples in schools catering to the white American was much softer, if not mute. More often advocates of assimilation challenged the segregated peoples to prove their worthiness for inclusion. Similar to French conditions for assimilation, American white society demanded that Native Americans replace their "tribal life" with one recognized as "civilized" (learn the English language and adopt Christianity) before they would consider them for citizenship. Black success encouraged whites to raise the standards for their assimilation. Southern American society rewarded their success by codifying segregation in passing the racist Jim Crow laws.[42]

THE MOTIVATION TO ASSIMILATE

A legitimate question regarding assimilation policy involves the intentions that colonizers brought to their administration of the foreign territory. Did they envision the colonized ever advancing to assume positions as their equals? If so, what policies did they enact to encourage and assist the peoples' advancement? If not, why did they introduce an intrusive policy that surpassed the less meddlesome external colonial approach both financially and in effort? The answers to these questions lie in security concerns: the closer the colony to the geographic and ethnic interests of the colonizers, the more intrusive the administrative rule. State security, specifically the need to secure potentially threatening peripheral territories (lest a rival gain control over them), encouraged the colonizer's drive to introduce this intrusive administrative policy. France, which identified assimilation in universal terms, introduced the policy to a greater diversity of states. Its practice did not necessarily reap impressive success rates, as it was willing to assimilate so few of its colonial subjects. We can only speculate the extent to which this deception further encouraged the bloody wars of liberation following the end of World War II.

We see this concern of security most clearly in the formation of the United Kingdom, a series of unions formed in part to prevent England's immediate neighbors from allying with France. England finalized "unions" with Scotland (1707) and Ireland (1800) during a period of virtually continuous war with France. Between 1689 and 1815 England fought a total of seven major wars, and participated in a number of minor scuffles, with its neighbor to the south.[43] A Scottish or Irish alliance with the French would have opened a second front that would have spelled disaster for the English. Welsh and Scottish relationships with France date back to at least the thirteenth century. Wales allied with France early in the century when England attacked North Wales.[44] Scotland signed with France the first "Auld Alliance" in 1295. French influence lingered in the Scottish Highland and island regions up through the mid-eighteenth century, when the government actively assisted the Jacobites in their final attempt to drive the English from northern Scotland. In 1745 the French supplied Bonnie Prince Charles Stuart (the "Pretender") with soldiers, financial support, and (after defeat) refuge.[45]

The possible "papal connection" between the Irish and the French was of greater concern to the English as witnessed by their treatment of Irish Catholics over the centuries. Discriminative practices underlined English policy toward Catholics in both Ireland and other parts of the United Kingdom. Up until 1829, Linda Colley writes, British Catholics were treated as "potential traitors, as un-British": they could not vote or hold public office and were also discriminated against in areas such as education, taxation, and military duty.[46] Some believed that these discriminative policies required reform. The barrister Theobald McKenna argued just after the turn of the nineteenth century that the English forging closer ties with the Irish Catholics was in the security interests of both countries:

> The circumstances of Europe and the state of Ireland render it the essential interest of Ireland to be closely combined with Britain; and 2d, an incorporation of all powers of the two states, executive and legislative, is the most permanent and eligible form of connection. I do apprehend that, in the actual circumstances of Europe, every motive, by which man, in a state of nature, is induced to abridge his native rights, and associate for mutual security with his neighbor, does urge Ireland to cling to the sister island, and cultivate the connection with every reasonable assiduity!

Those who favored the status quo, McKenna continued, exaggerated the religious factor while closing their eyes to Catholic incidences of loyalty. If this alliance had any potential, he observed, the Irish and French would have exploited it during the extraordinary opportunity provided by the American War.[47]

Security concerns also motivated peripheral expansion in continental Europe and the United States. The French and German governments both fortified their internal situations in the aftermath of the Franco-Prussian War by strengthening holds over peripheral territories. The French government redefined its relationship with its Algerian neighbor by assuming direct control over this territory. The Prussian government directly incorporated the residents of its newest acquisitions, Alsace and Lorraine. The ethnic base of the people was inconsequential; it was their strategic location that mattered. The German nationalist historian Henrich von Treitschke said as much when he noted that even "if the Alsatians had been Japanese . . . Germany would have annexed them anyway in order to capitalize on the military value of Metz and Strasbourg."[48]

The confusion in the aftermath of the devastating American Civil War in part inspired government officials and missionaries to assimilate the recently liberated black slaves and the Native American. As we shall see in Japan's case, peripheral expansion as a security measure was not a lesson the state had to learn; it appeared as a natural reaction to a threat—real or perceived—well before it began to envision the Korean Peninsula as a potential source of trouble.

Economic ambitions, over security issues, motivated external colonialism. When security did factor in, it generally addressed protecting a state's other external territories. Projected competition from the rising German state, for example, compelled the British government to extend its presence on the Malay Peninsula from 1873 as, in the words of Lord Kimberley, "it would be impossible to consent to any European Power assuming Protectorate of any State in the Malaya Peninsula." The volume of trade that passed through the Straits of Malacca, coupled with the peninsula's proximity to India, rendered the territory indispensable to the empire.[49]

The primary inspiration for this expansion factored at best indirectly into the colonial homeland's equation for its national security. The potential loss of territory in southern Africa, while trying to the ego and state coffers, did not advance anything near the debate generated over Irish independence that took place in the early twentieth century. Instead, according to D. L. Fieldhouse, the need for external colonies was explained as filling other national needs, particularly—but not limited to—economic ones related to the industrialization of continental Europe, such as surplus capital investment and raw material sources. These acquisitions also encouraged expressions of nationalism.[50] Pride in one's homeland waxed and waned in accordance with the gains and loses of a country's overseas holdings.

Fieldhouse prefers diplomatic, to economic, reasons to explain the increase in territorial expansion during the Age of Empire. He credits German post-Franco-Prussian War expansion with creating a domino effect that sent other states scurrying for new territorial possessions.[51] The issues that require consideration reflected the ways that the colonial powers integrated peripheral and external territories into their empires, and how they governed these territories. The close geographical and psychological proximity of the subjects residing in territories required them to assume a role of cultural, and in times of war physical, buffer to protect the homeland from external threat or invasion. This required colonizers to forge stronger linguistic, cultural, and social relationships with this "foreign" people than with those at the external level. It required the colonizer to present the people with the idea that membership in the homeland's extended community was possible. It did not necessarily require them following through with their promises.

ASSIMILATION TOOLS: EDUCATING THE "SAVAGE"

Formal education provided colonial administrations with their most important vehicle for assimilating peoples at internal and peripheral levels. The educational systems for the two levels, however, differed remarkably. Generally, the peripheral subject received an education inferior to that of the internal subject: it was noncompulsory, shorter in duration, and often taught in a foreign language.[52] These demerits impeded this group's opportunities to compete with their internal counterpart for occupational and social status within the empire.

The Prussians, following their defeat to the French at Jena-Auerstadt in 1806, were recognized as pioneers at introducing state-sponsored compulsory education for nation-building purposes. According to Ludwig Natorp, this education, created as "an establishment of the nation and the teacher, the educator, and the servant of the nation," in 1831 was the envy of the modern world.[53] That year the Frenchman Victor Cousin traveled to Prussia to study this system; his report influenced not only the French system but also education in England and the United States following his publication's English translation. Cousin applauded Prussian education for linking *Schulpflichtigkeit* (school duty) and *Dienstpflichtigkeit* (military service duty), the "two bases of true civilization."[54] Stiff competition from the Catholic school system prevented the French from instituting a national education system. A Colonel Stoffel wrote four decades later that this failure contributed to France's 1871 humiliation in the Franco-Prussian War. Stoffel, who spent three years in Prussia prior to the outbreak of war, wrote that compulsory education and universal military conscription had provided the Prussians with a huge military advantage as the institution diffused a "strong sense of duty through the Prussian people." The "Prussian nation," he continued, "is the most enlightened in Europe, that is, that in which education is most widely diffused through all classes." France could boast intellectual activity and production in only a few great cities. His report, however, remained sealed until after the war.[55]

The national education system that the French instituted from this time sought first to integrate peoples of the southern provinces who previously had managed to remain distanced from French culture, as well as to spread a sense of national pride to bond the citizens of the state. The new curriculum aimed to expand the people's national awareness by instructing them on the "manners, morals, literacy, a knowledge of French and of France, a sense of the legal and institutional structure beyond their immediate community." With the promulgation of Premier Jules Ferry's education reforms in the early 1880s the French made patriotic education the foundation of their national curriculum. This legislation made schools "free, compulsory, secular, and intensely nationalistic." Roger Brubaker argues that primary schools became the "great engines of assimilation welding France for the first time into a unified nation."[56] Patriotism appeared throughout the curriculum. Schools taught that a unified France was a country that was strong and powerful, a point emphasized in the songs taught in music classes. The curriculum instructed teachers that "their first duty is to make [their students] love and understand the fatherland." Later, appended instructions taught that the school was to be seen as "an instrument of unity," an "answer to dangerous centrifugal tendencies," and the "keystone of national defense." Instructors were to teach to instill a "love of France" in their students, rather than a love of their individual academic specialty.[57]

This education system contrasted greatly with that of its peripheral system. In both cases, French legislators considered the object of their efforts — the provincial as well as the colonized—to be of a quality inferior to that of the core Parisian French. The different education policies initiated in the two colonized regions can best be understood as fulfilling the aims of two different colonizing visions. Contemporary historiography on France's peripheral acquisitions questions the seriousness of the state's efforts to incorporate the native residents of these territories, even though colonized rhetoric advertised the people's conditioned "right" to claim French citizenship, as opposed to the southern French residents' obligation to participate to fulfill their duties as French citizens.

French education policies in Algeria and Vietnam present two illustrative examples. Both histories demonstrate a direct French administration reducing relatively well educated societies to illiteracy. John Ruedy proposes that the strong emphasis on scriptural reading and the high attendance rates at Koran schools probably developed a literacy rate among Algerians that even surpassed French levels at the time of the colonial power's arrival. The French government replaced this traditional school system with Christian-parochial and public education schools for French expatriates, European settlers, and a few sons of Algerian notables. Alexis de Tocqueville lamented: "Around us the [Algerian] lights are going out. . . . We have made Muslim society much poorer, more disorganized, more ignorant and barbarous than it was before it knew us."[58]

A similar sequence of events is seen in Vietnam. Precolonial Vietnam housed at least two schools in each district. Ngō Viñh Long estimates that pre-French-era rural literacy rates may even have surpassed urban literacy.[59] David G. Marr estimates that up to 25 percent of Vietnamese could read enough characters to decipher basic contracts and other records. Yet by the mid-1920s, he bemoaned, it "seems unlikely . . . [that] more than five percent . . . could read a newspaper, proclamation, or letter in any language."[60] French administration simply did not pay much attention to native education until after the First World War. Reforms initiated under the administration of Albert Sarraut, one of Vietnam's more progressive governor generals, increased school attendance. By 1930, a total of 323,759 Vietnamese children (out of a total population of 17 million) attended public schools, and another 60,000 attended private schools.[61] Long credits Vietnamese gentry, who interpreted Japan's military successes against China and Russia as resulting from its introduction of Western education, with having pressured the French to reform the colonial education system. Two issues that affected assimilation policy drove the debate on education policy. The first was language, specifically what language—Chinese, French, *nom* (demotic writing), or *quoc ngu* (Romanized script)—textbooks would use. In the end *quoc ngu* gained favor as a "transitional script" from Vietnamese to French.[62] A second issue concerned the depth of Vietnamese education: whether to provide basic education for more, or advanced education for a few. The French administration settled for the former, closing many of the colony's "overdeveloped" secondary schools in the mid-1920s.[63] This fit the French need to fill lower bureaucratic positions.[64] Students in even the lower grades became exposed to a wider variety of subjects that included French history, math, geography, and general science. However, even after a series of reforms between1920 and 1938, the vast majority of Vietnamese students (90 percent) never advanced beyond the third grade.[65]

Literature on colonial policy in Alsace and Lorraine suggests that the Germans made greater efforts than the French to educate their peripheral residents. This education system is also criticized for its inferiority to that offered in the German homeland. Coleman Phillipson wrote in 1918 that public instruction at all levels was "admirably organized and adequately endowed." An elementary system of 3,846 schools served 320,000 students; 10,000 students more attended schools at the secondary level. The one university, the University of Strasburg, enrolled 2,200 students. Phillipson described the education system, along with the other infrastructural advancements made by the Germans, as a "wonderful fairy of initiative and intelligence."[66]

Other observers were not so kind. Charles Hazen, writing a year earlier, questioned whether this school system served the needs of the colonized or the colonizers. Concentrating attention on the university, he argued the institution's purpose as placing in "the conquered territory a German university of the first rank, a center of the 'German spirit,' of 'German science.'" Of its 175 faculty members, he continued, only 15 were Alsatian.[67] Hazen also criticized the German decision to abolish French-based education in the primarily French-speaking region, particularly because of the economic advantage French speakers could have provided the Germans in their business dealings with their neighbors. While this is perhaps an understandable criticism in practical terms, suggesting that a peripheral colonizing administration permit the people to retain the language of the enemy would have conflicted with the grander assimilating ambitions of the core state and left unattended a security risk within its imperial borders.[68]

The assimilation policy employed by the United States during the Age of Reconstruction offers a situation different from the above cases in that the peoples to be assimilated had resided in U.S. territory as external subjects for centuries. In this case, assimilation efforts attempted to upgrade a minority people to a peripheral relationship with internal residents. *The Nation* enthusiastically explained this thinking as a "consciousness of sovereignty in the nation which is ready to assert its power on behalf of the general welfare, and the progress of the nation in regard to the recognition of human rights, the exaltation of manhood for its own sake, irrespective of race, color, or position."[69] The argument that unfortunately captured the spirit of these times was much less righteous: some calculated it cheaper to extinguish the people by integrating them culturally than by exterminating them physically.[70]

Between 1878 and 1887 the United States government increased its funding for Native American education from $20,000 to $1.2 million. It also increased the number of schools for them by one hundred; enrollment almost tripled.[71] Many of these schools transported (often by force) students from "primitive" reservation lifestyles to a "civilized" environment to separate the "children from the negative influences . . . to ensure their eventual success as citizens of the American nation." As General Richard H. Pratt, the founder of one such school, put it, this education was designed to "immerse [the Indian] in civilization and keep him there until well soaked."[72]

The Nation in 1868 also lectured on the importance of black education, particularly as a stepping-stone toward blacks gaining respect in American society. Black people, the magazine explained, had been provided in the past with "protection and education," benefits that allowed them a head start at becoming "familiarized with the machinery of free society." Their free ride was now over. From now on, blacks must work to "win a good position in the way that other races have won it; and when it has its roll of poets, orators, scholars, and statesmen to show, people will greatly respect" them.[73] Education for blacks prospered in the early years of Reconstruction, just at the time the Iwakura Mission tour visited the United States. Between 1869 and 1870 the number of school buildings, as well as children in attendance, doubled. By 1871, the state of Mississippi had built 399 schools for freed slaves. New state governments also expended much time and effort toward education matters. Robert Selph Henry, however, described their efforts as having found "a fuller expression on paper than in fact." White opposition toward black education, both in mixed (black and white) and racially segregated schools, turned violent. Whites burned the schools and intimidated the teachers hired to work in them. A congressional committee examining southern black education learned that in one county no one was permitted to teach in a school for blacks, and that all schoolhouses save for one had been burned.[74] As in other situations, the fear that assimilation could prove successful encouraged the hegemonic majority to hijack its progress.

Education policy for both Native Americans and blacks focused on, as Commissioner of Indian Affairs Thomas Morgan put it in 1889, creating "fervent patriotism." He continued: they should be "taught to look upon America as their home and upon the United States Government as their friend and benefactor." Culturally, they should become "more familiar with the lives of great and good men and women in American history, and be taught to feel a pride in their achievements."[75] This instruction would prepare them for cultural introduction to American society; it would not, however, guarantee their social inclusion. While the content of the education introduced these peoples to the heroes and tenets of American-ness, the fact that the majority of the students studied in an environment segregated from the majority white population diluted efforts made to ease black and Native American integration into American society. These efforts gained the praise of Iwakura Mission tour participants, who optimistically predicted that American blacks would someday surpass lazy whites. By the end of World War I, Japanese used U.S. discrimination against blacks as an example to criticize Japan's treatment of its Korean colonial subjects.[76]

IMAGINING THE PERIPHERAL SUBJECT

The eradication of the advances made by minorities during the period of U.S. Reconstruction exemplifies the paradox of assimilation: the perpetuation of segregation compromised the colonizers' rhetoric of inclusiveness. This rhetoric teased its recipients into believing that their acceptance by the dominant society was imminent. The decision to assimilate, this voice suggested, rested upon the colonized people's willingness to embrace civilization, as defined by the colonizer. This ruse encouraged a subset of the population to cooperate with the colonizers: they adopted the culture and language of the majority, preached the colonizers' messages, and sacrificed themselves in their wars. Yet, their efforts failed to erase the inferior images that their colonizers held, primarily because the colonizing population was ill prepared to recognize the peripheral subject as its equal. In Frantz Fanon's words, the colonized and the colonizers "behave in accordance with a neurotic orientation" with the former "enslaved by his inferiority, [and the latter] by his superiority."[77]

Colonizers established a set of cultural and social representations that distinguished the peripheral subjects from the internal citizen to frustrate their advancement. These barriers assumed a variety of forms, from the physical to the psychological. The colonizers juggled a concoction of geographical, biological, historical, and linguistic images to piece together a composite sketch of the peripheral subject as inferior. These images suggested as necessary the institutional segregation that placed the people in unequal school systems, and formed the segregated social system within which they later became entrapped.

The key variable here demonstrates an ironic twist in assimilation policy: while colonizers defined the colonizer-colonized relationship in historical and cultural terms, their insistence on this people's inferiority justified in their minds the need to delay assimilation, at least until the people "caught up." The colonized people's efforts to adapt their lives to that of their colonizers did not necessarily lead to greater integration. Often, the colonized people's equal inclusion as citizens remained a vaguely defined goal that situated strategic and malleable hurdles to ensure that all but a select few came close to attaining. In this regard, the colonizer developed a rhetoric that preached the goals of internal colonialism, yet in practice adopted policy that approached external colonialism.

The geographically defined borders that differentiated the territories of the two peoples constituted one of the more visible barriers drawn for this purpose.[78] Those traveling to the external colony generally reached their destination after crossing wide oceans or unfriendly terrains, to encounter a people that they found to be so different they characterized them as "subhuman." To create a distinction from peripheral lands and people required greater imagination, especially when these lands were contiguously linked to their own. The Englishman H. V. Morton left us the following description of his encounter with the Scottish border in 1935, more than two centuries after the country's "union" with England.

> I am alone at the Border, one foot in England, the other in Scotland. There is a metal post with "Scotland" written on it. It is a superfluous post. You do not need to be told that you have come to the end of England. Carter Bar is indeed a gate: the historic barrier between Celt and Saxon; it is the gateway to Scotland.

And

> The border is haunted indeed. It sleeps, but—with one eye open! And it is growing cold. I dip down into Scotland.[79]

Borders, of course, were not restricted to the geopolitical; ethnic zoning and urban segregation provided their own physical, economic, and social barriers. Colonizers mapped urban divisions by describing the primitive architectural designs of their buildings and the squalid conditions and unique odors that eked from their houses and eateries, as well as by the psychological feelings of apprehension that they imagined as they approached these ethnic zones. Edmund Burt, traveling to Scotland in 1730, alluded to this in a letter wherein the English captain criticized his fellow countrymen for being "so prejudiced that they will not allow (or not own) there is anything good on this side of the Tweed River."[80] The colonizers' control over infrastructural improvements ensured that the zones they inhabited remained superior to those of the colonized.

Ethnic or racial zoning also surfaced in the interpersonal relations that colonizers shared with the colonized as differentiated across levels of schooling, professional enterprise, and forms of recreation. Such divisions can also be explained partly in terms of social class, but also by ethnic difference. Here the particular characteristics of the hegemonic relationship determined the colonized subjects' inferior position, and consequently justified colonizer-colonized segregation. The importance of education cannot be overstated. Denied access to educational opportunities seriously blocked the roads that the colonized peoples needed to travel to stand as equals with their colonizer counterpart; it critically limited their employment opportunities, living arrangements, and consequently social contacts that might have elevated their social status. Segregation also justified (in the eyes of the colonizer) the people's low social standing. Jim Crow-era whites saw blacks as inferior simply because they used inferior toilets and lived in inferior neighborhoods.[81]

Another critical factor that fortified ethnic divisions was representation—the picture that the colonizing peoples drew of their subjugated charges. The "lazy native" represents one image that enjoyed extensive employment in the discourse of colonization at all levels of colonial activity. Archbishop Peckham, in a letter to King Edward I in 1284, attributed Welsh wickedness to their "idleness: because they are idle they think up their wicked deeds."[82] Ronald Takaki found similarities between English images of Irish laziness and those employed by the Puritans in their descriptions of Native Americans.[83] E. Merton Caulter wrote on the "idleness" of the blacks during Reconstruction who, as General Robert E. Lee put it, enjoyed their "ease and comfort."[84] Syed Hussein Alatas explained this image as follows:

> In its historical empirical manifestation the colonial ideology utilized the idea of the lazy native to justify compulsion and unjust practices in the mobilization of labour in the colonies. It portrayed a negative image of the natives and their society to justify and rationalize European conquest and domination of the area. It distorted elements of social and human reality to ensure a comfortable construction of the ideology.[85]

Rather than question what incentive the "lazy native" might have found in working for the colonizers' benefit, the discourse defined their "laziness" as an innate personality defect that begged intervention from the foreign agency—their lazy character in and of itself justified their subjugation. This character flaw also explained the primitive environment in which they resided—leisure was a luxury not afforded people of a civilized land. Finally, it vindicated a second rationalization for this colonization—the inability of the governing body to instill within its subjects the will to work for the betterment of the collective whole. Better guidance was required to guide the "natives" toward adopting sound moral characters and encourage their willingness to work.

Negative images often intensified as the colonizers' relations with the colonized became intimate through a closer spatial proximity that challenged the colonizers' images. Linda Colley interprets the very popular English MP John Wilkes's "noisy Scottophobia" as a "deeply misleading reassurance" that "traditional Englishness *and* English primacy within the Union would remain intact." In truth, she argues, "the real significance of Wilkite complaints that Scots were invading the British polity . . . is, quite simply, that they were true."[86] Reconstruction-era whites responded to black advancements with increased violence and segregation. Enslaved blacks, argues Grace Elizabeth Hale, "constructed masks of simplemindedness and sycophancy, loyalty and laziness to play to their owners' fantasies and desires." Liberation brought a sizeable number of former slaves success in political, economic, and consequently social arenas that, according to one contributor to *Colored American Magazine,* only seemed to antagonize whites: "'Impediments became more numerous' and white crimes more vile." Hale argues that the white countered this success by creating a "culture of segregation," to solidify a "myth of absolute difference, to stop the rising." She concludes that since "southern black inferiority and white supremacy could not, despite whites' desires, be assumed, southern whites created a modern social order in which this difference would instead be continually performed."[87] Rather than simply justifying the image of the inferior black, Jim Crow created it.

Inferiority as an image defined the nature of the contacts that members of the two groups would engage across the psychological zones created to protect colonizer from colonized. The most frequent contacts that the colonized experienced with their subjugators put them in an inferior position: social morals preaching against intermarriage to preserve racial purity often degraded the role of the colonized female to that of the colonizer's mistress or prostitute.[88] Encounters between female members of the two groups, occurring primarily in the household, often formed a relationship of colonizer mistress and colonized maid. The latter ensured that her duties would not taint the purity of the household. The image of the unclean Muslim Algerian maid, for example, rendered her unfit to prepare the food for the European table.[89]

The realization of the goals as proclaimed in the colonizers' assimilation rhetoric required the colonizers to dismantle the walls that cemented the hierarchical relationship separating the two peoples. Considering that the very foundation laid by the formation of this relationship assumed inferiority, it was much easier to preach this task than it was to realize it. Dismantling ethnic boundaries represented internal expansion activity—the inclusion of different peoples to establish images of intimate sameness. Peripheral colonial activity fortified barriers of difference to maintain the peoples' segregated existence. Coordination of assimilation rhetoric and practice demanded that the colonized adopt the cultural identity of the colonizer, as well as that the colonizers reorganize this people's identity as worthy of inclusion. With few exceptions this step of inclusion was one that the colonizers avoided, and lobbied against, lest their privileged position be compromised.[90]

THE COLONIZED RESPONSE

Discussion painting the colonizer-colonized relationship as one of victim verses victimizer often neglects the important role that the subjugated people played in influencing the direction of their fate. Their response to this foreign intrusion was mixed: they naively cooperated, they passively endured, they silently resisted, and they passionately rebelled. Because the administrators were often in the minority and had to rely on a less stable ideological base to justify their status, enlisting the assistance of the colonized was essential for their efforts to realize any success.

The colonized demonstrated creativity and flexibility in their efforts to counter the foreign culture imposed upon them. The Welsh and the Irish used myth to counter English claims of superiority. They both traced their historical lineages back to the ancient state of Israel. The Welsh resistance traced its linguistic roots to the Hebrew language, their people's origins to the descendents of Noah.[91] Other versions of Welsh national history described the people as the "true inheritors of the whole island of Britain, the descendents of Brutus the Trojan, a people defeated by the Saxons, but only out of treachery."[92] The Irish emphasized their "ancient historic rights" partly to distinguish their individuality as an Irish nation with its "peculiar linguistic social and racial characteristics." As one unidentified Irish home ruler put it, "Ireland was a nation 'civilized and highly educated, when England was sunk in barbarism.'"[93] This laid common cultural ground for Irish of different political persuasions to adopt to prevent absorption by a foreign—here English—entity.[94]

Colonial subjugation also forced people to maintain distance from the intruders by exaggerating the practice of their traditional culture. The Moroccan people exaggerated the use of their cultural dress—the veil worn by females and the *chechia* cap donned by males—to an extent that would have been considered excessive outside of the colonial context. Amal Vinogradov writes that Moroccans, similar to other North African Muslim peoples, responded to the French arrival by holding "fast to the veil and general confinement of women and insisted on a fanatic observation of the fast, Ramadan."[95] The Scottish kilt, invented by an English Quaker, surfaced as a sign of anti-British protest during the Great Rebellion of 1745, so much so that the English declared it illegal to don the garment.[96]

National language played a mixed role in the efforts of the colonized to retain and develop nationalist sentiment. On the one hand, Welsh nationalism was fueled largely by its ability to retain the traditional language of its people, at times in the face of scathing verbal attacks from their English neighbors.[97] In contrast, the Irish and the Scots managed to survive as a distinct people despite their reliance on the English language. In the case of the Irish, English translations of traditional Gaelic literature and music served as vital carriers of their national identity. "Anglicization," writes D. George Boyce, "far from destroying nationalist Ireland, made possible its creation."[98]

The colonized also used the instruments of the hegemonic culture to preserve their traditional culture. In 1824 the Cherokee people drafted a constitution to demonstrate their ability to incorporate modern institutions to the advancing Americans, a fruitless activity as the intruders preferred territory to civilized neighbors. From 1828 the Cherokee nation used the press to disseminate its laws to its members.[99] Cherokees also increased educational opportunities to preserve their traditional culture in the face of the external colonizing threat. The Scots, in the early nineteenth century, built an extensive school system along their border with England. George Lewis, writing in 1834, acknowledged this institution's crucial value by admitting, "all but our parochial churches and schools, we have lost our nationality. In these alone we survive as a nation—stand apart from and superior to England."[100] In this sense schools shared a similar role of cultural preservation with indigenous language newspapers. Aled Jones's evaluation of Welsh-language journalism serving as an "effective cultural barrier that isolated Welsh-speaking Wales from the debilitating effects of English values"[101] is a good example of the colonizer adopting institutions of the hegemonic power to resist assimilation.

Finally, travel throughout the empire provided the colonized with opportunities to contribute both positively and negatively to the colonizer's grand imperial schemes. Some participated as government officials or members of other organizations in external colonizing efforts active in these territories. Others used the opportunity to preach their message of independence to residents of these areas. Members of the Irish Home Rule movement participated actively in the Indian independence movement. The inspiration of nationalism and patriotism that they displayed by "going native" was seen as a serious threat to the British administration. These "white sisters" and "holy mothers," who came to be known by the Indians as "white goddesses," traveled to the subcontinent to preach modernity in the arts and in education, alongside their messages on Indian independence.[102]

Those allowed to travel to the homeland for schooling often supplemented their studies with lessons in leftist ideology that camouflaged their nationalist ambitions. Interest in Marxist thinking, for example, increased after Lenin published his treatise *Imperialism: The Highest Stage of Capitalism* in 1916. Revolutionary leaders established their legitimacy by adopting a globally recognized ideology. This was true of the Vietnamese leader Ho Chi Minh but also of members of the Socialist Party in Alsace and Lorraine. Algerian workers living in Paris organized in 1926 as the Étoile Nord-Africaine (North African Star), a communist group that soon expanded into a much larger nationalist movement called El Oumma (The Muslim People).[103]

The colonized also demonstrated their approval of colonial rule by cooperating with their colonizers to an extent that exceeded that needed simply to survive. Much of this cooperation, as was the case with businessmen in the German colonies of Alsace and Lorraine, was contingent on favors they anticipated receiving as compensation, in this case, access to German markets.[104] The Young Algerians demanded French citizenship in return for their cooperation in fighting the colonizers' wars and relocating to their imperial outposts. The colonizer's failure to properly recognize these efforts often provoked a backlash as collaborators quickly turned to anticolonial rebels.

In 1919, the colonized, disillusioned by the behavior of their colonizers during the First World War, and encouraged by a rising anti-imperialist sentiment, initiated anticolonial independence movements. These acts of rebellion previously suffered from their isolation; weak (or weakened) nationalist sentiment prevented the movements from expanding to the level that might have produced revolutionary change. Division among the colonized ranks compromised their effectiveness. The year 1919 was different in that a unique arrangement of events—at both the international and local levels—momentarily convinced a wide variety of peoples that, first, they had a right to self-determination and, second, that a united demonstration would attract international support for their local cause. The processes that generated nationalist sentiment at this time also managed to incorporate those traditionally excluded from political and social participation, most notably women, who not only marched alongside their male counterparts, but also accompanied them to the jails, torture chambers, and graveyards.

The breadth of these movements was remarkable considering the variety of participants over this limited time period. In early February Korean students in Tokyo issued a Korean declaration of independence. On March 1, thousands of Koreans took to the streets of Seoul to protest Japanese colonial rule. On March 9, hundreds of Egyptian women "poured out of their harems, clad in veils, onto the streets to demonstrate."[105] One month later in Amritsar, India, British forces killed more than four hundred Indian demonstrators participating in "one of the most widespread and effective demonstrations against British rule since the Mutiny of 1857."[106] In early May the Chinese students, inspired by the Korean uprising against the Japanese, initiated a cultural movement to condemn Japan's wartime initiative to push upon China its twenty-one demands and for its occupation of the Shantung Peninsula. The period also saw a rise in nationalism among the colonized in these countries, as well as in West Africa, the Sudan, and Vietnam.[107] Many of these groups submitted their appeals for global recognition of their right to self-determination to participants at the Paris peace conference who had gathered to decide the fate of post-World War I global geopolitics.

In many cases—but not all—the wrath of the colonized was induced by the poor treatment they continued to receive at the hands of their occupiers even after the two had battled side by side in the recently ended world war. The colonies, like the homeland, had been placed under wartime restrictions. Many of the colonized, aspiring to improve their status, had endured displacement for labor or even military purposes; a disproportionate number had succumbed to the fighting. The French transported more than 140,000 Vietnamese to France during the war years for labor purposes. From Algeria 173,000 men saw combat duty while another 119,000 performed work detail in France. Peripheral and external territories of the British Empire contributed their share of soldiers, as well. More than 1.4 million Indians fought in the war, of whom 62,000 perished; British East and West Africa sent 34,000 and 25,000 men to arms, respectively. The Welsh, whose men were subject to conscription, put 280,000 of their finest in uniform. Many more served in a noncombative capacity alongside 82,000 Egyptians.[108]

In addition to engaging in mass movements, some territories used this opportunity to debate the weak and strong points of seeking independence; these discussions were significant in their revelations of just how dependent these territories had become on the homeland. One such discussion took place in Wales from mid-March 1919. An editorial that appeared in the March 15 issue of the *North Wales Times* called for the independence issue to be debated in terms of the advantages and disadvantages it would bring to Welsh education, finance, and health. This debate continued for at least one month when on June 14 the newspaper argued against the selection of Cardiff as a location for an independent Welsh parliament: the city was "not, in any sense, a Welsh town" as, the editorial calculated, one hears more Welsh in Liverpool. Geographically, the article continued, Cardiff was far less accessible to North Wales than to London.[109] In the end the Welsh opted to remain with England.

Indeed, very few peoples gained independence as a result of these efforts, two of the most noted examples being Ireland and Egypt. In a manner similar to their union, the Irish obtained their independence through compromise: the English acknowledged its "Free State" status in return for Irish acceptance of division (as Northern Ireland remains a member of the United Kingdom). One member of Parliament, Sir Henry Wilson, complained that the loss of Ireland signaled the empire's "doom."[110] The argument can also be made that the British Empire's ability to sustain such a critical loss partly resulted from its improved relationship with France; Ireland's membership in the British Empire thus became more a matter of imperial pride than a security necessity. In contrast, we see the resilience of the institution in the number of territories over which the British and other colonial powers administered, despite demands by these subjugated peoples for recognition of their right to self-determination as put forth in President Woodrow Wilson's fourteen points.

Western assimilation practices offered Japanese administrators a number of options in their colonies: the English political assimilation model and the French and German cultural assimilation model. A third option, advanced by the French after World War I, suggested that the colonized people's assimilation need not be "total." Colonizers could gain the security they required from incorporating these peripheral peoples without requiring their complete cultural makeover. History suggests that English political assimilation proved most successful. While they initially resisted, the Welsh, the Scots, and even the Irish proved loyal in at least two important ways: they refrained from allying with England's enemies (France and then Germany) and they contributed both natural and human resources to England's colonial and military endeavors. Following the failure of the 1745 rebellion in the Scottish Highlands, the Welsh and Scots generally refrained from battling English forces for independence. Indeed, while other colonized peoples, including their Irish cousins, took to the streets to protest colonial rule, the Welsh debated their future in the press. The relationship appears to have benefited both colonized and colonizers over the centuries.

This model contrasted with the more intrusive French and German models that attempted to change the cultural fabric of their colonial subjects, while offering them at best limited political participation rights in return for their cooperation. Their peripheral colonization contrasted remarkably with the internal colonization these two states introduced to their southern territories that allowed these peoples full political rights in exchange for their cooperation. As we shall see in chapter 2, the Japanese frequently invoked these examples to justify their decision to assimilate their colonial subjects. The cultural similarities that Japanese shared with the Taiwanese and Koreans afforded them an advantage over those colonizers who attempted to assimilate peoples of different religious, linguistic, and social backgrounds. European and American practitioners of cultural assimilation failed, first, because they were unable to match policy rhetoric with policy practice and, second, because they were unable to gain the support of the expatriate population for assimilation practices. Thus, the most significant lessons that Japanese should have learned from these examples were the importance of gaining the support of the colonized, as well as the need to convince their own people of the colonized people's new imperial position.

2

JAPAN'S DEVELOPMENT OF INTERNAL AND PERIPHERAL ASSIMILATION

WHEN CONSIDERING THE PLACE OF EZO AND RYUKYU IN THE STORY OF Japan's expansion, the conventional interpretation that Japan was a "late starter" that got into the business of expansion only with the acquisition of Taiwan after its victory in the Sino-Japanese War in 1895 becomes untenable. Akira Iriye, for example, remarks that expansionist thinking was "never a major strand [of Japan] prior to this time."[1] Others acknowledge that these territories maintained a status different from Tokugawa-era domains, but shy from classifying this difference as "colonial." Mark R. Peattie writes that their Meiji-era incorporation constituted a "clarification of national boundaries of the sort common to nation building in nineteenth and twentieth century Europe."[2] Ōe Shinobu classifies Ezo and Ryukyu as Tokugawa-era "pre-modern colonies" that had been incorporated as part of the Japanese "mainland" by early Meiji.[3] More recent research, however, has argued the two territories' modern history of colonial subjugation.[4]

Expansionist aspirations by Japan predate the Meiji period, and intensified as Western encroachment increased in the nineteenth century. Tokugawa visionaries and statesmen outlined plans for Japanese expansion that painted a future Japanese empire extending as far south as Australia.[5] The late eighteenth-century Russian encroachment on islands to Japan's north compelled the government to temporarily occupy the territory and attempt to assimilate the local residents. The mid-nineteenth-century increase in global expansion further stimulated interest among Japanese who believed that their country should grab territory while there was still land left to grab.

Peattie correctly notes that Japan acquired lands generally "near at hand," rather than "empty stretches of jungle or desert," that were "well populated lands whose inhabitants were racially akin" to the Japanese.[6] But this constitutes an "anomaly"[7] only in a limited (external) colonial context. Colonial activity at the internal and peripheral levels includes numerous cases in which a hegemonic people imposed their culture on an "inferior," yet "racially akin," people. The Meiji Restoration provides one such example. The modernization that the Meiji regime introduced constituted an intense effort to impose new political, social, and cultural institutions on residents of former Tokugawa domains.[8] Soon after inaugurating this effort, this same regime initiated efforts to integrate Ezo and Ryukyu; the Tokugawa regime had demonstrated ambitions to exert influence over these territories, yet saw greater political and economic benefit in recognizing them as sovereign.[9] By incorporating Ezo and Ryukyu as Hokkaido and Okinawa, the Meiji government assumed responsibility for assimilating the territories' residents as Japanese. The acquisition of Taiwan in 1895 led a cautious Japan to affirm its administration policy by seeking foreign guidance and by debating the content of its assimilation policy. Lessons learned over this four-decade period of colonial activity proved instrumental in helping Japan determine its form of administration in Korea from 1910.

THE IWAKURA MISSION AND JAPANESE INTERNAL EXPANSION

Takekoshi Yosaburō, founder of the journal *Sekai no Nihon* (Japan for the World) and Seiyūkai political party member, wrote in 1881 that during the Edo period, "the idea of a Japanese nation did not exist. It only came to be realized in 1853 with the arrival of Commodore Matthew Perry when the 300 or so domains became siblings and the many tens of thousands of people realized that they were one people."[10] Takekoshi deserves credit for recognizing, amid the growing assertion of the Japanese nation's eternal existence, the freshness of his country's perception of nationhood. His shortsighted contention that it only took the arrival of a fleet of black ships to suddenly shape this people into a nation was, however, a gross simplification of an extremely complex process. The process that forged the Japanese people into a modern nation took more than a half century to realize, and periodically required renewed efforts as Japan's global position became increasingly precarious from the late 1920s.[11]

Meiji Japan's expansion efforts were driven in part by the global expansion that characterized the period in which it came to power. To avoid its own colonization, and to strengthen its chances of Western states rescinding the humiliating "unequal treaties" that they imposed upon Japan, Meiji Japan believed it necessary to prove the nation's capacity to both adopt modern institutions and disseminate them throughout the territory it recognized as internal. Its Tokugawa predecessors initiated efforts to learn from the West soon after signing a series of these treaties. The Meiji regime continued this effort. In 1871 it assembled a group of seasoned diplomats and young students (one being a six-year-old girl, Tsuda Umeko) to circle the globe in search of information. The Iwakura Mission returned in 1873 with a strong sense of the state's requirements to secure its internal and peripheral territories, as well as an acute understanding of the consequences should this expansion turn reckless. The mission's itinerary, placing the group in the capitals of the most important practitioners of assimilation at the time, offered the travelers a greater understanding of this policy's nuts and bolts just as Japan prepared to incorporate residents of Ezo and Ryukyu.

The tour's historian, Kume Kunitake, entered into his five-volume history its members' encounters with both internal and peripheral colonization. In the United States, he noted the efforts that Reconstruction-era America made to educate a diverse range of its citizens. The schools, he observed, did not separate men from women, and strove to educate blacks, Native Americans, and even the physically challenged. Education in the United States transformed even the rougher elements of the population into responsible adults.[12] Kume wrote: "Clearly, the colour of a one's skin has nothing to do with intelligence. People with insight have recognized that education is the key to improvement." He optimistically predicted that "in a decade or two, talented black people will rise and white people who do not study and work hard will fall by the wayside."[13]

The tour crossed over to England, where participants encountered representations of colonial expansion as history when they toured London's museums. At the museum, Kume noted, progress and its virtues could best be observed. He wrote the following after touring the British Museum:

> Progress does not mean discarding what is old and contriving
> something which is entirely new. In the forming of a nation, there-
> fore, customs and practices arise whose value is tested by constant
> use, so that when new knowledge arises it naturally does so from
> [existing] sources, and it is from these sources that it derives its

value. Nothing is better than a museum for showing clearly the stages by which these processes happen.[14]

The Japanese travelers also observed this progress at the South Kensington Museum (renamed the Victoria and Albert Museum in 1899), which displayed exhibitions on England of forty years past and England of the present. The museum served as a place where this "vast difference [between these two periods of English history] . . . can be imagined," and showed how England came to assume the wealthy status it now enjoys.[15] The foundation of its wealth was a product of its overseas acquisitions.

Kume reflected on the value of a strong military to protect this wealth after viewing a grand military review at London's Beacon Hill. Pondering the question of why civilized countries continued to prepare for war, Kume wrote that civilized people must retain standing armies not because they have yet to emerge from barbarism but because barbarian people relish battle. Sound and economical military security required keeping one's "external enemies . . . at a distance." England could concentrate its resources in its navy because, in contrast to France, Germany, and Russia, it had no enemies at its land borders. Kume then defined two critical military objectives: the state's attainment of both internal and peripheral security. To achieve internal security, the state must guide its people to "be at peace with one another, [to] work hard at productive enterprises, [to] be imbued with the spirit of patriotism and [to] regard it as shameful to submit to another country." The state must also secure its periphery: "A country which was threatened by no enemies on land or sea on any side and had no need of an unproductive army to maintain domestic peace would be a happy land indeed."[16]

The tour then advanced across the English Channel and into France, England's lone peripheral concern. The group's arrival in Paris came at a time of France's heightened awareness over the need to strengthen national allegiances (particularly in its southern provinces) and ties with its colonies through assimilation. The Japanese refrained from openly criticizing their hosts' recent setback to Prussia, even in Kume's official record of the mission. Richard Sims explains that the Japanese still believed the French to be the most enlightened European state. Kume complemented the French: "British industry depends on machinery; in France there is a balance between human skills and machines." The British could not match the French in "elegance and delicacy."[17]

Kume devoted extensive attention to the French colonial network and the products that each possession delivered to the French people. The historian diverged from his encyclopedic, fact-centered discourse style to comment briefly on the geographic similarity between Algeria's proximity to France and Korea's to Japan. His blunt mention of Korea here perhaps reflected the mounting debate taking place in Japan over whether Korea's "insult"—its refusal to meet Japanese envoys seeking to modernize Japan-Korea diplomacy—warranted military action on Japan's part. Kume's writing does not reveal the side of the debate to which he leaned. Later in his career the historian would support annexation: for Kume, the existence of a thalassocracy predating Japan's first mythical emperor, Jinmu (660–585 B.C.), that encompassed Korea, Kyushu, and southern China acted as a precedent to Japan's modern colonial ambitions.[18]

In Prussia the Japanese travelers encountered an example of progress that in many ways resembled their country's own situation. Recent military victories by the Prussian military over Austria and France had created for the new German state a double-edged sword: success had rallied the German states to unification but its neighbors to concern over the growing German threat. No one understood the challenges that the nascent German state faced better than its architect, Chancellor Otto von Bismarck, who cautioned his Japanese guests over the threats that the strong states wielded over weaker ones. The laws of nations, he warned, were only as good as their usefulness to the particular countries in dispute.[19] At this meeting Bismarck hinted at expansion's necessity when he informed his guests that "it is our hope that, motivated solely by respect for national rights, each nation may be independent and conduct diplomatic relations on equal terms, living within its just territories without its borders being violated." He added that Germany had (fortunately) learned in time that this is not always the case, and it must use force to protect its sovereign rights. International law was to be invoked "if [the great power] stood to benefit."[20]

The information collected by the tour participants reflected ideas that had been voiced from centuries previous. Honda Toshiaki had written in his eighteenth-century *Seiki monogatari* (Tales of the West) on the duplicity of strong nations who gained power by first assimilating peoples in their immediate environment, before extending their efforts to territories at their periphery. The Tokugawa regime employed assimilation in Ezo to protect areas at its northern periphery from foreign intrusion. Nineteenth-century intensification of global expansion encouraged the nascent Meiji government to incorporate ways to unify the peoples within its internal territories as subjects, while expanding its reach to incorporate those at its peripheral territories. The tour returned to Japan just in time to prevent a similar effort, a military campaign to punish Korea. Those against this operation hardly sympathized with Korea, but felt Japan ill prepared at this time to confront Korea militarily. Ōkubo Toshimichi listed the following reasons: weak state foundation, insufficient state revenue, underdeveloped domestic institutions, insufficient gold reserves, increased debt with England placing internal affairs at further risk, and the lingering unequal treaties. He later included the risk of Russian and Chinese intervention as yet another reason for Japan to cancel these plans.[21] More work needed to be done closer to home.

Japan's nation-building process resembled colonial expansion in that it replaced local cultural and political institutions with central hegemonic institutions. It replaced local gods, dialects, costumes, cuisine, holidays, and other customs with those determined by the core elite to be "civilized," and defined them as "national." Compulsory education and universal male conscription— open in theory (but in practice only over time) to all Japanese residents— became the primary vehicles that introduced this culture to the people. Print culture reinforced these messages to literate Japanese, who in turn read to the illiterate.[22] Policies initiated by the Tokugawa regime inadvertently assisted the Meiji government's centralizing efforts. Its *sankin kōtai* (a Shogunal control mechanism that forced *daimyo* to spend alternate years in the capital) policy developed economic and transportation networks along the routes the *daimyo* and their samurai entourage traveled to reach Edo, but also strengthened the domain lords' allegiance to a central shogun entity.[23] The central Meiji government's task was to secure the allegiance that commoners had previously reserved for their local *daimyo*.

This task was not completed overnight, nor was it free from opposition. The Tokugawa regime, ever vigilant against potential rival alliances forming, had instituted policies that stratified Japanese society by separating the military and peasant classes politically, socially, and culturally.[24] The scholar Fukuzawa Yukichi described this society as "many millions of people throughout Japan sealed up in many millions of separate boxes or separated by millions of walls."[25] Expansionists used similar criticisms in their commentaries on the "bad governments" that administrated territories targeted by Japan for annexation. The Meiji government sought to reconfigure these boxes into one large pyramid-like structure that affixed Japan's political, social, and cultural core at its apex.

The repulsion that Meiji leaders held toward the regime they overthrew, as well as their desire to restructure the state anew, was evident in their depictions of the antiquated Tokugawa state as barbarous; Japan's isolated existence kept it out of step with the progress of modern civilization. The German physician Erwin von Baelz observed that the Japanese "did not want to know anything about their past; in fact they declared that any civilized person could only be embarrassed by it." He quoted a Japanese acquaintance as saying that "everything in our past is completely barbaric. . . . We have no history, for our history is just about to begin."[26] All social customs were subject to reform, from eating and bathing practices, to linguistic writing systems, to even spouse selection. The multilayered screening that accompanied the changes examined innovation in terms of its capacity to distance modern Meiji Japan from traditional Tokugawa Japan, by its utility to redefine Japan as "civilized," and by the state's capacity to rally the people's patriotic awareness. In this narrative, *kaikoku* (open country) served as the perfect antonym for *sakoku* (closed country). The key to this movement's success was the alternative legitimate force—the imperial household—to which the Japanese could turn to consummate the process. The Meiji government would have found it rather difficult—as did Korea at this time—to institute the necessary reforms had this revolutionary regime change failed to materialize.

The great diversity that existed throughout the archipelago required social, political, and cultural forces to create a Japanese identity among the new state's constituents. Interdomain differences, evident before the Meiji Restoration, became even more acute after travel restrictions were eased to allow people greater access to different parts of the islands, as well as to each other. Japanese "dialects" and appearance seemed so different that, on one occasion, a Japanese girl from the countryside mistook the language she heard Japanese speaking upon her arrival in Tokyo as French.[27] One resident of present-day Toyama Prefecture observed Satsuma soldiers in the following way:

> The hair of the Kagoshima warriors was thick and shaggy; they
> wore beards. . . . Furthermore, among them were those who had
> haircuts [in the foreigner's style]. The occasion was the first time
> I had seen such a haircut. Their words were gibberish and I could
> not understand a single thing. It was truly like encountering Westerners (*seiyōjin*).[28]

In spite of these differences the central administration was motivated to include all residents of the archipelago first as *shinmin* (subject) and later as *kokumin* (national subject). Nurturing this identity tied the Japanese people more closely to the central administration's needs, be it for purposes of tax-ing them or enlisting them in the military, but also for gaining their support (as opposed to fighting the system). Their amalgamation also strengthened state security that would have been compromised should a particular region have allied with a foreign state. Finally, it demonstrated to the international community the legitimacy of the Meiji regime and Japan's advancement to civilization, both goals dependent on the central state's ability to establish control over its internal residents. Iwakura Tomomi, the leader of the tour that bears his name, emphasized the ill effects that political differences could have on statecraft.

> Within a body under autonomous rule (*jishū dokusai*), it is not debated whether a country is big or small, strong or weak. Its inde-pendent, absolute rule is based on whether there are places in the empire in which its orders are not reached. Even if the country is large, if a king's orders deviate and do not extend throughout [his realm], if political orders are different in every place, if the orders given are different from the king's orders, the country suffers from divided sovereignty (*han shukoku*). Even a big country like China has not fallen to this state; on the other hand, it is possible for a small country like Holland to lose its autonomy.[29]

Iwakura listed as one of his tour's purposes to search for the know-how to "unite [Japan]'s policy leaving no divisions."[30]

A second major task involved determining state membership. Fukuzawa emphasized this in his 1875 *Bunmeiron no gairaku* (Outline on a Theory of Civilization). Japan's most important interpreter of Western civilization defined national polity formation as a process of

> grouping together of a race of people of similar feelings, the cre-ation of a distinction between fellow countrymen and foreigners, the fostering of more cordial and stronger bonds with one's coun-trymen than with foreigners. It is living under the same govern-ment, enjoying self-rule, and disliking the idea of being subject to foreign rule; it involves independence and responsibility for the welfare of one's own country.[31]

Not all residents of the new Meiji state received the benefits and responsibili-ties of state membership at the same time. The Meiji-era selection process was hardly free from discrimination. Yet, in theory they all were granted unqualified membership in the newly reconstructed Japanese state. Their membership was not articulated as a process of becoming Japanese, but as their learning what being Japanese meant. The state's newly formed institutions would iron out any wrinkles in their allegiance, dialects, and mannerisms.

Education and the media formed two of the more important institutions created to, as Sheldon Garon puts it, "mold Japanese minds."[32] Both fed off of each other in the three-stage acculturation process that began in the home, continued in the schools, and was reinforced in society. Universal compulsory education, initiated with the 1872 Fundamental Code of Education, sought to instill in students the basic tenets of the national polity while instructing them in the three Rs. Social education (*shakai kyōiku*) used the media and study sessions to reinforce these messages. Educating women perpetuated this cycle by preparing future mothers for their role as preschool teachers for their children.

Meiji education specialists offered few kind words to describe the education their system replaced. The new Ministry of Education claimed that Tokugawa-era *terakoya* (temple school) "teachers are scoundrels for the most part, having fallen from the nobler ranks and were no longer able to support themselves." It added, "with no inkling of what education really is, they profess to be teachers of arithmetic, writing and reading, 'even though' their instruction is so superficial and shallow that [pupils] leave [just as] ignorant of the principle of things (*butsuri*) as when they entered."[33] Although left out of this commentary, the most critical shortcoming of this education system was its absence of a central coordinating entity to control its operations, as well as a compulsory element to bring all school-age children to the classroom.

The Iwakura Mission agenda gave high priority to investigating education systems. Iwakura Tomomi articulated this goal as examining

> every country's regulations and methods for educating its people;
> the building of both private and public schools; the ordering of
> various curriculums; and the holding of ceremonies for presenta-
> tions of class and rules. . . . The best situation will be [determined]
> and implemented throughout [Japan].

The government's paving the "road to education" provided Japan with a "united road to enlightenment," as well as concrete criteria for other states to view "Japan as a nation advancing toward enlightenment and thus ready for treaty revision."[34]

The spirit of the 1872 Fundamental Code of Education that established Japan's education system emphasized the importance of education in statecraft: expanding the talents of an enlightened people served as the foundation of a state that intended to become rich, strong, and stable. The most effective way to accomplish this goal was to build schools and establish education methodology.[35] The often-quoted mantra that defined this long-term ambition pledged complete literacy: "no community with an illiterate family, nor a family with an illiterate person." Meiji education, initially focused on individual development, like education in France shifted from the 1880s to emphasize the subject's contribution to the larger national body. An early reference to this change in direction is found in a July 1881 publication titled the "Memorandum for Elementary School Teachers" that instructed teachers to place "particular emphasis on moral education and [making] the students gain the most complete mastery of the great path of human morality, which includes such virtues as loyalty to the Emperor, love of country, [and] filial piety toward parents."[36]

Itō Hirobumi, traveling through Europe in 1882 to study constitutional law, also returned to Japan with ideas on the role of national education in developing state prosperity and power, as employed by the German Rudolf von Gneist and the Austrian Lorenz von Stein. Convinced of the misguided direction in Japan's education policy, Itō met with Mori Arinori, Japan's ambassador to England, to discuss reform. The fruits of this discussion are apparent in the Education Ordinance of 1885, promulgated soon after the inauguration of the first Itō cabinet, which included Mori as minister of education. Mori's instruction to Wakayama Prefecture teachers on Japan's education reforms mirrored directives issued by French education officials at the time Jules Ferry's reforms appeared.

> Reading, writing and arithmetic are not our major concerns in the education and instruction of the young. . . . Education is entirely a matter of bringing up men of character. And who are these men of character?—they are those persons who live up fully to their responsibilities as Imperial subjects. The fulfillment [of these duties] requires a steady disposition in carrying out the tasks of the nation and in extending oneself to the full extent of one's capacities.[37]

The trend that pushed Japan's education system toward moral-based instruction climaxed in 1890 with the promulgation of the Imperial Rescript on Education. The document, which was enshrined in every school, offered minimal attention to academic learning itself. Rather it focused on the students' filial and social responsibilities, lessons that school curriculums reinforced by introducing the document in textbooks and daily lessons.

Print media provided a medium of instruction for people outside the formal education system.[38] The national press introduced and reinforced similar messages in the Japanese media. The steps that the government took to control the press indicate the power of sway that it believed this institution held. Suzuki Kenji writes that the government funded newspapers to enhance their development; when one took a route that diverted from its intentions, it corrected and punished the wayward newspaper. He claims the newspaper "along with war served as levers to unite the people by cultural and political assimilation."[39] James L. Huffman adds that "no single institution did more to create a modern citizenry than the Meiji newspaper press."[40] The newspaper's most important value lay in its ability to simultaneously deliver to all people, both urbanites and rural dwellers, the information they needed to strengthen national ties. Its pages enabled people to participate in the nation's military battles, its territorial acquisitions, and its imperial celebrations without leaving their cities, towns, and villages. It demarcated state borders by offering simple graphic representations of the state in the form of a map, which both informed and reminded people of their country's size and shape, as well as its geopolitical relations with other states.[41]

The early Japanese press also assumed a socializing mission. One of the early issues of the *Tokyo nichi-nichi* in 1871 carried an order from the Tokyo municipal government instructing that *jinrikusha* drivers and day laborers dress appropriately to avoid serving as the butt of foreigners' jokes.[42] In November 1874, the very first issue of the *Yomiuri shinbun* carried a Home Ministry decree instructing people to "observe decorum and show respect to the emperor during his progress through the streets of Tokyo."[43] Huffman observes that those writing for the newspaper often chose topics that instructed readers on what "civilized" people did: they instructed Japanese on what they should eat and drink, as well as what they should read.[44]

These messages reveal as much about the government's views on the purpose of the media as they do assumptions regarding the newspaper's readership. It was clear that Japan's print media had tapped an increasingly literate population.[45] While it is inherently difficult to determine just how many people read each newspaper (purchasing a newspaper did not ensure it being read; one did not have to purchase a newspaper to read one), it does appear that more people read the news than purchased a newspaper. Japanese society attempted to create opportunities to ensure this. "Reading rooms" provided free access to newspapers. The illiterate gained access to the news when Buddhist monks and other literate Japanese read and explained the news to them.[46]

The potential sway that the press held over the public alerted the Meiji government to its threat potential. It soon pushed through legislation to control this effect. In 1868 the state gained the authority to punish journalists responsible for "serious slips of the pen." It also banned foreigners from holding publisher or editor positions to curtail criticism from abroad.[47] The Japanese government issued another set of publication restrictions in April 1883 that made it illegal for newspapers to criticize the military or foreign ministry. This legislation also prohibited journalists serving a publishing ban from switching newspapers during the duration of their penalty.[48]

The government enjoyed press support, rather than criticism, during its military campaigns and overseas expansion activities. The jingoist press often encouraged the government in these activities. In 1894, the press prepared the homeland for the battles to come, and then led the chorus of cheers that rose with every victory.[49] This support continued over the next half century: as the Japanese Empire expanded across the Asian continent, the press rallied the people to support Japan's new acquisitions, informing them of the advantages these new possessions provided for their individual welfare as well as their country's position in the world.[50]

The central government envisioned education and the media as potential tools for directing the people's attention toward its nation-building aspirations. These institutions also provided the Japanese people with the tools to lobby their interests. A literate population provided an expanding market for the growing print culture. This empowered a civil society that demanded attention be given to individual needs and interests, rather than simply to those that the government deemed essential for the broader interests of the state.[51] The Japanese public demonstrated on numerous occasions its willingness to take to the streets in protest if local and national officials failed to meet the people's demands. This empowered public sphere, notes Carol Gluck, produced "the strongest views—the hard line" that "produced a disproportionate amount of the 'public opinion' (*yoron*) of the period."[52] This potentially hostile element could not be tamed merely by legislation to establish learning and publication boundaries, but required prior consideration when the government made decisions regarding the domestic and overseas activities of the state.

EARLY MEIJI PERIPHERAL EXPANSION

The Meiji government's second task—after redefining the political allegiance of its constituents—was to strengthen its national security by incorporating potentially unstable peripheral territories. The first stage incorporated territories with which Tokugawa Japan maintained suzerain relations but had never officially annexed into "Japan" proper. Control over two such territories— Ezo and the Ryukyu kingdom—was subject to negotiation with two of Japan's neighboring threats, Russia and China. Japan's subsequent success in assimilating these peoples has camouflaged their colonial roots.

The two territories assumed critical roles in Tokugawa diplomacy even though they remained outside its domain-centered geopolitical system. Indeed, their value to the Tokugawa rested in their independent status. The Ryukyu kingdom facilitated Japan's trade with China and kingdoms in present-day Southeast Asia. Through Satsuma, the Tokugawa subjected the northernmost island, Okinawa, to a protectorate-style relationship. After consolidating power, the Ryukyu king, Shō Nei, was ordered to pay his respects to Tokugawa Ieyesu, the new shogun. The king refused and the *bakufu* ordered Satsuma to punish the kingdom for his disobedience. Satsuma officials kidnapped the king and held him hostage for three years, until he agreed to offer allegiance to Satsuma. Shō relinquished economic autonomy to the domain when he accepted a fifteen-article ordinance that legislated such areas as Ryukyu trade, tax collection, and slave policies.[53] The confusion of late Tokugawa and early Meiji provided the kingdom with an opportunity to establish its independence from Satsuma. It welcomed Western visitors to the islands, and even signed treaties with these visiting states.[54] For a short period Ryukyu also managed to deflect "requests" by the new Meiji administration that the king demonstrate his realm's allegiance to the new Meiji regime by making a visit, similar to Satsuma's demands in the early 1600s. King Shō Tai initially resisted but in the end succumbed to Japanese pressure.

The Chinese government challenged Japan's claims to these islands. This alternative provided the Ryukyu kingdom with hope for protection from Japanese intrusions. The Qing, citing China's historical tributary relations with Ryukyu, claimed them as its territory. The Japanese government offered its own historical narrative to justify its claims. Inoue Kaoru, a member of the Chōshū faction who served in both the foreign and finance ministries, drafted a statement that first argued the historic roots of Japan's control from the Keichō Period (1596–1615). Second, he asserted that China forfeited its claim to control when it failed to act against the kingdom's signing international treaties with foreign states. Japan, on the other hand, demonstrated its concern for the Ryukyu people when in March 1874 it dispatched its military to Taiwan after tribesmen massacred shipwrecked Ryukyu sailors.[55]

The Chinese requested that former U.S. president Ulysses S. Grant, then on a world tour, arbitrate the dispute over the Ryukyu Islands. He arrived in mid-1879 and, after hearing both China and Japan's cases, proposed a three-way partition, with Okinawa remaining sovereign and Japan and China dividing islands to its north and south. Both parties rejected Grant's initial proposal, and the Chinese court rejected a counter two-way partition. Japan used the delay to strengthen its hold on the territory, and annexed the entire island chain soon after. The islands' residents continued to maintain hope that China would come to their rescue until its defeat by Japan in 1895.[56]

Meiji Japan did not face the same challenges with Ezo as it did Ryukyu, primarily because its predecessor had completed negotiations with the Russian government to determine Japan-Russia borders. The initial Russian threat, half a century previous, did force the Tokugawa to reconsider policy that allowed Ezo its sovereignty. Both governments initiated assimilation policies to counter Russian encroachment on this territory. Brett L. Walker writes that as early as 1802 the Tokugawa regime adopted a "more 'modern' [administration in Ezo] with the central government participating in the planning of economic policy and overseeing the deculturation and assimilation of the Ainu." After two decades it relaxed its hold on the island, despite advice that it strengthen its grip on this strategically vital area. Soon after Perry's arrival, Tokugawa forces returned to Ezo and reinitiated their earlier efforts.[57] In 1855 Japan and Russia drew their territorial border between the islands of Etrofu and Uruppu, with Sakhalin remaining a common possession to be resolved through further negotiations, which were conducted in 1875.[58]

The Meiji administration reintroduced assimilation to solidify Japan's hold over Ezo, now renamed Hokkaido. As before, the Japanese government imposed upon the indigenous peoples the fundamental elements of "Japanese-ness" by banning outright all signs of what it considered to be "barbarous." The magnitude of this task was far greater than that required in Japan's internal regions, which required the molding of regional dialect and custom. David Howell describes this process as follows:

During the first decade in power, the new [Meiji] regime not only banned visible markers of Ainu ethnicity, such as earrings and tattoos, but also forbade the Ainu their religion or to hunt in their ancestral hunting-grounds. In November 1878 the state stripped the Ainu of their ethnicity in legal terms by renaming them "former aborigines" (*kyū dojin*); during the next several years the Ainu became subject to taxation, civil and criminal law and conscription under the same conditions as other Japanese subjects.[59]

In both Okinawa and Hokkaido education served as the primary vehicle to rid the peoples of their unacceptable characteristics to prepare them for assimilation as Japanese subjects, even if it meant transfering them to "civilized" environments. In 1872 the Japanese government physically transported thirty-six Ainu children to the mainland and admitted them to the Tokyo Kaitakushi karigakkō (literally the Tokyo temporary development school). Kuroda Kiyotaka, an early formulator of Japan's Ainu and Korean policies, explained this relocation as necessary in order to encourage the children to overcome differences that existed between the Ainu and Japanese languages, customs, and mannerisms by placing them in a civilized environment. The school assigned to the students nine faculty members, three of whom assumed responsibility for "indigenous control" (*dojin torishimari*).[60] A second fundamental purpose of the school was to instruct the Ainu students to "receive gracefully" the imperial grace, as well as to advertise to Japanese their subjugation over the Ainu peoples.[61] In 1873 the school welcomed members of the imperial family who visited to observe the Ainu students. The school treated its guests to a fashion show that displayed the students in both their traditional garb and modern (Western) dress. This display emphasized Ainu backwardness to underline the progress that the Japanese had made since the Meiji Restoration, while suggesting Ainu potential for advancing as a civilized people. In the end, though, this relocation experiment failed. Four of the original thirty-six students died before finishing the course; in 1875 the government transferred the school to Hokkaido and renamed it Sapporo Agriculture School. The Japanese situated future schools in places familiar to the students, but segregated the indigenous students from the newly arriving children of Japanese settlers once they constructed the necessary facilities. They also adjusted the curriculum for the Ainu students, reasoning that they required an education tailored to meet their special cultural needs. Visitors to these schools noted the students' training in "diligence, order, and cleanliness [to] improve their personalities."[62]

From 1901 the Japanese government established in Hokkaido two separate elementary school curriculums, one for resettled Japanese and the other for the indigenous Ainu.[63] Unlike the Ainu, Japanese settlers received an education that matched the curriculum established by the Ministry of Education. The administration at first limited Ainu education to three years, before raising it to four. Either case was shorter than the six-year curriculum that Japanese students had to complete to graduate. The curriculum concentrated on practical areas such as ethics, arithmetic, Japanese language, sewing (for women), and farming (for men), while neglecting content instruction on history, geography, and the sciences. Providing instruction in these latter areas would, education thinkers explained, stimulate the minds of Ainu children in a dangerous way. Exposing them to history and geography would reveal their inferior status vis-à-vis the Japanese and awaken them to a sense of ethnic identity. It was not until the mid-1920s that the Japanese integrated the school systems to allow Ainu and Japanese children to study together.[64]

The education system that the Japanese government established in Okinawa prefecture from the early 1880s appeared advanced when compared to that of the Ainu in Hokkaido. It established language schools from 1880; within five years there were a total of fifty-seven such institutions in operation. Ryukyu children were offered five to six years of elementary school education. Students who advanced to junior high school received instruction in geography, history, art, and elementary physics.[65] Schools also endeavored to eradicate all traces of Ryukyu tradition by introducing them to areas of Japanese culture. They also forbade any display of indigenous culture, such as in their traditional dress and hairstyle, which the schools taught as inferior to Japanese fashion. This "imperialization" education aimed to replace local traditions and histories to mold the people, as Kinjō Shigeaki concludes, "into a framework for which they had no roots."[66]

The Japanese developed "social education" as a follow-up to the people's formal education. The administration encouraged this instruction in Okinawa by establishing various associations to bring together young men and women, army reserve units, and farmer associations, along with other groups for various patriotic purposes. It also encouraged efforts in people's Japanese language learning. The "great dialect debate" that took place over the last decade of the nineteenth century devised ways to foster Japanese language use. One technique displayed posters decorated with slogans reading "Always clearly in standard Japanese" (*Itsumo hakihaki hyōjungo*), and "All members of the family using standard Japanese" (*Ikka sorotte hyōjungo*).[67]

The press also assisted in this Japanization process. The *Ryukyu shinpō*, a Japanese language newspaper founded in 1893, strengthened Okinawa's identity with the Japanese mainland by providing its readers with coverage of the Diet proceedings and important speeches by prominent Japanese statesmen. The important market price of sugar (determined in Osaka) became a daily fixture of the newspaper. After Japan acquired Taiwan, the newspaper serialized a discussion on the similarities shared by the Okinawan and Taiwanese peoples. The *Ryukyu shinpō* also assumed the capacity of a social education textbook by providing commentaries on new legislation that pertained to Okinawa residents. From October to November 1898 the newspaper lectured on the new Family Register Law (*kosekihō*). On October 11, it explained legislation that protected families of men drafted into the Japanese military. It also provided its readers with extensive coverage of imperial events, such as the Meiji Emperor's birthday celebration. This newspaper thus served as an essential nationalizing tool, similar to the function that the mainland press assumed from early Meiji.

The Japanese government also used the imperial family to forge ties with the indigenous peoples. Imperial tours made their way to Hokkaido on four occasions, in 1876, 1881, 1911, and 1916. En route the participants, on occasion the emperor himself and at other times simply members of the imperial family, visited Ainu schools. Reports from these excursions demonstrate changes in the Japanese images of this people. Early tours emphasized the Ainu being observed as colonized "others," while later tours emphasized the progress that Japanese had made in the assimilation process. Members of the first few tours brought Japanese gifts such as sake to reward the Ainu for their performance in traditional rituals, such as the popular Bear Festival. Visitors on the later tours did not request these performances, nor did they bring their hosts any gifts.[68] The initial tours emphasizing the Ainu-as-primitive image celebrated the Japanese people's successful transformation to civilization. Expansion into Taiwan and Korea pressed the Japanese to revise the Ainu narrative, to demonstrate Japan's ability to assimilate a foreign people.

Rather than making imperial visits (to date no sitting emperor has visited Okinawa), the Japanese used ancient Ryukyu relations with Japanese governments to strengthen claims to the islands. From ancient times the Ryukyu people had, they argued, accepted Japanese suzerainty. Iwakura Tomomi, citing a passage from the *Nihongi*, argued that Ryukyu-Japanese relations dated back to the reign of Suiko (592–628), when about thirty representatives from the islands visited Kyoto to offer tribute. He further noted that the Ryukyu people provided Hideyoshi with supplies and soldiers to aid Japan's sixteenth-century invasion of Korea.[69] Both claims are problematic. First, Iwakura misconstrued Japan's ancient historical text. The cited passage reported that groups of people from the island of Yaku "came hither as emigrants" during this era. Yaku, just south of Kyushu, is not considered part of the Ryukyu island chain. Also its residents did not bear tribute, but came as migrants. The *Nihongi* explains: "they were all settled in Enowi (now a part of Nara). They never went back again, but all died there."[70] Iwakura's second rationalization—Ryukyu assistance to Hideyoshi's military adventures—neglected to mention that this people refused his demands, and that Satsuma used the natives' intransigence in 1609 to invade the islands and to incarcerate King Shō Nei.[71] Grant, who hosted Iwakura during the prince's world tour and was asked to act as arbitrator over this dispute, was without grounds to challenge the historical interpretations of a person of Iwakura's stature.

The Japanese also invented symbols to demonstrate their historical links to the islands. After the turn of the century, the Meiji government replaced Buddhism with Shintoism as the island chain's state religion. It officially designated the Nami-on-ue shrine as the center of Ryukyu religious affairs, rededicating the shrine to the island's four great kings and to Tametomo (1166–?), a shady member of Japan's Minamoto family who allegedly fathered the first of these kings, Shunten.[72] Inventing this link suggested to the Ryukyu people the historic precedent of imperial ties that Meiji Japan sought to rebuild. Japan's modern diplomacy with Okinawa thus attempted to "restore" Japan's historical relations with Ryukyu.[73] As elsewhere in the empire, the Japanese government turned Emperor Meiji's death, and the enthronement of his son, into opportunity by using the funeral and coronation to gather Okinawans at "worship from afar" ceremonies organized to strengthen their bonds with the homeland.[74]

Japanese attitudes toward both the Ainu and Ryukyu peoples conflicted with their rhetoric for inclusion. They considered the Ainu to be a race that would eventually "die out," and thus, as Diet member Katō Masanosuke expressed in 1893, "there was no need to protect them."[75] Iwano Hōmei, a writer who traveled to Hokkaido in 1909, posited a similar view: "Even though a few of them may have achieved something it is not desirable to have them mix with *wajin* (Japanese) to produce hybrids. In my opinion, it is sufficient to keep them alive like livestock."[76] Textbooks used by Ainu children unabashedly characterized the people as separate from the Japanese, as a distinct race living within the Japanese Empire.[77] Their Japanese neighbors absorbed this discriminative attitude. In 1900 they filed a petition requesting further segregation, noting that, among other factors, the "ignorant and filthy Ainu" might "be happier on more suitable lands."[78]

Positive responses by Ainu and Ryukyu peoples did not decrease Japanese discrimination toward them. One telling sign was the categorical distinction that the Japanese government maintained between "Ainu" and "Ryukyu" with "Japanese." In the case of the Ainu, not only the indigenous population but also children raised by mixed Ainu-Japanese couples were registered as "non-Japanese." This even included children who were biologically Japanese—that is born to Japanese parents—but raised by their adopted Ainu parents. Richard Siddle writes that by the Showa era "Ainu" had become synonymous with "dying race." The assimilationist Kita Masaaki lamented in 1937 as follows:

> Ainu! Whenever this word is written, it is attached without fail
> to the phrase "dying race." Ainu! Whenever the average person
> hears this word, preconceptions of "primitive, hairy men, simple-
> tons" flash like lightning through his mind and echo there.[79]

Japanese also viewed the Ryukyuan as different, as the Okinawa-born instructor Takara Rintoku noted in an 1886 issue of *Dai Nihon kyōiku zasshi* (The Greater Japan Education Magazine) titled "Ryukyu kyōiku ni tsuite" (Concerning Ryukyu Education). Takara identified the Ryukyu people as members of the Yamato race (*Yamato minzoku*), but a people not yet molded together with the Japanese as one nationality (*ichi kokumin*). The article stressed that the ultimate goal of Ryukyu education was to complete this unification process.[80] The Meiji general Yamagata Aritomo identified the people's hybrid Chinese-Japanese way of thinking as the weakness that prevented their inclusion in the Japanese military.[81] The Ryukyu people also faced discrimination when traveling to Japan's mainland. Here signs greeted them with the message that (along with the Korean people) their employment application was not welcome. Their fellow Japanese also refused to lodge them, and some questioned aloud whether it was the Korean or the "Rikijin who was the lesser breed of person."[82] Alan S. Christy notes the irony that "as more Okinawans began to identify themselves more frequently and forcefully as 'Japanese' from the 1920s, they began to face more trenchant denials, particularly from government officials and potential employers."[83] This phenomenon—the dominant people rejecting the minority people's bid to accept assimilation—we saw in the French Algerian case; we will see other examples in Taiwanese and Korean colonial histories.

Mochiki Kanjin's 1917 article published in *Fujin kōron* (Women Review) illustrates Japan's disparaging attitude toward Ryukyuans. Though focused on Ryukyu women, Mochiki's discussion also incorporated Ryukyu men, as well as other peoples that the Japanese considered their inferior. He began by asking the rhetorical question "Who are the Ryukyuans?" He responded: they were a cocktail of minority aboriginal Ainu, Korean, and Chinese blood that had mixed with the blood of the majority Japanese. Consequently, the people remained inferior despite the similarity that their customs and mannerisms showed with those of the Japanese. Their cultural habits established them at a lower level of civilization: they bathed less frequently; they walked barefoot; they tattooed their bodies. The Ryukyu family structure was also inferior, as was their work ethic. Ryukyu males used their women as "fields (*hatake*) for child production"; traditionally they prevented them from getting an education. Before Japanese males could consider intermarrying with Ryukyu women, Mochiki concluded, the two peoples needed to pass a period of closer contact to erase stubborn differences.[84]

Others, such as the Okinawan scholar Iha Fuyū, attempted to interpret his people's customs and history for the Japanese to draw the two peoples closer together. Iha first drew distinction between the Ryukyu and the Ainu. In 1911 he wrote that, like the Koreans, Ryukyuans from ancient times constituted a "nation." The Ainu, on the other hand, existed only as a "people."[85] He criticized Japan's assimilation policy on two points: its failure to recognize Japanese-Okinawan differences (despite the two people being born from the same mother), and its failure to recognize their shared elements. He identified assimilation as a process of positive, combined in certain cases with negative, socialization (*shakaika*). In the case of Okinawa, its separate past encouraged Japan's scrap-and-build process: the Japanese must obliterate certain "state characteristics" (*kokusei*) before they could proceed with positive socialization—teaching the people how to be Japanese.

Iha also advised the Japanese government to recognize that there were certain genetic elements of the Ryukyu people that could not be communized; to do so would encourage the people's "spiritual suicide" (*seishinteki jisatsu*). He reasoned that other parts of the empire also contained regional pockets of this "individuality" (*kosei*). Could not the Ryukyu also retain their identity within the context of a Japanese identity? A great nation's success, he cautioned, was measured by its ability to unify the extended nation, rather than its capacity to obliterate all individual characteristics.[86] The Ryukyu could gain Japanese identity by their less-than-total assimilation.

Iha offered intermarriage as one of the more practical ways to encourage assimilation. Using the pig as a metaphor, he instructed that English specimens grew stronger by diversity—that is, by mating with stronger pigs. Okinawan pigs' mating opportunities were limited to their own population, and thus that pig was a weak specimen. Japan's incorporation of the islands from 1880 into its prefecture system gave the Japanese and Ryukyuan the opportunity to mix and thus produce bigger and healthier pigs—that is, children. The Ryukyuan must appreciate, rather than rebel against, Japan's efforts to rescue undernourished old Ryukyu. To complete their mission the Japanese must now guide the people's spiritual liberation from their oppressive past.[87]

Iha's concern reflected the demonstrations that Ryukyans carried out in opposition to Japan's intrusions in 1881, 1885, and 1893. China's defeat by the Japanese military in 1895 ended any lingering hope of Chinese assistance and represents a turning point in Japan-Ryukyu relations. Iha wrote that this defeat persuaded even those who opposed Japanese rule to join others in "yelling *banzai*."[88] From this time Ryukyuans began to Japanize their appearance, with men changing their hairstyles and dress to present themselves as Japanese. They also began to adopt Japanese surnames, and women began to add *ko* to their given names. The Japanese government offered the Okinawan military conscription rights in 1898, but made the people wait until 1912 to gain representation in the lower house of the Japanese Diet.[89]

Japan's success in integrating Ezo and Ryukyu virtually hides the colonial pasts of these two territories. This book's treatment of the early relationship between "mainland" Japan and incorporated territories suggests their acquisition to be more than simply, as Mark Peattie puts it, a "reassertion of national authority over territory traditionally within the Japanese cultural sphere."[90] Ezo and Ryukyu had long been territories strategically regarded as being outside Japan. Faced with challenges from China and Russia, the Meiji regime annexed the territories and introduced an assimilation policy to mold the people in Japanese likeness. Its effort, however, was superficial. Assimilation did not gain the Ainu or the Ryukyu status equal to that of "pure" Japanese; they encountered prejudice by Japanese who considered them foreign. The education system designed to mold domain peoples into a single nation segregated the people from Japanese migrants. Even today, after more than a century of these two peoples being part of Japan, whether they are completely integrated as Japanese nationals remains a question worthy of careful consideration.

TAIWAN ASSIMILATION: RHETORIC AND PRACTICE

Victory over China in 1895 provided Japan with another opportunity to extend what Yamagata Aritomo, as prime minister in 1890, defined before the Japanese Diet as the country's "line of sovereignty" (*shukensen*) when China ceded Taiwan, along with the Pescadore Islands and the Liaotung Peninsula, to Japan as part of the war reparations it paid. This acquisition further extended Japan's "line of interest" (*riekisen*) into China proper. The Japanese government demonstrated its interest in Chinese territory across from Taiwan. It demanded that China not cede Fujian province to a foreign power and laid plans to invade this territory.[91] The Japanese navy began to demand Taiwan's inclusion in the peace terms once it became clear that the Sino-Japanese War would end in Japan's favor. Recalling the French use of Taiwan to blockade southern China during the Sino-French War, it warned of the dangers to Okinawa and to southwest Japan should Taiwan fall into enemy hands.[92] The journalist Tokutomi Sohō, in his newspaper the *Kokumin shinbun* (The People's Newspaper), began calling for Japan to demand Taiwan even earlier, just after war broke out. He saw the island's value as a natural "footing for the expansion of Greater Japan," and a way to reopen travel and exploration paths that Japanese had followed three hundred years earlier.[93]

Psychologically, Japan's military victory and colonial acquisition were instrumental in Japan's national reformation. These two events represented critical components to rectify its "conflicting needs" as described by Kenneth B. Pyle: Japan's need to be "both modern and Japanese."[94] Military victory and colonial acquisition teamed together to demonstrate to the world the existence of an alternative (Japanese) road to modernity and civilization. The journalist Takekoshi Yosaburō crowed that Western nations "have long believed that on their shoulders alone rested the responsibility of colonizing the yet-unopened portions of the globe and extending the inhabitants the benefits of civilization; but now we Japanese, rising from the ocean in the extreme Orient, wish as a nation to take part in this great and glorious work."[95]

Successfully fulfilling this "glorious work" required the Japanese to adopt an administrative policy that the colonial powers recognized as appropriate. Japan's new acquisitions differed from Ryukyu and Ezo in that Japan could not claim past suzerain relations of any sort with these former Chinese possessions. In the Japanese mind, this left little margin for error lest the European powers sweep the territories from their grasp at the first hint of Japan's failure to fulfill its colonial responsibilities. Prior to the war, the powers had agreed to relax certain provisions of the "unequal treaties" signed at midcentury. Yet, the Triple Intervention, in which Germany, France, and Russia forced Japan to return to China the Liaotung Peninsula, acted as a cold reminder of Japan's delicate position in global affairs.

Concern over foreign reaction encouraged a cautious Prime Minister Itō Hirobumi to solicit advice from prominent foreign advisors regarding Japan's administrative approach in Taiwan. Searching overseas for knowledge was nothing new to Itō. He was among the first to be sent by the Chōshū domain for study abroad. He also joined the Iwakura Mission as a vice ambassador in the early 1870s, and toured Europe in the 1880s to research constitutional law. Regarding colonial administration, Itō received opinion papers from representatives of England, France, and the United States, as well as from prominent Japanese statesmen. These essays were later bound as volume three of Itō's "secret papers" (*hisho ruisan*).

Montague Kirkwood was entrusted with the task of delivering the British perspective. Kirkwood, a British lawyer employed as advisor to Japan's Ministry of Justice, recommended that Japan adopt the indirect association policy that his country employed in its external colonies. He suggested that Japan place strong emphasis on the emperor–governor general relationship. The Japanese emperor should appoint a chief colonial administrator who would report directly to him. The emperor would empower the governor general to establish, abolish, and reinstate laws in the colony as he saw fit. The administration's success would be contingent on the governor general's ability to make effective use of a legislative council composed in part of native (Chinese) subjects. Finally, Kirkwood recommended that the Japanese rely on Chinese residents for local administration while appointing a Japanese court to handle civil appeals. To the extent possible, he advised, the Japanese should preserve local laws, civil administration, and customs.[96]

Itō solicited a second opinion from a French advisor, Michel Lubon, who presented the Japanese with two different policy suggestions based on Japan's "logical limitations." Lubon warned of the dangers that accompanied an insular state exceeding these limitations by directly annexing continental territory as internal territory. The Liaotung Peninsula, he advised, could remain a part of Japan's colonial empire, but the Japanese should govern it as an external colony with an administration that protected the freedom, customs, and conventions of its residents. This acquisition should be governed indirectly, as an external colony. The Japanese administration of Taiwan, he continued, should be direct. As the territory shared Japan's insular quality, it could be absorbed as a "true prefecture" of Japan. Specifically, Lubon recommended that Japan impose upon its "new national subjects" the criminal and legal codes of the homeland. Their introduction should be gradual in consideration of the traditional distinctions that the people held. We see in Lubon's advice the influence of scientific colonialism by his recommending that the Japanese determine national policy by geographical quantity. It is also interesting to note the timing of Lubon's report, dated April 22, 1895, one day before France, Russia, and Germany demanded that Japan return this continental acquisition to China.[97]

Henry Willard Denison provided a third perspective. The New England lawyer served as legal advisor in Japan's Foreign Ministry from 1880 to 1914. His advice would later prove critical in helping Japan negotiate the 1902 Anglo-Japanese Treaty and the 1905 Treaty of Portsmouth that ended the Russo-Japanese War.[98] Denison prefaced his remarks by drawing attention to the United States' western territorial possessions acquired from Mexico. Japan should refrain from incorporating conquered peoples into the nation. Just because a state acquired this land, it does not follow that its residents should naturally be granted the citizenship of the conquering nation. Mexicans residing in California and New Mexico would never gain United States citizenship; they would always be considered foreigners. Denison criticized a European policy that allowed conquered peoples to choose their nationality, citing provisions of the Austrian-Italian Treaty (1866) and the Franco-German Treaty (1871). Should Japan adopt this policy, he predicted, it would cause confusion. Would it truly accept as Japanese citizens those Chinese who opted to remain in Taiwan? What would happen to these subjects should they elect to return to China, or migrate to Japan? Likewise, what status would the government offer to Japanese residents who relocated to Taiwan? Denison recommended an "American policy" as an alternative to this "European policy": citizenship determined by the nationality of the parents, rather than by individual choice.[99]

The Japanese government managed to insert parts of all three plans into the colonial administrations it introduced to Taiwan (and later Korea). In both territories Japan declared its policy to be assimilation, yet it never recognized the Taiwanese or Koreans as Japanese subjects. Nor did it export to the territories Japan's prefecture system. The Japanese government initially honored Kirkwood's advice that the governor general report directly to the emperor. It also formed assemblies staffed by indigenous Taiwanese and Koreans. These assemblies, however, never gained the degree of influence envisioned by the British advisor. The Japanese administration in Taiwan did adopt the provision of the "European model" that allowed the indigenous people to choose whether to reside under Japanese administration or relocate to China. Yet, till the end the Japanese government determined the nationality of the colonized by paternal heritage, rather by than individual choice.

Soon after Itō collected these papers, Japan began its administration of its new island colony. As with Ryukyu, Japanese scholars attempted to legitimize their new possession historically. Fujizaki Sainosuke, in a 1930 publication titled *Taiwan no hanzoku* (Taiwan's Tribes), described Japan's three-hundred-year relationship with this island, a history that dated back to Japan's Warring States period. Again revisionists focused on Hideyoshi claiming that in 1593, the generalissimo sent books to the island's residents and demanded in return that they offer tribute to Japan.[100] Fujizaki claimed that Japan forged strong ties with the island's tribal residents during this time as Hideyoshi permitted Japanese limited travel to Taiwan for trade purposes. Many of these trade missions established strongholds on the island. Later, the Tokugawa regime also sponsored missions to survey the islands and their residents; Japanese even ventured into the interior to subjugate indigenous residents, contacts that constituted a "colonial" (*shokuminchi*) relationship between Japanese and Taiwanese. The Japanese were eventually forced off the island by attacks from indigenous peoples residing on the island's west coast. However, they resumed their former relationship with the territory's tribesmen in 1874, when they avenged the murder of fifty-four Ryukyu sailors.[101]

As with Iwakura Tomomi's account of ancient Japan-Ryukyu relations, Fujizaki's history of past Taiwan-Japan relations stretched the truth. He did not detail the extent to which the Japanese "colonized" Taiwan's tribal peoples, only that the occupiers were soon driven off the island by a rival force. Japan's punishment of the island's inhabitants in 1874 hardly led to the resumption of a former relationship. Upon accomplishing their mission the surviving Japanese soldiers returned home and Japan maintained limited contact with the island until 1895, when the Treaty of Shimonoseki dropped the island into Japan's empire. Nitobe Inazō claimed that the Japanese even tried selling this "white elephant" shortly after acquiring it.[102] The series of administrative trials and errors that followed Taiwan's annexation may explain the caution Japan took when planning Korea's annexation.

Governing the colony proved challenging, particularly during the initial decade. In May 1895, the former navy minister Vice-Admiral Kabayama Sukenori left Japan to assume his post as Taiwan's first governor general. He stopped en route in Okinawa to confer with officials over the task that lay ahead. Kabayama was particularly interested in advice on how to control the "savages" who resided in Taiwan's interior: had Okinawan officials learned anything useful in this regard?[103] One often-mentioned problem was the island's ethnic diversity. In addition to the ethnic differences among the Chinese residents, Taiwan was also home to a large number of aboriginal tribes. Gotō Shinpei described this diversity in 1909 as about "twenty different tongues . . . being spoken by the savages [and] three different . . . dialects" by the Chinese inhabitants. As these people were "descendents of rebels and insurgents . . . [they] lack the character of a people who have lived ordinary lives under a hereditary government."[104]

The island's residents wasted little time in challenging Japanese rule. On May 25—just over one month after the signing of the peace treaty—one group drafted a statement that announced the formation of the Taiwan Democratic State.[105] The governor general borrowed a page from German rule in Alsace and Lorraine (Kabayama had studied in Germany) to combat anti-Japanese sentiment. He gave Chinese residents the choice of remaining in the colony or relocating to China. Kabayama also had to deal with fierce opposition to Japan's presence by the island's tribal peoples.[106] In addition, the governor general inherited a critical health problem. The malaria that had killed many of Japan's military forces in 1874 remained a problem for Japanese arriving after annexation.

Problems with the island's non-Chinese populations were not easily resolved. Fukuzawa Yukichi was particularly active in voicing opinion on how these peoples should be handled. In January 1896 he offered two "long-term plans for Taiwan": the British approach that preserved culture and custom or the United States alternative that "thrust aside the native entirely."[107] Five months later, frustrated over the lack of progress, Fukuzawa threw his support behind the U.S. approach.

If the island people cannot accept [Japanese] regulations they must leave the island. If they cannot accept the laws of Japan, we do not have to wait for their voluntary departure but must order them to leave the island. Our purpose is the prosperity of the island and even though it is the Japanese who are directing this prosperity, the cooperation of the island people is essential. We cannot allow for even one person who is unable to accept our laws. We should continue to bring people from the homeland to secure the island with the same level of prosperity and happiness that is found in Japan. It is to this task that Japan's administrators should focus their attention in governing Taiwan.[108]

Eventually the government-general separated the island into two zones: one housing the "civilized" and the other containing the "barbarian." The Japanese fortified this division with armed security guards instructed to shoot any "savage" who violated this border.[109]

Gotō Shinpei's 1898 arrival marked a major turning point in Japan's Taiwan administration. Gotō was introduced to colonial thinking while a medical student in Berlin and Munich, where he studied hygiene from 1890 to 1892. During this time he was granted an audience with Chancellor Otto von Bismarck, who advised the young student to expand his attention beyond his medical interests to include political matters. Bismarck left a deep impression on Gotō, who devoted his life to creating, as he put it "Japan's Japan, the world's Japan, and Japan's world." By this he meant that Japan's first goal was to forge a Japan accepted by the homeland residents before extending the polished image of Japan globally by expansion. Japan's success at home would gain it recognition as a model for the rest of the world to follow.[110]

Gotō's ideas on Japan's global position suggest support for assimilation, even though this policy's tenets conflicted with his interest in scientific colonialism.[111] He used the biological differences found in the sea bream, which has eyes on both sides of its head, and the flounder, which has both eyes on one side of its head, to explain his philosophy on human development.[112] All social customs and systems have their reasons. The enforcement of a system devised by a civilized nation upon an unenlightened people required a "destructive administrative police" to eliminate these differences. Edward I-te Chen describes Gotō's thinking as an effort to "paint himself as a scientist who would formulate policies based on realistic investigation of native customs and traditions." Gotō also sought to "paint policy-makers in Tokyo (with whom he had numerous policy disputes) as inflexible officials interested only in the appearance of integration." Gotō's strategy in Taiwan was an ego-driven effort to prove the practicality of his ideas to those who opposed him when he served in the Tokyo bureaucracy.[113]

Gotō's list of accomplishments includes his pacification plan to control tribal insurrection. This effort, which included the colonial government offering bribes to resistance leaders, helped reduce attacks on Japanese by about one-third.[114] The government-general's policy of drawing an artificial border that separated the "civilized" from the "barbarian" suggests the Japanese official introducing both peripheral and external colonizing policies to the island. Those residing beyond this border could live as they pleased so long as they remained in "barbarian" territory. Others in "civilized" territory would be governed under direct assimilation. Fujizaki Sainosuke described Japanese rule during this initial period as the Japanese drawing distinction between those who obeyed and those who did not, rather than as one between Chinese and indigenous peoples. From around 1916, he noticed, Japanese policy attempted to gain compliance by nurturing (buiku), by emphasizing education, job placement, health treatment, and trade and commerce.[115]

As in Ryukyu and Ezo, the Japanese extended education networks to assimilate the Taiwanese people that were an inferior rendition of those offered to Japanese. The physical investment in education demonstrated to observers the importance that the colonizers placed upon bringing civilization to the residents of this backward area. In addition, the instruction conducted in these buildings provided participants with the essential foundation they needed to assume their roles in the empire, and the psychological ties they needed to imagine their place in the advanced Japanese community to which they were to be assimilated.

This system also segregated Japanese from Taiwanese. The government-general first provided an integrated system for Japanese and Taiwanese children until, as in Hokkaido, expatriate Japanese objected. Their children hardly needed the education that Taiwanese most urgently required—basic Japanese language instruction. Language instruction dominated the curriculum to the extent that by 1921 first-year Taiwanese students were receiving twelve full hours of Japanese instruction every week. In later grades, they received less direct instruction, but more indirect attention, to this study. All subject areas in theory were to be taught in the colonizers' language rather than in the indigenous language. As in Okinawa, some schools practiced total language and cultural immersion that required students to live in dormitories where they were forced to eat only Japanese food, to dress only in Japanese costume, and to speak only in Japanese even with their Taiwanese friends.[116] This colonial education also emphasized "ethics," a subject thematically structured under the idea of "individual and social morals to national greatness." In the two hours per week devoted to this subject, schools introduced students to such topics as "the duties of citizens," "our country," "Yasukuni shrine," and "the Meiji Emperor." Textbooks published after 1933 emphasized the "way of the subject," a topic that portrayed the "ideal Japanese" as one who was "obedient and loyal to the emperor and state and true to the 'national essence' (*kokutai*)."[117]

On paper Japan provided Taiwanese children with a rather comprehensive education system. By 1944, Japanese policies had managed to provide elementary education to 71 percent of the Taiwanese school-age population.[118] High enrollments increased the number of Taiwanese residents becoming fluent in the "national language" (*kokugo*). One study showed that by the end of Japanese rule, a full 85 percent of the population could speak Japanese.[119] Missing from the report were the criteria used to determine language proficiency. If similar to the criterion used in Korea—school enrollment—then this figure raises suspicions. School attendance alone did not guarantee successful language acquisition.

The system's biggest shortcoming was its failure to provide an environment within which Taiwanese children could compete with their Japanese counterparts as equals. The heavy concentration on Japanese language instruction took valuable time away from the instruction students needed in other areas. It also set back students wishing to continue their education, who had to attend a separate preparatory school before advancing.[120] E. Patricia Tsurumi questions the degree that this education passed on to students its intended messages. She concludes her useful study on Japan's colonial education in Taiwan by surmising that the schools "probably convinced more Taiwanese of the importance of boiling water and washing one's hands after using the toilet than the majesty of the Japanese emperor."[121]

The government-general created "social education" networks to supplement the instruction provided by elementary schools. As in Okinawa, this extended instruction pressured the people to speak the national language. William Kirk, writing in 1941, observed that the colonial government kept a record of the names of Taiwanese "struggling to acquire Japanese." It decorated houses dedicated to speaking Japanese with a banner advertising that "this house speaks the national language," and hung signs in public places to encourage people to "speak only the national language." A number of institutions in the colony, including the Young Men's Association, offered Japanese language instruction for adults; Taiwanese more fluent in Japanese helped those less advanced in their language studies. By 1939 there were more than seven thousand national language-training institutions (*kōshūjo*) run by Taiwanese offering tuition-free Japanese language instruction to their compatriots.[122]

Japanese tours provided another mechanism for acculturating the Taiwanese people. Including the Taiwanese on homeland tours permitted a minority of people to witness firsthand the colonizers' superiority by allowing them a glimpse at Japan's accomplishments. The effect of this experience spilled over to those who remained behind as newspapers reported on their travels, and the participants relayed stories of their experiences to friends and acquaintances upon their return.[123] Tour participants assembled in Taihoku (Taipei). For many this was their first urban experience. After receiving presents for their cooperation, they set sail for the homeland. Their tour took them through Nagasaki, Osaka, Tokyo, and Yokosuka (to see the naval yards). These excursions generally lasted about one month and included up to, and on one occasion more than, a hundred participants. The *Taiwan nichi-nichi* (Taiwan Daily) covered the 1897 tour by providing descriptions of the travelers' daily experiences in a column titled "The Diary of the Native Tribesmen Tour" (*Banjin kankō nisshi*). The newspaper escorted its readers through Yasukuni Shrine and other stops, describing what the travelers saw, as well as their reactions to the sites they visited.

The *Japan Times* took a different perspective in its reportage of this tour. Commentary that accompanied the news reaffirmed the backward images that contemporary Japanese held of Taiwanese at the time. It commented on their strange dress and the multilingual makeup of the group, adding that these guests arrived unarmed, and that they displayed "childlike and pitiable" reactions to the trains that they rode.[124] The *Japan Times* emphasized Japanese-Taiwanese differences rather than suggesting the potential for the two peoples to assimilate. The molding of images by the Japanese in this way suggest the tours' dual purpose. In addition to instructing the Taiwanese on civilization, the visits also confirmed to Japanese their superiority over the colonized. This in turn legitimized Japanese subjugation over their lives. To maximize the domestic impact, the Japanese limited the tours to members of

Taiwan's indigenous tribes, rather than include ethnic Chinese. The Japanese also displayed these peoples at the 1910 exhibition held in London. Along with the Ainu, Taiwanese were provided with a natural village setting to demonstrate their culture. Their space, however, was physically separated from the "Japanese village."[125] The 1922 Tokyo Peace Exhibition held in Ueno Park went one step further by separating Japanese from colonized exhibits spatially and economically—visitors had to pay an extra twenty *sen* to take the escalator that transported them across this division.[126]

Successful assimilation also required the example of Japanese residents to act as role models. Though Japanese were generally isolated from the local residents, a few occasions permitted fraternization between the two. The membership roster of the Patriotic Women's Club, established by Gotō Shinpei's wife, Kazuko, in 1905 contained a few Japanese names. The majority of the members, however, were Taiwanese. The Japanese administration's general dissatisfaction with the behavior of the Japanese who entered the colony may have discouraged it from promoting contacts between the two peoples. Takenaka Nobuko's study reveals that nonadministrative Japanese migrants were not necessarily Japan's best and brightest. In 1902 the Japanese authorities estimated that almost half of the Japanese female residents between the ages of fifteen and thirty-five were "impure ladies" (*fuketsu no fujin*), or ladies who drew their salaries from night professions.[127] Japanese male expatriates also faced criticism. At one point the administration enacted legislation to force Japanese residents to cover their naked bodies. Gotō described problems regarding Japanese residents to be the "biggest cancer of the administration." He added, "those Japanese crossing over are, compared to the [Taiwanese], definitely not superior residents."[128] This suggests a serious problem with Japan's assimilation aspirations—Japanese migration being advanced to rid the archipelago of potential troublemakers rather than to dispatch Japanese capable of serving as role models for the Taiwanese to emulate.

The Japanese community, set on protecting its newly elevated status, also resisted efforts to incorporate the indigenous people as its assimilated peers to protect its enhanced status over the Taiwanese. The case of the Assimilation Association (*dōkakai*) is revealing in this sense. Formed in 1910 by two Japanese residents, the association aspired to replace the administration's superficial assimilation policies with those that more genuinely sought the two peoples' integration. The campaign grew rapidly: its membership soon exceeded three thousand and gained endorsement from many prominent Taiwanese. It did not, however, receive the support of the Japanese community, which contributed but forty-four members. Many more Japanese—according to the *Taiwan nichi-nichi* more than a hundred thousand—opposed the association's objectives. Governor General Sakuma Samata finally ordered the association to disband and had its Japanese supporters arrested on unrelated charges. Dismayed over this failure, many Taiwanese enthusiasts refocused their energy toward organizing a home-rule movement.[129] Other governor generals followed this pattern of preaching assimilation while enacting policy that perpetuated and reinforced Japanese and Taiwanese segregation. In the fifty years of Japanese rule, none of the island's native residents ever rose to a political position higher than county head. We see the government-general's utter lack of trust in this people in the degree to which it controlled them: on a per capita basis more policemen patrolled the streets in Taiwan (14 percent) than in Korea (8 percent).[130]

Over the four decades that followed its rise to power, the Meiji regime administered its imperial territories under two separate policies—internal colonization for Japanese and peripheral colonization for incorporated peoples. While it recognized regional differences within the Japanese archipelago, all were required to assume an identity as Japanese subjects. Their loyalties would be honed by the newly instituted compulsory education system and tested in times of national emergency, such as war. Residents of Japan's annexed peripheral territories required extended training before they could be given the status of Japanese subjecthood. The Meiji government rejected alternative approaches that envisioned Japan as a diplomatically savvy state that secured its borders by maintaining strong relations with global powers, or that imagined Japan forming a pan-Asian community with its Northeast Asian neighbors. By the end of the nineteenth century, Japan had clearly determined its interest in a third alternative, territorial expansion, as its eyes trained on the last peripheral territory that lay well within its line of interest, but just beyond its line of sovereignty—the Korean Peninsula.[131]

3

FORMING KOREAN ASSIMILATION POLICY

THE FRONT PAGE OF THE AUGUST 30, 1910, EDITION OF THE *TOKYO ASAHI*
shinbun introduced its readers to the expanded parameters of the Japanese
empire. On this day the newspaper displayed Japan's sovereignty extending
onto continental territory, suggesting that Korea, shaded in the same dark
color as the Japanese archipelago, was now to be considered an integral part
of Japan. This map also added lines that extended well into China and
Manchuria to the west, and into the Pacific Ocean to the east, to articulate the
extent to which the acquisition of the Korean Peninsula had extended Japan's
lines of interest. Accompanying this graphic display of the Korean Peninsula
as an internal colonial addition to Japan, the newspaper appended commentary that emphasized the people's peripheral status: Koreans had the
potential to become Japanese over time.

The new administration in Korea defined its task as developing Korean
potential to assume a position of equality with Japanese imperial subjects.
Few writing at this time openly challenged this mission or the Japanese ability to complete it. An incompetent Korean government had stifled Korean
potential. Placing the people under a benevolent government would allow
them to realize their potential. Rather than questioning the appropriateness
of assimilating Korea, the Japanese debated the pace and approach of the
policy to be implemented. Should assimilation be gradual or radical? Most
agreed on the importance of a strong education system to properly assimilate Koreans, but raised questions about whether to mix Koreans with Japanese, about which language to be used in the classroom, and about the focus
of the curriculum. The government-general, which monopolized publicly

circulated messages over this initial decade of rule, filtered its messages of Korean and Japanese unity through the textbooks used in the schools and the newspapers sold on the streets. It engaged Koreans in public events of cele- bration and condolence to strengthen their identity as Japanese. Yet, this ini- tial decade ended with the Korean people marching down the streets of Seoul demanding their independence, and the Japanese groping for explanations as to how their policy had failed.

JUSTIFYING KOREAN ASSIMILATION

Japan moved with caution even after it finalized the treaty of annexation with Korea on August 22, 1910. It refrained from publicizing the break- through for another week, and chastised its media for leaking the news pre- maturely.[1] The newspapers, however, continued to fill their pages with discussion on administration policy. Japanese commentators situated the Korean people as peripheral subjects, a people not yet ready to assume a role as internal Japanese subjects. A minority argued the appropriate adminis- trative policy to be one that treated the Koreans as external subjects: it would be dangerous to arm this people with the tools of a civilized people lest they one day use them to undermine Japanese rule. On August 25, the *Tokyo Asahi shinbun* carried an article by Ebina Danjō, a leading Christian evan- gelist who later served as president of Dōshisha University, titled "Can the Koreans Be Assimilated to Japan?" Rather than critique the policy, Ebina set out to inform his readers about the policy's merits in Korea: the racial, lin- guistic, and religious similarities that the two people share will make the assimilation task relatively easy when compared to European attempts at implementing the policy. Japanese resolve (*kakugo*) to accomplish the mis- sion, he predicted, will ensure success.[2]

The idea that Korean assimilation would be easy gained a strong follow- ing at this time. Ukita Kazutami, editor of the magazine *Taiyō* (The Sun) who was a leading voice on Japanese imperialism, wrote that the differences in religion, race, customs, and habits prevented the Irish from assimilating with the English; the people of Posen (Poznan, in present-day Poland), Alsace, and Lorraine from assimilating with the Germans; and the Poles and Finns from assimilating with the Russians. The case of the Japanese and the Koreans, he asserted, was different, as the two peoples have been of the same race and of the same culture for centuries. He predicted that the Japanese would have relatively few problems in assimilating the Korean people, and that the relationship would evolve peacefully, like the relationship between England and Scotland, rather than become estranged, as with England and Ireland.[3]

Some observers noted resemblances between Japan's tasks in Korea and those the Meiji government faced after it replaced the Tokugawa regime. Count Hayashi Tadasu, an active participant in the Meiji government's diplomatic circles, put forth one such argument. Hayashi recalled the transition from Tokugawa to Meiji, a process he witnessed from its inception. Both situations, he began, required people to upgrade their dress, their living styles, and their eating habits. The inferior Korean people, he cautioned, also faced the challenge of assuming a "Japanese style"—they must adopt "Japanese spirit and thought." The historic similarities that the Korean and Japanese shared strengthened Japan's chances of success with assimilation. Hayashi concluded, "If the Japanese failed to assimilate the Koreans there must be something particularly inferior with our political skills."[4]

Others argued the merits of assimilation by drawing on the historical roots that the two peoples allegedly shared. Kita Sadakichi, employed by the Education Ministry, justified Korean assimilation by claiming Japan's success in assimilating the Ainu, a people he argued to be now "almost indistinguishable" from Yamato Japanese. This experience, he predicted, would be valuable to Japanese assimilation of Koreans. Kita's most important work, however, traced the shared origins of the Japanese and Korean peoples. He explained that assimilation was appropriate because it represented a return to the historical, and natural, relationship that the two peoples once shared. Writing for the journal *Minzoku to rekishi* (Ethos and History) he argued the Yamato people's origins to be a result of the "fusion" (*yūgō*) of several lesser peoples.[5] These peoples were absorbed by the Tenson people, the alleged descendents of Japan's sun-goddess (Amaterasu Ōmikami). The Japanese and Korean peoples, Kita reported, evolved from these roots: their differences were a "small branch" rather than a "large branch" division; they were ethnic rather than racial. He estimated that no two peoples shared as close a relationship as the Koreans and the Japanese. In fact, he surmised, it would not be incorrect to consider them the same people. Japanese argued that Korean-Japanese ties were found throughout the matrix of Japanese society, including at its apex. A November 1910 editorial in *Taiyō* drew a biological link between ancient Korea and the Japanese royal family when it announced, "Korean blood runs in the veins of many Japanese noble families, even those of the Imperial family."[6]

Not everyone endorsed Japanese assimilation policy. Shiratori Kurakichi, the Japanese "father of Oriental history" (*tōyōshi*), questioned whether Japanese attitudes toward the Korean people were conducive to creating the productive teacher-student relationship that this policy required. If the Japanese wished to win the sentiments of the Korean people, they would have to adopt an attitude of "caressing enticement" (*aibu shitaku*) to encourage the people to accept Japanese morals and culture. He further cautioned that other factors might frustrate Japanese efforts even if they adopted a proper attitude. Japanese, he reasoned, may also lack the ability to assimilate a foreign people: Japan was a nation of imitators; its people were not creative and thus were incapable of assimilating others. He reasoned that prior to annexation, Korea, unlike Okinawa, had been a "nation" with its own customs and mannerisms. For this reason Koreans might not be open to assimilation.[7] Takekoshi Yosaburō, a journalist who authored a book on Japanese history, wrote that the Korean people should be guided only to be able to fill their place in the empire's division of labor. Teaching Koreans the Japanese language, he advised, should be avoided at all costs, for this skill would access them to the writings of the French Revolution and other ideas put forth by members of the Irish independence movement. The Koreans, he concluded, should be educated to be farmers.[8]

Korea-based Japanese offered a more cautious endorsement of Japan's administrative policy, perhaps concerned that successful assimilation might compromise their position of superiority. Asahi Kunio, whose comments appeared in the popular magazine *Chōsen oyobi Manshū* (Korea and Manchuria), believed assimilation to be more than the responsibility of Japanese as nationals, but the Japanese "noble responsibility toward humankind" (*jinshū toshite no koshō naru gimu*). The author distinguished the status of Koreans by arguing that the Japanese must assimilate the backward Koreans as "imperial subjects" (*teikoku no shinmin*) rather than as "imperial nationals" (*teikoku no kokumin*).[9] This distinction—*shinmin* but not *kokumin*— had appeared in a *Keijō nippō* (Seoul Times) editorial one year earlier. The largest Japanese-language newspaper in Korea urged that Koreans be incorporated as colonial subjects (*shinmin*) rather than as simply Japanese (*Nihonjin*). The newspaper lobbied for the maintenance of this distinction even if the Korean people were to be admitted into the Japanese Empire on a basis of equality, as was the case with Japan's other colonized peoples in Taiwan and Karafuto. Complete Korean assimilation would not be as simple as some assumed. As a model, the editorial urged Japanese to consider the case of the United Kingdom. The English had assimilated the Welsh, Scots, and Irish not as English (*Eijin*) but as British subjects (*Buriten eikoku no shinmin*).[10] The message here was that assimilation was acceptable as long as categorical distinction separated the colonizers from the colonized. The importance of this argument is that it was put forth by Korea-based Japanese who, first, were more attuned than idealists in Tokyo to the reality of the Korean-Japanese relationship and, second, similar to colonial expatriates in other peripheral colonies, by showing concern over the level to which Koreans were to be assimilated, revealed much about their determination to protect their personal status in the colony.

One year after annexation, *Chōsen oyobi Manshū* published a discussion that introduced government-general views on assimilation. Predictably, the opinions tended to favor the general idea of assimilation. However, uncharacteristic of assimilation discourse, some opinions also emphasized the two people's differences. Vice Governor General Yamagata Isaburō noted Koreans as "lazy" (*taida*) and "heartless" (*mujō*). Division of Home Affairs Minister Usami Katsuō cited their "easygoing" (*ki ga nagai*) nature. He cautioned that although assimilation would not be easy, the Japanese people should join hands to "patiently guide" (*ki ga nagaku shidō*) the Korean people. Police Commissioner (*keimusōchō*) Akashi Genjirō argued that assimilation would be difficult, but not impossible. The Japanese must show the Korean people "love" (*ai*), but not too much love. A degree of tact (*tekagen*) was also needed to counter the Korean people's "pretentious nature" (*zōchō suru seijō*) if the Japanese were to deliver them from the effects of "inept government" (*akusei*) to make them good imperial subjects.[11]

These cautions reflected the idea that many advised the administration to adopt: assimilation need not be rushed. Yamashita Nankai, writing for the *Chōsen shinbun*, distinguished between those advocating "gradual" and "radical" assimilation: the former emphasized Korean-Japanese "difference" and the latter their "similarity." Supporters of radical assimilation policy, he explained, encouraged miscegenation to mix Korean and Japanese blood. Gradualists, who saw assimilation as a long-term process, urged patience.[12] At least at this initial stage, few were willing to advocate more practical measures to encourage Japanese-Korean assimilation, such as the integration of schools, neighborhoods, and even families. Despite the apparent ease that Japanese imagined in the people's assimilation, Koreans would first have to demonstrate their ability to rise to Japanese standards before they could be accepted into their inner circles.

FORMING A KOREAN IMAGE

Segregated environments that separated Koreans from Japanese reflected the aura of superiority that Japanese maintained. The Korean people might share similar origins with the Japanese people, but their ineffective government of the past centuries created a gap that had to be narrowed before the Japanese could accept Koreans as legitimate members of the Japanese Empire. Radical introduction of Japanese culture would overwhelm the Korean people and create chaos. The use (and often misuse) of negative imagery to justify colonial subjugation was not unique to Japan; indeed Japanese themselves had been the object of similar images created by Westerners contacting the Japanese after initiating modernization.[13] The interesting aspect of Japanese discourse regarding Koreans at this time, and particularly that which depicted the two peoples as ethnically similar, was its difference from the discourse of pre-Meiji times, when the two peoples engaged in diplomatic activity under relatively equal terms. Examining the evolution of Japanese images of Koreans from foreigner to kin demonstrates the flexibility and malleability of images to fit situation and purpose. Japanese who viewed Koreans visiting Japan during the Edo period saw them as foreigners so different that the *bakufu* felt it necessary to issue edicts warning the observers against "finger-pointing and laughing along the route where the Koreans passed." The visitors provided quite a sensation, a break in the mundane lives for those residing along the Tōkaidō road over which the embassies passed en route to Edo (Tokyo). Hong Ujae, a staff interpreter with one of the embassies, wrote that "a million onlookers swarmed like ants on the riverbanks . . . pontoon bridges spanned the water and countless thousands were lined up to watch us." Hirado *daimyo* Matsuura Seizan noted the large number of unattended shops when the Korean troupe passed through town. He wrote that the onlookers were as numerous as "blades of grass on a mountainside in spring."[14]

During this period, both sides believed their culture to hold superiority over the other. The Japanese described Korean tours as tributary to emphasize Japanese superiority; the Koreans noted their refusal to allow Japanese visits to the Korean capital as proof of their superiority. Kate Wildman Nakai notes that in the early eighteenth century the influential Tokugawa official Arai Hakuseki revised protocol during Korean embassies to "maneuver the envoys into playing the role of tributaries to Japan."[15] Ronald P. Toby describes the relationship as follows:

That Korea was superior to Tsushima in status is beyond dispute. But the relative status of Japan and Korea is very much in dispute and not at all clear. Many Japanese writers of the Edo period called the Korean embassies "tribute missions" (*raikō* or *raichō*), or saw Korea as "submitting to Edo," while others clearly saw the loss of Japan's right to visit Seoul as a diminution of Japanese status. While it is more difficult to find Koreans who admired Japan than Japanese who admired Korea, or specific Korean cultural achievements, it is no problem whatsoever to find disparaging remarks by each other, and each continually tried to assert superior status vis-à-vis the other in their relations throughout the Edo period. However, the protocol of the relationship between the two capitals was essentially that of a peer relationship.[16]

At the same time Japanese scholars held Korean scholarship in high regard. Hatada Takashi, one of the first in postwar Japan to reflect on Japanese historical images of Koreans, described the strong respect that Tokugawa scholars held for Korean culture, particularly students of Shushigaku (the Chu Hsi school of Neo-Confucianism). He noticed a major shift in the Korean-Japanese relationship over the last decade of Tokugawa Japan when Korea, Ryukyu, and Ezo came to be regarded as gates, or buffer zones, that the Japanese felt compelled to control to protect their borders from foreign intervention.[17]

Korea as a threatening image emerged in Japanese illustrations drawn over the second half of the nineteenth century. "Revisionist" Japanese art suggested Hideyoshi's sixteenth-century invasion of the Korean Peninsula to have been a preemptive attack to a possible Korean threat. One 1860 woodblock print, titled *Satō Masakiyo's Tiger Hunt*, pictured a tiger molded to the shape of the peninsula with its left paw encroaching on Japanese territory. Midlevel Japanese samurai kept the intruder at bay with a long spear aimed at the animal's throat. Japanese artists continued to represent Koreans as tigers well into the Meiji period. Katada Nagajirō's 1902 print titled *Katō Kiyomasa* [one of Hideyoshi's most trusted generals] *Taming the Wild Beast* [*mōjū*] *in Korea* displayed Kato cautiously advancing upon a tiger half hidden in deep snowdrifts. This suggested the need for Japan's direct (but cautious) intervention in the kingdom's state of affairs. In addition to suggesting Korea's subhuman quality, depicting the Korean as tiger hinted at the dangers of allowing the peninsula to remain wild and untamed.[18]

The threat at this time was not of a direct Korean invasion, but the potential for a neighboring state to compromise Japanese security by occupying Korean territory. Korea's "inept government" opened the door for this potential, which Japan exploited to establish a pretext for intervention. International law recognized intervention as a legitimate action to replace such governments. As we saw earlier, foreign voices began to encourage Japan to assume its responsibility around the turn of the century.[19]

One consequence of "inept government" that Japanese frequently wrote about was stagnation. A "competent government" promoted the growth and development that contemporary Korea, still lingering in ancient times, lacked. Nitobe Inazō, who traveled to Korea in 1906, described the country as a contemporary "Arcadia." Korea's romanticism lay in its preservation of the ancient.

> I feel as though I were living three thousand years back in the age of our *Kami*—so sedate, so dignified, so finely chiseled, and yet so devoid of expression. The very physiognomy and living of this people are so bland, unsophisticated and primitive, that they belong not to the twentieth century or the tenth—or indeed the first century. They belong to a prehistoric age.

Death, he concluded, "presides over the peninsula."[20]

"Inept government" also stifled the cultural development of its constituents. A stagnated culture made the people dirty and lazy. Travelers returning from the peninsula littered their descriptions of Korea with these images, as Peter Duus offers in his study on Japanese annexation of Korea.[21] The lazy Korean constituted another product of Korea's "inept government." One of the visual images most frequently disseminated displayed the Korean asleep by the roadside as his mule, overburdened with lumber, waited patiently beside him. Yamaji Aizen described Korean laborers as even more physically blessed than their Japanese counterparts, but much less useful when it came to using their natural talents.

> Korean laborers excel our countrymen in stature as well as in physical strength. However, they are extremely lazy. They get up and go out for work only when they feel hungry, but even then, as soon as they quench their hunger for the day, they begin to think about going home and having a nap. They do not know how to save things, nor do they have any will to change their dispositions.

Yamaji concluded upon arriving in Pusan that the management of this people would be far from easy.[22] As further evidence of Korean capability, and the government's responsibility for not mobilizing their talents, Japanese often contributed stories of the industrious behavior demonstrated by Koreans living abroad.

Despite the rhetoric of Korean-Japanese similarity provided by participants in the debate over assimilation policy, those painting images of Koreans portrayed the people in terms only slightly more encouraging than those that predated annexation. Koreans remained an underdeveloped people trapped in the distant past, a spiritless people in desperate need of enlightened government to awaken them to present reality. While some saw potential in the Korean people, the views of difference in others hardened as they observed one of the results of annexation: Japanese and Koreans residing in closer proximity. Nanba Kasui believed Koreatown to be "dirtier and smellier" than he had imagined when seen after observing bustling Japantown, with its "*oseibo* [year-end gift-giving season] sales dressed in red and white banners, red lanterns swaying in the wind."[23]

Post-annexation travelers such as Nanba provided one important source for the Korean image. Many Japanese returning from their sojourn to the peninsula found Japan's expanding print culture eager to publish their experiences. The archipelago's leading monthlies, such as *Chūō Kōron* and *Nihon oyobi Nihonjin*, as well as the Korea-based *Chōsen oyobi Manshū*, all found room to print even the more mundane travel accounts. These included transcriptions of speeches given by the authors and longer multi-issue accounts apparently written specifically for publication. In addition to the tourist activities, these reports inserted short anecdotes of Korea and the Korean people that revealed as much about the authors' pre-arrival prejudices as of their actual travel experiences. The trips were long, particularly if they were packaged as *Mansen* (Manchuria-Korea) tours. Between the eleven Japan Tourist Bureau offices (and a number of smaller offices) sprinkled across the peninsula and the bilingual magazine *Tourist* (or *Tsūrisuto*), travelers had access to ample information to plan their trips. The July 1919 issue of *Tsūrisuto* carried a short, three-page article that provided readers interested in visiting Korea with a set of general travel considerations that ranged from weather conditions to lodging opportunities. It also appended a list of cautions from a Genroku-era (1688–1704) Japanese pilgrimage anthology (*Nihon angya bunshū*) that warned travelers to refrain from lustful sex (*shinyoku*), fame seeking, and arrogance. Although the anthology was penned in ancient times, the magazine argued its relevance to those traveling to "newly opened places" (*shinkaichi*) such as Korea as a precaution from their encountering disappointment while on the road.[24] Japanese travelers mixed their disappointments among their impressions of Korea in articles that summarized their travels.

Even after annexation, travelers continued to depict the Korean Peninsula as trapped in a time warp. Seika Ayaka, traveling in 1912, described his experiences in *Chōsen oyobi Manshu* as "nostalgic" (*natsukashii*). He saw the Korean people as the remnants of Heike who "vanished with the waves of the western seas" in the Genpei Wars (1180–1185) that ushered in Japan's Kamakura period (1185–1333). Seika continued: "whether it was their world or another one is left with the impression that [Korea] was a different world that fluttered away its glory, one built through wind and string instruments. I think of Korea as nostalgic." This feeling, he admitted, differed from sentiments used by other Japanese who describe Korea as "primitive" (*genshiteki*), "wild" (*arappoi*), and, conversely, "delicate" (*yawarakai*).[25]

Japanese residents in Korea offered similar images of the Korean as primitive. Kubo Takeshi, who taught at Keijō medical school, contributed more than three hundred pages of medical research on Koreans to the *Korean Medical Journal* (Chōsen igakkai zasshi), the organ of the Korean Medical Association (Chōsen igakkai) founded in 1911. Kubo's research on the Korean anatomy depicted the people as weak in the physiological characteristics of the civilized, yet strong in those of the uncivilized. While their development in "expressive movement" (*hyōjō undō*) muscles remained inferior, the muscles required for basic survival—those for hearing and smelling—remained superior, when compared to those of the Japanese.[26] Many of his results boldly generalized the physiological construction of the Korean people based on autopsies performed on the limited number of cadavers that a local prison provided him. His attempt to characterize his Korean students accordingly—he accused them of stealing a skull bone based on his theory that the Korean head shape made them more prone to criminal activity—led to their boycott of his class.[27]

The Koreans' backwardness was reflected in their daily life. Nakajima Motojirō, also writing for the *Korean Medical Journal*, attributed the habit of Korean women carrying heavy loads on their heads to their pelvic bone being smaller in diameter than that expected for women their size.[28] Koreans also lacked the standards of hygiene and cleanliness acceptable to civilized people. Toriga Ramon, who authored a 1914 guidebook for potential

Japanese migrants to Korea titled *Chōsen e iku hito ni* (To People Going to Korea), advised his readers to expect Korean inns, like Korean houses, to be "dirty."[29] Hara Sōichirō criticized Korean houses as "narrow and suffering" (*semakurushii*). He added: "Japanese houses are small when compared to European houses. But when I see Korean houses I have to sink to another level in poverty [*binjyaku*]."[30]

Both Toriga and Hara cited the Korean lack of spirit (*tamashii*). Toriga believed this to be a characteristic shared by other underdeveloped peoples: in Japan there is a Japanese spirit, in Russia a Russian spirit, and in America an American spirit. It would sound strange (*hibiki ga warui*) to consider an Egyptian, Indian, or Chinese spirit. He then questioned whether there was a Korean spirit.

> A Korean spirit? No matter how hard we try to say this, it sounds totally strange. It is strange but, though the nation is dead, the country [rivers and mountains] live on. Does Korea have a spirit? In one sense it is said that Koreans are sly [*inken*] and suspicious [*saigishin*]. This is an interpretation that is well-meant and has been given the splendid title of Korean spirit. However, is this accurate? It is not that people cannot recognize this phenomenon. It resembles the shortsighted [*tanshi*] imprudence [*senryo*] of a woman [*fujoshi*]. The degree of [Korean] slyness and suspicion, however, cannot be seen as synonymous to the country.

"Such negative traits," he concluded, "do not constitute spirit."[31]

Toriga's images reflect those of Arakawa Gorō's 1906 distinction between the physical Korean—"they all look just like the Japanese"—and the psychological Korean—"they appear to be a bit vacant, their mouths open and their eyes dull, somewhat lacking."[32] The Korean Peninsula may be geographically close to the Japanese archipelago, and the Korean people physically similar to their Japanese counterparts, but the land and its people suffered from stagnation. Having diagnosed the symptom, the Japanese prescribed the remedy—competent government. The Meiji government, having deposed one inept government in the Tokugawa regime, accepted a similar challenge by annexing Korea.

None of these Japanese directly expressed opposition to assimilation. Yet, many indirectly hinted that it would be difficult. We may perhaps read into their thoughts suggestions of its impossibility, at least if assimilation was to be total—Koreans becoming indistinguishable from Japanese. The Korean

people were caught in a time warp that needed to be broken. Their lifestyle was antiquated: they retained customs that the Japanese had relinquished centuries ago. Those indicating the time frame needed to overcome
Japanese-Korean difference predicted it would take generations—fifty to one
hundred years—before the Koreans could catch up with the Japanese. Over
this time Koreans would have to be exposed to Japanese customs and language. Recruiting Japanese role models was one way to demonstrate to the
people the Japanese spirit. In addition the administration recognized the
importance of educating Koreans on the components of "Japanese," just as
Meiji Japan had emphasized this institution in its internal and peripheral
situations.

JAPAN'S EDUCATION POLICY UNDER MILITARY RULE

The Japanese administration that entered the government-general offices,
in accepting the challenge to assimilate Koreans also accepted the task of
delivering the people from their pitiful situation. Japanese guidance would
train the Korean to complete a full day's work, it would educate him in frugality, and it would motivate him to improve himself. It would further equip
women with the tools they needed to pass these critical attributes on to their
children in the home education they would direct. The classroom served as
one of the most important venues to accomplish this. Similar to the other
peripheral examples, Korean participation in this education was voluntary,
although the administration apparently pressured certain Korean families
to send their children to school.[33] Indeed, the government-general waited
until the late 1930s, just after it began accepting Koreans into the military,
to announce that it would institute a compulsory education system—and
then only after another decade.

Successful assimilation of Japan's colonized subjects required the government-general to create a system dedicated to integrating the colonized
people into this system. Instituting an integrated Japanese-Korean education
system would provide the newly annexed subjects with a foundation for
Japanese culture and language and graduates with networks required for
social and economic advancement. The system established by the government-general provided separate and unequal learning environments to iso-
late the colonizers from the colonized. It offered Korean children a four-year
elementary "common school" (futsū gakkō) curriculum and a "higher common school" (four years for males, three for females) curriculum. Students

could also enroll in technical schools and professional schools (*senmon gakkō*) on the peninsula. Those who crossed over to the archipelago to attend secondary schools were required to enroll in a two-year preparatory school before gaining admission to compensate for the shorter Korean curriculum. This preparatory education was not required of Japanese expatriates as the government-general provided them with a six-year public elementary school (*kōritsu shogakkō*) education that generally matched the homeland curriculum in content and duration. In addition, Korean children had the option of seeking enrollment in the private schools run primarily by Western missionaries or attending traditional Korean schools that had survived annexation.

The contribution of a solid education foundation to the social mobility of its recipient cannot be overstated. It is difficult to understand the entrepreneurial success that the Kim brothers, Sŏngsu and Yŏnsu, realized without considering the education they received in Japan. During their stays—Sŏngsu, for six years, attended Waseda University; Yŏnsu, for ten years, attended Kyoto Imperial University—the brothers received a solid education. But more important were the contacts they made, and the knowledge in Japanese language and customs that they acquired, which allowed them to comfortably mingle with Japanese of influence upon returning to Korea. These experiences proved indispensable to their success in forming the Kyŏngsŏng Spinning and Weaving Company. The Kim brothers, of course, were not alone. In 1920 only 1,230 Koreans were studying in Japan. By 1942 this figure had reached 29,427.[34] The small percentage of Koreans studying in Japan, when compared to the overall population of nearly 2 million Japan-based Koreans, suggests it to have been a luxury beyond the reach of the majority of Koreans who resided in Japan by the 1940s.

The role that education would play in advancing Koreans toward civilization formed the basis of a rather active debate in education journals and newspapers soon after the Japanese government announced Korea's annexation. The discussants, presuming the administration's goal to be integration, offered a rich variety of opinions. Some participants even questioned Japan's decision to assimilate Koreans. The discussion first entertained practical questions: the purpose of this education, the nature of the curriculum, and the language in which it would be conducted. Some argued for mixed Japanese-Korean education, an idea more seriously debated from the second decade of Japanese rule. Others who criticized the disparaging attitude of the Japanese toward their Korean charges echoed doubts over Japan's ability to assimilate Koreans.

One of the primary concerns voiced at this time centered on Korean-Japanese differences: they spoke different languages, they followed different customs, and Koreans were less developed. Whether these differences required their academic segregation from Japanese children constituted one important point of discussion. Terauchi Masatake, as Korea's last resident general, anticipated this issue prior to annexation:

> Koreans are on a different level from the Japanese and thus it is difficult to put them under the same [education] system right away. After they learn the conditions, customs, and mannerisms of the Japanese, after the welfare of the people is secured through improvements in their level of culture, and after they develop the required knowledge, gradually they can be assimilated as Japanese.[35]

Following annexation, few contested this characterization. The discussion centered on the best way to narrow this gap.

The journal *Kyōikukai* (Education World) advised in an editorial that Koreans complete a "special preparation course" (*junbi kyōiku*) before being allowed into the Japanese system. This special course was necessary because the different histories and sentiments of the Korean people rendered mixed education with Japanese impossible. Offering the people a "misguided education" would conjure "bad feelings" that would nurture a rebellious attitude among them. Equality in education, it concluded, would have to wait for another ten, twenty, or even one hundred years. This editorial next addressed the content of this special curriculum: practical over moral instruction. The author reasoned that as the Korean people were already trained in Confucian education principles, their education should concentrate on more practical areas, such as agriculture, industry, and manufacturing. This education would enable them to make a more useful contribution to the empire. The Korean people would attain happiness, the article reasoned, by becoming more autonomous and self-managing.

Linguistic capacity was also a factor. The linguistic differences that separated the two people required the Japanese offering Korean children a curriculum that, similar to that offered the Ryukyu and Ainu peoples, concentrated heavily on language study. The editorial lamented that, for the time being, the Japanese would have to endure the Korean people's bilingual existence—Japanese in the schools and Korean in the homes—until they adopted the colonizer's language as their native tongue. The colonized government should encourage the Korean people's gradual advancement: while the goal of this education was to remold the Korean people into loyal imperial subjects, it would be wrong to push this objective in a radical way.[36]

The *Maeil sinbo*, a Korean-language newspaper published by the government-general, echoed these views. Concerning curriculum design, the newspaper also advanced a Korean education system based on practical industrial skills. An "intellectual curriculum" that offered students courses in history and geography was valuable for nurturing within the students a "unified spirit" (*iltan chŏngsín*); practical education, however, established a foundation for this spirit and thus addressed the more immediate needs of the Korean people.[37]

Opinions offered by Mitsuchi Chūzo, a member of the Japanese Diet who had previously acted as a consultant for the Korean government's education offices, touched on similar issues but reached different conclusions. He acknowledged the intellectual gap that separated the two peoples but was more explicit in explaining its existence. The Korean people needed a "special education" to overcome what he termed a forty-year handicap, which incorrectly limited their education to the Korean *sŏdang* system. He advised that these schools required reform just as the Tokugawa-era local *terakoya* system had to be replaced by Meiji Japan. This gap had been historically induced: the Japanese simply had the good fortune to be introduced to "enlightened education" four decades earlier than the Korean people. Koreans having reformed at the pace of Japanese reforms would have eliminated gaps that presently separated the two peoples. His solution to narrowing this gap differed from the above opinions on two points. First, Mitsuchi argued that Korean children should be offered a curriculum based on moral, rather than practical, education. He also viewed the purpose of this education differently, suggesting opposition to assimilation: Koreans should be trained to be world citizens rather than Japanese subjects. Creating a moral-based curriculum would train Korean students in "obligation, honesty, moral character, and public spirit," rather than in loyalty to the Japanese state and subjugation to the Japanese emperor.[38]

Mitsuchi's arguments indirectly criticized Japanese arrogance toward Koreans by calling for Korean education to extend beyond simply cloning Japanese subjects. A number of participants in this debate echoed this criticism in more direct terms. Horio Mine advised the Japanese government to implement a curriculum that offered the Korean people what he called "incentive for national education" (*kokumin kyōikuteki dōki*). Koreans must be led to form their own nation with a foundation of common interests and equal prosperity, as a people holding "parity" and "equal sentiments" with the Japanese people. Above all, he continued, the Korean people must gain an understanding of their position as fellow countrymen and countrywomen. This was how the Japanese people came to stand shoulder to shoulder with the world powers; it explained why incentive for national education was so essential to the Korean people. Unless they acquired a sense for national polity, Horio warned, the road to assimilation would be lost. Korean education thus should be constructed with the ambition of training the people for positions of equality with, rather than subjugation to, their colonizers.

To Horio, the Japanese superficial understanding of their administrative mission constituted the primary obstacle to their realizing this goal. He criticized their advancing an assimilation policy without sufficiently considering its content, and noted the disturbing contradiction between their inclusive assimilation rhetoric and Japanese discriminatory views of superiority over Koreans. The lack of a genuine intention to either recognize or respect the Korean people's "potential character" was an attitude harbored by the Japanese that required more attention. Unless they bridged this superior-conqueror over the inferior-conquered gap, much like the Indians under British rule and the blacks and Native Americans under U.S. rule, the Koreans would have little chance of advancing as a people.[39]

Participants in this debate also addressed pedagogical issues such as whether the classrooms should be mixed or segregated, and the language that the instruction should assume. The English language *Seoul Press* linked the two issues by recommending that Koreans first demonstrate adequate Japanese language ability before being allowed into schools for Japanese expatriates. The newspaper argued that similarities between the Japanese and Korean languages, and Korean people's superiority in learning foreign languages, made Japanese, rather than Korean, the preferred language of instruction. The newspaper then argued the benefits of integrated classrooms: this arrangement offered Koreans the opportunity to study under a curriculum equal to that offered Japanese students, and Japanese students incentive to learn the Korean language.[40] The *Seoul Press* advised that the content of the curriculum remain Japanese-centered: history and geography lessons would concentrate attention on Japanese matters, with Korean history receiving attention only in events that demonstrated Japan-Korea connections.[41]

The idea that the Korean people were superior to Japanese in language learning capacity is one that appeared quite often. Language learning is a talent commonly attributed to colonized peoples (and women) based on the idea that these groups are less creative and more docile. Of course the incentives for the colonized to learn the language of the colonizer far outstripped those of the colonizer for learning the language of their poorer and less powerful colonies. In November the *Seoul Press* took this idea one step further in a feature article on the Hansŏng Higher Women's Institute. Here the newspaper contrasted the excellent progress being made by the students in the Japanese language, against the relatively slow progress they were making in music and math.[42] Similarities shared by the two languages also received attention. Some argued Korean to be a "dialect" (*hyōgen*) of Japan's "national language" (*kokugo*), one on a level similar to Japan's other regional dialects.[43] Yamada Kanto's recent review of Korean language study among Japanese reveals that Japanese officials, dissatisfied with the progress that Koreans were making in the Japanese language, felt obliged to provide incentives to encourage Japanese in Korea to study the Korean language. Employers rewarded their efforts by offering bonuses to those who passed a proficiency exam. It should come as no surprise that, given their task of censorship and their frequent contact with Koreans, the police generally faired best on these exams.[44]

The degree to which women were to be educated presented another issue for this discussion. Barring women from the classroom perpetuated traditional superstition and stifled development. Educating them enabled women to positively contribute to early child development by directing their "home schooling" (*katei kyōiku*) to prepare their children for classroom instruction. The *Maeil sinbo* emphasized this in September 1910, when it explained this education as pivotal to their future: "Whether a person will turn in life from a good to an evil road, or from an evil to a good road, depends upon whether they have been properly taught. If they are taught correct things (*chŏngsa*) they will become correct people (*chŏngʾin*)." This education, the editorial continued, began in the home: if the mother is educated, she can pass on correct knowledge to her children; if she is uneducated she will recycle to them superstitions of the past. It then linked the merits of home education to the health of the state: "it is not an overstatement to say that women's education is tied to the rises and falls of the state. If women do not have morals, then boys cannot be strictly directed. Without this foundation, it will be too late after to make him excel in his education." Women's education, the newspaper advised, should be limited to moral issues. The author did not consider knowledge-based education or physical training to hold particular importance for their role in society.[45]

Discussion over issues regarding the Korean education system proved to be much more creative than the dialogue over Japan's choice of assimilation as its administrative policy. Rather than simply mimicking the superficial idea that the Koreans would readily assimilate, participants challenged the Japanese qualifications for assimilating a foreign people: were they prepared to accept this task? They also challenged those responsible for forming Korea's education policy to guide students beyond the limited goal of molding imperial subjects. Education officials in the government-general apparently were unswayed by these arguments. The education system and curriculum that emerged as the First Education Ordinance on November 1, 1911, demonstrated a striking resemblance in content and duration to the education system that Japan offered its other peripheral subjects in its segregated and unequal characteristics. Elementary education for Korean children constituted a truncated version of that offered to Japanese children: the four-year program started the Koreans later (from age eight), and finished them earlier (at age twelve) than their Japanese counterparts. This difference required Koreans interested in continuing their education to enroll in extra schooling to compensate for this deficiency. The curriculum's content stressed moral education in the elementary stage, but practical education once the foundation had been laid. It thus emphasized the creation of the loyal subject before the prolific student; it instructed the students on the value of a hard day's work before preparing them for their life calling. Governor General Terauchi Masataka emphasized the "object of education" as "promot[ing] the intellect of the young people and enhancing their moral character so that they may become able govern themselves and their homes." Korea's backwardness required more emphasis on the latter:

> Hitherto many men of [Korea] have been led by the erroneous method of education pursued to dislike work and indulge in useless and empty talk. In the future, attention should be paid to the removal of this evil as well as to instilling in the minds of the young men the detestation of idleness and the love of real work, thrift, and diligence.[46]

The 1911 Education Ordinance reiterated this ambition.

> Educate Koreans on the basis of the Imperial Rescript on Education so that they may become good and loyal subjects of the Empire, fostering in them such characteristics and giving them such knowl-

edge and ability as will enable them to lead a respectable life and rise in society.[47]

Language study dominated both curriculums but the Japanese school curriculum exposed the students to a greater range of subjects (such as history and geography) than the shorter Korean school curriculum. Korean students having to study three languages (they also had six hours per week of a combined Korean and Classical Chinese class) cut into the time needed for these subjects. Science was only introduced as a two-hour class from their third year, an addition that added one hour to the school week and subtracted another hour from their Korean/Classical Chinese instruction.[48] The curriculum offered students ten hours per week of direct Japanese language instruction. Students indirectly received additional language instruction in their other classes. After the first year, the only textbooks that were not written in Japanese were those used in the Korean/Classical Chinese class. Teachers, in principle, were also expected to teach their classes in Japanese. If honored, this requirement further diluted the quality of the education, as it forced the children to study in a foreign language, and the teacher (if Korean) to instruct in a foreign language. The administration felt confident that this instruction achieved its goal of creating Japanese-speaking Koreans. It would base its estimates for Korean Japanese language proficiency simply on school enrollment figures rather than a more objective measure, such as a proficiency exam. Considering that the government-general provided teachers for the earlier grades with bilingual (Japanese-Korean) instruction manuals, and relied heavily on Korean teachers (1,206 Korean to 498 Japanese teachers in 1914),[49] one might question just how much of this instruction was being conducted in Japanese.

The elementary school curriculum offered but one hour per week in ethics. A glance at the content of other classes reveals lessons in ethics being presented across the curriculum. Language textbooks stressed thriftiness by portraying the Empress Dowager as a person who did not aspire to luxury, as a person who raised her own silkworms to demonstrate to the commoner ways of promoting Japan's national treasure. The same textbooks contained stories of Japanese-Korean harmony to promote the spirit of assimilation and Japanese-Korean communication. Kinan dutifully learned Tarō's language; the Korean boy's positive attitude inspired a similar attitude in his parents. Korean and Japanese language textbooks introduced students to Japanese myths and tales, and exposed them to essays on Shintoism, the

Japanese flag, and other important icons of Japanese culture.[50] E. Patricia Tsurumi notes that teachers in Korea, like teachers in Taiwan, were urged to include "the 'Japanese spirit' in everything they taught."[51]

Japanese officials could possibly explain the shorter duration, along with the crowded classrooms and underfunded instruction of Korean education, by logistics: constructing new school buildings and training qualified teachers could not be accomplished overnight.[52] Yet, this was also the case in Japan when the government first introduced its education policy in 1872. What separated Japanese education from Korean education was more fundamental—intention. Unlike Japan's 1872 Fundamental Code of Education, the Korean government-general's 1911 Education Ordinance contained no declaration that expressed an ambition to leave "no [Korean] community . . . with an uneducated household nor a [Korean] family with an uneducated person."[53] The Japanese administration did not express this ambition until the late 1930s, when it became necessary to begin inducting Korean boys into the Japanese military.

SOCIAL EDUCATION AND THE *MAEIL SINBO*

The government-general supplemented classroom education with a "social education" (*shakai kyōiku*) that disseminated similar messages to Korea's literate population. The primary outlet for this instruction was the *Maeil sinbo* (Daily News), a government-general newspaper that published its first issue on August 30, 1910, the day after annexation was announced. This education reinforced messages emphasized in "classroom education," and by extension "home education." In addition to print media, the government-general gradually introduced avenues such as ceremony, travel, and short seminars (*kōshūkai*) to spread its message. This effort would thrive in the 1920s after the government-general initiated revised publication legislation that greatly diversified the print culture. The administration again curtailed Korean publication during the wartime period (1937–45) as the government-general intensified its efforts to instill in Koreans "correct" messages crafted to gain their cooperation in those trying times.

The media provided the administration with a means of communicating its message to the Korean people and linked other components of Japan's social education system. In addition to delivering to its readers the news of the day, it also provided them with an explanation of their new position in the Japanese Empire, along with instruction on the cultural and social adjustments expected of them to raise their level of civilization to that of the Japanese. As in the case of internal expansion, the press played an indispensable role as instructor in the formation of an imagined community in the peripheral colony. Over the first decade, the *Maeil sinbo* enjoyed a virtual monopoly over the media, as the Japanese had ordered the major Korean newspapers closed at the time of annexation; the few minor publications allowed to continue operations soon went out of business.[54] It remained the primary legal Korean-language news outlet in the colony until the Saitō reforms expanded the vernacular press from 1920. The *Maeil sinbo* survived until 1945, when Japan's defeat forced it to stop its presses.

The *Maeil sinbo* joined the Japanese language *Keijō nippō* and the English language *Seoul Press*, which had been publishing since September 1906, as the primary government-general media outlets on the peninsula.[55] Its inaugural issue carried a Korean translation of the treaty of annexation, the Japanese Imperial Rescript that commemorated this event, a text of the law governing Korean royalty, and an editorial on the significance of the new Japanese-Korean relations. The newspaper's highly Sinified text in its early editions—which suggests the editorials to have been translated directly from an original Japanese text—demonstrates the government-general's intended audience to have been Korea's educated *yangban* elite. From March 1912 *Maeil sinbo* attempted to expand its readership by publishing a *han'gŭl* (Korean alphabetic script) version of the paper.[56] After the government-general expanded the number of vernacular newspapers in the colony, even its regular edition began to make greater use of *han'gŭl* and occasionally added miniaturized *han'gŭl* readings (similar to Japanese *furigana*) above the Chinese characters.[57]

The immediate value to the government-general's assimilation policy was the civilizing message that the *Maeil sinbo* advanced. Most often this message found its way into the daily editorials that graced the newspaper's front page. Lessons offered here repeated those provided in classroom textbooks: thriftiness, hard work, health and nutrition, and eradication of "feudal customs." The newspaper advertised itself as an organ of civilization: if one does not read the newspaper, it warned, your day is "dark."[58] Its journalists briefed Koreans on Governor General Terauchi's frequent trips to and from the Japanese capital by providing them with his departure and arrival times. It then led them into the imperial chambers where Terauchi reported directly to the Meiji Emperor on the colony's developments. Other articles reported on the amicable relations that the Korean royal family and the Japanese government-general shared, in anticipation of a similar relationship developing between the Korean Kims and the Japanese Suzukis.

One of the newspaper's first tasks was to introduce to its Korean readership the peninsula's new status in the empire. The newspaper instructed the Korean people on the connection between new ideas and Japan's peninsular policies, and explained why it was necessary for them to acquiesce to Japanese rule. One editorial described the new situation as a natural phenomenon of cycles: "The old rain ends and a new rain enters; the lingering moon fades and a new moon appears. The new rain and the new moon create the world for the new people." It advised that it was not necessary, or even expected, for the Korean people to do away with their past in toto. The old, it conceded, would never completely die away. The task facing the Korean people was to "do away with the rotten thoughts of yesteryear and let in the fresh ideas of today."[59] This point suggested an idea occasionally heard in Japanese colonial discourse: like different regions of Japan (such as Kyushu and Tohoku), Korea too should be allowed to maintain a local flavor. Assimilation did not require the Japanese to clone Koreans into a fictitious image of a "homogeneous" Japanese people.

One week later the *Maeil sinbo* preached that the Koreans and Japanese must join forces to survive the "era of reform" (*kaehyŏk ŭi sidae*) that challenged them. The present was an "era of new people" (*sinmin sidae*), an era defined by the thoughts of the people. Knowledge and its potential awaken people from their slumber and allow a fresh wind to enter. Our Korean and Japanese abodes, it instructed, presently rest side by side. Those who reside here will find happiness in sharing a drink together.[60] Their success depends on Korean cooperation. This editorial stressed that Koreans and Japanese were bound together by fate in a tight symbiotic relationship. "If Japan was strong," it reasoned, "then our country (*aguk*) is strong. If our country is weak, however, Japan is also weakened. . . . If the elder brother eats well, then the younger brother of the same house will not starve."[61]

The *Maeil sinbo* contextualized this relationship one week later. The two peoples shared a racial affinity: they were of the same family and of the same yellow race. In terms of dignity there existed no difference in status between them, nor was there to be any superior or inferior treatment between the peoples living on the peninsula. This editorial anticipated the day when Koreans would drop *wae* (dwarf barbarian) as a denigrating reference to Japanese, and when Japanese in turn would cease to refer to Koreans as *yŏbo*. Education, the author concluded, would guide the Korean people toward the imperialization to allow them to live in harmony with their Japanese neighbors.[62]

The *Maeil sinbo*'s views over this initial period on how assimilation should be implemented mirrored those held by other Japanese—gradual over radical. It acknowledged the differences that had emerged between the Korean and Japanese peoples to be a result of their historical separation. Linguistic, legal, dietary, and other such differences accounted for contemporary differences in the two peoples' character and thinking. Maintaining these differences complicated the formation of a trusting relationship between Koreans and Japanese. Intimacy, the newspaper explained, emerged through the assimilation of human nature and feelings. The close history shared by Koreans and Japanese provided a sufficient basis to stimulate natural progress toward the desired relationship. Devising a policy for this purpose was unnecessary. Likewise, the Korean people would not need to study the Japanese language morning, noon, and night. Rather the promotion of gradual acquisition provided the best way to encourage the Korean people to adopt the Japanese language.[63]

As in the debate on education policy, commentary often linked linguistic proficiency with cultural assimilation, and language capacity with mental capacity. Gaining the capacity for superior thinking required a people adopting a superior language. Ignoring the counter Irish example, the newspaper argued that if the Koreans adopted the Japanese language, the two peoples would be united in thought. One February 1911 editorial articulated this understanding as follows:

> If one is clever and the other is incompetent . . . ; if one is wise and
> the other foolish . . . ; if one is strong and the other weak, assimila-
> tion will not succeed. The glory of assimilation is when there exists
> no clever or incompetent, wise or fool, and strong or weak.

Common language, the editorial concluded, was the leveling agent of the two peoples' natural talents. Koreans studying the *Naeji* (homeland; Japanese *Naichi*) language was one important way for them to synchronize with Japan's efforts.[64]

In addition to Japanese language acquisition, the Korean people would also have to shed their "barbarous" customs and mannerisms to gain proper acceptance as Japanese subjects. Assimilation would fail if the Korean people did not adopt a lifestyle that attained the standards of civilization expected of them by Korea-based Japanese. Like the elementary school textbook, the

Maeil sinbo assumed responsibility for instructing its Korean readers on areas that the Japanese people considered to be uncivilized. As with language study, it advised gradual change. Radical change would disrupt the Korean social structure in a harmful way.

The newspaper targeted Korea's health and cleanliness standards as an area that required dramatic reform. In a rather patronizing editorial titled "Hygiene and ethics" (*wisaeng kwa susin*), the *Maeil sinbo* generalized that to date the Korean people had given insufficient attention to their health: "We are indifferent to the filth in our homes; we also do not seem to mind if our food is kept unclean." The editorial argued the primary cause of this unhealthy lifestyle to be Korean idleness. To correct this character flaw, it advised, Koreans must learn to better regulate their lives. There is a time and a place for everything—exercise, meals, enjoyment—and these activities must be regulated. Once our lifestyles are regulated, the editorial declared, we must follow our schedule no matter if the weather is "windy or rainy, hot or cold."

There were a number of other ways in which the Korean people could improve their health. The editorial urged them to exercise to allow their blood to flow more smoothly and their food to digest properly. Exercise also allowed a person to rest more deeply. It also helped prevent sickness. The newspaper advised the Korean people to establish healthy dietary habits: "Be careful over food selection and eat a little of everything." In particular, it advised, one's body, one's house, one's furniture, and one's food must be kept clean. This was important for the sake of cleanliness, as well as for one's personal hygiene.[65]

The *Maeil sinbo* also took issue on early marriage, framing the problem as one characteristic of Korean culture in general.[66] Forcing girls to marry as children prevented them from receiving a proper education, and thus perpetuated superstitious beliefs. The newspaper explained that this "corrupt custom" interfered with the development of the individual, as human beings generally progressed most rapidly in brightness and intelligence between the ages of seven and twenty. Its reference to legal edicts not encouraging a change in mind-set perhaps alluded to the fact that the Kabo Reform Edicts of 1894, which established a minimum age for marriage, had not produced a recognizable change in practice.[67] Parents, particularly among poor families, continued to marry their daughters off at an early age.[68] Emphasizing this practice as an innate part of Korean culture suggested the need for foreign intervention to correct it. Yet at the same time it ignored its economic aspect: families with limited incomes had to marry their daughters earlier, when the dowry price was more affordable.

In addition to correcting Koreans' shortcomings, the government-general encouraged their participation in Japan's imperial events. Holidays were to be observed; imperial birthdays, weddings, and coronations celebrated; and royal deaths mourned. The Japanese were also rather fond of numbers. They left volumes of statistics to quantify their administrative successes that suggested Korean advancement toward assimilation. They publicized the number of Koreans fluent in the Japanese language, the number of Korean visits to Shinto shrines, and the number of mixed (Korean-Japanese) marriages. Rather than extrapolate on the content of the statistics, the Japanese allowed the often-misleading numbers to speak for themselves. It did not matter why the Koreans may have visited the Shinto shrine; the increase in attendance alone demonstrated success in their administrative policy.[69] The Japanese colonial government encouraged participation as a means of instruction, as well. Here the media's role was crucial. It sponsored and publicized activities that required Korean participation. But it also instructed the people on the activities' significance, as well as the proper (Japanese) way to dress and act while participating. It also allowed those residing in remote locations to participate indirectly by bringing to them news on how Japanese and fellow Koreans commemorated special events such as imperial birthdays and coronations. Editors choreographed this reportage to strengthen the colonized people's identification with the people of the colonial homeland, the two peoples joined in communion by a shared purpose.

The media often advertised the relationship that Japan's imperial throne shared with the Korean people. As in Japan, many of the holidays celebrated in the colony were related to the throne, the most important being the imperial birthday. On this day the *Maeil sinbo* decorated its front pages with the imperial portrait and letters carrying the emperor's special message to the Korean people. Special occasions—imperial deaths and coronations— provided the government-general with additional opportunities to instruct the Korean people on the emperor's relationship with Korea. As the Meiji Emperor lay dying in July 1912, the *Maeil sinbo* detailed King Sunjong's behavior—he canceled all forms of entertainment and demanded information on the emperor's health—to instruct the common Korean on what constituted attitude and behavior appropriate for this dark time.[70]

The Meiji Emperor's birthday (November 3) provided the colonial government with its first opportunity to enlist the Korean people's participation just over two months after annexation. An "aristocratic tour" (*kwijok chegong*) organized by the government-general highlighted Korean celebrations for this occasion. The travelers' itinerary being set to bring them to Tokyo just in time to join the emperor's birthday celebrations appears intentional, as a way to demonstrate Korean acquiescence to Japanese rule. The list of participants included a number of Koreans who had cooperated with the Japanese in the past: former members of the recently dissolved Korean cabinet, including Pak Chesun (home minister) and Yi Yŏngjik (education minister), and members of the current General Council that included Kim Yongham, Ho Chin, Yi Wŏnsik, and So Sanghun. One other participant, Min Chŏngsik, had led righteous army revolts against the Japanese. The *Seoul Press*, always able to find space for feel-good stories to advertise Korean-Japanese benevolence, afforded Min's case special attention. The newspaper described him as an "ex-insurgent leader who once wrought havoc in 1906 in [the] Honju district." It noted that he had secured his position on the tour by appealing directly to Sunjong, the last Korean emperor, who warmly granted the ex-insurgent permission to join the troupe upon learning of Min's desire to "see the land of his erstwhile enemies."[71]

Two tours, separated into male and female members at the onset, traveled from Keijō to Tokyo, making brief stops en route at Shimonoseki, Miyajima, Kyoto, and Nagoya, where they were greeted and entertained by local dignitaries. Patriotic groups, such as the Patriotic Women's Association (*Aikoku fujinkai*), held luncheons and dinner parties in the visitors' honor. Local leaders led them on tours of schools, postal and telegraph offices, and police bureaus. They also treated the Korean guests to military demonstrations. Japanese implored their guests in speeches to study the Japanese language to promote Korean-Japanese friendship.[72] The tour received strong coverage in the Korean press. The *Kyŏngnam ilbo* ran a column titled "The Diary of the Tourist Group" (*Kwan'gwangdan ilji*) between October 29 and November 5. On October 20, the *Maeil sinbo* explained to its readers the tour's significance. It urged participants to return with information necessary to improve the lives of those Koreans who remained behind. Female participants were requested to transfer the latest information on the Japanese household to Korean housewives whose knowledge on this subject was shallow. Such information, it continued, offered Korean women the opportunity to engage in deeper discussion by presenting them with new ideas for improving their own households.[73]

The *Tokyo Asahi shinbun* observed the tour from the angle of the colonial homeland. An editorial carried in its November 3 edition characterized the tour as one organized to allow Korea's "new aristocracy" (*shin kizoku*) the opportunity to "express their gratitude (*shaon*) to the emperor on the occasion of his birthday." This opportunity came the following day when the male participants were granted their audience with the emperor, and the women participants with the empress.[74] The tour thus served a practical purpose, in that the Korean visitors gained direct instruction in modernity and Korea's new role in the empire, as well as a symbolic purpose in its demonstration to the Japanese people of Korean acceptance of their new position in the Japanese empire by a modern use of the ancient tributary mission.

While the Korean aristocrats toured the imperial capital, Koreans paraded the streets of the colonial capital in celebration. The *Maeil sinbo*, in conjunction with the *Keijō nippō*, began preparations for the Korean celebration of the first imperial birthday in late October. At this time the newspapers issued a call for participation in a parade that would wind through the city in his honor. Within a few days it received more than five thousand responses. A planning committee (composed of both Koreans and Japanese representing schools, enterprises, banks, and leading businesses) was quickly organized to coordinate the parade's participants and route. This committee created a list of rules and regulations to control the parade marching: it defined the event as a national flag and costume parade; it also banned children, the elderly, and women from participation. Regarding costumes, the committee determined that while in principle the marchers were free to dress as they pleased, it specifically forbade cross-dressing, as the practice could be potentially demoralizing.[75]

The committee also mapped out a parade route that passed the participants by the citadels of modernity that Japanese colonialism had introduced. The marchers would start at Honmachi, Japantown's main street, before passing through Eirakuchō, and Kotobukichō via Hinodechō. They would turn in to Yamatachō and enter the government-general compound to offer *banzai*s to the Japanese administration and then circle into Hasegawachō before dispersing. The parade thus passed directly through the heart of Keijō's Japan district, which was located on the north slopes of Namsan (southern mountain), where most Japanese resided.[76] On November 5, the *Maeil sinbo* reported that twenty thousand Japanese and Koreans participated in the parade from the start, with many more joining the marchers after the parade got under way.

Had the parade tradition survived into the 1920s, it would have contributed to the powerful statement of modernity that the Japanese assembled to legitimize their administration. The original parade course would have taken its participants past some of the finest examples of Japanese modern architecture in Korea—the Bank of Korea (1912), the Chōsen Hotel (1914), Keijō Station (1925), Keijō City Hall (1926), and the Mitsukoshi Department Store (1930). The parade route would no doubt have been altered to pass the participants by the colony's most powerful structure (in both construction and purpose), the government-general headquarters, which in 1926 moved out of the Namsan area (to be replaced by the city's most important Shinto shrine) to the grounds of the ancient Kyŏngbok palace, now drastically reduced in size to accommodate the new government-general building, gardens, and museum. (In 1995 the South Korean government imploded this building to accommodate the reconstruction of the original palace.) Newspapers reported at least one more formal newspaper-sponsored parade, held on the first observance of Annexation Day (August 29, 1911), and several spontaneous parades, organized less formally to honor imperial coronations. Soon after, however, the Japanese replaced the public display of celebrations with the more private garden party held in the government-general compound.

The first Annexation Day received heavy newspaper coverage, with the *Maeil sinbo* issuing a special edition to honor the day's significance in Japan-Korea relations. The lead editorial of this edition declared that this day would continue to be celebrated not just for a hundred years, or even a thousand years, but for as long as the Korean people remained subjects of the Japanese Empire. The next day it reported that fifty thousand people, including seventy-four Korean groups, participated in a lantern parade that the newspaper cosponsored in conjunction with the *Keijō nippō*. As in the earlier parade, the marchers paraded around the city shouting *banzai* as they passed by the important establishments of Japanese rule. The significance of August 29 as a day of celebration, however, soon faded. The Meiji Emperor's July 1912 death placed the entire empire in a state of mourning, thus canceling all demonstrative celebrations for that year. In 1913, the newspapers attempted to resurrect the holiday. The front-page coverage provided by the *Maeil sinbo* announced that the present (Taisho) emperor's "benevolent succession" and "benevolent message" were deep in the radiance passed on from the thread of the late Meiji Emperor. As in 1911, the newspaper also sponsored a lantern parade, which, it again reported, drew fifty thousand participants. Similar parades also took place in Inch'ŏn and P'yŏngyang. The following year the *Maeil sinbo* recognized this day's significance with simply a short message and a picture of the letter sent by the emperor to commemorate the anniversary. It also reported on a ceremony attended by members of the government-general and the Korean royal family. The newspaper did not sponsor a parade, nor did it offer an explanation for the cancellation of this activity. After this year, the newspaper refrained from carrying news directly related to the day's significance. By 1914 the significance of Annexation Day had been eclipsed by the October 1 anniversary of the formation of the government-general. As with Korea's celebration of imperial birthdays, the main events scheduled to commemorate Annexation Day apparently were confined to the walls of the government-general residence, and to invited Japanese and Korean guests who greeted the occasion with toasts and a round of *banzai*s.

The government-general used special occasions to engage the Korean residents', along with the colony's Japanese, participation in what it called "worship from afar" (*yōhai*). It built Shinto shrines throughout the peninsula, and then spent time and effort to encourage and even force Koreans to visit them. As mentioned above, the Japanese administration measured its success at assimilation by the rise and fall of shrine attendance figures. The Japanese linked the Shinto shrine directly to the imperial throne; the coronation of a new emperor provided an opportunity to instruct the people on this connection. During the wartime years shrines served as the most important venues for public ceremony in the colony, as well as the location where people were to obtain their food rations. After Japan's surrender these structures were the first to be destroyed by the liberated Korean people.

Coronation celebrations provided the Japanese with another opportunity to advertise the emperor's exalted position in Japan's polity. The first such opportunity came in November 1915, three years after the Meiji Emperor's death, when the Japanese staged the Taisho Emperor's coronation ceremonies. This ceremony received heavy coverage in all newspapers. The *Maeil sinbo* offered its readers a series of articles that focused attention on topics concerning Japanese polity and the emperor's indispensable role within this institution, including "Enthronement and National Polity," "The Imperial Throne," and "The Sacred Treasures." The newspaper appended to these lessons daily reports on the new emperor's journey from Tokyo to Kyoto, the venue of the coronation ceremonies, providing readers with the times he was to depart and arrive, as well as detailed descriptions of the train that would carry him and the hotels that would host him along the way. It published images—both sketched and photographed—of the sacred venues prepared for the ceremonies. The newspaper also reported on Korea's representation at these ceremonies. It included a picture of Governor General Terauchi at the ceremonies dressed in his ceremonial garb. Although Korea's royal family was not physically in attendance, their activities—primarily their visit to the government-general offices to extend their congratulations and to sign a guest book—consummated the Korean people's symbolic link to the events.

Japanese colonial rule in Korea during its first decade saw a cautious colonial administration use education and a monopolized press to introduce to the Korean people the idea of their gradual assimilation as Japanese. At the same time it strengthened geographic and social walls that separated the two peoples. By the end of the decade their progress hardly resembled the integration of peninsula to archipelago and Korean to Japanese, suggested by the map that graced the front page of the *Asahi shinbun*'s August 30, 1910, edition. The Korean-language media squared this apparent discrepancy by advising Koreans that assimilation rested on their shoulders: the sooner they advanced as a people, the sooner they would be able to reside, work, relax, and even intermarry with their Japanese counterparts. Yet the government-general also encouraged separation by instituting segregated education systems. Japanese civil servants, donned in required uniforms with swords at their sides, accented the military rule instituted by a government-general, much out of custom, but also out of fear of the trouble that previous colonial experiences taught them to expect.[77] The independence movement that erupted in March 1919 was but the most demonstrative sign of general Korean dissatisfaction with Japan's conspicuous presence and harsh administrative rule. Its magnitude and intensity forced many Japanese to reconsider their initial images of Koreans and the ease in which they believed they could be assimilated.

4

POST–MARCH FIRST POLICY REFORM
AND ASSIMILATION

FROM THE EARLY MORNING HOURS OF MARCH 1, 1919, JAPANESE IMAGES of the Koreans passively becoming assimilated like the supposedly docile Scots turned into an Irish nightmare. On that day thousands of Koreans marched through the streets of Keijō demanding their independence from Japanese rule. The Korean *mansei* (long live [Korea]) cacophony would reverberate in Japanese ears throughout the remainder of Japan's period of colonial rule as warnings to the colonizers against complacency. The demonstrations affected Japanese in different ways. To some they revealed (as the 1857 Indian Mutiny had to the English) the weaknesses of assimilation policy and its inappropriateness in Korea. To others, the demonstrations crystallized the difficulties of assimilation while still allowing for its possibility if administered correctly. The relatively vibrant print culture that characterized early Taisho Japan allowed for a much more dynamic discussion on Korean policy than that which occurred at the time of annexation.

The Korean demonstrations were critical in advancing the changes that in Governor General Saitō Makoto's cultural rule (*bunka seiji*) were ushered in over the next decade. The demonstrations, as well as the reforms that followed, were also a product of the times. Indirectly, Korean actions may also have been influenced by demonstrations that broke out across the Japanese archipelago following the end of World War I. The rice riots of 1918, which brought more than 2 million Japanese to the streets, required a hundred thousand troops to quell. Frederick R. Dickinson, who credits these riots with proving "the magnitude of the 'power of the people,'" notes the effect they had on other Japanese political activity, such as the universal suffrage demonstrations that drew fifty thousand students, merchants, and workers to Hibiya Park in March 1919.[1] One might speculate that this social unrest may also have encouraged the ambitions of the students who met in Tokyo in early February 1919 to draft the first Korean independence declaration, whose actions stimulated the March demonstrations in Korea. The rice riots had a more direct influence on two counts: they encouraged Japan to increase its imports of Korean rice,[2] and they ushered into the Japanese prime ministership one of Japan's more innovative political figures, Hara Takashi (Kei). An avid supporter of assimilation, the prime minister challenged the primary contradiction in Japanese rule: why it preached Korean inclusion as internal citizens, but provided a policy that encouraged discrimination that rendered them as peripheral, or even external, subjects. Hara's fingerprints are on many of the reforms introduced to Korea in the early 1920s.

In Korea, the most profound change that followed the March First demonstrations were attitudinal changes that Japanese held toward Koreans. The idea that over time the Korean people would naturally assimilate was replaced by the idea that the Japanese had to work to guide Koreans to this goal. Exposing them to culture—even their own—would develop within them the sophistication required to evaluate their culture against that of the Japanese. The Japanese expressed confidence that their more developed culture would prevail in the end. From this time, the Japanese enacted reforms that relaxed the psychological distance between the two people. Walls separating Koreans and Japanese by dress, education, and legislation were lowered to allow qualified Koreans to step over to join Japanese circles. Our concern in this chapter is whether the Japanese lowered these walls enough to encourage assimilation.

CHALLENGES TO ASSIMILATION POLICY

News of the government-general's harsh reaction to the Korean independence movement quickly spread throughout the empire and beyond. Criticism from abroad took a number of forms. Some critics specifically targeted Japan's colonial policy; others equated the harsh reaction by the Japanese to their uncivilized nature as a people. Criticism by Japanese also focused on their country's assimilation policy. While some faulted contradictions in the approach—assimilation rhetoric and segregation practice—others cast blame on the Korean people. Their "cacophony" (*sōjō*) demonstrations proved them to be unworthy of assimilation as Japanese. Dissent appeared even among Koreans who used the Japanese media to criticize Koreans who had encouraged an activity that held so little promise of success.[3]

Criticism by acting British consul in Korea, General William M. Royds, faulted Japanese assimilation rhetoric rather than Japanese effort:

> The Japanese policy at present openly aims at depriving the Core-
> ans of even their own language and customs, and their total assimi-
> lation by Japan, and their deliberate attempt to enforce this policy
> by every available means is the cause of the universal hatred in which
> the Japanese are held throughout the land.

Royds's advice reflected disdain for the brutal administration to which Japan subjected Koreans during its initial decade of colonial rule: "It seems evident that a few reasonable concessions and a more sympathetic attitude would do more to restore quiet and contentment than an attempt to stamp out the dissatisfaction by force."[4]

Some in the United States Congress believed that Japanese behavior demonstrated this people to be racially inferior, particularly after receiving news that Japanese had burned Koreans in Christian churches. George W. Norris, a senator from Nebraska, used Japan's barbaric behavior to justify attitudes against the United States joining the League of Nations. After reviewing Japan's history of deception in Korea that led to annexation, he presented an incriminating account of Japan's handling of the March First Movement. Norris characterized the plight of Korea—a country "on the eve of a great upheaval for Christianity and civilization when the Japanese took possession"—as a case of pagan Japanese persecution of Korean Christians. This alone, he claimed, made Japan's crimes much more heinous than the other atrocities conducted by other colonial powers at this time. The Korean case, claimed Norris, illustrated why the League of Nations treaty needed amendment before the United States could join. To accept the treaty as pro-posed would "put the clock of civilization back a thousand years," as was now happening in Korea.[5]

Neither the United States nor Great Britain took steps beyond this ver-bal criticism on Korea's behalf. To do so would have been hypocritical in light of the vast colonial holdings that they and their allies possessed, many of whom had confronted similar anticolonial rebellions in 1919. There was also the idea that these governments considered Japan's problems in Korea as domestic, and thus beyond their immediate influence. The British under-secretary of state for foreign affairs, Cecil Harmsworth, implied as much in remarking, "the subject matter would not appear to lie within the province of His Majesty's Government."[6] Congressman Henry Z. Osborne expressed this more directly in his report on a congressional tour that he led to Northeast Asia in August 1920. Frustrated at being prevented by Japanese from meeting Koreans, he lamented that America's hands were tied: the territory was "as fixedly a part [of the Japanese Empire] as California, Arizona, and New Mexico are a part of the United States."[7]

The independence demonstrations opened Japanese eyes to the realization that, first, they did not really know the Korean people and, second, that assimilation was not going to be as easy as anticipated. These realizations prompted many over Japan's second decade of colonial rule in Korea to offer more diverse commentaries on Japan's assimilation policy than had been given over the first decade. Many Japanese continued to support assimilation, claiming that the policy just needed more time and greater effort. Others admitted that Korean behavior had altered their opinion on the policy's merits. Still others argued that Korean behavior rendered the people unworthy of assimilation. To a few it demonstrated progress in the people's advancement toward civilization.

Editorials in the nationalist magazine *Nihon oyobi Nihonjin* (Japan and the Japanese) cautioned "patience" and offered suggestions for change: assimilation is the work of centuries; Japan and Korea have only been united for a decade. The magazine explained that even after thousands of years of Japanese history, there remained in Kyushu and Tohoku certain linguistic and cultural aspects that differed from those of "Japan." It noted two disadvantages facing Japan: Korea being separated from Japan by sea, and the limited number of Japanese who had crossed over to assimilate Koreans. The editorial concluded that "expecting results in such a short time is an extreme impatience."[8]

Newspaper editor Aoyagi Tsunatarō also urged patience while advising the Japanese administration to exercise "positive" (as opposed to "negative") assimilation practices. Such practices should aim to reform the education system to redirect the Korean people toward a civilized (Japanese) culture. It should work to establish a common (Japanese) language between the two peoples. It should encourage migration by Japanese farmers to the peninsula at a pace of thirty to fifty thousand people annually. These newcomers should instruct the Koreans in advanced farming techniques, while passing on to them by example the diligent habits of the Japanese people.

No friend to the Korean—his commentary on the people was extremely derogatory—Aoyagi concluded his remarks by reaffirming his belief that the Japanese people held the potential to uplift the Korean people and their society to civilization.

> Our great national abilities can advance the Korean culture; they
> can·also raise the achievements of Korean development. By creating
> a harmonious balance between intellectual and moral education,
> within 50 to 100 years that which is known to be Japanese-Korean
> will cease to exist, and we shall see on the Asian continent an inter-
> marriage assimilation (*tsūkon dōka*) of perfect harmony among the
> peoples of the greater Japanese race.

"Positive assimilation," he warned, would succeed only if the Japanese people shed their "island mentality" and extended their vision onto the Asian continent.[9]

Iwasa Zentarō, who delivered his opinions to the government-general in 1928, offered reasons to feel positive about Japan's chances of success, but also cautioned vigilance. The Korean people, he stated, "are now greatly imperialized and are reaping the benefits of this. They sing the praises of submission." His cautions suggested that the effects of the March First Independence Movement lingered.

> [Korean] ladies may sing "kimi ga yo" [the Japanese national
> anthem] at public meetings, but we cannot become complacent.
> Remember the 1919 *banzai sawagi*? . . . Even if you cover up
> something that smells foul, the stench will someday seep out.

He also warned that assimilation for Japan's benefit was dangerous. It must be directed toward the betterment of the Koreans. His proposal, however, was rather ambitious. It called for the mass migration of 20 million Japanese to the Korean Peninsula. The influx of Japanese to Korea would create economic demand. It would also "bathe the Korean people in the blessings of culture," the benefits of which would manifest in "Japanese-Korean harmony, cooperative accords, [and the beginnings of] co-habitation and intermarriage."[10] Aoyagi and Iwasaki's ideas on mass migration were high on vision, but limited in practical application. Japanese promoters of migration to Korea never addressed the key question of why similar ambitions had failed in the past; nor did they explain how best to convince this large number of Japanese to relocate to Korea.

The policy's critics attacking assimilation's inherent contradiction—a superior people attempting to assimilate a people deemed to be inferior—claimed that the European powers had all but abandoned assimilation; the Japanese should do so as well. This critical voice split into those who advised greater separation between the peoples and those who urged the Japanese administration to offer the Korean people more political autonomy. Akagi Kameichi and Hosoi Hajime offered two of the harshest critiques. Akagi's problem stemmed from the policy's goal of "equality." He conceded that the two people shared similarities in ancient times, but contended that this characterization did not hold at present. The two people had since evolved in different directions. Assimilation has proven to be a mistaken policy in the past (as seen in French Algeria); it would likewise prove to be a failure in Korea. Akagi addressed the U.S. president Woodrow Wilson's idea of self-determination, an idea he incorrectly equated with "racial equality." If the Korean people's call for independence were effectuated throughout the world, he reasoned, we would have to devise a system of "racial determination" in which Negroes in the United States would be given their own state to govern, and Russia, England, and other states would have to be divided to allow different peoples their own sovereign territories. Racial self-determination presupposed that minorities were capable of taking advantage of this privilege. They were not, Akagi claimed, and the world would be thrown into chaos should they be given this right. For this simple reason he believed it impossible for Japan to grant Koreans the independence they demanded.

Akagi proposed that ending discrimination constituted a credible alternative to granting them outright independence. This equality did not, he cautioned, constitute Japanese-Korean equality. The Korean Peninsula could not be redefined as an extension of the homeland, as a "second Kyushu." Such thinking only wrought ill fortune for both people.

> Korea must be ruled as Korea. Whether the Koreans are happy or not they must be governed as a colony. Discrimination between Koreans must end but discrimination between Japan and Korea must remain. The thousands of years that separated the two peoples cannot be done away with overnight. . . . Koreans must receive happiness as Koreans; Japanizing them will not bring them happiness.

Trying to assimilate the Korean, he imagined, was like trying to change a "wild boar to a pig; a wolf to a dog; and a lady to a man."[11]

The reporter and government-general advisor Hosoi Hajime experienced a revelation as he witnessed Koreans marching down Keijō's streets demanding their independence.[12] At that moment Hosoi "completely forgot the joy he experienced ten years previous when the lives of our 20 million Korean brothers and sisters were refocused as our compatriot siblings (*dōhō kyō-dai*)." To Hosoi, the March First demonstrations served as a lesson not only to him, but also to "naive Japan" (*wakaki Nihon*). Japanese had only themselves to blame, as they did not adequately fulfill their "elder brother" responsibilities. "We treat them as things at the bottom, shake our fists at them as if they were slaves, spit upon them, beat them with canes, and kick them with our shoes. We show no signs of love (*jinai*), chivalry (*kyōyū*), but only menace (*ihaku*)." The Japanese attitude toward the Korean peoples is a "stepchild mentality" (*keiji konsei*).[13]

Hosoi determined the problem in part to be Japanese unwillingness to learn about Koreans. Koreans have good points—such as their family relations—from which the Japanese can benefit. Governing the "simplistic (*soboku*) Korean is difficult." He explained:

> The stepmother has to toil for five, ten, twenty, and even thirty years. And then the time will come when the child's eyes and ears will open to understand for the first time that it can reconsider its distrust and attain repentance temporarily. And then from the great bosom of the stepmother fall passionate tears of appreciation. Based on the absolute vision of a united Orient (*tōyō ikka*) we find Japan's inevitable responsibility: annexing and assimilating other peoples. This is the global trial before which the Japanese nation stands.

The March First Movement complicated this process. The Korean people may misinterpret the tolerance (*ninyō*) shown by the Hara cabinet, which could blind them to the impotence of Korea's independence potential. Hosoi noted post-March First changes in Korean behavior. The traditional "cat-like attitude" of Korean clerks has turned to a "haughty tiger-like attitude" that challenges their Japanese colleagues with independence thinking. Koreans no longer feel obliged to attend parties sponsored by Japanese clerks. One thousand Koreans who ordered advance copies of the publication *Sōtoku seifu* (Government-General Administration) refused to honor their commitment after it appeared in print.[14]

Hosoi criticized Japan's initial decision to implement a "comprehensive assimilation" (*dōyō dōka*) policy as a telling sign of "naive Japan." The administration rushed into this policy without adequate preparation. It did not realize the determination of Korean public sentiment (*minshin*). It believed that if Japan did not subjugate Korea, Korea would subjugate Japan. Neither was the case. Rather the policy was designed to "deepen our sibling friendship and form a peaceful cooperative unification" based on terms of equality. This policy was no longer feasible. The two peoples stood at different levels of maturity, as before 1910 the Koreans had endured five centuries of "inept government" while the Japanese enjoyed steady advancement over three millenniums. Enforcing radical assimilation (*ikki ni dōka*), Hosoi forewarned, would drive Koreans either to "suffocation" from Japanese oppression or to a desperate resistance to Japanese rule.[15] Executing "the cultural rule of Japan extensionism" (*Naichi enchōshugi no bunka seiji*), he warned, would ensure "naive Japan's defeat in its global trial."

> Japan would have to retreat from its view of the relationship as mother country and child country (*bokoku kokoku*) to regard it as indispensable territory (*fukabun no ryōdo*). The Japanese would have to extend its prefecture system (*fuken seido*) to the peninsula and like Hokkaido rename [Korea] to something like Seihokudō [Northwest territory] or Seikaidō [West sea territory]. . . . Each prefecture on the peninsula would have to send representatives to the Imperial Diet's lower house. Local assemblies would have to be organized, and education, military service, and tax systems would have to be extended to Koreans on a basis equal to that of the homeland.

The problem here involved competence. "Could Japanese awaken to the broadmindedness and farsightedness needed to realize success?" Hosoi believed they could not. He urged Japan to reconsider its assimilation policy.[16]

Akagi and Hosoi challenged their readers to consider the inherent contradictions of this policy as social Darwinists had questioned French attraction for this policy the previous century. Were the Japanese prepared to accept Korea as an integral geographic and political addition to the Japanese state? Were they prepared to accept Koreans as their fellow subjects? Practices initiated over the previous decade suggested they were not. Thus, the more practical choice, they argued, would be to reject assimilation and govern the territory as an external element of the empire so as not to build Korean expectations or provide them with further reason for anti-Japanese sentiment.

Finally, the March First demonstrations produced a small group of Japanese who supported the Korean cause by urging the Japanese government to

The 1860 "Satō Masakiyo's tiger hunt," which depicted Hideyoshi's protection of the Japanese islands from attack by Korea, as represented by the peninsula-shaped tiger. Tokyo Keizai University, http://www.mdat.ff.tku.ac.jo/korea

韓國服の伊藤公と公爵夫人

Koreanization? Itō Hirobumi and his family dressed in Korean garb.

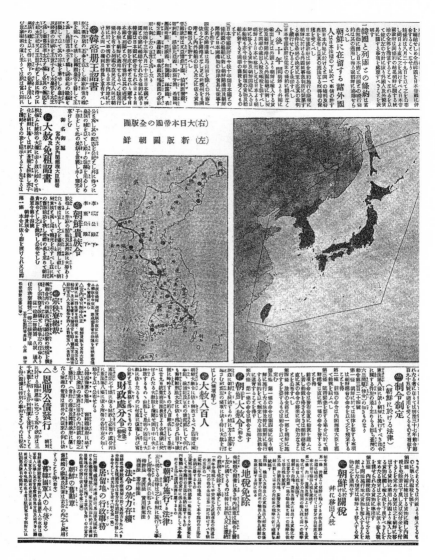

圖版全の國帝日本大(右)　鮮朝圖版新(左)

A map of "Japan" that appeared on the front page of Tokyo's *Asahi shinbun*, August 30, 1910.

朝鮮教育の進歩
Progress of Education in Chosen.

京城校洞公立普通學校舊校舍
Old School-House ef the Kyodong
Public Common sohool in Seoul.

書　堂
Old Fashioned Native School.

京城校洞公立普通學校新校舍
New School House of the Kyodong
Public Common School,

Japanese advertised the progress made under their watch by comparing
traditional Korean schools with modern Japanese schools.

Governor General Saitō Makoto (*left*) and Vice-Governor General Mizuno Rentarō.

Princess Nashimoto and Prince Ŭn. Theirs was the most successful royal marriage brokered by the Japanese government.

The *Tong'a ilbo* celebrated the accomplishments of Korea's first pilot, An Ch'angnam.

Korean New Year's Day. The magazine *Chōsen* was founded in part to introduce Koreans to the Japanese.

The Government-general building displayed in an article titled "Chosen: The Land of Happy People." The palace, situated behind this building, was drastically reduced in size to make way for Japan's colonial headquarters.

A farmer celebrating Japan's founding day (*kigensetsu*).

내선일체를 선전하는 엽서

A three-legged race with "nai" (Japan, *right*) and "sen" (Korea) "united in cooperation" as a "world of 100 million."

況狀會總會查調策對局時鮮朝

A meeting at which Koreans and Japanese discussed ways to strengthen *Naisen ittai*.

In the *Maeil sinbo*, Yun Ch'iho and Ch'oe Namsan advertise the role of Korea in Japan's struggle with China.

Advertisement for Korea's grand exhibition of 1940, the 2600th year of Japan's founding and the 30th year of Japan's rule over Korea. From *Kwŏn Hyokhŭi, Chosŏn eso on sajin yŏpso* (Seoul: Min'umsa, 2005)

A bilingual advertisement for Tomokawa, a medicine that prevents colds and upset stomachs.

Governor General Ugaki modeling Korean "homespun" clothes. Ugaki pushed Korea's industrial development.

Governor General Minami and his New Year's message: Korea-Manchuria unity.

Advertising the circumstances of the times. *Top:* The poster reads "The China incident and the peninsula home front." *Bottom:* Koreans receive instruction through picture stories (*kamishibai*).

Governor General Minami reviewing the Korean volunteer troops.

adopt a more congenial attitude toward the people. Moved by the determination displayed by Koreans, and appalled by Japan's suppression of this effort, they spoke out against Japan's present policy in Korea. Such Japanese agreed with the views of people like Akagi and Hosoi in one respect— assimilation policy had failed—but differed in their belief that the Koreans had demonstrated in March 1919 greater maturity since 1910. Their relatively liberal views would come to haunt them later in their careers. The pacifist views of Yanaihara Tadao, for example, cost him his teaching position at Tokyo Imperial University in the intellectual purges from the mid-1930s.[17]

Yoshino Sakuzō, professor of political history at Tokyo University, preached for greater equality between Koreans and Japanese but stopped short of backing their calls for independence. Described by one as the "guru of 'people's democracy'" in post-World War I Japan, Yoshino actively participated in debates on democratizing Japanese press and education at this time.[18] He directed his criticism at Japan's arrogance toward Koreans, and the unfounded negative images that they drew of Koreans. This attitude, normally directed toward a "defeated country" (*bōkoku*), provoked anti-Japanese sentiment in Korea. The Japanese and the Koreans, he wrote, have shared thousands of years of close contacts. Yet, since annexation the Japanese have ruled the country as "enemy land," an attitude that reflected the victors' treatment of Germany after World War I.[19] Yoshino chastised the Japanese for regarding as "enemy" anyone who voiced disagreement toward Japan's colonial policies. The government, he argued, considers the Korean people evil because they sought their independence. It immediately spits out the word "insubordinate" (*futei*) without considering the moral basis for this characterization. The Japanese administration holds the entire Korean population responsible for the actions of a few. Yoshino predicted that until the Japanese were ready to consider the relative strong points of each people the Koreans will never attain a peace of mind under Japanese rule.[20]

Yanaihara Tadao took this argument one step further by challenging the Japanese administration to cultivate within the Korean people a "spirit of independence" (*dokuritsu no seishin*). Nitobe Inazō's successor as professor of colonial studies at Tokyo Imperial University, Yanaihara, in a 1926 article, criticized the Japanese administration for instilling fear within Koreans by exaggerating the people's actions after the recent death of their last emperor, Sunjong. Japan has impoverished the Korean people, he said, in the name of "uplifting the people's cultural desires." It improved Korea's transportation, trade, and legal systems, but it also caused uncertainty among the people. The reforms initiated at this time also did not benefit the people unconditionally. They were also instituted for Japan's benefit. The motivation for "cultural rule" should be to advance coexistence and co-prosperity.[21]

Yanaihara's arguments reflected his distain for assimilation, a policy he regarded as impractical. In his lecture notes he wrote that assimilation, if attainable, was the "most stable form of equality." The approach was based on the belief that humanity originated as a single race that was divided by environmental differences. Colonial assimilation aimed to radically undo a gradual process that transpired over millions of years. Enforcing the policy injured the independent consciousness of its recipients. The "existence of prejudice" betrays the potential for the policy's success. Rather than assimilate under these circumstances, a policy based on the "principle of autonomy" (*jishu shugi*) that respected individuality held a better chance of success as it respected diversity.[22] Japanese administrative policies in Korea regarded this principle as the Koreans being given a more active role in determining their future with Japan. "The new society," Yanaihara wrote in 1931, "was one that the Korean people must build themselves." Thus Japanese attempts to foster "a feeling of dependence" among Koreans is extremely detrimental to their development. The inspiration that derives from the energy of independence is the "true patriot of the Korean people."[23]

Not all commentary criticized government-general policy. The policy retained its supporters, many stipulating that amendments were necessary if the Japanese hoped to succeed in their mission. The monthly magazine *Chōsen kōron* (Korean Review), for one, gave the government-general positive marks for its advances in such areas as education, health, and industry. It criticized this administration's development of the people's sentiment against its rule. To correct these faults, the Review said, the Japanese must research Korean needs and provide them a lifestyle of peace and comfort. Only after correcting its faults (the administration's most urgent task) can it expect Koreans to gain a capacity for self-rule. Only then could Japan expect to extend its prefecture system to Korea. Only then could Japan realize its mission—"Korean-Japanese impartial humaneness" (*Naisenjin isshi dōnin*).[24]

This discussion over assimilation policy in Korea challenged the government-general in a more diverse way than the discussions at the time of annexation, with many participants advising the administration to drop the policy altogether. These ideas were not necessarily new ones—we can expect that dissenters existed in 1910. However, the relatively freer atmosphere in

Japan to disseminate ideas at this time encouraged people to put forth a wider range of views on political, social, and cultural matters. While these views are interesting, the real question concerns the influence they had on their readers, as well as people with political influence. Can we see similar changes in Japanese images of Koreans? To what extent did these views influence colonial policy on the peninsula?

KOREAN IMAGE CONFIRMATION

The demonstrations did cause some to rethink their images of the Korean people. The Japanese, no longer confident that cultural and historical similarities alone would guarantee Korean assimilation, now believed it necessary to research this people and their customs. The demonstrations encouraged Kita Sadakichi to travel to Korea and Manchuria to verify his ideas on the two peoples' shared roots. His travelogue, published in January 1921, shared one important quality with those expressed by previous travelers in his image of Korea as a living museum of ancient Japan. But this conclusion reflected the nature of his research to date—a search for the common origins of Japanese and other Asians, including Koreans. Kita observed that contemporary Korean markets resembled those of Japan's past; the Korean practice of laying gravestones (rather than standing them) had also been practiced in premodern Japan.[25] His decision to verify his findings also reflected a trend encouraged by the March First demonstrators.

As during the first decade, travelers made frequent contributions to Japanese understanding of conditions in Korea. Travelogues of the 1920s reflected efforts by these Japanese to make direct contact with Koreans and to see Korea from Korean eyes, rather than simply as Japanese tourists. Kurosaka Katsumi, whose experiences appeared in *Chōsen*'s August 1921 issue, is illustrative of this trend. He crossed over to the colony with the explicit intention of learning about the Korean people. His ambition to do so resulted from a trip to Oki no shima, an island off the coast of Tottori Prefecture, where he discovered in shrines remnants of ancient Korean culture. The focus of his trip to Korea was to test the theory that Japanese and Koreans were of the same ethnic stock. He made his first trip to Korea in 1915, and returned to the peninsula every year thereafter. Believing that he could never really understand the people unless he assimilated, Kurosaka went "native": he dressed as a Korean; he rode a Korean horse; he read a Korean newspaper; he smoked Korean pipes. Kurosaka sought to learn about himself by tracing the path that his ancestors had trod to reach the Japanese islands. If the two people were ever the same, he calculated, they probably chose divergent paths from China's Han period. From this time Korea was not much more than a Chinese colony. Those who remained on the peninsula became Sinified; masses of others crossed over to Japan as refugees. Linguistic and social differences followed separation.[26]

Hozumi Shigetō, professor of civil law at Tokyo Imperial University, traveled to Korea later in the decade with a similar mission: to "learn to respect Korea and its people," an ambition he gained after reading a book on Korean history. Hozumi admitted that he admired the ancient Korean culture. He advised that efforts be made to preserve that which still remained. Respecting Korean culture, he determined, was fundamental to solving the "Korean problem." Like Kurosaka, Hozumi's discussion returned his readers to Korea's ancient culture, rather than view the people in a contemporary setting. Contemporary Koreans were the antithesis of the innovative Koreans of the thirteenth century, when they invented movable type. During his travels, Hozumi visited Koreans of different social standing, both the rich and the poor. He concluded that neither resided in homes as richly decorated as Japanese homes. Korean markets or villages had yet to be exposed to the mass entertainment or mass music industry. The children, he lamented, had no amusements whatsoever. It is extremely sad for a child to grow up without toys.[27] The second part of his essay addressed the need to preserve Korean culture: Koreans can be assimilated without succumbing completely to Japanese culture. It is not important, he began, for Koreans to be able to speak a language comprehensible to Japanese. People of northeastern Japan (*Tohokujin*) and Kyushu (*Kyushujin*) use dialects that are incomprehensible; their clothes are also different. Yet, both are considered fellow countrymen. More important was to understand the Koreans. Japanese prejudice stemmed from the people's failure in this regard.[28]

Toward the end of the decade signs appeared that suggested a return to the overtly negative attitudes that Japanese harbored toward Koreans. One article that appeared in October 1927 attacked Korean superstitions by describing their habit of drinking the urine of a child to remedy stomach ailments.[29] Another report that compared Koreans, Chinese, and Japanese crime found that Koreans accounted for a higher ratio of criminal activity than the other two groups. The article cited both economic and culture factors as the causes for the high occurrence of swindling, murder, obscenity, adultery, and polygamy found among Koreans.[30]

Travelogues that interpreted Korea as remnants of ancient Japan did not fade away. Sasagawa Rinfu's 1926 travelogue differed in his provincial attitude that colonized even Korean scenery: it was not Korean, he argued, but Japanese. Likewise, the *funa* (Prussian carp) and *higai* fish he ate in Heijō (P'yŏngyang) were not native "Korean." The Japanese must have brought them over after annexation.[31] The attitude that Kurosaka and Hozumi carried to the Korean Peninsula differed from that of Sasagawa and earlier travelers in that they believed the Koreans had something to teach the Japanese, that Korean culture was worth preserving, and that the Japanese administration should respect its value. Assimilation and cultural preservation, they argued, could advance in tandem. To the contrary, Sasagawa's presentation of assimilation as a one-way process reminds us of attitudes that prevailed at the time of annexation.

HARA TAKASHI, SAITŌ MAKOTO, AND CULTURAL RULE

As Japanese adjusted their images of the Korean people, the government-general gradually introduced policy revisions. Discussion on reforms began soon after the March First Movement was quelled. Prime Minister Hara Takashi, one of Japan's foremost advocates of assimilation, took the lead in pushing these reforms.[32] His statements blurred divisions between Japan's homeland and colonial subjects, whom he felt should be accorded equal positions in Japan's extended community. Hara contributed one of his earliest public statements on assimilation to Itō Hirobumi's "secret papers" (discussed in chapter 2). The deputy foreign minister made generous use of the European example in his arguments. Taiwan should be incorporated not as a "colony" in the British model, but as an extension of the homeland. Japanese administration policy should assimilate the Taiwanese as Japanese, as seen in German-controlled Alsace and Lorraine and in French Algeria. The cultural heritage shared by the Japanese and the Taiwanese rendered this policy appropriate. To implement this policy, Hara advised as follows: Japan's legal system being extended to the island, its governor general receiving orders from a Tokyo-based Taiwan administrative minister (*Taiwan jimu daijin*), and Japanese institutions holding jurisdiction over their respective counterparts in the colony. He thus advised that Taiwan's administration be organized as extensions of the capital, just like Japan's other prefectures.[33]

Hara reaffirmed his support for assimilation after Japan annexed Korea. In May 1911 he entered in his diary his belief that it would not be difficult to assimilate Koreans as they have a "strong passion (*netsubō*) to be Japanese." He also cautioned that assimilation would succeed only if the Japanese afforded the Korean equal education opportunities. Discrimination would compromise the policy's chances for success.[34] Hara expanded on this view after being named prime minister in September 1918. At this time Hara echoed the idea that Japanese-Korean affinity justified Japan's annexation of Korea and its assimilation of Koreans: Koreans and Japanese have close geographic relations; they also maintain close cultural affinity. "In their customs and feelings (*ninjō*) Koreans are not very different from [Japanese]."[35] His efforts to replace Hasegawa Yoshimichi, who tendered his resignation soon after the rice riots in Japan were quelled, with a civilian administrator suggests his recognition of the problems that military rule brought to Korea, and his determination to revise policy to bring the territory more in line with homeland policies.[36]

Hara placed blame for the March First disturbances squarely on military rule and, specifically, the barriers it erected to block integration of Korean and Japanese. In a 1919 opinion paper (*ikensho*), the prime minister defined the government-general's role as promoting integration not only in schools and workplaces, but also in the two people's living arrangements. Hara began his statement by criticizing the decision to use Western colonial practices as a base for Taiwan's administration policies, which were later exported to Korea. The ethnic relations between Korea and Japan were much closer and required a separate policy. The key word for this policy was "unity" (*tōitsu*): unity between the Japanese homeland and Korean colony to forge stronger financial, political, and educational ties. Hara recommended that the Japanese regional system of *fu* and *ken* (prefectural system), as well as the municipal distribution of *shi* (city), *machi* (town), and *mura* (village) be transposed upon the Korean geographical distribution, just as it had in Okinawa. In addition, he encouraged both peoples to work together to integrate neighborhoods, as well as households, through intermarriage.

Hara specifically targeted the education system that segregated Koreans from Japanese. One cannot expect a people to change, he stressed, while administering them as fools. Differences that the government-general had created in the two systems nurtured the discriminative attitude to which Japanese stubbornly clung. Hara further recommended that Koreans be taught their history to allow them to understand the progress made by the Japanese, and to be able to compare the past decade to the centuries of stagnation that their ancestors endured under Korean rule.[37]

The prime minister's most difficult decision rested on his choice of Hasegawa's replacement. The anti-Japanese demonstrations eliminated any chance of a civilian assuming this post—his first choice had been the present vice governor general and adopted son of Yamagata Aritomo, Yosaburō— as his selection required the army faction (Yamagata, Terauchi, Hasegawa, and Tanaka)'s backing. The new governor general also had to be distanced from this group to signal to Koreans and the critical international community Japan's willingness to push reform. His ultimate selection, Saitō Makoto, was different in a number of ways from other governor generals. First, Saitō was from the navy rather than the army. Also, Saitō was retired at the time of his appointment and thus technically civilian. However, after the appointment Hara had the admiral's name returned to the active roster to conform to the existing Organic Regulation of the Korean Government-General.[38]

Saitō also spoke excellent English, a talent that proved indispensable. It opened a direct line of communication with Korea's foreign residents, and thus an indirect line with their governments, to sell his reforms. After assuming office he welcomed discussions with missionaries on Japan's reform plans. His efforts received high marks from the foreign community. The U.S. consul-general, Ransford Miller, remarked in 1927 that "Viscount Saitō . . . has shown himself so approachable, straightforward, broad-minded, kindly, patient, conscientious and fair that he has won the confidence and respect of all classes, whether Japanese, Koreans, or foreigners."[39] Saitō served longer in office (1919–27, 1929–31) than any other governor general. After returning to Japan he replaced the assassinated Inukai Tsuyoshi as prime minister (1932–34), until scandal brought down his cabinet. He then served as Lord Privy Seal until his own assassination in the February 26 (1936) incident.

Saitō put his English to use soon after assuming office by authoring an article for the American magazine *The Independent* that explained Japan's new policy in Korea. Here Saitō first justified Japan's annexation of Korea as an action that had been determined by "mutual consent." Annexation also ended Korea's reign as the "storm center of the Far East." Japan had made mistakes. He explained the recent demonstrations as Korean "expressions of dissatisfaction with the existing regime." The government-general should have explained its reform ambitions earlier. Saitō also offered his readers a sneak preview of his reform plans. Those being considered would extend to Korean's self- (local) rule and even representation in the Japanese Diet, end Korean-Japanese discrimination, and deliver to the Korean people freedoms of speech and press.[40] Mizuno Rentarō, a key ally of Hara during the prime minister's tenure as home minister over the first two decades of the twentieth century, served as Saitō's deputy. Described by Hara as a "supporter of progressive politics," Mizuno remained in the government-general until June 1922. During his tenure in Korea, Mizuno was an active student of the Korean language, reportedly sitting for private lessons three times a week.[41]

The Saitō-Mizuno administration entered Keijō in September 1919 to assume its duties. At least one Korean was not impressed with the administration's talents. As Saitō rode into the city, Kang Ugyu rolled a bomb under his carriage. The explosion injured horses and spectators and left Saitō mentally shaken but physically unharmed. He dusted himself off and continued with the day's events, only to later find bomb fragments lodged in the thick belt that he had just changed into. Perhaps to signal a new direction in Korean rule, the administration responded with much more prudence than did the Terauchi regime when it uncovered an alleged assassination plot in 1910. Its investigation rounded up four Koreans, found them guilty, and quietly executed them.[42] Saitō announced soon after that the assassination attempt would not affect the reform package.[43] Tominaga Bun'ichi, an official in the government-general, later revealed that Saitō's inability to gain the upper hand over "outlaw Koreans," and the lack of positive responses toward Korean rule from Japan, discouraged him from pushing some of the more ambitious reforms.[44]

From his first days in office, Saitō maintained that he intended to honor the initial intention of annexation as articulated in the Rescript issued by the Meiji Emperor in 1910. In his 1921 New Year's address Saitō vowed that his administration would

> continue with the fundamental plan of Korean administration
> that remains unchanged, namely to honor the imperial words of
> "impartial humaneness (*isshi dōjin*), to integrate Korea into the
> general world situation, and to imperialize our 20 million brethren
> (*dōhō*) while constructing a paradise of peace over the 3,000 *ri* of
> rivers and mountains.[45]

He anchored his reforms with what came to be known as "cultural policy" (*bunka seiji*), a policy with five fundamental goals: the maintenance of public peace, the spread of education, the promotion of local rule, the development of industry and transportation, and the improvement of health. These goals sought to enhance the development of the peninsula and the prosperity of its people, both prerequisites to the Korean people assuming a status of equality with their Japanese counterparts in preparation for assimilation.[46]

The new government-general anticipated that passing cultural understanding on to the Koreans provided them with the tools they required to accept responsibility for their local affairs. This aspiration required closer Japanese and Korean relations. The people were required to learn to coordinate local administration with central policy to gain an understanding of general administrative policy. They also needed a sophisticated capacity to use the Japanese language and observe Japanese customs. Saitō planned to coordinate this education through local consultation committees (*hyōgikai*) and deliberation councils (*kyōgikai*), while enlisting cooperation from local government offices.[47]

The Korean people's "cultural advancement" became a central goal of the administration in the 1920s. Mizuno Rentarō expressed this ambition in a June 1922 report in which he emphasized the need to improve transportation networks to disseminate culture, and the role of the police system to promote cultural development.[48] The Japanese administration also hoped that the vernacular newspapers, permitted for the first time by the 1920 reforms, would assume responsibility for disseminating culture. A letter issued in September 1920 by the Police Bureau to the *Tong'a ilbo* offices announcing the newspaper's indefinite suspension listed its failure to promote culture as one of the reasons for this harsh penalty.[49] In fact, the newspaper included much discussion on culture in its pages; it was not the kind of culture, however, that the Japanese administration welcomed.

Publication legislation reforms constituted just one of the many reforms that the government-general would introduce in the years that followed the March First demonstrations. A 1920 report summarized the twenty-four reforms that it had enacted to date, and eight new reforms planned for implementation in the near future.[50] Many suggested the influence of Prime Minister Hara Takashi's opinion paper, but few reached the level of integration that Hara had recommended at this time. The reforms first eliminated important physical symbols of Japanese power that distinguished Japanese from Korean. They banned uniforms for most Japanese government-general officials. Although it was not specifically stated, these officials would presumably be disarmed of their swords, as well. The hated *kenpeitai*, the gendarmes who were most responsible for Japan's botched handling of the independence movement, were exiled to northern border patrol. A second round of reforms encouraged Japanese with pay incentives to learn Korean.

These developments relaxed two barriers—power symbols and language—
to encourage greater interaction between Koreans and Japanese. By revising
the nationality laws (*minsekihō*) the administration also hoped to make it
easier for Koreans and Japanese to intermarry. Other measures sought to
erase existing differences in the way colonized and colonizers were treated.
Bureaucrats would now be paid under the same salary scale, regardless of
ethnic origin. In its revisions of the police department, the administration
announced that Japanese had eliminated the title of "Chōsenjin junsaho"
(Korean patrol assistant) to erase Korean-Japanese distinction. Finally, Japanese ended the whipping of Korean prisoners, a punishment originally
believed by the Japanese to be fitting to their cultural level (*mindo*); the ban
would equalize Korean-Japanese punishment.

The reforms also targeted Korean education, both classroom and social.
We do not see efforts made to integrate Koreans and Japanese. Rather, the
reforms increased opportunity while maintaining (and even fortifying) segregation. The high enthusiasm that Koreans showed for this education
encouraged the government-general to increase the number of elementary
schools (from 556 to 870) as well to strengthen male and female higher education. It also vowed to add classes in the sciences and to upgrade English
from an elective to a required class. Most important, the administration
promised to examine the possibility of extending Korean education to six
years, the number of years then required of Japanese children. The reforms
also emphasized social education. The most visible change was its reforming
publication legislation to permit three new vernacular newspapers: the
Tonga' ilbo, the *Chosŏn ilbo*, and the *Chungang ilbo*. This revision ignited an
active print culture that oversaw publication of numerous journals and magazines of various genres that lasted up into the outbreak of war in the late
1930s. The Japanese headed a second element of social education as "Facilities to promote Japanese-Korean harmony" (*Naisen yūwa no tame no
shisetsu*), and listed four areas to be targeted to "gain [Japanese] acceptance
(*ryōkai*) of Koreans, and Korean understanding of Japan": bringing Korean
teachers and public officials to Japan, introducing Korea to Japanese people
through movies, organizing public seminars for Koreans on Japan, and promoting ways in which Japanese could observe Korea and Koreans.

The reforms advanced assimilation in a number of ways, yet in others
suggested the Japanese retreating temporarily from this policy. Calls for
greater Japanese-Korean interaction by Hara were answered by reform measures to promote greater understanding between Japanese and Koreans

through travel and seminars. The motivation behind the creation of *Chōsen* appears to have been this intended result. In February 1921, the new government-general publication solicited discussions that examined areas of Korean life and offered praiseworthy anecdotes of Korean and Japanese interactions. At the same time, other measures suggest the government-general retreating to safer administrative grounds. Did its expansion of the Korean-language media, and the incentives designed to encourage Korean language proficiency among Japanese signify a softening of Japan's total assimilation rhetoric, to allow a hybrid culture to emerge in Korea? Or did this administration truly believe that exposing the Korean people to their traditional culture would open their eyes to the merits of Japanese culture? Either way, by the end of the decade it came to realize that allowing Koreans access to their culture worked against the administration's vision of assimilation.

STEPS TOWARD JAPANESE-KOREAN COEDUCATION

On paper the reforms reflected the interests of the government-general to improve its position as a recognized colonial power internationally, and as a benevolent colonial administration in Korea. Understanding their practical intent requires further analysis beyond the optimism interjected in Japanese rhetoric. Our discussion returns to education, the area that the administration made its most important investment. In January 1921 the government-general established an educational investigation committee; in February 1922 Governor General Saitō announced the Second Education Ordinance to be introduced in classrooms the following April. The importance of this ordinance was reflected in its staying power: it would remain in effect until 1938, when the Third Education Ordinance reformed Korea's wartime education system.[51]

A November 21, 1921, draft of the Second Education Ordinance plan revealed its initial intention to reform the education system to promote equality between Japanese and Koreans children, but in separate facilities. Admitting Koreans to Japanese schools came only in the ordinance's last draft, no doubt the result of heated deliberation. We see in the proposal's margin "Japanese" crossed out, and "those who can function in *kokugo*" (literally "national language" but here to mean "the Japanese language") penciled in. To the Japanese "equality" may have meant equal access (by building more schools), equal instruction (by increasing the number of years in elementary education from four to six, and by integrating the two curriculums), and equal opportunity (by easing requirements for Koreans to enter institutions of higher education). Save for a small group of Koreans, the system did not necessarily promote equal experience (by integrating the Japanese and Korean education systems and classrooms), a critical step that the government-general needed to take to demonstrate sincerity in its assimilation policy.[52]

Over the course of the 1920s the Japanese administration did manage to build more schools to educate Korean children: by the end of the decade they had increased threefold, from 595 (in 1920) to 1,831 (1930). It follows that an increase in schoolhouses allowed more Koreans the opportunity for an education. Over this decade Korean attendance at least doubled at all levels from primary to higher education. The number of Korean elementary school students quadrupled over this period. Women also made significant gains in higher education enrollment, from 771 in 1920 to 4,422 in 1930.[53]

The two systems, however, remained unequal in a number of important ways. Most critical was the duration of the student's elementary school education. Shibata Zensaburō, who headed the government-general's education bureau (*gakumu kyokuchō*), noted that the administration could not be expected to offer students the six years of elementary education that the reforms promised, as rural areas were less developed culturally than others.[54] Students attending schools that offered the six-year program attained parity with their Japanese counterparts in at least duration of attendance, though there was lobbying in the homeland to increase elementary education to eight years, which was considered the international norm at the time.[55]

Integration, as encouraged by Hara Takashi, remained an important theme in educational circles throughout the 1920s. It constituted an important issue for the Chōsen kyōiku gakkai (Korean Education Association). The association used its journal, *Chōsen kyōiku* (Korean Education), to advertise "integrated education" (*kyōgaku*) to promote true understanding and conciliation between Japanese and Koreans.[56] Sawayanagi Setarō, a member of Japan's House of Peers, used this journal to criticize excuses — integration was "inconvenient" and "troublesome" — offered by school officials as insufficient for maintaining segregation. If the Koreans and Japanese were to unite as a single people, Sawayanagi reasoned, these problems should be subservient to the greater mission of social brotherhood (*shakai dōhō shugi*). The Japanese people must recognize, he concluded, that by providing Koreans with an integrated education system they offered the world a lesson in humanism, particularly to colonizers who maintained segregated systems.[57]

Kamada Eikichi, president of Keiō Gijuku University, also supported integrated education, and illustrated his aspiration by the example of a dog barking at strangers: the goal of education was to promote a situation in which a dog would show no difference in response to either the Japanese or Korean. Kamada's vision of integrated education did not simply Japanize Koreans, but also required Japanese to resemble the Korean. Both peoples would exchange their strong points to nurture, as Homi K. Bhabha terms it, "hybridization."[58] Kamada thus interpreted integrated education as a process that did not result in the unidirectional assimilation of the colonized, but a merging of the two peoples' linguistic and cultural characteristics.[59]

Integrated education served as the theme of the Conference of Japanese-Korean Union in Education, convened in November 1924 to promote "Japanese-Korean unity and friendship." Governor General Saitō Makoto's participation—he delivered a plenary address—demonstrated the government-general's support for this cause, as did the four-pledge document that participants drafted.

1   To encourage coeducation, particularly in the elementary schools.
2   To foster the development of Korean and Japanese strong points, and to correct their weak points to develop national dignity.
3   To disseminate information on the Korean people to promote a correct understanding of the people.
4   To cultivate mutual tolerance by promoting contacts between Koreans and Japanese, interaction through leisure activities, and by using the media to explain Korea's position.[60]

Statistics reveal modest gains in integrated education that nonetheless fell short of the visions expressed by those writing on education reform. Figures released in 1930 reveal almost twice as many Koreans entering predominantly Japanese public elementary schools (708) than graduating (364), suggesting either a rising trend in admissions or high dropout rates by Koreans admitted to these schools. An overwhelming majority of Koreans (66,000) continued to be educated in Korean-centered common elementary schools. In this same year, a total of 321 Japanese students entered these schools, and 55 graduated.[61] Japan is to be credited with building an educational system that surpassed many of its colonial peers. Yet more effort needed to be directed toward integrating Koreans and Japanese in the classroom.

Even these paltry results may have exaggerated the extent that integration progressed. Kang Pyŏngju, a bank manager from North P'yŏngan Province who attended Suwŏn College of Agriculture between 1929 and 1931, recalled the "symbiotic relationship" that Japanese and Koreans shared:

> At the college everybody was supposed to live in a dormitory—
> the West Dorm for the Japanese students and the East Dorm for
> Koreans. Each dorm was self-governing. For example, for meals in
> the cafeteria, the food committee hired a cook and purchased food
> supplies. The library committee purchased books, and both the
> Japanese and Koreans students were supposed to buy identical
> publications. Each dorm had its own Ping-Pong committee. . . .
> We studied together in class and did laboratory experiments
> together, but we seldom compared notes or talked to each other.

Korean students protested attempts by school officials to integrate rooms—two or three Japanese to every Korean—forcing the school to alternate the students by halls.[62] Experiments in "mixed schools" (*Naisen kyōgaku*) faired no better. Takasaki Sōji cites a survey that revealed that only a quarter of Japanese students attending mixed schools had Korean friends. Those who did tended to choose Koreans who did not know Korean or whose mother was Japanese.[63]

A number of reasons, apart from conscious efforts to keep Koreans out, explain this separation. First, lack of adequate Japanese language ability prevented more Korean students from enrolling in these schools. Another probable cause was cost: the higher tuition demanded by Japanese schools prevented Koreans from enrolling even if these schools were willing to accept them. One government official noted the "military training" (*kyōren*) required of all Japanese students at these schools as a factor. Unable to envision Korean students participating in this activity, he argued that subjecting only Japanese to this training would be discriminatory and harmful. On the other hand, subjecting them to this training would also presume their eligibility for military conscription, a task for which in 1925 Koreans were not ready.[64] Finally, Korean enrollment figures may also have been limited by Korean hesitation toward sending a child to a school that treated their children as inferior.[65] We can imagine that Koreans entering Japantown felt similar apprehensions.[66]

The colony's urban demographics reflected (and perhaps contributed to) the segregation in the school system. Hashiya Hiroshi estimates that 80 percent of the Korean and Japanese residents lived in neighborhoods defined by their ethnic identity.[67] Chongno Street, which lay in the heart of the city's Korean section, often was used as a metaphor for "Korean" as Kajiyama Toshiyuki demonstrates in his novel *Gei no naka* (Inside the Rainbow) through the character of Kaji.

> While living in Seoul, Kaji absolutely refused to walk in the world of Chongno. That was pure Koreatown. To walk in that part of town strangled him in depression. One could go so far as to describe this as a feeling of numbness (*bukimi*). This feeling did not stem from a fear of Korean hostility toward the Japanese. It was simply an extremely chilling feeling that passed through Kaji.[68]

Visitors to Keijō who did cross into this part of town left descriptions of its primitiveness. Nanba Kasui described one Chongno shop as follows:

> The stench of the shop was worse than I had been led to expect. The eves of the entrance were too low; its entrance was niggardly small. The colors of the posts and walls of the shop were badly faded, and the paper that did remain appeared to be—although it was hard to tell for sure—*daikichi* (good luck) signs. The proprietor squatting in front of the shop's entrance with his disorderly hairstyle seemed to fit in perfectly with the atmosphere of the scene: a picture that had not changed for at least 1000 years.[69]

The textbook revisions that accompanied educational reform reflected these developments. Textbooks accommodated the increase in Korean students by including more mentions of Korean icons, and promoting Japanese-Korean integration in the lessons. Yi Sukcha notes that the new texts carried more stories of famous Koreans. Those featured were primarily limited to scholars and social pioneers rather than military figures or members of royalty. The curriculum also used Japanese and Korean geographical comparisons to exemplify the relationship that they were to forge. One lesson, for example, introduced two industrial centers Hino (Japan) and Kaijō [Kaesŏng] (Korea) as two places that shared a tight industrial bond despite being spatially separated.[70] Women's civic textbooks encouraged cultural development by instructing that "home education" should be shared between husband and wife, and that there were benefits to women seeking employment.[71]

At the same time, textbooks also perpetuated the negative images that separated Korean from Japanese, areas that Koreans needed to change to "catch up" to the Japanese. Textbooks included stories such as "Three Reasons Why Korean Rice Is Bad," "Korean Houses Are Small and Weak," and "Koreans Do Not Take Baths." Ethics textbooks told the story of Japanese-Korean annexation as a tale of a troublesome Korea inhabited by a people with an impoverished national vitality. Japan, in the name of righteousness, fought off the Chinese and Russians for Korea's sake; its successes impressed the Korean people, who desired annexation with Japan. After the Korean emperor entrusted the rights of Korean administration to Japan, this fiction continued, the Meiji Emperor agreed in 1910 to merge the two countries.[72] This material reflected the arrogant attitude that Hara and others warned against, rather than the spirit of integration required for completing Japan's assimilation mission.

SOCIAL AND POLITICAL PARTICIPATION

The 1920 reforms continued to emphasize participation as a means of furthering assimilation, but centered more on the exchange of knowledge about each other's societies and cultures. Classroom education was the most important activity. But social education also offered adults, both Korean and Japanese, ways of participating. As during the previous decade, ceremonies provided the administration with opportunities to remind the Korean people of their place in the empire. The government-general also organized tours to bridge the cultural and social gaps that separated Japanese from Korean, as well as expatriate Korean from peninsular Korean. A new area of debate was political participation. Governor General Saitō proposed the possibility of Koreans gaining political representation in his 1920 contribution to *The Independent*. The government-general also included it in its list of future reforms.

The most symbolically important opportunities to remind Koreans and Japanese of their union directly involved the Korean royal family—the 1920 royal marriage between Korean Prince Ŭn and Japanese Princess Nashimoto Masako (Korean name Yi Pangja) and the 1926 state funeral for Korea's last emperor, Sunjong. Differing from ceremonies held during the initial decade of Japanese rule, events such as this marriage allowed the government-general to exploit their symbolic value regarding the Japanese-Korean relationship. On April 28, 1920, Prince Ŭn and Princess Nashimoto were married in

Tokyo after a one-year delay—their original nuptial ceremony was delayed by the death of Ŭn's father, Kojong. The prince had been taken to Tokyo by Itō Hirobumi at the age of ten to be educated at the prestigious Peer's School (Gakushūin). He served as his half-brother Sunjong's crown prince after their father's forced abdication in 1907. Princess Nashimoto was the daughter of Prince Morisamasa, the adopted heir of the Nashimoto family, whose brother, Kuni Kuniyoshi, sired the future wife of the Showa Emperor. Nashimoto reportedly had been rejected as a candidate for empress after her family's poor record for producing males was revealed.[73] This unfortunate history did not deter the plans of the Japanese imperial household to arrange this symbolic union. At an audience with the Taisho Empress, Nashimoto was first congratulated for her bravery before receiving her "sympathy" for the sacrifice that the young bride-to-be was to make. "We had to agree to this," she consoled, "for the sake of our country."[74]

The wedding was unpopular among Japanese. Nashimoto's family received numerous phone calls and telegrams from people expressing their displeasure over the Japanese princess marrying "a prince of such vehemently anti-Japanese Koreans." One Japanese fanatic attempted to blow up the royal carriage that carried them to and from the wedding ceremony. These threats followed them throughout their life together and turned to tragedy in 1922 when their newly born son was poisoned during a trip to Korea to present him to the Korean court.[75] The Japanese administration exploited the wedding for its symbolic value. Governor General Saitō noted in a congratulatory statement:

> We are blessed with the marriage of Crown Prince Yu (Ŭn) and Princess Nashimoto Nomiya. This [union] demonstrates the intimacy of the Korean and Japanese peoples as a united family [*Naisen ikka*]. . . . The Imperial Household has bestowed its benevolence upon the harmony of the Japanese and Korean people.[76]

The Japanese government arranged a European tour in May 1927 to display through the couple a Korean-Japanese harmony. Their marriage was the most successful of all Korean-Japanese royal unions, surviving even Korean liberation from Japanese rule.[77] Nashimoto acted quintessentially Japanese, while betraying the trajectory of assimilation, by adopting her husband's culture. She reportedly learned the Korean language, enjoyed Korean cuisine, and preferred Korean to Japanese dress.

Six years later, on April 26, 1926, Sunjong's death provided the Japanese with another opportunity to demonstrate Japanese-Korean unity. The Japanese went to great lengths to present his death and June funeral in the context of two peoples united in sorrow. Soon after, the Japanese government convened a special cabinet meeting to decide that Sunjong would receive a Korean-style state funeral and that Vice Governor General Yuasa Kurahei would chair the funeral committee.[78] The Crown Prince (the future Showa Emperor) announced that all celebration activities planned for his birthday (April 29) were to be canceled.

The Japanese administration also used the opportunity to retell the story of Japan's annexation of the Korean Peninsula, and to "credit" Sunjong with having arranged the union. Again, Governor General Saitō interpreted the event's significance. After describing Sunjong's long sickness as a period in which 80 million Japanese and Koreans joined together in prayer for his recovery, Saitō reviewed Sunjong's contribution to Japan-Korea relations.

His Highness [gyokudenka] Yi [Sunjong] ascended the Korean throne in Meiji 45 [1912] (sic 1907). He administered benevolent rule and maintained fraternity [shinwa] with Imperial Japan for a long time. Finally, in Meiji 43 [1910], in light of the domestic and foreign situation, he arranged the tremendous plan [kōbo] for Japan-Korea annexation before stepping down from the throne. His sacrifice preserved the divine millet [shinshoku], and strengthened the peaceful environment [kōnei] of the people's lives. His actions also established Oriental peace [tōyō heiwa].[79]

Newspapers played an important role in displaying this unity. They offered extensive coverage throughout the period from the time Sunjong lapsed into a coma. They provided readers with Sunjong's vital signs (his body temperature, pulse and breathing rates, and urine output), coverage normally reserved for Japan's imperial family members. They also covered the story from both the Korean and Japanese sides. The *Japan Times* carried a picture of people climbing the steps of the Japan-side site, Zojoji Temple, and advertised the occasion as Japanese and Koreans joining together in prayer.[80] The Tokyo *Asahi shinbun* ran the banner headline "Japanese and Koreans Share Equally in Grief" (*Naisen hitoshiku awareshimi wo wakatsu*). It arranged pictures of both peoples participating in ceremonies held in both the homeland and colonial capitals. The government-general magazine *Chōsen* displayed a picture of the bell that had been placed in Sunjong's honor in Nikko, the traditional burial grounds for the Tokugawa, the first government that the Meiji regime had overthrown.[81]

In addition to ceremony, the government-general also utilized tours to advertise its success in the colony. The more exploitable tours were those that returned overseas Koreans to their homeland to observe, and comment on, the advances that Korea had made under Japanese rule. The government-general anticipated that introducing these people to the "new Korea" would tame their anti-Japanese activities. The publicity that these tours generated demonstrated an image of Japan extending an olive branch to resolve the ongoing conflict with Koreans opposed to its rule. Inviting overseas Koreans to revisit their homeland added a new twist to one of the recommendations made in the Saitō reforms, to provide opportunities for Japanese to visit the peninsula and Koreans to visit the archipelago. Articles, penned in the Koreans' names and carried in *Chōsen*, advertised erstwhile anti-Japanese Koreans acknowledging Japanese success in Korea.

The journal *Chōsen* reported that between 1920 and 1921 the government-general organized at least three such tours. The first two groups (of seventy-two and twenty-two people) arrived from China, and a third group (with twenty participants) from Siberia. This particular group arrived in Genzan (Wŏnsan) and traveled by train to Keijō and Jinsen (Inch'ŏn) before returning home via Heijō (P'yŏngyang). The tour's itinerary included visits to the Chōsen government-general medical clinic, the royal palace and palace zoo, schools for the visually challenged, and various factories. The members of this tour also visited a museum exhibiting Korean products and viewed a military parade at the Yongsan training ground. They were also the dinner guests of the governor general at the plush Chōsen Hotel. Along the way dignitaries extended to them invitations to attend various functions.

The Japanese saw these tours as vital to overcoming the misunderstanding that inhibited the Korean people from accepting Japanese rule. Governor General Saitō wrote that Japanese-Korean harmony would fail to materialize unless the two peoples came to understand each other.[82] Remarks left by the Korean participants, and edited for publication in *Chōsen*, suggested success in this regard. Participants recognized progress in forestry preservation, industrial and manufacturing development, and education reform as impressive. Other comments suggest editorial assistance: the participants vowed to offer guidance to fellow expatriates to correct misunderstandings on Japanese rule, and a desire to "work with their [Japanese] brethren toward a greater plan of peace in the Orient."[83]

The Japanese were not as eager to enlist Korean participation in other areas commonly employed to develop national sentiment. Over the period of cultural rule, the administration increased the number of schools in the colony, but refused to make education compulsory. It was reluctant to engage Koreans in military training, much less enlistment in the military. The Japanese government also actively barred Korean political participation. In 1929 it faced challenges on this point as Japanese and Koreans petitioned for Korean representation in the Diet. The assembly's negative ruling sent the clearest message to date as to the extent the Japanese seriously considered Korean assimilation.[84]

The challenge came from seventeen Japanese legislators who formed the Chōsen sansei shingikai kōsein (Korean Political Participation Deliberation Committee). Their proposal challenged the Japanese government to act on its words: realizing the imperial will (*goseishi*) of "imperial humaneness" (*isshin dōjin*) and the "ideal" (*risō*) of the "unified Japanese-Korean family" (*Naisen ikka*), the petition argued, required the Japanese government to advance the political system beyond the present "infantile stage," in accordance with Korean people advancement. The text specifically called for investigation into the possibilities of (1) residents of Korea being granted rights of political participation, (2) the creation of a system to allow Imperial subjects residing in Korea to be seated in the Imperial Diet, and (3) Korean provinces being permitted under "Japan extensionism" to form regional assemblies (*chihō gikai*).

The decision rendered by the legislative body reflected previous images nurtured by Japanese to date: the Korean people were inappropriate for inclusion in the empire under terms of full and uncompromised membership. It deemed Korean participation in the Lower House (*sangiin*) to be inappropriate for two reasons. First, such representation would be "harmful" (*heigai*) to Japan as it could sway the council's present situation and thus provoke troublesome results. Second, since the Japanese could not provide the Korean people with sufficient political participation at this time, it was better to give them none at all. Limited participation would only provoke Korean dissatisfaction. One decision, to select up to five Korean males of high status for seats in Japan's House of Peers in the near future, did actualize, but not until the 1940s.

A proposal to allow Koreans local representation, a potential hinted at in the 1920 reforms, received cautious support. The Diet ruling argued that since Korea was a single region (*ichi chihō*), it was more appropriate to establish a single council than to form multiple local assemblies as found in Japan's prefectures. This decision determined that after ten years the government-general would organize such a body of one hundred representatives, one-third appointed by the Japanese administration and the remainder elected by eligible voters. Over this time the government-general was to reform the regional system and gradually acclimate the people toward regional self-administration.[85]

The 1919 Independence Movement challenged Japanese administration in a number of ways within the colony itself, but also domestically and, perhaps most importantly, among Japan's colonial peers. Japan's response to this challenge reflected its complexity. The reform package it delivered to the Korean people in many ways suggested a Japanese retreat from its total assimilation rhetoric, unless we understand the Japanese confidence that the superiority of their culture would in the end encourage Korean assimilation. Toward the end of this decade the Japanese indicated in two reports the failure of this idea and their realization that the Japanese could not expect success in assimilation while the Koreans were permitted access to their own culture.[86] Michael E. Robinson notes that these reforms "opened the way for a nationalist renaissance in the colony after 1920."[87]

The reforms served other purposes as well. They sent the important message to Japan's Western colleagues that it had its colony under control. As Frank Baldwin and others have argued, they manipulated the Korean resistance by "giving hope to the Korean people that Japanese rule would be more liberal and humane [and] effectively countered the Korean nationalist propaganda which demanded Japanese withdrawal."[88] The humane nature of the reforms camouflaged another control element—the degree to which they exposed the Korean people to the Japanese administration. Vice Governor General Mizuno Rentarō eloquently expressed this in his explanation of the value of Korea's indigenous press to the Japanese administration. One reason the March First demonstrations surprised the Japanese was that the colonizers lacked a chimney to allow Korean smoke to escape. Articles and editorials appearing in indigenous newspapers, Mizuno wrote, "allowed [Japanese] access to Korean thought. Koreans expressed their personal opinions in their newspapers. . . . Without these chimneys the room smolders in darkness. [The newspapers] made these rooms bright, and [Korean] feelings clear (*azayaka*). Without the chimney the firewood will not burn which causes [the room to catch on] fire. This was why the "*banzai undō* broke out."[89] More Japanese fluent in Korean and knowledgeable about Korean culture displayed important signs of Japanese willingness to accommodate Koreans; they also showed the Japanese seeking more chimneys to observe Korean smoke. These reforms did not bring Koreans much closer to assimilation, but they did provide the Japanese with important means to observe and control their indigenous independence movement.

5

RADICAL ASSIMILATION UNDER
WARTIME CONDITIONS

PARTS OF CULTURAL RULE LINGERED INTO THE LATE 1930S, WHEN THE Japanese finally ordered the indigenous newspapers to cease publication. However, cultural rule displayed signs of waning as early as the mid-1920s. Peace preservation legislation initiated in 1925 severely restricted activities deemed by the government-general to be anti-Japanese. By the end of the decade most Koreans active in the independence movement were either in jail or in exile. Tighter censorship erased more articles from Korean newspapers toward the latter part of the decade; the drop in newspaper seizures in the early 1930s properly indicated more conscious self-censorship than greater leniency on the part of the censors.[1] Also from the mid-1920s, the government-general lowered incentives for Japanese studying Korean; from 1940, it eliminated this allocation entirely.[2]

Japan's mounting crisis on the Asian continent initiated yet another review of its Korean administrative policies. Aware of the Korean Peninsula's strategically critical geographic location, the Japanese government realized that success on the Asian continent could not be realized without Korean support and cooperation. In 1938 the government-general produced an extensive report that advised measures to strengthen *Naisen ittai* (Japan-Korea, one body). The report, distributed just over a year after the Japanese military's July 1937 encounter with the Chinese at the Marco Polo Bridge, introduced measures required for Japan to realize a "complete strengthening" of Korean assimilation in accordance with the circumstances of the times. The document emphasized the importance of Japan forming internal-peripheral links to ensure its ties to the Asian continent. Securing these links further required Japan to step up its assimilation policies to ensure Korean cooperation.

This acceleration of Japanese assimilation in Korea during the final seven years of its rule witnessed the colonial administration adopting hitherto unprecedented measures to eradicate Korean culture and identity. Many of the measures introduced by the Japanese over this period—particularly its Korean language and family name policies—are among those cited most often in criticisms of Japanese colonial rule. At the same time, this latter period also saw Koreans making unprecedented advances in their economic and social standing in the Japanese Empire. As suggested by Cho Pyŏngsang and others who invested loved ones and money in Japan's war efforts, it was now time for the Japanese to demonstrate their sincerity to the assimilation process their rhetoric had been preaching since annexation.

SIGNS FOR OPTIMISM AMID DARKENING CLOUDS

Saitō Makoto, relieved of his position as governor general, returned to Japan in June 1931. Less than a year later he assumed the role of Japanese prime minister. His replacement, General Ugaki Kazushige, was not new to the position. He had temporarily replaced Saitō in 1927 when the admiral left Korea to represent Japan at the Geneva arms limitations meetings. Prior to assuming this position, Ugaki had served as Japan's war minister on a number of cabinets. Like Saitō, Ugaki's record was also tainted by scandal. His involvement in the aborted March (1931) incident (*sangatsu jiken*), an effort to install a military government by coup, forced him from homeland government but cleared the way for his return to Korea. His tenure in office, which lasted until August 1936, oversaw increased emphasis on the peninsula's industrial development.[3]

The governor general linked Japan's continental crisis with Korea's industrial development in a number of speeches. In a 1934 speech, he predicted that Korea would soon be known not simply as a country of agriculture, but also as one of industry. The Manchurian situation, Ugaki continued, had "heightened the peninsula's significance and mission."[4] In another speech made at Keijō Imperial University, the governor general emphasized the uplifting of rural Korea and the industrialization of the Korean Peninsula as a whole.[5] Ugaki joined others in acknowledging the advancements that Koreans had made since the 1931 Manchurian Incident to assimilate Japanese culture and practices. He provided a list of telling signs that demonstrated this success: more Koreans were donning colorful clothing, choosing modern hairstyles, and displaying the Japanese flag on holidays. He also complemented their spiritual attitudinal change that incorporated many of the characteristics emphasized in Korean education: sacrificial service; a love of labor, frugality, and savings; and a socially cooperative lifestyle.[6]

Longtime peninsula resident Nakanishi Inosuke, writing in October 1933, also noted progress. Over the past twenty years, he wrote, the Koreans have emerged from being a "people of indolence" (*yūda no tami*). He now saw them as a people who had gained a more positive attitude toward the Japanese. Nakanishi cited Japan's successful military campaigns as having encouraged this change. They first weakened Korea's traditional attachment to China, which in turn caused them to amend their view of Japan in a positive way. The Korean people now had a sense of appreciation for the colonial efforts that Japan extended to the peninsula.[7]

The economist Takahashi Kamekichi, upon completing a month-long tour of the peninsula, echoed this praise. During his travels he observed that Koreans had experienced a "rebirth" (*umarefukeru*). Like Ugaki and Nakanishi, he also attributed their resurrection to developments since the 1931 Manchurian Incident, which had since elevated Korea's status in the empire. Takahashi explained that the incident helped "Koreans understand the advantages of possessing Japanese nationality." He noted that he now "felt the spirit of the people as well as a sense of security through their [political and economic] developments."[8]

Participants in discussions on Japan's education policies drew from this positive imagery of Korean progress to emphasize unity between homeland and colony. Under Ugaki's watch the term "civic education" (*kōmin kyōiku*)—education to strengthen the students' concept of citizenship—frequently appeared in these discussions. They first focused on the value of the Japanese cooperative system as a tool against (Western) individual personalities. Nonaka Sainosuke cited the hypocrisy of European colonial practices to emphasize Japan's efforts to integrate its "outer territories" (*gaichi*): the Europeans preach freedom and equality but they practice discrimination. The Japanese, on the other hand, administered their territories by the principle of *isshi dōnin*, a spirit that unifies these outer people with the *Naichi* (Japanese) spirit. Japan, he predicted, would surely rise as a nation once this process was completed. Takebe Kin'ichi linked Japanese groupism to political participation in suggesting that more work needed to be done: the Korean people gaining political participation rights required their "discarding the self and dedicating [themselves] to the public" to attain the goals of coexistence and co-prosperity with the Japanese.[9]

Nakamura Sei, a principal at a common school in South Chŏlla province, defined civic education in social terms, emphasizing the "plurality" of people in the family village, society, or state over the individual. He summarized the essence of this education as "cooperation, connection, and shared responsibility."[10] These values were emphasized in the content of the civic education curriculum that centered on both intellectual and moral education. Students required instruction on the political and economic infrastructures of the peninsula, as well as the proper behavior they must adopt in their interactions with the relevant institutions. Kamatsuka Tamotsu summarized the practical content of this curriculum as follows: morally it should emphasize the traditional responsibilities that family members share among each other—the love that children hold toward their parents and the affection that parents return to their children; legally it should emphasize the people's responsibility to perform their civic duties, such as registering births, deaths, and marriages; and economically it should stress ways that traditional customs could be integrated with the present circumstances by instructing people to accept their economic and social responsibilities. This curriculum also emphasized religious concerns, primarily the need for Koreans to make Shinto shrine visits a part of their daily routine. It instructed that they should consider ways to link industry and manufacturing with the demands of society and with moral principles, rather than simply with economics. These ideas, advised Kamatsuka, should constitute an integral part of both classroom and social education.[11]

Nakamura introduced practical ways in which to implement civic education in schools. At his school the first and the fifteenth of every month were designated "civic days," which began with a ceremony that included the following activities: bowing in unison, singing the national anthem (*kimi ga yo*), raising the flag, bowing to the flag, worshiping from afar (facing east), listening to a lecture, singing *Hi no maru* (the rising sun, or Japanese flag), and bowing a third time. Afterward, participants joined the peninsula and archipelago in radio calisthenics. Nakamura assigned a different teacher to deliver the lecture each time and required speakers to submit copies of their lectures in advance for his inspection. A sample of topics addressed in these lectures included "on the raising of the flag," "on the establishment of civics day," and "on the Imperial Rescript on Education."[12] This description offers a more pragmatic example of civic education as patriotic education, a curriculum introduced to instill loyalty to the empire as a logical extension of familial piety, than was found in previous discussions on education policy. It differed in its depiction of the Western ideals as the "other" to be avoided, rather than a model to be followed. Such discussion would intensify as Japan extended further onto the Asian continent and plunged deeper into war, both developments that increasingly required tighter Korean-Japanese cooperation.

THE MOVEMENT TO STRENGTHEN *NAISEN ITTAI*

In September 1938 the government-general issued two documents designed to guide revisions in its colonial administration, a 100–page "reference report" (*sankōsho*)[13] and a 262–page proposed titled "Chōsen sōtokufu jikyoku taisaku chōsakai shimon tōshinan shian" (Korean Government-General Investigative Meeting to Devise a Counterplan to Meet the Present Situation) (hereafter known as Counterplan Proposal).[14] Together the two documents outlined strategy for the administration to meet what Japanese euphemistically referred to as the "circumstances of the times" (*jikyoku*) presented by the military crisis that Japan faced on the Asian continent. The Japanese defined this crisis as "total" (*sōryoku*): total victory depended on Japan's ability to utilize the empire's total resources. Korea's strategic position between the homeland and the battlefields required the people's total participation and cooperation in the war efforts. These reports outlined, first, Japan's successes to date and, second, what needed to be accomplished from now to prepare the Korean people for their responsibilities.

The "reference report" outlined recent developments that demonstrated Japanese success in assimilating Koreans. It also announced plans to further strengthen Korean identity with the colonial homeland. This publication summarized the extent to which the administration had advanced toward this goal. The news carried in this report was encouraging for Koreans who supported Japan's efforts. Shrine visitations had increased dramatically between 1935 (4,156,119) and 1937 (5,541,367).[15] Likewise, the number of Korean boys and girls who "no longer experienced difficulty with basic [Japanese] conversation" had risen from just over 760,000 (1933) to just under 1.2 million (1937),[16] a reflection of the increase in education facilities, and particularly in school attendance. Increases in numbers of educated Korean males expanded the potential pool of candidates for the recently initiated Korean volunteer military corps (*shinganhei*). Their graduation from elementary school assumed Japanese language fluency, the primary prerequisite for their eligibility to the volunteer corps. This publication also announced plans to increase the education and worship opportunities for Koreans. The government-general planned to increase the number of schools, particularly at the higher levels, and to establish a Korean Yasukuni Shrine to enshrine souls sacrificed while serving in Korea since annexation.[17] This summary established a foundation to advance Japan's Counterplan Proposal to strengthen *Naisen ittai*.

Vice Governor General Ōno Rokuichirō headed the committee designated to draft policy recommendations to be included in this second document. This committee consisted of distinguished Japanese and Koreans in the areas of business, education, and government administration. The contents of the Counterplan Proposal indicated the growing crisis in northern China that had evolved from the Marco Polo Incident, a relatively minor confrontation between Japanese and Chinese troops that escalated into a prolonged battle. The strategic proximity of the Korean Peninsula resting between the Asian continent and the Japanese archipelago required the Japanese government to more closely integrate the Korean people into its empire. The consequences of failure would be most critical to the empire's future.

The Counterplan Proposal addressed a major concern emphasized in two reports penned just after Sunjong's 1926 funeral: the futility of expecting Koreans to assimilate as Japanese should they be provided access to their traditional culture, including the Korean language-based media.[18] The situation of the times no longer afforded the luxury of gradual assimilation, but required procedures that expedited the process. The first chapter of the Counterplan Proposal quoted from the 1910 Imperial Rescript on annexation. It then projected the extent to which the Korean people must be assimilated, before concluding by detailing how Koreans and Japanese would benefit from a closer relationship:

> The roots (*konpon*) of [Japan's] administration of Korea are grounded in the sacred words *isshi dōnin* (imperial benevolence) extended to our peninsula brothers. It aims to bathe them in the immeasurable imperial favors (*kōtaku*), to attain in both name and reality (*meijitsu*) their complete imperialization (*teikoku kōminka*). Leaving not the slightest gap, we will forge a Japanese-Korean unified body to confront future complications initiated by the circumstances of the times (*jikyoku*). Together we will advance the mission of realizing the great spirit (*taiseishin*) of international

brotherhood (*hakkō ichiū*) from a commissary base to be established [in Korea] to assist in the Empire's continental management.

The Counterplan Proposal centered on three broad areas: education, participation, and unity. It encouraged the administration to provide the Korean people with proper "guidance and enlightenment" (*shido keihatsu*). It advised ways to strengthen Korean links with Japan by engaging their participation in nation-building activities, specifically highlighting holidays and Japanese calendar use. It proposed ways for the government-general to forge ties between Koreans and other peoples of Japan's continental empire, particularly with Manchurians and Chinese.[19]

Education facilities again provided the most important places to disseminate to Koreans the spirit that the present circumstances required. The Counterplan Proposal advised that this instruction be based on three fundamental principles: clarification (*meichō*) of the national polity, endurance (*ninku*) of *Naisen ittai*, and discipline. The instruction was to emphasize history, particularly the diplomatic, cultural, and blood connections that the Japanese and Korean peoples have shared from ancient times. It would encourage national language acquisition. And it would foster within Korea's youth the "spirit of industry and patriotism."[20] The Counterplan Proposal called for an expansion of education facilities to "allow everyone to attend school," and suggested ways to engage Koreans further in social education activities. Museums should be built, movies produced, and seminars organized to educate Korean adults. This instruction aimed to provide means for the Korean people to "rationalize their lifestyles and soften (*yūka*) their [Korean] mannerisms."

The Counterplan Proposal also envisioned ways to enlist and control Korean participation. In a section titled "*Naisen ittai* in everyday life," it outlined the administration's role in extending the lessons Koreans learned to their livelihoods. Instruction on the true meaning of holidays would enhance Korean observance of these days in more meaningful ways. They were also to be encouraged to replace their Western calendars with Japanese calendars based on Japanese imperial reigns. To integrate Japanese and Korean lives, the Counterplan Proposal encouraged greater emphasis on national language acquisition, as well as Korean observances of Japanese customs and mannerisms. By spreading Japanese martial arts, for example, the Korean people would cultivate the Japanese spirit both spiritually and physically. Finally, it advised the Japanese administration on "managing [censoring?] documents, speech and behavior, resources, movies, and music that obstructed *Naisen ittai.*"[21]

A third area that the Counterplan Proposal targeted was imperial unification. Its authors recognized the need to establish links not just between Japanese and Koreans, but also between Koreans and continental Asians, devoting far greater attention to this latter concern. It advised that ties be established through educational and cultural exchanges between instructors at universities and professional schools, students and youth leagues, as well as information disseminated through the media and exhibitions. These suggestions depicted Koreans serving as living testaments of Japanese success, a display to allow the Chinese and Manchurians the opportunity to view their potential development should they choose to cooperate.[22]

The Counterplan Proposal dedicated far less attention to the segregated environments in which the Korean and Japanese people existed. Two exceptions were the document's call to "reorganize social stratums to abolish (*kaihai*) all differences in treatment of Koreans and Japanese," and to "encourage Japanese-Korean marriage" by lecturing Koreans on the topic.[23] Its call for an increase in Japanese migration to the peninsula presumably was meant to encourage interactions between the Japanese and Koreans. The Counterplan Proposal recycled ideas that had been circulated since annexation, including many proposed in the 1920 reforms. The one major exception— strengthening Korean, Manchurian, and Chinese exchanges—reflected recent changes in Japan's Asia continent policies. Once again, the Japanese administration demonstrated an understanding of what had to be done to advance assimilation. As in previous reform proposals, this advice appeared to be short on practical suggestions needed to ensure its success.

The most original part of the Counterplan Proposal addressed directly how the Korean Peninsula was to contribute to Japan's continental war. This, of course, involved the long-term need to prepare the Korean people as loyal subjects. A more immediate need involved preparing the peninsula and the people for military operations. The plan described here dovetailed with Japan's greater total war preparation efforts in its urge to "prepare the people for times of national emergency (*yūji*) such as incidents (*jihen*) or even war."[24] It further emphasized the people being prepared to keep "confusion and unrest to a bare minimum to maintain order."[25] This required augmenting the police forces and facilities. Preparation of the Korean people would emphasize taking measures to defend the colony against communism and countering espionage (*bōchō*) both within and beyond Korea's borders.

Preparation for total war also required that the administration limit physical and social problems. Japan was to increase the peninsula's health facilities to handle wartime casualties. This investment was also required to ensure that imperial subjects remained healthy enough to continue working, to produce strong offspring, and to engage in battle. The Counterplan Proposal added the need to create health institutions to research, prevent, and cure sicknesses such as tuberculosis, leprosy, "prostitutes diseases" (*karyūbyō*), and other infectious diseases.[26] Koreans could prepare by making simple adjustments in their everyday lives. They should be encouraged to walk rather than take public transportation, as well as participate in regular radio calisthenics sessions held at established times during the day.

These two adjustments to Korean social habits repeated ideas that the government-general had been pushing since annexation. Walking more would save money and fuel; it would also teach frugality. Participation in radio exercise sessions would generate a group activity (particularly with those who worked) that also helped regulate the Korean people's daily lives. The Counterplan Proposal repeated other such "lifestyle reforms" (*seikatsu no sasshin*), including having Koreans change their eating, dressing, and living styles to coincide with those of imperialization (*kōminka*). They should wear colorful clothing (to limit laundry tasks), eat simple foods, and practice budgetary economics. Rules prohibiting alcohol and smoking by minors were to be strictly enforced.[27] A more productive people that strove to strengthen themselves physically while limiting their extravagances increased their capacity to make a more productive contribution to the empire in its time of need. Connecting these activities to imperial needs strengthened the participants' identity with the greater cause and advanced their assimilation.

Strengthening Japanese-Korean ties contributed to the military role that the Japanese envisioned the Korean Peninsula assuming. The Counterplan Proposal revealed ideas on how Korea's northern provinces could serve the Japanese military. The region contained valuable coal mines and industrial facilities that the enemy might target for bombing. Fortifying this region militarily both protected this critical resource and strengthened the Japanese war-waging capacity on the Asian continent. The Counterplan Proposal envisioned the militarization of this region strengthening the Japanese capacity to "distribute weapons in a flash" to troops fighting in China.[28] Implied, but not directly stated, was the importance of the empire gaining Korean cooperation and establishing military facilities on the peninsula. The Japanese could not expect to succeed on the Asian continent unless it tamed this region, often described as wild and uncivilized; it harbored many insubordinate (*futei*) Koreans.[29]

Soon after completing the Counterplan Proposal, the government-general organized a series of meetings attended by primarily Japanese, but also a handful of Koreans, to evaluate its contents and to suggest ways to implement its goals. Governor General Minami Jirō opened the general meeting by reminding participants of the primary reason for this proposal's existence: the present total war (*sōgō kokuryokusen*) that required national spirit capacity (*kokumin seishinryoku*) and national economic capacity (*kokumin keizairyoku*). Although progress had been made, more work needed to be done to strengthen Japan-Korea cooperation. He concluded by encouraging the participants to imagine the Sea of Japan as an enclosed lake (*kosui*), rather than an open sea.[30] We will consider Japanese commentary here, and the Korean recommendations in chapter 6 when we discuss general Korean reaction to Japanese assimilation policy.

Discussion at these meetings, which were chaired by Vice Governor General Ōno Rokuichirō, generally centered on the ideas included in the Counterplan Proposal but at times diverted to consider ideas that it had overlooked. In total 105 Japanese and Koreans joined these discussions, with Koreans representing just over 10 percent (12) of the participants. Participants represented the colony's political and business interests. Most of the Korean participants served on a central advisory committee (*chūsūin sangi*) established by the government-general in the early 1920s. A small number of Japanese appear to have traveled from the homeland to participate.[31] Perhaps to promote equality between Japanese and Koreans, each participant was assigned a number to which he was referred (rather than by name) during the discussions. This precaution was unnecessary as the Korean participants who were less than fluent in Japanese (the transcript apparently did not correct their Japanese but offered what appears to be a direct transcription of their words) surely revealed their ethnic background.

Commentary by Japanese participants tended to honor the Counterplan Proposal's content. House of Peers councilor Shitamura Hiroshi emphasized integrating the empire's "outer regions" (*gaichi*) and Hokkaido as a bloc to enlist the cooperation of these peoples. Shitamura cited Japan's declining population, due to lower Japanese longevity (a full ten years less than Europeans), lower birth rates, and sickness (tuberculosis), as the primary reason for requiring colonial participation.[32] Kada Naoji, chairman of the Korean Chamber of Commerce and Industry (Chōsen shōkō kaigisho kaitō), emphasized industrial and commercial links. Despite this progress he believed that Korean and Japan remained "poles apart" (*kakusei no kan naki*). He continued: the "infantile" (*yōchi*) Korean industry could not develop alone but required Japanese participation. He recommended that Korean industrial and financial organs be linked directly to those of the homeland. Failure to develop Korea in harmony with Japan, he warned, would prove harmful to the empire's economic and national capacity.[33]

Few Japanese participants addressed the contradictions in Japan's administrative policy. Tagawa Jōjirō was exceptional when the president of Ryūsan Industrial limited (Ryūsan kōsaku kabushiki gaisha) questioned how Japanese could expect to strengthen Japanese-Korean ties while they maintained differences in such fundamental areas as family registration legislation (*kosekihō*) and writing scripts. Tagawa noted that the practice of Korean women maintaining their maiden name complicated the inclusion of Korean families in the Japanese family register system. Miyamoto Gen, who headed the Korean Government-general Justice Division (Chōsen Sōtokufu Hōmu Kyoku), corrected Tagawa: this was a problem of the "family substantive legislation" (*shinzoku jittaihō*) rather than of the family registration law, and announced that his department was now looking into this very problem.[34] Mitsuhashi Kōichirō of the police bureau responded to Tagawa's suggestion that all publications be published in Japanese by saying that this would be convenient but impractical. While one goal was to encourage Korean use of the national language, Korean language was still necessary to instruct Koreans on the present situation. Evidently Korean development in Japanese language capabilities remained insufficient.

The general meeting ended with this comment and the group divided into several smaller groups. It is worth noting that among the Koreans at this session, only Han Sangnyong of Chōsen Trust (Chōsen seimei hoken) managed to interject his opinion. His rather long contribution centered on Japan's industrial strategy (*sangyo seisaku*) and advised that Japanese allow the Korean people to assume a role in the empire's industrial development. Smaller discussion groups offered Korean participants a less threatening environment in which to contribute, as we shall see in chapter 6. One subgroup was given the task of discussing specific ways to strengthen *Naisen ittai*. Nine Koreans joined this group, which totaled forty-six members. This discussion first focused on education. Enhara Jisaburō, head of the government-general's education division, reminded participants that this *Naisen ittai* idea was not new. Its foundation is the "fundamental spirit" (*konpan seishin*) behind Japan's 1910 annexation of Korea. Enhara acknowledged the need for the Japanese to shed their superior mentality. But more important, his remarks placed the responsibility on Korean shoulders: Koreans must "incorporate deeply the self-realization that they were imperial subjects." Education—both classroom and social—provided the key to *Naisen ittai* success, as properly targeted by the Counterplan Proposal.[35]

Yamazaki Iwao, focusing on Japan-based Koreans, linked low Korean education rates (and by extension their low Japanese language ability) to their high crime rates. The 730,000 or more *hantōjin* (peninsulars) who had migrated to Japan occupied a low social status due to their low level of education. Both their scholastic records and literacy rates were quite low; consequently their unemployment and crime rates were rather high. He advised Japanese officials to work harder to educate the Koreans. Their unemployment problem had to be addressed, but Koreans residing in Korea and Japan must understand the importance of learning Japanese.[36] Enhara Jisaburō came to Yamazaki's rescue when challenged by Yi Sŭngu to explain how Japanese expected to solve this problem when they projected to provide education only to half of all Korean children by 1942. Enhara attributed the present situation to budgetary concerns, and then revealed his office's aim to reach complete attendance by the year 1950. More schools needed to be built; more teachers needed to be trained. The education official then briefed the participants on the administration's thoughts concerning other areas addressed primarily by Korean participants: opportunities for Koreans to serve in a conscripted military, visit shrines, and intermarry with Japanese. He advised that Korean boys needed to qualify as "complete imperial subjects" before the volunteer military could be extended to compulsory military participation could be considered. Similar to Korean education, the Japanese needed more time to build shrines to accommodate Korean needs; as for intermarriage, Enhara contended that it was not as if Koreans and Japanese were not marrying—they were. They just were not registering their marriages at the city office.[37]

Enhara's comments reflect the predicament that pro-Japanese Koreans faced. Unlike the case of internal subjects, for whom institutions such as the military were deemed essential to hone their national identity, the colonizers required peripheral subjects to first demonstrate their national sentiments before the colonial government was prepared to enlist their participation in these nation-building institutions. Yet, even after Koreans demonstrated their advancement in this regard, and even after the Japanese had opened doors to their admission to these institutions, their colonial sub-jugators still regarded them as less than complete Japanese *kokumin*. Indeed, as Koreans occasionally lamented, Japanese often accented their Koreanness when Japanese-Korean ethnic divisions began to fade.

"NATIONAL EDUCATION" AND *NAISSEN ITTAI* STRENGTHENING POLICY

Both social and classroom education were affected by the government-general's efforts to strengthen Japan-Korea ties. Later in the decade education circles replaced "civic education" with "national education" (*kokumin kyōiku*) as the focus of their discussion. Thus, the focus of Korean education shifted from training students as members of the local (Korean) commu-nity to training them as members of Japan's extended empire. The spirit behind this movement was manifested in the superficial merging of the hith-erto separated Japanese public (*kōritsu*) and Korean common (*futsū*) ele-mentary schools under a single system—*kokumin gakkō*, or national schools. In theory, merging the two school systems suggested the government-general's aim to eradicate lingering differences between Japanese and Korean schools on the peninsula, as well as archipelago and peninsula schools. In practice the reform produced little change in the general makeup of the schools: as before Japanese and Koreans occupied the vast majority of seats in their respective schools. Indeed, merging the two systems rendered less necessary the integrating of classrooms, as on paper, Korean students were being educated on equal terms with their Japanese counterpart. From the early 1940s, Japanese education statistics merged Korean and Japanese stu-dent figures into one category—"students" (*seito*), separated by gender but not by ethnicity.[38] We thus do not know how these trends continued over the last years of Japanese rule.

Merging the two school systems introduced a number of changes to the Korean curriculum. "Japanese history and geography" simply became "his-tory and geography," as it was no longer necessary to specify whose history the students were studying. More important, the Korean language, no longer necessary, became an elective class (*zuii kamoku*). A combined phys-ical education and singing class occupied part of the time that had previ-ously been devoted to Korean as a required subject. By 1943 all Korean language classes had been phased out. Gym class (*taisōka*) now focused on "military arts" (*budō*) in grades 1–2 and 5–6, and regular physical education in grades 3–4.[39] Changes in focus reflected the new role that the Koreans were expected to fill in the empire. The greater presence of Koreans in the Japanese factories and male admittance (first voluntary and later compulsory) into the Japanese military required that Koreans attain a more sophisticated level of Japanese and develop healthier bodies. This education also targeted the Korean women's primary responsibilities: producing healthier babies and then properly training them prior to their admittance into the Japanese education system.

The education division of the government-general reflected both the letter and spirit of the Counterplan Proposal in its textbook revisions. One example is found in its treatment of "employment" in women's civic education (*kōmin kyōiku*) textbooks. The Counterplan Proposal emphasized in "lifestyle reforms" that women be "enlightened (*kyōka*) in the doctrine of "good wife, wise mother" (*ryōsai kenbo*), and specifically advised that they be "domesticated" (*junchi*) from their outside activities to allow them to devote their energy to raising their children and caring for home-related matters. The 1938 textbooks instructed that the women's "first mission to the state and society [was] in the home—housekeeping and child upbringing." It added that she could work outside the home if it did not interfere with this most important task. However, she must choose her employment carefully and choose a job that is appropriate for women. Textbooks printed in 1943 repeated the above message and warned that this work should train her for her "basic mission": to build a fine house (*rippa na katei*). This edition more strongly emphasized her home education responsibilities, quoting the German philosopher Johann Friedrich Herbart, who taught "one mother is worth 100 school teachers."[40]

Critics of these education reforms reveal their limitations. Tanaka Kōzō targeted the Japanese administration decision to merge the two educational systems. He also voiced his disappointment over the government-general's neglect to make Korean education compulsory and to give Korean students a six-year curriculum.[41] Funata Kyōji doubted that a simple merger of names would do much to unify the systems: surely, he challenged, the administration had something more substantial to offer. Could anyone realistically imagine the Korean education system equaling in quality that of the homeland? He criticized officials for "only looking at the surface to treat this problem. There were much more serious issues that required attention."[42]

Indeed, to expect that Korean-Japanese discrimination would be eradicated simply by merging the names of the Korean and Japanese school systems appears shortsighted. Even if the two curriculums could be successfully merged, little progress would be made toward assimilation unless the schools integrated Japanese and Koreans into the same classrooms, a step that the Japanese apparently were not prepared to take. More important than the school system as a whole, the individual school's reputation—a critical factor in determining higher education admittance and employment opportunities—would remain unchanged unless the individual schools shed their reputations as either a Japanese or a Korean school.

Those interested in a school's student makeup did not have to dig too deep to obtain this information. Government-general records reveal that even after the two education systems were merged, the distinction between schools that predominantly catered to Japanese and Korean children remained, this time by cost. Government-general statistics reveal that Japanese students attended "primary (high) expense" (*daiichibu keihi*) schools, and Koreans "secondary (low) expense" (*dainibu keihi*) schools at ratios similar to those under the two systems.[43] Indeed, school integration improved but slightly over that of the late 1930s: Koreans studying in predominantly Japanese schools doubled from 5.0 to 10.8 percent between 1935 and 1940, which suggested advancement, as did the numbers of Japanese studying in predominantly Korean schools, which rose from 0.8 to 2.4.[44] Yet, these figures hardly suggest integration progressing with the urgency that the Counterplan Proposal suggested as necessary to meet the circumstances of the times.

The government-general did make public in 1938 its intention to introduce compulsory education to the colony, but Koreans would have to wait another ten years. In 1944 it revised this estimate by two years: Korean elementary education would be made compulsory from 1946 to coincide with universal military conscription, which was slated to start that year. Takahashi Hamakichi put these two developments into perspective: "Serving in the imperial army was the highest responsibility of the people. Compulsory education, however, was not to be interpreted as compensation for this service, but as preparation for it." The government-general's plan for Korean compulsory education did not, however, envision full participation, but participation by only 90 percent of males and 50 percent of females.[45] Japan's defeat in 1945 robbed the government-general of the opportunity to demonstrate its sincerity in following through with this promise.

Suggestions for strengthening Korean social education included in the 1938 Counterplan Proposal stressed "total": few aspects of the Korean people's lives would escape the administration's influence. Upon Koreans entering society, the media, places of employment, and the general community would assume responsibility for continuing their education (and educating those who failed to attend school) to inform them of their duties to the empire. These activities ranged from neighborhood seminars to government-general sponsored special retreats that offered intensive Japanese language instruction and indoctrination on the Japanese spirit.

The media served as an important outlet for this purpose. From 1940 the government-general revised its publication policy to close all major Korean newspapers, save for the *Maeil sinbo*, which continued to publish up until the day Japan surrendered. The Japanese authorities did allow a number of Korean magazines to continue operation, one being *Siningan* (New Person), the organ of the Religion of the Heavenly Way (Ch'ondogyo).[46] The Korean press was instrumental in both instructing the people of the present circumstances that the empire faced (including wartime news), and instructing them on their special duties as imperial subjects. In August 1937, just after the Marco Polo Incident, the *Maeil sinbo* published photos and endorsements for Japan's military efforts by two prominent Koreans. The educator Yun Ch'iho declared that the Japanese and Korean people shared the same fate. The popular historian Ch'oe Namsŏn advised that the Korean people's "understanding of the times (*siguk*) was fundamentally [necessary for them to enjoy] the promise of a bright future."[47] One can only imagine the impact that their messages had on Koreans.[48]

This same newspaper also enlisted the help of Korean women to advise its female readers of their duties. In January 1938 the *Maeil sinbo* carried the advice of thirty-four women over three pages who all advertised messages included in the Counterplan Proposal. Pak Yŏnghŭi, for example, advised women to walk instead of using public transportation. Their efforts would save precious gasoline, but also provide them with inexpensive physical exercise. Paek Hahŏ reinforced the administration's call for thriftiness by encouraging "total economizing in one's correspondence, one's association with others, and in one's entertainment practices." Yi Chŏnghŭi's advice to "serve your husband" characterized the "good-wife, good-mother" message that the government-general pushed in its Counterplan Proposal as well as in its more recent textbook revisions.[49]

These messages were also found in advertisements carried by the *Maeil sinbo*. In contrast to those of the 1920s that often advertised beauty items (such as soap and cosmetics), leisure activities, and education seminars, ads that appeared in the 1930s advertised personal health, pregnancy, children's

health, and even husband-wife intimacy. Wakamoto insisted that its medic-
inal products would strengthen children. Their consumption would increase
a child's appetite and lessen any fatigue they might experience from study
and exercise. To drive home the military message, the company decorated its
advertisement with a picture of a child-soldier wielding a bayonet decorated
with Japan's rising sun flag. Other advertisements encouraged pregnancy
and congenial family relations. One example of the former featured a group
of women sitting in a circle contemplating getting pregnant by the end of
February, their last chance to give birth to a son during the year of the tiger.[50]
Again, the implied message here was military related: boys born under this
sign matured into fierce fighters. Products that promised to stimulate (or
rekindle) sex drives encouraged not only reproduction, but also healthier
families through less promiscuity and closer husband-wife relations.

Radio broadcasting, which flourished following the start in early 1927 of
the Korean Broadcast Corporation (just in time for the Showa Emperor's
coronation), also contributed to this process. Encouraged by the Ministry
of Communication, this medium contributed to Korea's cultural, educational, and entertainment forums. While the broadcast schedule included
Japanese music, it also set aside spots for lectures on ethics, agriculture
improvement, and women's education. From 1937, increased airtime for
Japanese-language broadcasting decreased the time available to Korean-
language programs (which ceased altogether in 1944) and pushed programs
that promoted Korean culture off the air. Michael E. Robinson summarizes
the role that this medium played in colonial Korea as "part of a more complicated (Japanese) colonial hegemony constructed of both physical coer-
cion and cultural/political attraction." Like the vernacular newspaper, the
radio allowed Koreans the space to "construct culture."[51] This worked
against the Japanese original intention for introducing culture to Koreans
in the first place, and against Japanese confidence that Koreans would choose
Japanese culture over their own should they be exposed to both.

The government-general initiated more concentrated efforts to educate the Korean people, as summarized in a twenty-seven-page pamphlet
titled "Korean Administration and the Advancement of Imperial Training"
(Chōsen tōchi to kōmin rensei no shinten) published in 1944.[52] This pamphlet described daily activities established to remind the people of their
imperial duties. Every morning at an established time the authorities set off
a siren to engage the people in Shinto worship. A noon whistle announced
the time for silent prayer on behalf of the military heroes who protected the

country. The pamphlet also described government-general sponsored lectures, exhibitions, movies, picture-card shows (*kamishibai*), and discussions to remind the people of the increasingly dire circumstances and their role in the empire.

The administration also set aside special days on a weekly, monthly, and yearly basis to remind Koreans of the greater cause that required their undivided attention. On these days Koreans were required to wake up early to gather under the flag for regular meetings held at schools, places of employment, public offices, department stores, and other designated locations. Here they listened to speeches, recited a pledge to the emperor, and worshiped at shrines. From 1937 one day every month was set aside as "patriotic day" (*aikokubi*). In "January 1942 the entire country celebrated the establishment of a day to honor their receiving the Imperial Rescript" (*taishō hōtaibi*); from March 1943, every Monday had been designated "Drilling Day" (*renseibi*), when 25 million Koreans throughout the peninsula joined together in training.[53]

Newly created holidays, some being redirected traditional days of commemoration, offered the administration additional opportunities to assemble people for patriotic indoctrination. From the 1930s, April 3, a day traditionally set aside in memory of Japan's first emperor (Jinmu), came to be known as "Spirit Promotion Day for Educators" (*Kyōikusha seishin sakkō kinenbi*). November 3 continued to be observed in the memory of the Meiji Emperor. On July 7 Yun Ch'iho, ironically as he was a Christian, observed, "Shinto Thanksgiving Services" day, which commemorated the anniversary of the Marco Polo Incident. On these occasions people gathered at Shinto shrines to listen to speeches by both Koreans and Japanese, and participate in a series of *banzai*s directed at the imperial capital.[54] It is difficult today to ascertain the extent to which these activities encouraged (or discouraged) Korean solidarity with the Japanese, or the degree to which the participation was coerced or voluntary, as the war's result and subsequent Korean liberation greatly influenced the negative way these events are recalled by Koreans who experienced them.

A more practical function initiated by the government-general was a movement that aimed to engage the Korean people in concentrated Japanese language (*kokugo*) study. Japanese since the time of annexation had written that assimilation required a unified language shared between Koreans and Japanese. Mild disagreement arose over which language this would be, with the vast majority arguing that for Koreans to learn Japanese would be more practical than for either the Japanese to adopt Korean or both people to agree on a hybrid (Japanese-Korean) language. The wartime period put a sudden end to this discussion. Japanese grew in dominance as Korean language mediums gradually disappeared. From May 1942, just at the time that plans for a military conscription system were being finalized, the Japanese administration initiated a program of intensive Japanese language study. The report "Korean Administration and the Advancement of Imperial Training" argued Korean capacity in Japanese to be essential for their "grasping the Japanese spirit." The fact that the colonizers' Korean brethren (*Chōsen dōhō*) occupied "one-quarter of the Japanese territorial population" only magnified this concern. This report designated "the language dissemination movement plan as one critical element of the . . . general strength movement [*sōryoku undō*]" in what it termed the national general strengthening federation (*kokumin sōryoku renmei*).[55]

Another pamphlet, "Korea in Training" (Rensei suru Chōsen), also published in 1944 outlined one such program that drew direct links between the spiritual and physical training.[56] The document informed readers that throughout Korea Mondays had been designated as a training day. On this day the workplace and schools arranged activities that emphasized both physical (military training) and spiritual (public ceremony) exercises. One schedule followed what had become an established pattern: flag raisings, worship from afar, silent prayer, speeches, and radio exercise.[57] "Korean Youth Training" (Chōsen no seinen rensei) also described Korean youth training programs as an institution new to the Korean people due to their "custom of early marriage." The document advertised this training as instruction of a lesser quality than that taught in higher education, but a

> place where youth working in factories can learn and train during their spare time. It was a place for imperial subjects to raise their stature (*shishitsu*), an opportunity for them to receive technical skills for their occupation as they underwent basic military training and honed their ability to protect the nation.

It added that this training operated for the "same purpose as that which took place in the homeland."[58]

The number of training centers increased dramatically following the Manchurian Incident and the escalation of Japan's war on the Asian continent. By 1944 they numbered over two thousand and accommodated over 120,000 participants.[59] Youth corps (*seinentai*) incorporated Korean boys (under thirty) and girls (under twenty-five), both educated and illiterate, who were not currently engaged in formal education. These sessions, which lasted from two hundred to six hundred hours, centered on the following goals: character training of imperial subjects, domesticating a *Naisen ittai* lifestyle, physical training for national defense purposes, and extending the production ability of imperial subjects. The government-general also organized compulsory "special youth training" (*seinen tokubetsu rensei*) sessions for all Korean males between the ages of seventeen and twenty-one, with provisions being made to include volunteers up to age thirty. Those who attempted to avoid this compulsory training were punished.[60]

The pamphlet "Korean Administration and the Advancement of Imperial Training" did provide passing attention to the colonizer's need to initiate a compulsory education system to complement the compulsory military service that the colonial government now required of all young Korean males by reminding its readers of plans to initiate compulsory education in 1946. The pamphlet stated that the increased patriotic zeal displayed by Koreans since the Manchurian Incident had allowed for the institution of conscription military service. Many more Koreans, it explained, now came to define themselves as "Imperial subjects" (*kōkoku shinmin*) who wished "to join the front line of battle to protect the homeland."[61] This conclusion was based on the numbers of applicants for the volunteer corps, which had increased steadily since the military first began accepting Koreans (from 12,000 in 1939 to 250,000 in 1942). The Korean people required a conscription system to propel them toward a "higher and more patriotic devotion." It underlined this point by quoting former governor general Minami Jirō: "The shape of military conscription allowed *Naisen ittai* to reach a climax. Our past efforts were spent to attain this end."[62] "Korean Administration and the Advancement of Imperial Training" concluded by repeating other institutional changes for successful Korean assimilation. First, it stipulated that successful conscription required that Koreans maintain their family registers, which it considered to be the "foundation of the military service." As of 1942 as many as half of all Koreans living in various places throughout the empire had neglected to fulfill this obligation. By March 1943, the government-general, in cooperation with the Patriotic Society, reported that it had managed to register "without exception" all males under the age of twenty.[63]

This pamphlet also noted that differences in Korean and Japanese names had caused problems with the family register system. This was resolved when the government-general began permitting Koreans to adopt the Japanese *uji* (surname) system, a "gift to the people" presented to commemorate the 2600 anniversary of Japan's founding. Previously Koreans had been limited by the "inconvenient system" that prohibited them from marrying someone with the same last surname, particularly troublesome given that Kim and Yi constituted 21 and 15 percent of all Korean surnames. The pamphlet further stated that "the majority of the general public supported the establishment of a Japanese name (*seimei*) system."[64] As typical of the period of colonial occupation, Japanese officials publicized statistics by their face value without explaining the reality behind the numbers. That more Koreans had obtained Japanese names, were visiting the local shrines, or enlisting their boys in the military, regardless of the reasoning that led them to cooperate, was proof enough that assimilation was taking hold in Korea. Left out were the stories of Korean resistance and Japanese opposition to Korean advancement.[65]

As in previous written declarations and pronouncements, the Japanese colonial authorities were extremely talented at articulating the steps needed to enlist Korean support for their efforts. They also had accumulated a wealth of statistics that documented their successes to date: the number of Koreans participating in Japanese education and customs such as visiting shrines was increasing. They provided, however, no means for quantitatively assessing the relationship between these increases and the stated goal of Japan's colonial administration—Korean assimilation. Numbers alone tell us little about the attitudes that Koreans carried with their participation. Many perhaps did visit Shinto shrines to pray to Japanese gods, particularly if their sons were fighting for the empire. Still others visited to enjoy the vistas that their prime location provided. Regardless of Koreans' intentions, the Japanese forced most Koreans into entering the shrines simply by placing ration collection points on their grounds.[66] The Japanese also increased Korean participation at camps to teach them how to be good Japanese, but these camps failed to make full use of the opportunity because they were limited to Koreans only. Furthermore, these data do not help us understand whether Koreans' participation encouraged Japanese to adopt a more favorable attitude toward them.

JAPANESE WARTIME IMAGES OF KOREANS

Many of the reforms made by the government-general from the late 1930s aimed to erase distinctions that separated Koreans from Japanese. The assumption was that if Koreans attended the same school system, answered to similar names, and offered the same devotion to the empire by praying alongside Japanese at Shinto shrines and fighting alongside Japanese in the trenches, then eventually discrimination toward Koreans would diminish. Assimilation required as much. By examining Japanese attitudes toward Koreans at this time we learn the opposite. Similar to other cases of assimilation, acceptance of Japan's assimilation policy by Koreans (and in some cases Japanese) was a development that the colonizers generally did not welcome.

Occasional signs suggested progress. Shiohara Tokisaburō offered in his preface to Hyŏn Yŏngsŏp's *Chōsenjin no susumu beki michi* (The Path That the Korean Must Tread) that the road for Korean advancement was one that "our 90 million brethren" must take together, indicating that the fate of 70 million Japanese was linked to that of 20 million Koreans.[67] The government-general organ, *Chōsen*, also demonstrated evidence of change in attitude. As indicated earlier, over the journal's first decade it focused attention toward understanding Korean uniqueness. As the military situation moved from "incident" to crisis to warfare, the journal increasingly analyzed the Korean people by their capacity to contribute to Japan's military efforts. Discussions in the publication often referred to Koreans in terms of their value as "resources" (*shigen*). Mitarai Tatsuo's article on the new "Korean mission" (*Chōsen shimei*) predicted that Korea's "number one mission (after the Asian people were united) would not be its underground resources, nor its food products, but in its human resources (*jinteki shigen*), particularly as a hardcore group of people who had mastered the Japanese spirit."[68]

The Japanese wartime situation no doubt fueled much of the optimism expressed in the journal. Japan's plan to locate military bases on the Korean Peninsula to ease their continental advancement required their adopting a more congenial attitude toward Koreans. Japanese leaders emphasized this message during the 1938 *Naisen ittai* strengthening meetings discussed above. For example, Vice Governor General Ōno Rokuichirō warned that Korea's military fortification required an equal fortification of Korean patriotism.[69] This message was repeated after Japan became embroiled in a multifront war with China and the United States in the early 1940s. The 1944 pamphlet titled "Korean Administration Past and Present" (Chōsen tōchi no kako to genzai) quoted Governor General Koiso Kuniaki's declaration that *Naisen ittai* was not simply a formality or surface equality, but the "completion of [Korean] Imperial subjectification (*Kōmin shinminka no kansei*) . . . the underlining principle of an equal Japanese-Korean national polity."[70]

Japanese attitudes proved far more stubborn, as noted by a group of Japanese professors during a roundtable discussion published in the June 1939 issue of the monthly journal *Bungei shunju*.[71] The discussion suggested that Koreans had advanced in their acceptance of Japanese colonial rule. Yet, despite these advances, the Japanese continued to reject the Koreans as their fellow imperial subjects. The panelists were asked to focus their discussion on Korean culture, but were also free to introduce other related subjects. One question addressed to the panel concerned the Korean desire to become Japanese. Referring to Hyŏn Yŏngsŏp's book, this participant, identified only as a reporter (*kisha*), suggested that the "image of the Korean intellectual was their desire to be Japanese." University president Hayami Kon commented that ever since the Manchurian Incident this seemed to be the case. Funata Kyōji, a professor of law, noted that many of his Korean students seemed eager to fit in: they "eat and dress just like Japanese." Ōkuhira Takehiko, who taught diplomatic history, observed that Hyŏn's writing reminded him of Korean eagerness to study Japanese classical literature to compensate for a void that they saw in Korean literature.[72]

Ōkuhira proposed the idea that Japanese rule had stabilized Korean lives and fortunes. Unlike in the "old [Chosŏn era] days," the Japanese were not about to plunder their fortunes. The Koreans, he continued, "then compare their life to that of the Japanese and attempt to add a spiritual side to it." He noted as signs of assimilation Korean homes adding Japanese alcoves (*toko no ma*) and staggered shelves. They have also begun to demonstrate, he added, an appreciation for their traditional culture—specifically their literature and pottery—since the Japanese arrived. More Koreans now collect Korean pottery, whereas in the recent past they ignored it. They use Yi-era vases to perform Japanese *ikebana* (flower arrangement).[73]

Part of the more positive attitude the Keijō Imperial University professors observed could perhaps be attributable to the increase in opportunity, a point mentioned at the onset of this roundtable discussion. Hayami commented that Japanese (*Naichijin*) returning home opened opportunities for more Korean students to gain admission to the university. He complimented the students for their hard work—they were "good students." He wondered, however, how long this situation would continue. Philosophy professor Abe Kazunari and Funata linked Korean advances to changes in government-general education policy, specifically the integration of the two school systems, but quickly added their doubts that Korean education would ever equal that of the homeland. Funata's comments echoed concerns introduced earlier in this chapter:

I am afraid that the [unification of school systems] might end with simply a name change. The Education Act revision stipulating that *Naisen* education should be unified is a step in the right direction. However, it is difficult to imagine that the education here will ever come to match that of the *Naichi*. When you look at the details, many difficult problems remain. . . . Many people only look at the surface in treating this problem. In actuality there are many difficult problems.[74]

Problems still remained once the Korean student graduated and attempted to secure employment. Funata bemoaned the fact that employers would accept Japanese, but not Korean, graduates. Toriyama Kiichi, who taught Oriental history at the university, remarked that even Koreans prefer Japanese over Korean university students as home tutors for their children. He added that patients in hospitals—both Japanese and Korean—feel the same. "Among Koreans (*hantōjin*), there is a tendency to hate Koreans."[75]

The discussion then focused on the superiority of the Japanese race, and the need to encourage superior Japanese to come to the peninsula. Abe lectured:

The question of equal treatment of Koreans and Japanese presents much confusion. In theory it [Japanese superiority] is correct. But practically speaking, equal treatment should be conditioned on whether superior Japanese move to the peninsula. In my opinion, if the Korean student with an excellent academic record is afforded worse treatment than the Japanese student with the poor record, then we cannot excuse this blatant unfairness. It is necessary that Japanese be considered [the Korean's] superior at some point. To realize this we must encourage superior Japanese to move without hesitation to the peninsula. At the same time, if Japanese do not consider how to reform the treatment we afford excellent and faithful (*chūjitsu*) Koreans they will not improve. Japanese cannot be considered superior just because they are Japanese, but because there is confidence in their actual reliability and excellence. If the Korean does not recognize this, then the Japanese will never be able to administer the peninsula.[76]

The professors demonstrated the rigidity of a number of generalizations often directed toward Koreans. Koreans excelled in law, remarked statistics professor Ōuchi Takeji, because they were superior at memorization, a quality often used to argue their advantage as foreign language learners. Hayami questioned the moral character of Korean students: even though their level of knowledge had risen, their moral character remained unchanged. Ōuchi chastised Koreans for their failure to greet Japanese properly, as well as their tendency to be hyperbolic.[77] On one occasion a panelist attempted to criticize these negative images as stereotyping. Kuroda Akira, a professor of psychology, noted Abe's tendency to depict the Koreans as a homogeneous people and added that different parts of the Korean Peninsula maintained diversity similar to that found in Japan's Tohoku and Kyushu regions. Abe retorted by patronizing the professor: people who hold such sentiments normally are ones without much contact with the Korean people. Once they made this contact they soon lose such idealistic thinking.[78]

The discussion ended with the professors exchanging ideas on how to better encourage Japanese-Korean unity. Abe and Funata resurrected views more commonly heard during the first two decades of Japanese rule, suggesting that present attempts to strengthen *Naisen ittai* were premature. Abe commented that Japanese-Korean unity would not come quickly. He questioned whether Japan's policy was to "unify with . . .or to rule over the *hantōjin*."

> Either way the Japanese had to realize the importance of Korea as a cardinal point from which to develop the Asian continent. For this success to transpire Japanese must demonstrate, even if but minimally, respect for Korean customs and take what good they have to offer. They will naturally adopt the good things that [Japanese] have to offer. . . . This, however, cannot be rushed.

Funata agreed, and added that he heard too much talk of turning Korea into a military base. Rather, Japanese should focus on its value as a cultural base, a requirement if the Japanese government wished to encourage superior Japanese youth to study here.[79]

The diversity of perspectives that the participants introduced during this discussion is its greatest contribution to our inquiry. The professors were able to offer their own views, as well as those they experienced by observing both Japanese and Korean residents in and out of their classrooms. Their perceptions revealed that a deep caste-like social stratum had emerged to physically and psychologically separate Japanese from Korean. Advances had been made. Yet, the lingering negative impressions toward Koreans that Japanese held, and that even Koreans had adopted, compromised this progress. The content of this roundtable discussion further suggested that the main pillar of Japan's assimilation policy—formal education—would have but a minimal effect unless efforts were made to correct these prejudicial attitudes.

Literature published by Korea-based Japanese authors reaffirmed these negative attitudes at a time when print restrictions rendered scarce negative commentary in the media. This writing often emphasized the discrepancy the author saw between Japanese official rhetoric, in support of Japanese-Korean unity, and the prejudicial attitudes that strengthened the two people's segregated living environments. It introduced a dimension of peninsula society often ignored in official documents and the media, the everyday interactions between Korean and Japanese youth. Kajiyama Toshiyuki, a novelist who was born in Seoul, where he attended elementary school (he turned fifteen when the war ended), authored a number of short stories based on his experiences in wartime Korea. These stories emphasized the expatriate population clinging to the high status that they had gained simply by having relocated to a Japanese colonial territory. His stories describe the resistance shown by longtime Japanese residents toward any policy designed to promote Korean-Japanese equality or that narrowed ethnic distinction. Regarding the Japanization of Korean names, Japanese considered this a "right" that allowed the Korean to "speak and be spoken to as equals." It was one that "longtime Japanese residents of Korea did not welcome."[80]

Kajiyama's stories bring his readers into the homes and classrooms of Japanese students. This education, rather than encouraging expatriate Japanese students to accept their Korean classmates as equals, actually hardened existing stereotypes. The untrustworthy Korean students participated in military drills using wooden "weapons," rather than the authentic steel ones distributed to the Japanese students. Kajiyama notes the humor felt by some Japanese who giggled when given the order to "present arms": "The contrast between the steel weapons and those wooden 'rifles' . . . created a tragicomic effect that made many Japanese students giggle and terribly shamed all Korean students." Kajiyama uses his schoolboy character to innocently question the motives driving this discrimination, only to sacrifice him to a scolding by his father who yells, "Don't be a fool! Don't you know those Koreans will cause riots and rise in rebellion as soon as they get their hands on real rifles?" The boy's request for clarification—does not assimilation policy make them Japanese "just as we are?"—further enrages his father, who asks his son to consider the wartime circumstances facing Japan.[81]

Kajiyama's fictional account of Korean mistrust by Japanese actualized in their real-life experiences in the Japanese military. Universal male conscription of Korean males began in 1944. As we saw earlier in Cho Pyŏngsang's contribution to *Chōsen*, Koreans welcomed this development as a sign of the Japanese recognizing advances made by the Korean people. Many Korean boys who legitimately enlisted into the military saw their service as a means of social advancement upon their release from their duties. However, Japanese mistrust cast its dark shadow even over those Koreans who fought alongside them. Rather than as a Korean regiment (as was the case of colonized peoples in the British military, or minorities in the United States military) Korean soldiers were distributed into different units where, similar to peninsula-based schools, many found themselves as the minority. Koreans were capped at 20 percent for frontline units, 40 percent for rear units, and 80 percent for noncombatant units.[82] While senior harassment of junior subordinates infiltrated all parts of the Japanese military, evidence suggests that colonial recruits from the colonies were forced to endure this to a greater extent than their Japanese counterpart. One report described a Korean recruit who was bashed with a bat so brutally that even his "parents and siblings found it hard to recognize him."[83] Following the war's end a relatively high proportion of civilian and military Koreans and Taiwanese (7.2 percent) were convicted of war crimes than Japanese. This was mainly due to the nature of their duties: carrying out Japanese-issued punishments to allied prisoners of war. After the war the Japanese government made these POWs ineligible for benefits afforded to other Japanese POWs.[84]

A second theme in Japanese-authored fiction pursued fledgling, yet unfulfilled, romances between Koreans and Japanese, perhaps as much for the symbolism of Japan's unfulfilled promises of assimilation as to illustrate the negative Japanese reactions to such liaisons. Yuasa Katsuei's 1934 "Kannani" depicts the relationship that the Japanese boy Ryūji sought with the short story's namesake, the Korean girl Kannani. Born in Japan months before Korea's annexation, Yuasa's family moved to Korea when he was just six, where he stayed until he left to attend Waseda University in Tokyo. He would later return to the peninsula in 1939. His main Japanese character, Ryuji, was the son of a Japanese policeman who harbors many of the derogatory attitudes Japanese held toward Koreans—their houses he saw as "really small, like the piles of dirt used for burial mounds." Then he meets Kannani. Kannani, whose father was a retainer in the service of a Korean count, speaks Japanese fluently enough to recognize Ryūji's interesting (Shikoku) dialect.

Their conversations target differences in impressions that separate Korean from Japanese:

> KANNANI: My father said that I can't play with the kids of Japanese policemen . . . Because my father hates Japanese; he hates the Japanese military police the most and he hates the Japanese regular police the second most. He says they abuse Korean people and they're mean.

> RYŪJI: Policemen don't do mean things. Their job is to *get rid* of bad people who do mean things. Even my father says that. My father also says not to abuse any Koreans. Japanese don't do bad things, because we're subjects of the emperor and also because the great deity of Ise is watching us.

Kannani then reveals to Ryūji the roots of her anger: the Japanese overtook their fields and the police arrested her father, before nailing shut the private school that he had started. Her family was able to survive only because her father accepted a job as a gatekeeper for a Korean count. She confesses both her hate for Japanese in general and her fondness for Ryūji, taking his face in her hands and imploring him to learn Korean as she has learned Japanese.[85] Kannani thus embodies the Koreans who had done their part, only to be let down by the Japanese who failed to fulfill their promises.

Korean and Japanese reactions to their affection represent the schisms that separated the two peoples. Kannani's friends welcome the development, describing Ryūji in a chant as "clearly the best" and "the very best groom in the world." Japanese boys view their romance as an ethnic disgrace. Upon seeing the two walking together they break out with the chant, "Ryuchan and Kannani are totally strange; falling for a Korean slut puts all Japanese to shame." In the end, Kannani disappears. Her father pleads with Ryūji's policeman father to find her. Ryūji and his father's conflicting theories regarding who was responsible for her pitiful fate—she was murdered—represents different views held by Japanese as to why assimilation failed: Ryūji blaming it on "those crazy Japanese swinging their swords around like lunatics" and his father on "a young Korean kid having himself a little fun."[86]

The inconclusive ending to this story coincides with Yuasa's views on Japan's mission on the Korean Peninsula. He supported Japan's *Naisen ittai* movement and maintained hope that the younger generation would realize this goal. His characterization of Kannani and Ryūji reflected his disdain for Japanese arrogance—both in their attitude toward the Korean people and their insistence on their total capitulation to Japanese culture—as the barrier that prevented assimilation. The couple's story is reflected in the experiences of Japanese living on the Korean Peninsula. The government-general actively encouraged Japanese-Korean intermarriage in the name of *Naisen ittai* both in the 1920 reforms and the 1938 Counterplan Proposal. Its efforts demonstrated results—a slight increase in Korean-Japanese marriage. Yet, individual experiences suggest that social pressure discouraged many couples from intermarrying. The real-life case of Tauchi Chizuko is illustrative. She writes that after she decided to marry a Korean, her close friends began to ignore her even when they met on the street. Once she was married, her Japanese friends showed cold feelings toward her. Osada Kanako recalls that she entertained the idea of marrying a Korean to demonstrate her support of *Naisen ittai* until she discussed this plan with her parents, who scolded her severely.[87]

The wartime years (1931–45) represented for Koreans the harshest times of the colonial period. The most demeaning policies—name changes, efforts to eradicate the Korean language, forced labor, and sex slavery—were all products of the latter half of this period. It was also a time when the Korean people made their biggest strides, particularly after the escalation of war forced many Japanese home to serve in the military. The void in labor and even management offered unprecedented opportunity for Koreans both in schools and the factories. Soon-Won Park notes a competition for skilled Korean labor during the war years that resulted in managers "head hunting" capable Korean laborers, and rewarding workers who stayed with more responsible jobs.[88]

Statistics suggest increased interest among Koreans in Japanese efforts. The pamphlet "Korean Administration Past and Present" noted increases in the number of people entering Japanese shrines since the 1937 Marco Polo Bridge Incident (from just under 1.2 million in 1936, and just over 2 million in 1937, to more than 3.6 million in 1939, before dipping to over 2.3 million in 1941).[89] An increasing number of Korean children were entering Japanese-run schools, and Korean boys (now certified as capable in the Japanese language) were volunteering in greater numbers to join the Japanese military.[90] Increases in the number of intermarriages (50 couples in 1937 and 1,416 in 1941), although still low and overwhelmingly Korean males with Japanese women,[91] suggested that the efforts of the administration's *Naisen ittai* strengthening movement were taking effect. Japanese writing on colonial policy observed the positive efforts that Koreans had been making since 1931, following the Manchurian Incident.

Our inquiry into Japanese wartime attitudes toward Koreans reveals a different story: closer contacts contributed to a Japanese hardening of anti-Korean views that had plagued this colonial relationship since its inception. Trust appeared repeatedly as a factor that prevented tighter relations from emerging, as evident in fictional accounts such as those left by Kajiyama and Yuasa. Memories of the March 1919 independence movement imprinted within the Japanese an image of the Korean too dangerous to allow to shoulder firearms unless very closely supervised.[92] Japanese who contemplated marrying a Korean were forced to consider the effect that their decision would have on their relations with Japanese friends and family members. The discrepancy between Japanese rhetoric and policy, one that characterized other peripheral colonization situations, was not overlooked by Japanese, who since the time of annexation recognized it as a flaw in Japanese administration in Korea. As we shall see in the next chapter, it was one that even those Koreans who supported Japanese presence in their country criticized, as well.

6

KOREAN CRITIQUES OF JAPANESE ASSIMILATION POLICY

POSTLIBERATION ACCOUNTS LEFT BY KOREANS WHO ENDURED JAPANESE rule tell stories of a proud people united under a single cause—to oust the Japanese invaders from their homeland. If they (or their parents) were not at the forefront of the independence movement, they were committing other acts of resistance: they bravely defied their Japanese interrogators, irreverently poked holes in imperial portraits, or passively avoided their assimilation activities.[1] Koreans place this thirty-six-year struggle in the context of a much larger narrative that portrays Korean history as a series of struggles by a united Korean people to protect their peninsula from foreign invaders. This interpretation gave birth to the metaphor of Korea existing as a passive shrimp among aggressive whales. Few struggles are so neatly defined, and the Korean reaction to Japanese rule is no exception. It has been only recently that the activities of not so patriotic Koreans have been publicized.[2]

Postliberation governments in North and South Korea differed in their treatment of collaborators. While the North Korean government soon purged the majority of those who assisted the Japanese, the South Korean government, until recently, discouraged investigation into their activities and retained many in their positions. Democratization has encouraged a reevaluation of this history, including the identification of those who assisted the Japanese. Like most colonial situations, foreign invasion forced Koreans to rethink their identity, a process that produced a kaleidoscope of responses that often clashed with the more patriotic accounts of the Korean response to Japanese rule. More often than not, the identity many Koreans settled upon blurred the lines that separated "patriot" from "collaborator," as they adjusted their existence to accommodate the circumstances that they confronted.[3]

My intention here is not to diminish the patriotic actions of Koreans during this period, nor is it to exonerate the actions of collaborators. Rather it is to reveal Korean critiques of Japan as critical voices to our understanding of Japanese assimilation policy and implementation. Both types of reactions offer interesting appraisals that contribute to this study's aim of understanding the appropriateness and effectiveness of Japanese assimilation in Korea. Korean opposition to Japanese rule, most vocal from the early 1920s to the early 1930s, criticized colonial assimilation ambitions in the newly formed indigenous press by informing their readers of the policy's inappropriateness to the Korean people. Japan's supporters, on the other hand, used the Japanese language media to applaud the government-general's efforts, but also to urge the administration to correct contradictions they saw between its rhetoric and practice. Korean self-characterization intersected often with the images that Japanese drew of them as a people. Reform-minded Koreans were unable to unite behind a unified agent—either the Japanese colonizers or a single Korean reform group. Nor could they unite behind a desired result—either as subjects under a sovereign Korean state or as assimilated subjects under the Japanese. The value of Korean critiques of Japanese rule is in their perspective as the object of this policy. Their position allowed Koreans to cut through the contradictions that Japanese critiques either failed to see or chose to ignore.

KOREAN RESPONSES TO JAPANESE ASSIMILATION POLICY

Korean responses to Japan's threat differed from the initial attempt to modernize Japanese-Korean diplomatic relations soon after the 1868 Meiji Restoration. At this time, divisions over the shape of Korean modernity hardened as Japanese intrusions intensified over the late nineteenth and early twentieth centuries. Factions generally gravitated toward the different rivals that sought to influence Korean development. Loyalties shifted with the waxing and waning of influence by Korea's neighbors, creating at times interesting—but complicated—relationships. (In 1895, the Japanese even recruited the Taewŏngun, who had kept Japanese envoys from the capital in the late 1860s, to participate in Queen Min's murder.) Following annexation these factions split first over when Koreans should seek their independence (gradually or radically), and who should lead Korean development (Koreans or Japanese). Koreans from different factions differed also over the political context under which a future Korea should exist: Could Korea maintain a sovereign state should it gain independence? If so, should Koreans seek to gain their independence through diplomatic or military means? If not, should Korea support its assimilation by Japan or as a member of a greater pan-Asian confederacy? These questions divided families and friends, but also individuals who drifted in and out of different factions over the course of Japanese rule.

This division is illustrated in the Hyŏn family. Peter Hyun (Hyŏn Chunsŏp)'s popular *Man Sei! The Making of a Korean American* provides a fictional account of the author's struggles as a boy in occupied Korea. His title, *Man Sei!* (literally, may you live for ten thousand years), echoes the chants of the Koreans who in March 1919 braved Japan's military rule to demand their independence from colonial rule. Indeed, his story opens with scenes of the demonstration.[4] Occupying a minor role in his story is his unnamed cousin (probably Hyŏn Yŏngsŏp) who disgraced his family by marrying a Japanese and fathering two "half-breeds." This cousin's family was confined to the rear house, the gate padlocked, when his father entertained guests.[5] Hyŏn Yŏngsŏp also authored a book. His, titled *The Path That the Koreans Must Take* (Chōsenjin no susumu beki michi), argued why the Korean people must support Japan's *Naisen ittai* policies: Koreans should reject their Chinese-influenced traditional culture and accept a Japanese-influenced modern culture.[6]

The Japanese (and Koreans) recognized the 1931 Manchurian Incident as being instrumental in changing Korean perceptions toward Japanese rule. A number of changes accompanied this event. Japan's expansion onto the Asian continent increased Korean economic opportunity both in Korea and in Manchuria as the government-general placed stronger emphasis on industry. Increased opportunity, along with stronger assimilation rhetoric, encouraged Koreans to consider their ethnic (Korean) identity in a broader racial (Asian or "yellow") context. The present Korean government investigation into the "pro-Japanese" actions of these Koreans condemns those it identifies to be "pro-Japanese" Koreans for their traitorous actions to the Korean state and people: rather than join other Koreans in the fight for Korean liberation, these Koreans profited from Japanese colonial rule. Contributors to this discussion must consider the circumstances under which all Koreans made their life choices. With the world quickly moving toward war, did it make more sense for Korea to seek independence or to seek autonomy within the context of a greater East Asian alliance?

Korean responses to Japanese rule were diverse. They ranged from acceptance to disapproval; the latter differed in approach: some actively demonstrated their disapproval by violent means, others by seeking diplomatic assistance, still others by more passive measures such as civil disobedience, product boycotts, and school strikes. In addition to disagreeing about methods, Korean resistance groups also argued over the timing of Korean independence: should Koreans demand Japan's immediate retreat or strengthen to ensure greater chances of success when independence came? Analyzing the vast array of responses to Japanese rule is a rather complicated task. Our goal is challenging but simpler: to consider the value of these voices in our evaluation of Japanese assimilation policy. We will pursue this question by considering Koreans' responses based on their images of Korea's future: either as independent state or a part of the greater Japanese empire. The groups whose opinions are most fitting are those most directly affected by Japanese rule—those who remained on the Korean Peninsula. These groups were gradualists in that they generally believed, whether they favored independence or assimilation, that greater efforts by Koreans were necessary if they were to attain either result. Both groups benefited from Korea's expanding print culture to publicize their views, particularly in the early 1920s when Japanese censorship was relatively generous in what it allowed the Koreans to publish.

THE CULTURAL NATIONALIST CRITIQUE OF ASSIMILATION

Strict government-general censorship of the Korean voice over its first decade of colonial rule reflects the opposition it anticipated to its assimilation policy. Indeed, every attempt by Japan to assimilate other peoples in both its internal and peripheral territories had been met with varying degrees of resistance. The Japanese decision to relax its publication legislation following the March First Independence Movement provided Korean groups with a forum through which to voice their opinions on Japanese administrative practices. The Japanese police subjected the Korean media to strict censorship throughout this period, although they appeared more lenient during the initial half decade of indigenous press than after the administration enacted peace preservation legislation in 1925, and again after Japan went to war with China in 1937. By 1940 it had ordered all indigenous newspapers (except the *Maeil sinbo*) and many indigenous magazines to cease publication. As during the first decade of Japanese rule, we can assume that underground newspapers resumed operation (if they had ever ceased publication in the first place) after the Japanese reinstated the ban on non-government newspapers.[7]

Those who strove to prepare Koreans for their eventual independence, among which cultural nationalists formed the most important group, provided the most detailed critiques of Japanese assimilation policy. Michael E. Robinson describes the cultural nationalist movement as a collection of interests united in the belief that Korea's best chance for survival rested in the advancement of "a gradual program of education and economic development . . . to lay the basis for future national independence."[8] These efforts, which necessarily clashed with Japan's assimilation-directed education, made good use of the opportunities offered by Japan's relaxing its publication legislation. The Tong'a ilbo (East Asian Daily), one of the newspapers granted publication rights as part of the reforms enacted by Saitō's "cultural rule" (bunka seiji) policy, was particularly useful for this purpose. Over the early 1920s, the peak of the cultural nationalist movement, the newspaper sold more copies daily (37,802) than any of the other three Korean-language newspapers.[9] The Tong'a ilbo attacked Japanese rule directly from a variety of angles. It kept the idea of liberation alive among its readers by introducing other independence movements. It also attempted to build a Korean identity by introducing Korean history (it serialized an article on Korea's mythical founder titled "Tan'gun non" [Tan'gun Thesis] from April 1926, just as Korea's last emperor lay dying), by creating Korean heroes (one of the most popular was An Ch'angman, Korea's first aviator), and by promoting Korean self-strengthening by critiquing shortcomings in Korean society and culture.[10]

The newspaper frequently criticized Japan's fundamental policy, as well as its components. In April 1924 the Tong'a ilbo attacked the Saitō regime's "cultural rule" policies as the "rule of violence" (mokhaeng chŏngch'aek) that was driving the Korean people to anguish. Such a "narrow-minded policy," it remarked, could not possibly be considered "cultural."[11] The following August it challenged the legitimacy of Japan's assimilation policy. Why, the newspaper questioned, would Koreans want to become Japanese? The editorial explained: it is "hard to understand the life and customs of the Japanese." Their kimono and geta are not very practical items of clothing, the article stated. There also is nothing among Japanese customs that the Korean people find very attractive, at least not anything that would attract their voluntary acceptance of Japanese assimilation overtures.

The editorial then turned to Japan's education system: the school system is not very useful for building "youth character" as it does little to enhance the students' scientific knowledge. The institution's sole purpose was to Japanize Korean youth. What's more, the children are witness to Japanese deception.

> They know of its dishonesty. . . . Furthermore, they know that their teachers are the enemy. They know that their grandfathers and fathers have had to endure cruel persecution at the hands of the Japanese. They have observed the Japanese police passing through their house and committing brutal acts against their parents. Can such children ever be Japanized?[12]

The *Tong'a ilbo* often exploited the system's fundamental purpose, to Japanize Korean youth, to attack Japan's fundamental assimilation policy. Not only did it rob the Korean people of their heritage, but it also placed them at a severe disadvantage in that they had to study in a foreign environment and language. This extra burden "stifled the natural development of Koreans." The newspaper instructed: as education was most important for a people's modernization, and as the ages between five and twelve were critical for a child's development, schools were required to provide students with an education in the language that is most natural to them. The Japanese system fails miserably in this regard.[13]

Other Koreans joined the newspaper in attacking the education system. In 1930, Chu Yosŏp, in his 1930 publication titled *Chosŏn kyoyuk ŭi kyŏrham* (Deficiencies in Korean Education), challenged Japan's stated dedication to educating Koreans by questioning why it provided space for only 20 percent of Korean children, while it found room to accommodate 99.5 percent of the Japanese student population. Why, he continued, does it employ over three times as many spies as teachers (30,000 to 8,111)? He calculated Saitō's plan to build one school per village (*myŏn*) as insufficient: with the size of Korean villages ranging from 220 to 5,300 children, and the average number of students attending a single school being 280, the Japanese would have to build an average of three to four schools per village to sufficiently meet Korean needs.[14]

Chu believed the problem to be one of priorities rather than revenue. Was, he inquired, the 50 million yen spent on railroad work a greater priority than the Korean children who could not attend school? Did the peninsula need an imperial university that absorbed 2 million yen to educate ten thousand (primarily) Japanese students? Would not the reallocation of these funds to elementary education better serve the needs of the Korean people?[15] The problem was more acute in women's education: only 7 percent of Korean girls could attend elementary school. He instructed that a "healthy development of Korea could not take place if Korean men and women are [educated] at the present pace. . . . Korea's advancement awaits the awakening of the Korean woman."[16] Messages by the *Tong'a ilbo* and Chu resembled those delivered by the Japanese and pro-Japanese Koreans, but differed in the envisioned result. Questions that divided the two reflected those considered prior to annexation: how much outside assistance was required for Koreans to attain these goals? Some, like Yun Ch'iho, believed Japanese presence to be beneficial if only the colonizers could shed their arrogant attitude toward the Korean people and realize their ultimate goal as Korean independence.[17]

The Christian independence leader Yŏ Unhyŏng delivered to the Japanese a similar message during his trip to Japan soon after the March First demonstrations. At this time Yŏ had been invited to Tokyo to meet with government and military officials to discuss Korea's relations with Japan. His invitation proved to be highly controversial on both sides. Many Japanese questioned why their government was inviting to Japan a "criminal" who had participated in the anti-Japanese demonstrations and was now a member of the illegal Provisional Government of the Republic of Korea.[18] His Korean compatriots urged him to decline this offer, some going so far as to call his visit "the people's shame" (*minzoku no haji*).[19] Reasons provided by Christian missionary Fujita Kyūkō, who was instrumental in arranging Yŏ's visit, offered cooptation as a reason for Japanese inviting Yŏ to Japan. He explained in a letter to Colonial Chief Koga Renzō that appeasing Yŏ offered the "most peaceful approach to running the administration." Fujita advised Koga to "inform Yŏ of Japan's intentions to declare [Korea's right to] self-determination in due time, and to warmly welcome him and guarantee absolutely his security." At any rate, he suggested, "just keep him coming back, even with his associates, so as to make him your tool" (*rakuryōchū*).[20]

Yŏ arrived in Tokyo on November 17, 1919, to begin his two-week stay. While in Tokyo, he was granted audience with members of the Hara cabinet, including Prime Minister Hara Takashi, Koga, and War Minister Tanaka Giichi, as well as with private citizens such as Yoshino Sakuzō.[21] He also gave a public lecture at the Imperial Hotel and met with Korean students. At the Imperial Hotel he spoke on the divine rights of freedom and equality. Yŏ began by inquiring as to what authority allowed the Japanese to restrict these

rights from the Korean people. At present, he continued, the global movement is toward female and labor liberation in both Japanese and Korean
societies. These demands, Yŏ attested, had gained "even God's approval."[22]

Yŏ continued to press liberation in his discussions with Japanese political leaders. He reminded Koga that it had been the Japanese who from
ancient times had imported Korean culture. More recently Japan had fought
two wars allegedly to protect Korea's independence. Yet it had been the Japanese who violated Korea's sovereignty by annexing the peninsula. Yŏ's Christian influence emerged when he warned Koga of the ill fortune that awaited
Japan as retribution for its having sowed the seeds of calamity on the Korean
Peninsula.[23] His discussions with the colonial minister were relatively
congenial—Koga even invited Yŏ to his house—compared to those with
General Tanaka Giichi. Tanaka was an influential member of the Seiyūkai
political party; in the late 1920s he would serve as Japan's prime minister
until dismissed by the emperor.[24] Before Tanaka Yŏ boldly declared that the
Japanese could "murder all of us at once; they could even cut off my head.
They could not, however, kill the spirit of Korea's 20 million people; nor
could they sever my spirit." He likened Japan to the recently sunken *Titanic*,
a ship of whose splendor people boasted to the world. Similar to its fate, the
Japanese were heading straight for disaster even though the iceberg floated
directly in front of their eyes.[25]

During these discussions Yŏ argued that peace and stability in East Asia
were dependent on, rather than threatened by, an independent Korea. The
Korean people's long history, unified language and customs, and homogeneous population made it impossible for Japan's assimilation policy to succeed. Yet, he also emphasized that independence did not mean isolation.
Rather, he believed that a policy designed to awaken East Asia—Japan, Korea,
and China—was required to advance a political world of peace. Should Japan
fail to heed this warning, he (correctly) predicted, the world will once again
experience the disaster of war.[26] But, as Yŏ emphasized in his Imperial Hotel
speech, if Japan were to grant Korea its independence, it would be in Korea's
interests to join Japan and China in an "Oriental group."[27]

The *Tong'a ilbo*, as well, focused on the message of liberation, so much so
that within months of its first publication the government-general slapped
the newspaper with its harshest penalty—indefinite closure. On occasion the
newspaper directly advocated Korean independence. More often it kindled
this message by invoking other colonial liberation movements. The *Tong'a
ilbo* used its very first issue, printed on April 1, 1920, to declare imperialism

to be an institution in its twilight years. Declarations by the Russian V. I. Lenin and President Woodrow Wilson, along with the recent uprisings by colonized peoples around the world were telltale signs of its imminent demise. The newspaper editorialized: "with the coming of spring the hard packed snow melts" and a hundred flowers bloom. Nothing can be done to prevent this new spring as its trajectory is natural rather than artificial. A new world, it concluded, is unfolding. So in the dark we fight to give birth to this child. The shape of this "new culture" and the "rays of the dawn of this new era can be seen in the distance."[28]

The *Tong'a ilbo* followed a practical manifestation of the new era's rays in the Irish liberation movement, at the time the most active independence movement. The newspaper saw in the Irish example a European reflection of Korea's fate. The two peoples shared geographical and historical similarities in that both peoples were subjugated by colonizers who crossed a body of water to colonize them; both peoples had also been betrayed by treacherous traitors. That the Japanese and the English, both island nations, shared a political alliance at the time of Korean annexation no doubt strengthened Korean identification with the Irish example.[29] In September 1924 the *Tong'a ilbo* used Ireland's success at gaining its independence to warn the Japanese of their fate.

> The fatal blow [annexation] was dealt to Ireland. At the same time, an equally fatal curse was voluntarily invoked upon the British Empire. The crushing of a neighboring nation must have been gloated over by the leaders of the English government. But they knew little of what their joy would cost their country in subsequent centuries.[30]

The newspaper followed this editorial with one the next month that compared the nationalist activities of the 3 million Koreans who had migrated to Manchuria and Siberia with the guerrilla warfare that Irish nationalists conducted to secure their nation's independence.[31]

The Indian liberation movement provided the newspaper with another, albeit less frequent, example to strengthen its readers' aspirations of liberation. On one occasion the newspaper introduced Mahatma Gandhi as the "bare footed saint and the maker of new India, along with his efforts to liberate India from British rule."[32] It occasionally reported on secret meetings organized by independence groups, as well as news of Indian demonstrations against their British subjugators. We find signs that these messages were reaching their intended audience. In December 1927 the *Tong'a ilbo* carried a story of a Korean elementary school student who was punished for suggesting that India faced the same repressive predicament as Korea.[33]

In addition to contemporary examples, the newspaper also ran historical accounts of successful independence movements, particularly those of nations that were in a position to help Korea. In addition to instilling hope within its readers, these articles—often written about the United States example and in English—also served to remind people that the dream of the Koreans was one that their forefathers cherished. Authors decorated these messages with rhetoric familiar to Americans—"taxation without representation," "freedom," and "democracy"—to emphasize their shared values. One such display appeared in the *Tong'a ilbo*'s August 24, 1920, issue, just as the United States congressional tour arrived in Keijō. Had the American guests obtained a copy of this edition (and chances are they did not) the congressmen could not have missed the banner English-language headline that welcomed Korea's "brothers" to the peninsula. Nor could they have missed the lengthy article, again in English, that emphasized freedom and democracy. It lectured: the United States has been from early on a "refuge for the oppressed. . . . That is why America has been loved and respected by the troubled and the tyrannized." The Korean people, it continued, were ready to "make sacrifice for . . . the principle of *democracy*." This welcome concluded by imploring the tour members to "carry our hopes" back to the United States. Although Koreans and Americans are separated geographically, "there can be nothing which can separate us in our love and common ideals."[34] The government-general tried to discourage the tour from passing through Korea by sending it reports of an alleged cholera outbreak in the colony. It succeeded in wooing the American guests with tours that displayed their progress in the colony. But Koreans remained out of their reach. The one member who made contact with Koreans, Congressman Hugh S. Hersman of California, attended a reception scheduled to be held (but canceled) at the YMCA in the congressional tour's honor. Police broke up the meeting, but Hersman left only after his Korean hosts, who had been beaten and arrested, were released.[35]

The *Tong'a ilbo* did not fool Japanese officials by its attempt to camouflage its Korean independence advertisements with news of foreign liberation movements. In a September 1920 letter announcing its decision to indefinitely halt the newspaper's operations, the government-general listed two serious infractions that forced its hand. First, the newspaper was guilty of characterizing as superstition the Japanese worship of the three imperial treasures, the mirror, the jewel, and the sword. Secondly, it accused the *Tong'a ilbo* of using "cryptic language" (*ŭnŏ*) and "antonyms" (*panŏ*) to mask its true intention—to promote interest in Korean independence, and specified its use of the Irish example for this purpose. The *Tong'a ilbo* had violated the Japanese intention behind allowing the newspapers publication rights—to promote culture among Koreans.[36] The ban successfully halted the newspaper's publication up through the following April.

Calls for Korean liberation from social and cultural practices viewed as uncivilized served two purposes: in addition to providing more "cryptic language" to promote liberation, they addressed areas that reform-minded Koreans believed required attention if Korean capability for independence was to be respected outside its borders. Without a modern culture Koreans could hardly expect foreign powers, much less the Japanese, to recognize their appeals for sovereignty. Not surprisingly, many topics addressed by the Korean media overlapped with those in the Japanese media.[37] Gender relations provide one such example. By stressing the importance of gender reform, Korean writers joined a global movement that encouraged the emergence of a liberated "new woman." The *Tong'a ilbo* characterized the "new [Korean] woman" as the saving grace of the Korean people: Korean society could not properly advance without female liberation from the inner quarters. A woman's liberation required her being properly educated for her own advancement, rather than simply to improve her marriage portfolio. This was the theme of a series of articles offered by Ok Sunch'ŏl in October 1926. The Korean woman, Ok began, must properly prepare herself to be treated as her male counterpart's equal. She could not expect perfect equality unless she earned this right. Although education provided the opportunity to prepare herself to be regarded as equal, many women, Ok said, have abused this privilege by using it as an "ornament to upgrade [their] marriage choices." If a woman engaged in learning only for this purpose, she was merely "applying a new color to an existing doll; her education thus serves as a new cosmetic. The inner remains unchanged as the outer undergoes this beautification process."[38] Part of the problem lay in the content of the education that Japanese schools offered. Educating women as Japanese, rather than Korean, would compromise their ability to serve Korea. In September 1929 the *Tong'a ilbo* demanded that Korean women be trained for use in Korean, rather than Japanese, society. She must be taught how to serve tea on a Korean *ondol* floor rather than a Japanese *tatami* floor.[39]

Those critiquing women's education in other media went further. Paek Pa, writing for the *Hyŏndae p'yŏngnon* (Contemporary Review), also blamed Japanese schools for the pitiful plight that it led the "so-called new woman": it failed to produce anything "new." Instead this "new woman's education" is no more than a ruse to promote "good wife-wise mother" ideology. Universal education, Paek offered, was one way that the controlling class sought its benefits. The "ideal returns" targeted by this education system were the creation of a "good wife" to serve her husband, and a "wise mother" to educate her children.[40]

Critics also targeted the traditional "good wife" expectation of Korean men; specifically, the barriers that this expectation erected prevented them from advancing in society, and consequently Korea from advancing its feudal society. Under fire were the double standards that traditional Korean society maintained—it permitted husbands to engage in extramarital affairs while it chastised women for any display of jealousy over men's infidelity, and punished her severely if she was unfaithful. Hong Kwon criticized the Korean male for not living up to his own expectations of his wife. This caused decay in male-female sexual morals. Korean society, Hong explained, expected the female to remain physically loyal to her male partner before, during, and after marriage (in the case of widowhood). Korean society did not, however, believe it necessary to insist on this same loyalty from the male, whose sexual promiscuity contributed to his personal honor, and criticized the jealous wife who questioned or complained of her husband's extramarital affairs; it discriminated against the divorced women and any children that she might bear following separation, while remaining silent over the husband's remarriage and postseparation offspring.[41]

Korean writers linked gender reform directly to Korean social reform. The liberation of Korean society from its traditional past rested on its ability to reform its gender relations. Yi Kiwon warned in the *Tong'a ilbo* that progress could not be expected unless it liberated the female from her "slave-like existence."[42] Another Korean, who preferred to remain anonymous, blamed gender inequality for Korea's social weakness, and linked this shortcoming to the degeneration of Korea's "unique and beautiful customs." The Japanese and Chinese, the author lamented, have been able to absorb the new culture delivered by the West. In Korea, "our people sleep." The article continued: "Our culture and industry have disappeared. How will we survive?" The solution lay in the antithesis of Japanese assimilation—Koreans' "regeneration" as a people. This task required the Korean people to embark on a bidirectional path: the study of Korea's ancient culture and the adoption of the new global culture. The author emphasized the former. All people have their history as well as their spirit. "If the people are ignorant of that which made them Korean they cannot be considered individuals." As they come to understand their national character and talents they come to understand their national spirit. Through this process they gain confidence as a people.[43] This argument, of course, embraced the primary question that all reformers of this time faced—how to "catch up" with a foreign culture and still maintain one's ethnic roots. The Japanese had answered this question by resurrecting the imperial household; the author of this article believed Koreans were still at a loss as to how best to untangle this riddle.

Koreans used the media to propose their visions of a utopian postliberated Korea.[44] In May 1920 the *Tong'a ilbo* offered its own proposal. Its vision first criticized the traditional "machine-like society" that had frustrated Korean advancement to date. The editorial likened this society to a honeybee colony that prohibited individual expression by placing royalty at its apex and military and labor at its nadir. Such a social structure blocked individuals from acquiring a consciousness or any potential for self-reliance. The ideal society to replace this traditional system resembled an orchestra in which all sounds emitted from the various instruments maintained their unique characteristics, but harmonized into a single unit when the conductor raised his baton. Similarly, members of this society merge their individual talents to create a harmonious social orchestra. Gaining liberation from the mechanical social structure required the Koreans to accomplish two goals: individuals shedding their dependency on others, and the congregation of self-reliant individuals harmonizing in social communion.[45]

This editorial never reached the public, as Japanese censors ordered it erased from the newspaper's May 17, 1920, edition. Just what in this editorial irked the censors is not clear. The editorial came at a rather lenient time in terms of censorship. This particular editorial paled in the face of other more blatant calls for Korean liberation that, along with attacks on the emperor system, generally encouraged the censor's knife.[46] Censors perhaps interpreted the message as yet another case of "cryptic language" that characterized Japan's imperial system as "machine-like." The editorial was vague in this regard: it could just as easily have had contemporary Japan, Chosŏn Korea, or both, in mind. While the newspaper never shied from voicing its distain for Japanese rule, among its writers were those who blamed Korea's past rulers for obstructing the Korean people from attaining the self-reliance they needed to assemble their social orchestra. The realization that these traditional and contemporary barriers could not be overcome any time soon encouraged many prominent members of the cultural movement to shed nationalist sentiment for cooperation with the Japanese, particularly after Japan's continental advancement provided enhanced opportunity for Koreans.

CRITIQUES BY KOREAN "COLLABORATORS"

Collaboration has proven to be problematic in all occupational situations;[47] Korean collaboration served as the antithesis to the critical response examined above. The North and South Korean governments handled pro-Japanese (*ch'inilp'a*) elements rather differently following liberation. North Korea purged most Koreans deemed to have collaborated with the Japanese occupiers, while South Korea utilized the talents and experiences they had acquired over this period. Although the South Korean government carried out investigations in 1949 and 1960, this work was never completed to the satisfaction of all Koreans. From the 1990s, private and government groups initiated new efforts to identify these people.[48] Examining the "collaborator" requires consideration of their vision of Korea's future: did they advocate Korean absorption by the Japanese or, rather, their inclusion under more equal terms in a greater pan-Asian community? Those seen as guilty of collaboration are criticized for their support of a policy that refused to recognize the Korean culture's right of existence. Some, no doubt harbored this aspiration. With others, however, their vision of the future more accurately resembled a partnership, a union of the Korean and Japanese cultures within the context of a broader Asian alliance. This interpretation helps us understand the sentiments behind Cho Pyŏngsang's pride in sending his son to the Japanese military, as well as his claim that more Koreans had come to accept Japanese rule since the 1931 Manchurian Incident, a time from which Korean opportunities on the Asian continent increased dramatically.[49] It also helps explain the support voiced by Koreans for Japan's *Naisei ittai* strengthening movement, those who, in attendance at meetings convened to critique this document, generally voiced support for its contents but questioned whether it was in Japan's interests to push the policy to its logical limits. And it would explain the glee expressed by Yun Ch'iho on December 8, 1941, over the "electrifying news" that Japan had attacked both English and American territories: "A new Day has indeed dawned on the Old World! This is a real war of races—the Yellow against the White."[50]

Regardless of whether collaborating Koreans interpreted assimilation as their integration into a Japanese or larger Asian community, it was their view that Koreans could not manage their own country that drew them to the Japanese. Korea, as a small and weak territory, could hardly be expected to retain its sovereignty should it gain independence. Its merger into a larger geopolitical community, either as a Japanese prefecture or a member of a pan-Asian alliance, provided the better chance for Korean prosperity. Inquiry into collaborator motivations, as well as their guilt or innocence, is beyond the parameters of this study. Instead, our purpose is to abstract from their views the strengths and weaknesses of Japanese assimilation policy. As supporters of a policy that sought their allegiance, collaborators' critiques advised its improvement rather than its abolishment.

Koreans became attracted to Japan's Meiji reform movement soon after Japan "opened" Korea in 1876. Many came to see their country's future as part of either Japan or a larger pan-Asian bloc from the protectorate period. The Russo-Japanese War served as a critical turning point in Korean thinking. Son Pyŏnghŭi, a leader of the Ch'ondogyo (Religion of the Heavenly Way), saw Korea's fate as determined by the results of the Russo-Japanese War: Korea would merge with the victor. Kim Tohyŏng writes that Japan's victory made certain Koreans realize the advantages of being controlled by a Japanese yellow race over a Russian white one. He quotes Kim Kajin, who served as vice minister of foreign affairs at the time Japan negotiated the protectorate treaty, as arguing that Korea could survive only if it forged stronger ties with Japan to preserve East Asian peace.[51] Han Myŏnggŭn remarks that Yi Wanyong, who as prime minister signed the 1910 annexation treaty and later accepted a peerage title, praised Itō Hirobumi's "Korea-Japan one family" (*Ilhan ilga*) idea as the saving grace for East Asian peace and prosperity.[52] Recent research has even considered the Ilchinhoe, who lobbied for Japan's annexation of Korea, in this light.[53]

The post-March First government-general monthly organ, *Chōsen*, offered Japan's Korean supporters a chance to voice their opinions on Japanese administration practices should they prove capable of delivering their manuscripts in Japanese. Predictably Korean contributions gave Japanese policy positive appraisals; their criticism tended to be constructive. Much of their writing parroted the administration's line that annexation was necessary to secure regional peace and prosperity. The periodical occasionally grouped articles thematically in special issues, thus suggesting that the government-general often solicited writing from Koreans.[54] Han Yun's contribution to the September 1921 issue, which argued that Japanese rule in Korea "created order out of the dark government's disorder of the past," is typical. Han complimented the Meiji Emperor's ability to "see the entire Orient as one family, and love entirely the Korean people as his subjects." Reflecting on the participants in the March First Movement, he chastised those who sought Korean independence from Japan as "climbing a tree to look for a fish."[55]

A second contributor to this particular issue, Ch'ae Mandal, was more critical of the Japanese than Han, but arrived at a similar conclusion. After warning that Japanese might find it hard to accept what he was about to argue, he implored them to adopt a more progressive attitude toward the Korean people. Koreans are not all troublemakers; yet, Japanese tend to look at only their bad points. He particularly cited Korea-based Japanese who treated Koreans with contempt. Where was the Japanese warmth that he had felt when he resided in Japan? Ch'ae offered the administration a few words of advice. First, the Japanese concept of *yūwa* (unity) required clarification. Both sides needed to reflect on its meaning. He contextualized his second piece of advice in greater Japan: invoking the British use of the Irish in their empire, he advised the Japanese to make better use of Koreans in their empire. It was, after all, Korea's existence that had made Japan's military wars with China and Russia possible and had gained Japan a place of prominence in world affairs.[56]

Others offered their opinions directly to the government-general in the form of private "opinion papers" (*ikensho*). These opinions, apparently not solicited and less public, were generally less conciliatory in tone. Kim Yŏng-sun, a self-proclaimed former "insubordinate Korean" (*futei senjin*), accused the government-general of treating Koreans as Japanese "stepchildren" (*mamako*). Yet, rather than advocate Japan's retreat, Kim explored a more useful Japanese-Korean relationship, one he likened to that which a "strict father and a benevolent mother would nurture with their [biological] children."[57] Other criticism simply requested that the Japanese administration provide the Korean people with the means to enjoy a humane life, as demonstrated by Han Ŭn's pithy, but poignant, list of requests:

1   Listen to the voice of the Korean people.
2   Utilize the intentions of the Korean masses. (An organ for public opinion is needed.)
3   Please let something [food?] pass through our stomachs.

4   Don't let the unrest of the so-called lawless Koreans persist.
(Don't let a person's position be a problem; if they have qualifications use them.)

5   Put off construction projects that are not critical until later,
including unnecessary road repairs, railroads, office buildings,
and school construction.[58]

In a word, Kim's requests encouraged the Japanese to construct practical
policy that lent an empathetic ear to Korean concerns.

Others made use of the Japanese media to voice their criticisms. Yi Yŏng-
sun's remarks, carried in the May 1937 issue of *Jiyū* (Freedom), are most
valuable as they appeared just two months before the Marco Polo Incident
initiated more stringent wartime publication controls as the fighting on the
continent intensified. Yi's thoughts suggest a person whose efforts to blend
into Japanese society had been rebuked by even Japanese he counted among
his acquaintances, if not friends. His search for clues to Japanese-Korean
unity (*Naisen yūwa*) assumes a sarcastic tone as he questions the Japanese
dedication to the unity they preach. If Japanese valued unity,

> why are Koreans not offered military duty rights? Is it because
> Koreans do not have patriotism? Why can't Koreans participate
> in elections? Is it because Koreans are uneducated? If the Japanese
> truly wish to attain Japanese and Korean unity they first have to
> consider Koreans as their equal. . . . In the colony there are Japanese
> schools and Korean schools. It would be better if both people stud-
> ied together. However, the Japanese do not want their cute child
> studying with dirty mischievous [Korean] child. . . . Where is this
> Japanese-Korean unity?

Yi's appraisal of his Japanese acquaintances suggests his relatively successful
integration into Japanese society. Yet, his integration had only created more
frustrations. He interpreted the low sense of obligation and human feeling
that he saw in his Japanese acquaintances as indicative of Japanese as a whole.
Japanese, considering themselves to be superior, regularly took advantage of
the merchants' ignorance by cheating them. Japanese who had stayed at his
house, and had even borrowed money from him, often left without saying
good-bye and neglected to repay their debt. Yi pondered, are obligation and
human feeling character traits that Japanese practice only among their own
people? Are they not applicable to their relations with Koreans as well?

Yi felt Japanese inconsideration to be anything but unique. He compared it to the relations existing between blacks and whites in the United States. He noted that the Korean people greeted the news of their fellow country-man Son Kijŏng winning the 1936 Olympic marathon not as a victory for Japan, under whose flag the runner participated, but one for the Korean people. Blacks in the United States, he surmised, must have enjoyed a simi-lar feeling when Joe Louis scored a knockout victory over a white boxer. Rather than as a problem unique to Japanese and Koreans, Yi recognized discrimination as endemic to many different peoples throughout the world.[59] These comments suggest little progress in the challenge made by the now deceased Hara Takashi in 1919 when the prime minister warned of the harm to Japan's mission in Korea should they fail to properly integrate the Korean people into their lives.

From 1937, war escalation forced the government-general to once again reevaluate its Korean policy. The review of the *Naisen ittai*-strengthening document gave Koreans another example to critique Japanese assimilation policy. Discussion meetings held behind closed doors empowered the Kore-ans in attendance to voice their opinions rather bluntly, and many directly challenged Japanese policy for failing to live up to its hype. The twelve Korean participants selected by the government-general were among the Japanese administration's most trusted Korean allies, people who had staked their future and their reputation on Japan maintaining long-term control over the Korean Peninsula. To them, Korean independence represented the worst possible scenario. Rather, Korean liberation from their traditional roots, and Japanese recognition of Koreans as imperial subjects, constituted the scenario that would best secure their fortunes and dignity. Carter J. Eckert describes these Koreans as individuals who "had to abandon whatever nationalist aspirations they might once have had and were ready to embrace a new Japanese order that left no room for the expression of a separate Korean identity."[60]

The Japanese requesting input on such an important policy revision must have encouraged Korean confidence regarding the colonizers' sincerity in their assimilation mission. The *Naisen ittai* document must have reinforced their confidence by emphasizing Japan's role on the Asian continent and the need to enlist Korean assistance to secure Japan's interests. The meetings, which convened from early September 1938, entertained the following top-ics for discussion: strengthening and completing *Naisen ittai*; advancing social links between Korea, Manchuria, and China; providing protection and guidance for China-based Koreans; and improving Korean (*hantōjin*) physical strength and reforming their lifestyles. Compared to the rather positive opinions offered by the Japanese at this meeting (as introduced in chapter 5), Korean commentary reflected back to Japan's original administrative vows to uplift Koreans in preparation for their assimilation. Given that very few changes were made from the original draft to the final version of the document, it is fair to question the sincerity of the Japanese interests in hearing Korean views. Was their purpose not, once again, to co-opt?[61]

The first issue—strengthening and completing *Naisen ittai*—occupied the better part of the discussion. Ch'oe Rin, a central organizer of the 1919 independence movement but now president of the *Maeil sinbo*, offered that Koreans required the Japanese to better "clarify Japan's national polity" (*kokutai*). He advised that Koreans and Chinese (*Han minzoku*) would embrace this polity because they cannot boast the equivalent of the Japanese unbroken line of emperors. More practical changes, however, presented problems for Koreans born before annexation. He used as an example his family's reluctance to change. The Japanese and Korean cultures were different and older people were having difficulties adjusting. Women objected to wearing socks in summer, and they did not like walking in Japanese traditional *geta* shoes. He predicted that those born after annexation would find the transition easier.[62] Here Ch'oe seemed to be encouraging the Japanese to maintain its gradual pace, despite the urgency suggested in the Counterplan Proposal.

Han Kyubok, a member of the Korean central advisory committee (*chūsūin sangi*) to the government-general, agreed with Ch'oe in principle but differed with him on the contention that younger Koreans would prove to be more cooperative. He explained that it had only been recently, since the 1931 Manchurian Incident, that Koreans had made advances. Korean education must begin with the basics. "Even if Japanese push '*Naisen ittai*,' Koreans have to realize that they have become a subject (*shinmin*) of the great Japanese Empire (*Dai Nippon teikoku*). But first they have to gain an understanding of the fundamental terms *country* and *my country*.[63] Here Han seemed to be tacitly underscoring the need for the government-general to extend its education program to more Koreans.

The most valuable comments made by the Korean participants targeted not only the core problem of Japanese administrative practices, but of assimilation as a policy in general: the reluctance of the colonized to introduce practices that would actually integrate the colonized with the colonizer. Yi Sŭngu's comments attacked two such issues: family registration and marriage registration. He noted the problem of Koreans who migrated to Japan having to maintain their legal addresses (*honseki*) in Korea. This prevented them from gaining full status as Japanese subjects (*kokumin*), which required their being permitted to transfer their family register (*koseki*) to their place of residence. This would seriously affect Japan-based Koreans who wished to join Japan's volunteer corps, because to complete their applications they had to travel to their Korean hometowns to obtain copies of their family registrations. Also, Japanese law prevented Korean males married to Japanese females from forming a family register in Japan, but allowed Korean wives to be included on their Japanese husband's register. This legislation—which served in Japan proper as well as throughout the empire—characterized the Koreans as different and even foreign. It required amending to unify peninsula-archipelago family registration laws (*kosekihō*).[64]

Yi also redirected the assimilation problem from Korean involvement to Japanese recognition of Korean inclusion. The government-general's Counterplan Proposal had focused on improving Korean understanding but offered little in the way of instructing the Japanese people on Korea's place in the empire. The Japanese, too, needed to be better informed. Yi began by making the extraordinary claim that "there was not a single Korean who did not agree with, or welcome, *Naisen ittai*," before adding the conditional caveat: "If this means that [Koreans] will be at the same level as Japanese (*Naichi to onaji teido*) then they will not run to communism or nationalism." He continued: "What about the Japanese? Naturally, there are many who embrace *Naisen ittai*, but there are others who disagree with it. Some feel that it would not work, while others feel troubled that Koreans and Japanese were to be considered as equals." He explained:

> I have traveled here and there in Japan, and save for the minority
> of those who travel frequently to Korea, the majority of Japanese
> have not the slightest idea about what Korea is. Some believe that
> because they have been to Korea a while back they know the coun-
> try. Some are talking about a time twenty years ago. They may
> know Korea of twenty years ago but they do not know contempo-
> rary Korea. . . . It is important for Japanese to understand Korea's
> present situation, the present state of the Korean people, and the
> value of the Korean Peninsula to the Japanese Empire.

He also cautioned that the Japanese have to come to accept Koreans as their ethnic brothers: people can go around saying *Naisen ittai! Naisen ittai*, but if they respond to Korean efforts to identify themselves as Japanese by refusing to accept them as such then people "will go about as they like" (*kattei ni suru*).[65]

The question that united Japanese and Korean commentary at these meetings was how to narrow the gap between Japanese and Koreans to allow both peoples to contribute better to the East Asian community that Japanese advertised. The question that divided them was one often found in different assimilation situations—when, if ever, would the colonizers allow the colonized to participate as equal members in the empire? In addition to offering the general impressions described above, Korean participants also advised more practical ways for the Japanese to accomplish this. Korean participants suggested that the Japanese make the peninsula's infrastructure more accessible to a greater number of Koreans. Yi Sŭngu advised the Japanese to build more Shinto shrines, one per village (*myŏn*), to shorten the distance that Koreans had to travel to pray.[66] Others advised that the government-general increase its efforts to appease rural Korea. Pak Chungyang of the Korean Industrial Bank (*Chōsen sangyō ginkō*) suggested that the Japanese locate more factories in rural areas to increase employment potential; Ch'oe Rin lobbied for more health facilities.[67] These changes would offer the Koreans more equal opportunity, which they believed would eventually bring them equal status.

The Koreans provided their Japanese hosts with a list of matters that required their attention should they hope to bridge gaps that separated the two peoples. Yi Kich'an, who also served on the central advisory committee, questioned why the Japanese could not unify professional credential systems. Why were credentials earned in Japan not recognized in Korea and vise versa?[68] Yi later advised changing a reverse-discrimination practice—higher tax rates being assessed in Japan than in Korea. Yi informed his fellow participants that Korean income tax was half that paid by homeland residents. Even if it took extra money out of Korean pockets, taxing them the same rate as Japanese would increase their economic asset to the empire. Korea's residents, too, must carry an equal share of the burden.[69]

Integration of neighborhoods remained an issue with the Korean participants. Pak Chungyang's contribution to these discussions echoed criticism put forth by Hara Takashi nineteen years previous: strengthening and completing *Naisen ittai* required the two people to associate with each other on a daily basis. Realizing this ambition required a substantial relocation of people. Pak requested his audience to "look at Honmachi," the center of Keijō's Japantown.

Even though Japanese have been coming more and more to Korea, as seen in places like Honmachi, they form groups that are exclusively Japanese. They form no ties with the Korean villages. There is no possible way for the two people to come together under these circumstances. I believe that the Japanese must enter Korean farm villages . . . to mix with the Korean people. A bureaucratic-civilian company under the Oriental Development Company must be formed. The Japanese government can place Japanese in the Korean villages. In this way Koreans will come to understand Japanese, and Japanese will come to understand Koreans. Their spirits (*tamashii*) will bond.

Echoing suggestions from others, Pak's plan required amendments to this piece of legislation that inhibited assimilation, such as easing requirements that complicated Koreans' travel to Japan. His plan also called for the relocation of 10 million Koreans (half its population) to places in Japan, Manchuria, and China to make way for Japanese farmers arriving from the archipelago.[70] This plan was not unique. The Japanese had offered similar migration plans since the era of protectorate rule. These plans failed to encourage Japanese migration as, based on faulty population estimates, the available land for these Japanese to farm simply did not exist.[71] Opportunities increased after the Japanese established a puppet government in Manchuria. As one Japanese commented, "old pessimism toward migration was suddenly transferred into optimism."[72]

The twelve Korean participants at these sessions, rather than challenging Japan's fundamental idea of strengthening *Naisen ittai*, embraced it. Indeed, their comments reflected disappointment over the plan's fundamental omission—providing the tools and guidance to fell barriers that sustained Japanese and Korean segregation. As Yi Sŭngu's comments suggested, it mattered little that Koreans attended Japan's schools, learned to speak Japan's "national language," and adapted to Japan's "national customs" if the Japanese themselves failed to recognize these Koreans as their fellow subjects. Their concerns targeted a major omission in the lengthy Counterplan Proposal—its neglect to suggest ways to instruct the Japanese on the Korean people's new position in the empire. This omission, far from being unique to the 1938 document, underlay decisions and statements issued by Japanese government officials as well as civilians throughout the duration of Japan's rule. In the Japanese mind, as with other colonizer administrations, the responsibility for assimilation depended on the rise of the colonized to the colonizers' standards, rather than a broadening of the colonizers' identity to accept the colonized as fellow subjects. While the Japanese debated the pace at which Koreans should be assimilated, they neglected to consider the criteria under which to gauge Korean progress toward this goal. Korean participants focused on what the Counterplan Proposal omitted rather than what it emphasized: the practical steps needed to desegregate Japanese and Korean lifestyles to build this community. This focus suggests Korean aspirations that Japan's long-term plans include their being recognized as Japanese' equals, that is as internally colonized subjects.

The impact that the comments made by Koreans had on Japanese is hard to assess. As we saw in the previous chapter, the government-general established ways to elicit Korean participation as recommended by the Counterplan Proposal, particularly by establishing local seminars, regular exercise sessions (*rajio taisō*), and extended sessions to study Japanese language and culture. Other practices, including education system mergers, military inclusion, and family name changes, were also endorsed in these discussions. The government-general also pushed northern Korean development more intensely from this time.[73] Koreans continued to write to Japanese audiences to demonstrate their support for Japan's imperial mission. However, prejudices lingered and suspicions intensified as the war escalated from continental confrontation to global warfare.

Hyŏn Yŏngsŏp's *The Path That the Koreans Must Take* represents one of the more comprehensive efforts by a Korean to demonstrate support for Japan's assimilation plan. The book, first published in 1938, apparently enjoyed success. By 1940 it had already reached its twelfth printing. Hyŏn's motivation was to delineate reasons why the Koreans must change: to narrow the gap separating the deprived Korean and the advanced Japanese. He then prescribed a remedy: the actions that Koreans must take to become "complete imperial subjects."[74] Hyŏn, who acknowledged his thoughts to be a result of his quest for truth that led him to read widely in Marxist, anarchist, and nationalist thought during his school days, became attracted to Japanese group-centeredness (over individualism) upon arriving in Tokyo. He now described himself as "one Japanese national" (*Nihon kokumin no hitori*) who felt a heavy concern for the people of his birthplace. Since the 1937 China Incident, he explained, the term *Naisen ittai* had injected optimism within the Korean population. However, optimism alone will not bring this union; much work needed to be done. He saw his book as his contribution toward helping Koreans understand their responsibilities.[75]

He began his monograph by describing the historical significance of what he termed Korea's "Meiji Restoration"—the Japanese annexation of the Korean Peninsula. Hyŏn's summary of pre-annexation Korean history proved harsher (but just as misinformed) than that offered by the Japanese: Korean history before 1910 was "hell": it had passed through a "dark history" as a "colony" under the Han Chinese; its culture did not even begin until the Three Kingdoms period; unlike Tokugawa Japan, Korea had never developed a popular culture. The people experienced little joy as they eked out a living without scripts or arts. Hyŏn then questioned why the people endured such a miserable existence. He offered a number of possible reasons: Korean character defects were at fault, but also their political, economic, and geographic situations. China's traditional influence, which had stifled Korea's development of a unique culture from the Silla period (698–935), must also be considered. Those who doubted this point, he challenged, need only go to China, where they will find the mold for any particular aspect of "original" Korean culture. Unlike the Japanese, Koreans produced no great works of literature such as the *Tale of Genji* or the eighth-century *Manyōshū* poetry collection. While the Japanese awoke from their *sakoku* (isolation) slumber in time to initiate a Meiji Restoration that positively incorporated European and American culture, the Koreans maintained their ill-directed era of a closed country.[76]

The Korean people had occasionally demonstrated potential. They introduced Buddhism to the Japanese. They developed movable type two centuries before the West developed it. However, these advances were limited to a "certain era and certain places rather than the total people, the total nation, and their total history." Buddhism began to fade in Koryŏ Korea (935–1392); Chosŏn Korea situated Buddhist monks at the lowest social rungs. Korea's invention of movable type did not initiate a boom in Korean literature.[77]

Japan's annexation of Korea allowed Koreans the opportunity to be rejuvenated as a new Korea (*shin Chōsen*) to replace that of their previous "half-Chinese" (*han Shinajin*) existence. But first Korea must break away from its narrowly conceptualized "familial ideology" (*kazokushugi*) ideals. Hyŏn quoted one Chinese critic, Rin Yu-tang, as saying the Chinese people would die for their family, but not for the state of the world, to explain Korean family-centered ideology. It was the Japanese "family spirit" (*kazoku seishin*)—

an idea that transcended the local for the national—which the Korean must adopt to embark on the path of their destiny. Hyŏn explained: the Japanese spirit was comprehensive (*zentai seishin*); the people would die for their country. The Korean, on the other hand, would die only for his wife, parents, or children.[78] The Japanese concept was one honored in the West, as demonstrated in Bertrand Russell's *The Problems of China*. The Westerner, he generalized, kisses his wife before paying the ultimate sacrifice; the Japanese yells *banzai* to his emperor before meeting his death in battle; the Korean (if he is to head for battle) thinks only of his wife and children before confronting his fate.

Both Japanese and Koreans honor a *kazokushugi*, Hyŏn stated, but of different kinds. The Japanese place themselves as children of the imperial family. Japanese raise their children with the idea of making them great members of the nation, even if it means beating them every day to produce this result. They, like the English, would never dream of rescuing their children from their duties to the nation. This fosters a sense of mutual respect between elder and youth. Korea's overconcentration on Confucian ideology in its society has thus had a negative effect. If Japanese society had not relied on a variety of ideologies, including Buddhism, Shintoism, and modern science, it would face consequences similar to those that hindered Koreans of today.[79] Lacking this sense of nation-as-family influenced the Koreans' lack of national sentiment: their selfish disposition eventually sacrifices the whole.

Hyŏn identified Korean society's biggest flaw as its total lack of responsibility. Korean banks have not performed as expected. Newspapers have been ordered to cease operations after they failed to live up to their promises. The entirety of Korean society has had to sacrifice at the expense of these institutions. He cited the 1936 Berlin Olympics, and specifically Son Kijŏng's victory in the marathon, as an example. Hyŏn reminded his readers that Son participated in the Olympics as a Korean, but a Korean raised as a Japanese. It was thus improper for the Korean people to celebrate his accomplishment as a victory for Korea. His criticism no doubt was fueled by Korean vernacular newspapers that superimposed a Korean flag over the Japanese flag on Son's uniform. This mentality needed to be amended along the path that the Koreans must take.

This path must begin, Hyŏn explained, with Koreans coming to understand the Japanese. They must first realize the "majestic existence" (*genzen to sonzai shiteiru*) of Japanese culture that synthesized different cultures. They must endeavor to "become Japanese" (as he had). That is, they must "shed the

Chinese *kanbun* culture and widely accept Japanese culture."[80] This was but the first step leading Koreans toward becoming "complete imperial subjects." Koreans must also recognize the "historic significance" of annexation and "thank Japan" for admitting their territory into its empire. Finally, the Korean people must recognize the "fate that the two peoples share [and] adopt a feeling of being Japanese." Like the Japanese, Hyŏn placed full responsibility on the Korean people embarking on this change. As Korea, he predicted, would never again return to the status of "independent country," it is Koreans' responsibility to adopt the spirit of Japanese subjects (*Nihon kokumin*) if they wished to attain full political rights, be provided with compulsory education, participate in Japan's military service, and gain freedom of residence. Koreans must "demonstrate their heightened respect and admiration for the emperor" (by making pilgrimages to the homeland and to Ise and Meiji shrines), embrace the Japanese language as their own, and discard their more obvious signs of Korean-ness (such as Korean dress, cuisine, and housing).[81] Admittedly this process would take time: Hyŏn calculated it would take hundreds of years of hardship. If Koreans were to accomplish what Japanese have accomplished over the past seventy years, he warned, they "must endure frantic efforts to study even harder than the Japanese did."[82] It was thus not the Japanese that blocked Korean progress, but the Koreans themselves. They just had to work harder at becoming Japanese.

If the Japanese required a poster boy to advertise the fruits of Korean cooperation, Hyŏn appears appropriate. He met all the basic criteria for assimilation: Japanese schooling, Japanese language fluency, and a Japanese family. His attitude was also very correct: not only did he consider himself assimilated as "one Japanese national," he also believed strongly that all Koreans should join him. If Hyŏn practiced what he preached, we can assume that his lifestyle blended closely with that of his Japanese neighbors, that he raised his children to speak and act like loyal Japanese subjects of the empire. We envision Hyŏn carousing with a close circle of Japanese friends—former classmates and business associates, making regular visits to the local shrine, and proudly observing proper protocol during Japanese holidays. We might suspect that one reason for his choosing to write in Japanese was necessity: his level of Korean was perhaps not good enough for him to do otherwise.

Yet, despite his apparent successful immersion into Japanese society, Hyŏn remained a legal alien in his adopted country. As a male Korean head of his household, he was unable to perform his most basic requirement of a

Japanese subject: registering his family record at the local ward office. This document he had to file and maintain in Korea, where he returned anytime he made changes in his or his children's (but not his Japanese wife's) status,[83] or anytime he required a copy. He was reminded of his Korean heritage every time he had to produce papers at a public office, and every time he passed to and from Korea. Despite his efforts to assimilate (he chose Amano Michiō as his Japanese name), the local police box no doubt recognized him as Korean, perhaps even penciling *senjin* (Korean) beside his Japanese name just to be on the safe side. They may also have subjected him on occasion to ethnicity tests that required people to answer questions designed to differentiate Koreans from Japanese (such as having them pronounce a word containing sounds difficult for Koreans to reproduce). People in his Japanese neighborhood, no doubt aware of his Korean heritage, perhaps made passing jokes regarding his ethnic roots either directly to him or behind his back. May we further speculate that Hyŏn's decision to write in Japanese stemmed from his desire to inform Japanese that among Koreans there were some who wished to be accepted by Japanese as their equals?[84]

The voices of many Koreans introduced here unite with those of the Young Algerians and of the Taiwan Assimilation Association in their acceptance of the colonizers' assimilation rhetoric, and their demands that their colonizers match their idealistic words with practical policy. They all saw their fates as resting in the hands of their subjugators, whose culture, politics, and society offered them the best road to civilization. Yet, all three experienced the occasion when, as Frantz Fanon writes, the colonized "suddenly discovers that he is rejected by a civilization which he has none the less assimilated."[85] Although advances were made, commentary by pro-Japanese Koreans exposed the rift that separated Japanese rhetoric from that country's true intentions. A fatal flaw with Japan's policy was that, despite efforts to unify school systems and personal names, its administration refused to allow Koreans to forget that they were indeed Korean, and not Japanese. Its bureaucracy stamped "Korean" over Japanized names on official documents.[86] Its police devised tests that focused on telltale characteristics of Koreans. Social Darwinists thus had it wrong in attributing assimilation's weakness to the expectation that the colonized could rise to the colonizer's level. Rather, it was an inflated self-image that prevented the colonizers from entertaining the idea, or made them fear the consequences, of their accepting a colonized people who had adopted their culture and language as their equal.

CONCLUSION: EVALUATING PERIPHERAL COLONIZATION

THE JAPANESE TOOK CONTROL OVER THE KOREAN PENINSULA, EXPRESSING confidence that in time their assimilation policy would eradicate differences between colonizer and colonized. Japanese and Koreans, they predicted, would one day unite as a single body. Koreans such as civil defense chief Cho Pyŏngsang, who offered his son to the Japanese military, and the author Hyŏn Yŏngsŏp, who mapped the path that Koreans must take to gain Japanese acceptance, now identified themselves as assimilated Japanese rather than Korean subjects. Their stories suggest that the Japanese assimilation policy realized success over Japan's tenure of colonial rule in Korea.

Other indicators compromised these success stories. Japanese rhetoric may have preached the merits of assimilation, but Japan's policy decisions often strengthened the differences that separated Koreans from Japanese. Koreans such as Yi Sŭngu, who supported assimilation, expressed doubts as to whether it was in the Japanese interests to accept Koreans as Japanese. Many more Koreans resisted assimilation altogether; others fled the peninsula to avoid it. Cho and Hyŏn's support for Japanese rule hardly represented the majority view among Koreans. Lingering segregation in schools, neighborhoods, and workplaces demonstrate that the government-general had not properly heeded Prime Minister Hara Takashi's 1919 warning of the perils that Japan's rule would confront should it fail to properly integrate the two peoples.

These problems, hardly unique to the Japanese-Korean relationship, reflected those found in other examples of peripheral colonization that adopted assimilation as its administrative policy. Forced assimilation at any level, internal or peripheral, provoked protests and demonstrations. The discriminative nature of peripheral colonialism, which preached a qualified internal colonialism but practiced a glorified external colonialism, satisfied few. Understanding Japan's assimilation policy in Korea requires inquiry into what prevented the Japanese from matching their ambitious rhetoric with an appropriate policy.

CAUTIOUS STEPS TOWARD ASSIMILATION

Dong Wonmo's study on social mobilization in colonial Korea concludes by stating that the Japanese had realized a "definite positive effect on [Korean] political integration of the native population." He based this conclusion on indicators in areas that suggested greater Japanese acceptance of Koreans: rising school attendance, more Koreans speaking Japanese, increased Korean-Japanese intermarriage, and more Korean employment in the government-general, to name a few.[1] These trends were certainly encouraging to Japanese officials, as well as to Japan's Korean supporters, both of whom cited the 1931 Manchurian Incident as a turning point in this process. Statistics, however, offer only the quantity dimension of the story. They are not useful for helping us understand the quality dimension: Did greater Korean participation in Japanese institutions increase their appreciation for things Japanese? Did this participation strengthen their identity as Japanese subjects? And to what extent were these increases due to the wartime situation that repatriated Japanese males to fight the war? Would these trends have continued had Japanese rule in Korea survived the war?

The Japanese made important gains in the physical integration of archipelago with peninsula, and then peninsula with continent. These infrastructural advancements encouraged interest in Japan's colonial administration both at home and abroad. Western observers gave the Japanese high marks for their improvements in Korea's transportation, communication, and health infrastructures.[2] The Japanese treated Western visitors, such as the 1920 congressional delegation, to tours that highlighted these advancements. The government-general continued to improve the education system that from the mid-1920s included a national university in Keijō Imperial University. Japanese today laud these improvements to combat criticisms over their harsh rule in Korea. These claims, however, suggest two suspicious conclusions. First, they suggest that Koreans could not have accomplished these advancements without Japanese assistance; they required Japanese colonial rule. We, of course, cannot turn back the clock to support or refute this statement. Yet, we must observe that since liberation the Korean people have proven themselves to be rather capable in this regard. This claim also suggests that the colonial government constructed its colonial infrastructure with Korean interests in mind. However, this defies logic. As with other colonizers, Japan's blueprint for this infrastructure clearly demonstrates the colonizer's plan to create peninsula-archipelago links. The Korea Peninsula unquestionably benefited from Japan's infrastructural initiatives after liberation. Yet, these initiatives were inadvertent, rather than deliberate, contributions to postliberation South Korea, and highly contingent on postwar decisions made by the United States to re-create Japan as its primary Asian ally after China was "lost." Japan's education system provides further counterevidence. Like the French in Vietnam and Algeria, the Japanese replaced Korean schools with Japanese schools. The system Japan introduced clearly favored Japanese expatriates over Korean children, as discussed throughout this book. This trend continued even in Keijō Imperial University (present-day Seoul National University), which opened in 1928. Between 1929 and 1938 the university enrolled more Japanese (68 percent) and employed more Japanese faculty (76 percent in 1938) than Koreans. The Japanese are to be credited with founding the university, which provided qualified Korean youth greater education opportunities. Yet, it would be overstating Japan's purpose to claim credit for the emerging of this university as South Korea's leading institute of higher education following liberation from Japanese rule.

Japan's colonial message also attracted interest among Koreans. The actions of the more active Koreans who publicly declared their support for Japan's war effort also constitute an important positive development of the period. Their motivations behind their participation were diverse. Personal gain certainly was one motivation. In many of these cases, as Carter J. Eckert demonstrates, capitalist interests trumped national interests.[3] Kyeong-Hee Choi suggests that a Korean "urge for modernity" attracted Koreans to the Japanese mission.[4] Other Koreans, convinced that small states such as Korea (and perhaps Japan) stood little chance of independent survival, welcomed the possibility of joining Japan in a pan-Asian community. These ambitions suggest the question of "pro-Japanese" Korean to be far more complicated than the idea of Koreans simply acting as traitorous Japanese lackeys. It further suggests that the Japanese and Koreans may have harbored conflicting images of "assimilation," with the Japanese envisioning a vertical cultural integration and the Koreans a more horizontal political and economic amalgamation.

Japan's engagement in total war from the late 1930s served as an important test for its assimilation experiment. The 1938 Counterplan Proposal to strengthen *Naisen ittai* emphasized the need for the government-general to intensify its infrastructural, as well as human development, efforts. Securing Korean loyalty presented Japan with its biggest challenge. As in the English and French cases with their colonies, the possibility of Koreans forming a fifth column to disrupt Japan's wartime efforts concerned the Japanese. This never materialized, although United States government documents reveal efforts being made to explore this potential.[5] Advancements realized by Koreans at this time surely helped secure their cooperation. In addition to occupational gains, the chance to enlist in the Japanese military provided Koreans with a hope for a brighter future should the Japanese emerge victorious.[6]

Victory draws a community together. It was instrumental in solidifying the United Kingdom and the British Empire; it sent Japanese out into the streets in celebration, and encouraged many of Japan's Ryukyu subjects to accept their fate as Japanese. We can imagine victory having a similar effect on Koreans. One Korean convicted of war crimes, Kasayama Yoshikichi (Korean name unknown), suggested the euphoria that might have erupted in Korea had the Japanese military returned in triumph in 1945. "Japan was victorious [after his induction and assignment to Java], and we all shared in the uproar and excitement. If you wore a Japanese star on your cap, you were really something."[7] We will never know the euphoria that Koreans might have felt had they been given the opportunity to witness Japanese and Korean boys marching side by side in a victory parade through the heart of Keijō's Japantown. Japan's total defeat encouraged equally negative Japanese images. Koreans reasoned that if they were a second-class people, the soundly defeated Japanese must be a fourth-class people.[8]

The argument can also be made that Japan's peripheral colonies succeeded in their most important role: protecting the security of the homeland. Intense Allied aerial bombing could not commence until the Allied forces drew near enough to safely conduct their bombing raids on Japanese cities. This required their battling Japanese forces up through the Pacific Islands that Japan occupied. One of its earliest peripheral acquisitions, the Ryukyu Islands, endured the war's bloodiest ground battle. Japan's occupation of the Korean Peninsula opened a corridor to the Asian continent; it also protected the homeland from direct Allied attacks from its western flank. Japan's military presence in its northern peripheral territories—Korea and Hokkaido—

would have detained the Soviet military had the Allied forces initiated their planned ground invasion of the archipelago. The war's sudden conclusion saved Japan from this tragedy, and perhaps division, had the Soviets been positioned to accept Japanese surrender in its northern prefectures. Japanese sometimes credit the atomic bombs for saving their country from this result; Koreans offer that it was Japan's late surrender that divided their country. Yet we can also argue that Japan's military presence in Korea, requiring disarming and repatriation, limited the Soviet Union's advance to northern Korea, allowing the United States to dominate the occupations of Japan and southern Korea. Seen in this way, the divided Korean Peninsula serves as an ongoing reminder of Korea's sacrifice to the Japanese people.

FLAWS AND OVERSIGHTS IN JAPAN'S ASSIMILATION POLICY

One important factor that complicates our ability to evaluate Japanese assimilation policy in Korea was its short duration. By Japanese estimates it would have taken from fifty to one hundred years to assimilate Koreans. Yet their tenure on the peninsula ended abruptly after thirty-six years. Dong's findings, and the writings of pro-Japanese Koreans, suggest that given time the Japanese could have achieved total assimilation. Considering the advances that Japan made over this period we cannot deny this possibility. However, our examination of Japanese assimilation policy revealed several fatal flaws that, if left unattended, would have inhibited Japanese ability to realize its assimilation goals. Here we will consider three such flaws: misconceptions of colonial realities, conflict between rhetoric and practice, and Japan's failure to consider alternatives approaches.

The first major flaw was Japan's misperceptions of the European examples and their implications for Korean assimilation. A closer examination of these examples might have enlightened their rule in Korea. Here Japanese interpreters erred in two ways: in the conclusions they drew about European assimilation relationships and their comparisons in their colonial practices, such as the English administrations in Wales, Scotland, and Ireland. Japanese reliance on these examples was not surprising, given the efforts they made to learn from Western institutions throughout the Meiji period. Other fledging colonial powers also turned to English and French experiences for guidance. Japan's mistake was in its drawing conclusions from a superficial understanding of their histories. Hara Takashi's 1895 arguments (which he later amended) present a case in point. While Hara invoked the European example, he never properly critiqued the policy but simply ascertained that these states practiced assimilation and Japan should do so as well. Rather than argue the factors that would allow Japan to succeed where others had failed, Japanese might have reflected on why states succeeded or failed to enlighten their application of the policy.

Japan's use of the United Kingdom example is illustrative. A closer look at the content of English practices beyond the simplistic Wales and Scotland success stories against the failed Irish example would have yielded invaluable insight as to why the Irish battled the English for independence while the Welsh and the Scots appeared to accept English rule. The lone conclusion offered by those who invoked this example considered the all-too-obvious (but at the same time misleading) religious difference—the clash between the Protestant English and the Catholic Irish. A more thorough review of these histories would have revealed to the Japanese that the early decades of English intrusion provoked resistance by the Welsh and Scots, as well.

Inquiry into the history of Irish-English relations would have enlightened Japanese on the background of Irish resistance. The English barred Catholics from civil rights available to Protestants. They also "transported" them from Ireland to make room for English migrants. Those who refused to relocate were subjected to painful and humiliating deaths.[9] Certain aspects of Japan's administration of Korea resembled this harsh treatment, a point that did not go unnoticed by Koreans. Japan also limited Korean participation in civil institutions. Many Japanese (and Koreans) proposed rather large-scale (albeit less violent) transportation plans in which Japanese migrants to Korea would push Korean migrants into Manchuria.

Further inquiry into the content of English administrations in Wales, Scotland, and Ireland would have also offered Japanese an alternative to total cultural assimilation that they pursued. Rather than encourage the intrusive policy that sought to replace the peoples' cultural foundation, the English pursued a positive policy that granted them a political voice (albeit a minority one) in the British Parliament. The English also incorporated these people as British, rather than as English (or "Engelsh" [English and Welsh]). In this sense, these peoples' incorporation assumed a hybrid identity into an exalted entity rendered superior to the core English. The more positive Korean responses to Japanese ambitions suggest this alternative to have held greater attraction than simply one that proposed Koreans' absorption as Japanese.

Japanese might have gained insight over its administrative policies in

Korea had it turned more to its own experiences for guidance. Curiously these comparisons rarely appeared in print.[10] Kita Sadakichi used the Ainu example to argue Japanese qualifications as practitioners of assimilation. Nitobe Inazō examined differences between Japanese colonial rule over Korea and Taiwan in a January 1920 article titled "Japanese colonization." His description of their differences—their vastly different histories— suggests why Japanese relied on the European example over Japanese examples. Nitobe wrote that the short Taiwanese history could not compare with Korean pride "on being one of the oldest nations on earth." For this reason, he added, "self-determination" is far more popular in Korea than in Taiwan.[11] Despite the lack of attention, the Japanese rule in Korea benefited from governing experiments and policy decisions made in Taiwan before Korea's annexation, including the very decision to adopt assimilation as its governing mechanism.

The more often used comparison drew from Japan's internal population, which suggests that Korea's assimilation could be less than total and still be successful. Japanese, after all, accepted residents of Kyushu and the northeast regions as "Japanese" even though their customs and language differed from that which Japanese had come to regard as standard. This idea recognized the Japanese people as a heterogeneous mix of cultures. Koreans, too, could contribute to this cultural potpourri by maintaining their unique language and culture. Their doing so, proponents of this idea suggested, should not compromise their chances of becoming Japanese. Though this argument was not popular in government-general circles, the 1920 reforms that allowed an indigenous Korean press and encouraged Korean language study among Japanese suggest Japanese policy makers tacitly accepted this possibility, at least until the following decade.

Finally, Japanese misperceptions are also evident in the images that they drew of the Korean Peninsula and its people. In Japanese and Western eyes, Korea was in a state of political decline over the last half of the nineteenth century. Many Korean reformers believed this to be the case as well. The Japanese imagining the government it replaced as incapable of reform was as predictable—most newly installed rulers, including the Meiji regime, tend to characterize their predecessors as such—as it was self-serving. Painting the entire people as inept worked against their stated intentions and supported arguments that encouraged segregation. Many Koreans recognized that the Japanese had something to offer the Korean people. Even the "anti-Japanese" *Korean Daily News* suggested as much by offering a potential Japanese-Korean relationship akin to a "father to a son, or an elder brother to a younger brother," before cautioning that Japanese residents would have to abandon their arrogance toward Koreans for this relationship to material-ize.[12] Although images fluctuated during Japan's tenure in Korea, they con-tinued to portray Koreans as a people below Japanese standard.

The image of the Korean Peninsula as the source of regional instability, the reason that Japan gave for fighting wars with China and Russia, also requires deeper consideration. Regardless of whether Russia aimed to annex Korea, realist thinking informed Japan that this possibility required their concern, particularly when Korea's military remained weak. Korea's turning to Russia for assistance only heightened Japan's security fears. Japan's post-annexation history, however, demonstrates that while Korea's addition may have strengthened Japan's domestic security, it decisively weakened its impe-rial security. Following Yamagata Aritomo's idea that the state extending its line of sovereignty also required it extending its line of interest, Japan's annexation of Korea required it extending its interests into continental Asia to protect its new acquisition. Extending this line risked Japan infringing on the sovereignty and interests of neighboring China and Western imperialists, thus exponentially increasing the probability of war. In this sense, Korean an-nexation weakened Japanese security and by extension Northeast Asian secu-rity, as evident by the reckless wars that Japan fought in the 1930s and 1940s.

A second critical flaw was in the discrepancy between what the Japanese claimed as their intention and what they actually did. Why, as even Japan's Korean supporters questioned, did so many barriers remain between Japa-nese and Koreans? These barriers impeded Korean-Japanese assimilation by preventing, as the *Maeil sinbo* so eloquently put it, Japanese and Koreans "finding happiness in sharing a drink (or a meal or even a conversation) together."[13] How were the two peoples to unite if they lived, studied, and worked in separate environments? How could the Japanese advertise the fra-ternal brotherhood of Japanese-Korean unity while treating the Koreans as inferior? Our inquiry considers factors that prevented the Japanese from establishing adequate procedures to allow the two peoples to fraternize more.

Hara Takashi cited the segregated environments in which the two peoples existed as a critical impediment to Korean assimilation. This in part can be explained by an economic factor: Koreans and Japanese traveled in separate circles because they were of different economic classes. The 1920 reforms established that Japanese and Korean officials would be compensated under the same wage scale. This reform no doubt pressured other Japanese employers to follow suit. Leveling salaries would have rendered differences as based on class, rather than ethnicity, and theoretically allowed more Koreans access to Japanese-centered neighborhoods and schools. Yet this apparently did not happen. One reason for this reform's failure was that it considered only base salary; it neglected the stipends that the government and businesses offered Japanese as incentive to relocate to the peninsula. Japanese dispatched to the northern regions received an additional 30 percent "hardship" stipend, and those to border regions an extra 7 percent stipend.[14] Many professions also continued to offer Japanese higher salaries than Koreans, and others (as suggested by the roundtable discussion by Keijō Imperial University professors) limited Korean access simply by preferences that favored Japanese over Korean, regardless of skill.

Segregation persisted even within the appearance of apparent integration, as seen in schools where Korean and Japanese students maintained segregated lifestyles even within the integrated campus. Yet little evidence exists that shows the government-general actively trying to integrate Japanese and Koreans. More research into the daily lives of Korea's Japanese population is required to determine the extent to which this segregation resulted from conscious efforts by Japanese and Koreans to maintain the two peoples' separate existences.

Japan's disparaging images of Koreans may also have kept Koreans away from Japanese neighborhoods and schools. The Japanese stubbornly continued practices that accented Japanese-Korean difference even while making efforts to reduce these differences by unifying school systems and having Koreans adopt Japanese names. This was evident in the regulation that forced Japan-based Koreans to maintain their family registers on the peninsula. A subtler example was the semantic use of *kokumin* for Japanese and *shinmin* for Koreans. The two terms mean "subject," but while both Japanese and Korean were *shinmin*, *kokumin* appears to be a term more appropriate for Japanese. Official documents encouraged Korean adoption of a *kokumin seishin* (national spirit) that would unite both Japanese and Korean. But Koreans would gain this as *kōkoku shinmin* (imperial subjects) rather than as *kokumin* (national subjects), as the *Chōsen oyobi Manshū* argued in November 1911.[15]

Our study has directed primary attention toward distinctions made in Japan's education system given the institution's importance in Japan's assimilation mission, as well as its potential as a social leveling institution. The administration is to be credited for the importance it placed on educating

Koreans, but not for the system that it created to accomplish this goal. Despite frequent calls to integrate classrooms, the schools remained virtually segregated throughout the period. The government-general claimed that the number of Koreans fluent in Japanese was rising. It would follow that this result would lead to increases in the number of Koreans entering Japanese schools. Yet, the figure hovered between 5 and 10 percent of the total enrollment throughout the duration of Japanese rule. Korean education also remained voluntary (as opposed to compulsory), and inferior to the education offered to Japanese children: its classroom populations were larger and the per student budgetary allocations smaller. Lower quality education placed Koreans at a serious disadvantage when they competed against Japanese for scholastic or employment opportunities. The product of two separate and unequal education systems is rather predictable—a two-tiered society constructed primarily of a privileged colonizer minority over a handicapped colonized majority.

We can only speculate as to why the Japanese failed to back their assimilation rhetoric with appropriate policy. One reason may lie in their persistent negative images of the Koreans. According to the Japanese, Korean inferiority rendered the people unfit for inclusion as subjects of equal status, as indicated in the June 1939 discussion held by Keijō Imperial University professors. Subscribers to this belief argued that Japanese could not revise their attitudes until the Korean people attained a suitable level of civilization. Perceived cultural inferiority also fed the idea that Korean assimilation should progress gradually, suggesting that Koreans could not handle the radical changes expected of the internally colonized. Total assimilation would take as long as a century to realize success. History, rather than incompetence, robbed the Japanese of their chance to complete their mission.

Negative portrayals of the Korean also contributed to Korean-Japanese divisions. Painting the Korean side of town as antiquated, filthy, and unhealthy, and the residents as lazy, mentally stagnated, and untrustworthy taught Japanese to honor lines of division. Those who crossed this divide risked being ostracized by their compatriots, as Tauchi Chizuko discovered after she married a Korean.[16] This is not to say that these images were completely untrue—there were lazy Koreans who lived in unsanitary quarters (just as there were Japanese). But to extend this image to characterize the entire Korean population is irresponsibly self-serving. Japanese and Koreans also fraternized; they intermarried probably at a level higher than official records indicate. Some relations blossomed into lifelong friendships that remain strong to this day. These occurrences appeared less frequently than one would expect given that Japan's stated goal aimed to assimilate Koreans and Japanese.[17]

To sustain this argument required the Japanese to compile a composite image of the assimilated Korean. Japanese articulated the kinds of activities that they desired of the Korean that suggested prerequisites to Korean assimilation. Japanese shying from compiling a checklist of concrete requirements suggests that Korean assimilation was dependent more on Japanese delivering images of the people as their fellow subjects, rather than the efforts that Koreans made to gain Japanese acceptance. To the pro-Japanese Korean, Japanese rhetoric nurtured an expectation that eventually they would stand shoulder to shoulder with Japanese as equals, perhaps as colleagues in a greater Asian community. To the anti-Japanese forces this unattractive rhetoric needlessly fueled their rhetorical (or even armed) attacks on Japanese and their interests.

A lack of confidence in the strength of Korea-based Japanese national identity may have provided a second reason for the discrepancy between Japan's colonial rhetoric and policy. Increased contact with Koreans risked producing a result counter to Japan's assimilation intentions: Japanese Koreanization. At stake here was Japan's image of its cultural superiority over Korean culture, on the basis of which they justified their colonization of Korea. Warnings of the dangers that Sawanō Kyokuhō called *Chōsenka* or *yoboka* first appeared in the peninsula-based media over the first decade of Japanese rule.[18] Evidence of this appears in children raised in rural areas who had more contact with Korean people, as well as with Korean culture. Togawa Akio, raised on Cheju Island, lived a bilingual, bicultural lifestyle differentiated by his at-home and at-play environments.[19]

A third flaw in Japanese colonial thinking was its failure to consider alternatives to total cultural assimilation. The government-general was warned of the consequences should it fail to coordinate rhetoric and policy. These warnings offered three alternatives: administer its assimilation efforts more intensely, end this policy altogether, or relax its total assimilation ambitions to allow Koreans to maintain a distinct identity within the empire. The administration, however, continued to preach its gradual assimilation policy until 1938 when it intensified its efforts. But was this the best choice?

Koreans presented the Japanese with alternatives to their relationship even before annexation. One such alternative required that the two peoples form a more horizontal relationship that would help Koreans preserve their independence (Japan's stated goal at the time) and strengthen Japanese-Korean bonds. This proposal, advanced by the *Independent* in April 1896, offered a more horizontal division-of-labor relationship in which Koreans would provide Japan with the raw materials its burgeoning industry required.[20] Presumably tighter economic relations would bond the two peoples without Japan assuming political control over the peninsula. Annexation ended the possibility of independent economic coexistence but not the possibility of Japanese and Koreans defining their relationship on more horizontal terms. Koreans recognized Japan's accomplishments and the potential role the people could play in guiding Korean development. Yet, throughout this history the prime obstacle to their forming a more equal relationship remained unchanged: the arrogant attitude that Japanese held toward Koreans. A less arrogant Japanese mentor would have stood a better chance of encouraging Koreans to accept the merits of its culture, while generating greater Korean support for its efforts.

The Japanese could also have relaxed their total cultural assimilation rhetoric. Less intrusive goals would have limited direct Japanese influence over the Korean people, and might have left Japan's more ardent supporters among Koreans dissatisfied. It could also have gained them broader support from Koreans, particularly if they believed this administration to be more sympathetic to their culture and traditions. The British model that Japanese so frequently invoked comes to mind. The political assimilation introduced by the English inadvertently brought the Scots, the Welsh, and even the Irish closer to England culturally, perhaps because the policy gave something (political participation) rather than threatening to take something (cultural heritage). Governing the Korean people under a political assimilation policy would have required at a minimum the Japanese accepting Korean representation in their national assembly. It would have required the Japanese to extend suffrage rights to Koreans eligible to vote by Japanese laws. It would also have squared Japanese rhetoric and practice. Granting Koreans political participation would have sent a more positive message to Koreans than the negative emotions that accompanied Japanese plans to replace Korea's traditional (and supposedly inferior) heritage. Properly introducing political assimilation might also have encouraged warmer participation by *naichijin*, *hantōjin*, and *tairajin* (continental, Manchurian) under a broader pan-Asian umbrella as the idea of "British" united the Celts and Anglos.

We cannot write the scenario for how Japanese administrations might have evolved had Japan retained control over the Korean Peninsula following the war's end. The enormous impact that defeat had on the attitudes and images of both Koreans and Japanese precludes our predicting whether Japanese would have followed through with their promises, or what policy adjustments they might have made under new circumstances. Even defeat did not humble Japanese views on this history. As early as 1958, Liberal Democratic Party vice president Ōno Banboku called for its return in commenting that "the emphasis of Japanese diplomacy should be given to close cooperation with America. In order to do this, the ROK and Formosa will have to be closely related. If feasible it would be nice to form the United States of Japan with the ROK and Formosa."[21] Ōno's remark, far from isolated, is one of a number of similar remarks that Japanese political figures have made since Korean liberation. Such opinions neutralize the sincerity of apologies that Japanese prime ministers and emperors periodically offer to Korean dignitaries. They also suggest that prewar attitudes of Japanese superiority over inferior Koreans would have continued in our imagined scenario of a postwar Japanese Korea colony.

ASSIMILATION OF PERIPHERAL PEOPLES

Can a people assimilate a people that it considers to be inferior? Our examination of Japan's assimilation policy argues this to be rather difficult, if not impossible. While similar images of inferiority existed in the more intimate internal colonial example, these images gradually weakened as the peoples lived, studied, worked, and fought alongside one another. Peripheral and external colonized peoples generally were denied the opportunity to fraternize with the internal subject to this extent. Even today Japanese harbor images of their differences with the Ainu and Ryukyu peoples, whom they claimed to have assimilated decades ago. Indeed, it still seems natural to consider as distinct cultural and linguistic categories the Ryukyu or Ainu examples (as opposed to the Kyushu or Tohoku ones).

This appears to have been the case in non-Japanese examples, as well. Like the Japanese, Germans had their assimilation experiment prematurely ended by defeat in two world wars, after which Alsace and Lorraine passed to French hands. The French, after eight decades of imposing assimilation on Algerians and Vietnamese, were driven out by bloody independence movements. The English, after centuries of rule over the Welsh and the Scots, found these people opting to form their own national assemblies after the creation of the European Union provided them with an alternative political identity to that of British subject. Even under relatively favorable conditions, peripheral colonial assimilation, while providing a framework more nurturing than that offered the external colonial subject, lacked the intimacy required to absorb the people as internal colonized citizens.

The American civil rights movement provides an example of assimilation in progress. Although blacks are by no means completely integrated into American society, the strides they have made since they began gaining admission to traditionally white institutions in the late 1940s instruct us in the kinds of actions that the assimilation process requires to reap success. From this history we learn that assimilation does not simply emerge passively; it must be actively nurtured by determined guidance and direction. Negative legislation from above, designed to prevent discrimination, is but a first step to dismantle the barriers that separate majority from minority. Orlando Patterson argues that this alone is insufficient:

> Interpersonal relations are still plagued by distrust and confusion. If there is to be greater integration we must establish clear-cut rules to facilitate the crossing of ethnic barriers erected over the centuries. Simply ridding oneself of ethnic prejudice and enforcing laws against discrimination are not enough. Antidiscrimination laws tell us what not to do and how to behave under specific formal circumstances. They do not, and cannot, dictate how we are to interact in everyday encounters.[22]

In this sense Hara Takashi had it right. Positive guidance to create opportunity is required from above to counter negative images. Integration of livelihood, such as through school integration and affirmative action policies, place the two peoples in situations that require more intimate encounters and gradually reduces socioeconomic gaps. Generally seen as a policy for balancing "numerical representation" of low performing groups,[23] affirmative action provides a closer proximity that forces the majority to confront their own stereotypes of the minority, many of which have been developed, strengthened, and sustained by an ignorance hardened by the two peoples' segregated existences. Providing individuals with the opportunity to confront these stereotypes, to learn how to cross ethnic barriers, is a crucial step in the process of the majority's eventual acceptance of the minority as their equal.

Herein lies the primary flaw of Japanese assimilation policies. While it succeeded in convincing a significant number of influential Koreans of Japan's cultural and political merits, it failed to rally the Japanese people around the idea of including Koreans in their livelihoods as fellow imperial subjects. Successful assimilation required the government-general to articulate policies that brought Koreans and Japanese together in neighborhoods, schools, and occupations under circumstances that championed their equality, rather than simply producing rhetoric that predicted their eventual equality. Japanese calculated that Korean assimilation could take up to a century to complete. The histories of other assimilating efforts suggest that progress toward this goal does not begin with the colonizers' annexation of their territory, or with a simple declaration of their intention to assimilate. Rather, the hands of this clock begin to turn only after the governing body initiates proactive legislation to encourage integration on both sides. This study found insufficient evidence to conclude that the Japanese administration prepared to initiate this process over its thirty-six-year rule of the Korean Peninsula. In this regard the Japanese were not unique, but were in step with other practitioners of peripheral colonization.

NOTES

INTRODUCTION: COLONIAL ADMINISTRATION DECISIONS

1   Cho Pyŏngsang, "Shiganhei wo ko ni mochite" (My Son the Volunteer Soldier), *Chōsen* (March 1940): 61–63. Cho's second son entered the military as a student draftee (*gakuto shutsujin*). For information on Cho Pyŏngsang, see Kim Yŏlchin, ed., *Panminja tae kongp'an'gi* (A Record of the Great Trial of Treason), vol. 1 (Seoul: Hanp'ung ch'ulp'ansa, 1986), 89. Kyeong-Hee Choi addresses the idea of compromised nationalism in her "Another Layer of the Pro-Japanese Literature: Ch'oe Chŏnghŭi's 'The Wild Chrysanthemum,'" *Poetica* 52 (1999): 61–87.

2   Koreans previously served as "volunteer" (*giyū*) translators and drivers in the Japanese military. As many as 200 Koreans accompanied Japanese forces in the 1932 Shanghai Incident. From 1938 they were included as volunteer soldiers, and from 1944 as conscripted soldiers. During the war, 154,907 Koreans served in the Japanese military; 6,377 died in battle. Higuchi Yūichi, *Kōgun heishi ni sareta Chōsenjin* (Koreans Enlisted in the Imperial Army) (Tokyo: Hyōronsha, 1992), 12–13, 16. Government-general documents reveal that in 1938, 3,000 Koreans applied for the 400 positions in the Korean volunteer corps. In 1942, the Japanese military received as many as 250,000 applications. "Chōsen tōchi to kōmin rensei no shinten" (Korean Administration and the Advancement of Imperial Training), in *Ilcheha chibae chŏngch'aek charyojip*, vol. 17, edited by Sin Chubaek (Seoul: Koryŏ sŏrim, 1993), 701.

3   Cho's extreme groups correspond with Gi-Wook Shin's pan-Asianists and independence-seeking nationalist groups. Gi-Wook Shin, *Ethnic Nationalism in Korea: Genealogy, Politics, and Legacy* (Stanford, Calif.: Stanford University Press, 2006), chap. 1.

4   Cho, "Shiganhei wo ko ni mochite," 61, 62.

5   I address accusations of Yun Ch'iho as a Japanese collaborator in my "Loyal Patriot or Traitorous Collaborator? Reassessing Yun Ch'iho's Colonial Activities in Contemporary Japan-Korea Relations," *Journal of Colonialism and Colonial History* (e-journal, December 2006). Koen de Ceuster offers a broader treatment of Korean collaboration in his "The Nation Exorcised: The Historiography of Collaboration in South Korea," *Korean Studies* 25, no. 2 (2001): 207–42. For a negative appraisal see the three-volume *Ch'inilp'a 99 in* (99 Members of the Pro-Japanese Group), edited by Panminjok munje yŏn'guso (1993; Seoul: Tosŏ ch'ulgwan tol pegge, 2002).

6   Sŏ Ch'un, "Chōheisei jisshi to hantōjin no kangeki" (The Enforcement of the Korean Conscription System and the Peninsular People's Emotional Inspiration), *Chōsen* (July 1942): 55–57.

7   Yun Ch'iho, *Yun Ch'iho ilgi* (Yun Ch'iho Diary), vol. 11 (July 3, 1939) (Seoul: Kuksa p'yŏnch'an wiwŏnhoe, 1986), 196.

8   Sŏ, "Chōheisei jisshi to hantōjin no kangeki," 56.

9   Lawrence James's *The Rise and Fall of the British Empire* (London: Little Brown, 1994) includes separate chapters on India, Egypt, South Africa, India, and the white dominions (Canada, Australia, and New Zealand), but only pages on Ireland, Scotland, and Wales.

10   Bruce Cumings, *The Origins of the Korean War: Liberation and the Emergence of Separate Regimes, 1945–1947* (Princeton, N.J.: Princeton University Press, 1981), 7. See also Gregory Henderson, *Korea: The Politics of the Vortex* (Cambridge, Mass.: Harvard University Press, 1968), 72; and Carter J. Eckert, Ki-baik Lee, Young Ick Lew, Michael Robinson, and Edward W. Wagner, *Korea Old and New: A History* (Cambridge, Mass.: Harvard University Press, 1990), 256. Among Japanese historians, see Eguchi Keiichi, *Nihon teikokushugishi kenkyū* (Research in the History of Japanese Imperialism) (Tokyo: Aoki shoten, 1998), 31, 122. Cumings later suggests similarity with the England-Ireland relationship in his *Korea's Place in the Sun: A History* (New York: W. W. Norton, 1997), 140.

11   Hannah Arendt, *The Origins of Totalitarianism* (Orlando: Harcourt Brace, 1979), 223.

12   Michael Hechter, *Internal Colonialism: The Celtic Fringe in British National Development, 1536–1966* (Berkeley: University of California Press, 1975).

13   Harold Wolpe, "The Theory of Internal Colonialism: The South African Case," in *Beyond the Sociology of Development: Economy and Society in Latin America and Africa*, edited by Ivar Oxaal, Tony Barnett, and David Booth (London: Routledge & Kegan Paul, 1975), 231. See also Elia T. Zureik, *The Palestinians in Israel: A Study of Internal Colonialism* (London: Routledge & Kegan Paul, 1979).

14   Pratha Chatterjee, *The Nation and Its Fragments: Colonial and Postcolonial Histories* (Princeton, N.J.: Princeton University Press, 1993), 14.

15   Partha Chatterjee quotes from Ernest Gellner's *Nations and Nationalism* to refute the idea that Western states such as Italy and Germany were better equipped to incorporate nationalism's "universal standards" than Asian peoples in his *Nationalist Thought and the Colonial World: A Derivative Discourse* (Minneapolis: University of Minnesota Press, 1986), 5–6.

16   Benedict Anderson, *Imagined Communities: Reflections on the Origin and Spread of Nationalism* (London: Verso, 1991), 6.

17   Eamonn Callan addresses some of these questions in his "The Ethics of Assimilation," *Ethics* 115 (April 2005): 471–500.

18   Examples of external colonialism, far too numerous to list here, include European "land grabbing" efforts in Africa and Asia over the decades leading up to World War I.

19   John D. Fage, "British and German Colonial Rule: A Synthesis and Summary," in *Britain and Germany in Africa: Imperial Rivalry and Colonial Rule*, edited by Prosser Gifford and William Roger Louis, 691–706 (New Haven, Conn.: Yale University Press, 1967).

20   England justified many of its external acquisitions as necessary to protect its colonial "jewel" and "lifeline," India. James, *The Rise and Fall of the British Empire*, 204.

21   Internal colonialism included integrating efforts by Prussian officials to form the German state, by the Piedmont monarchy to integrate the Italian peninsula, and by Satsuma and Chōshū leaders to integrate the Tokugawa-era domains in Japan.

22 Peripheral colonialism occurred in the following situations: English "unions" with Wales, Scotland, and Ireland; the French subjugation of Algeria; the Prussian annexation of Alsace and Lorraine; and the United States' brief Reconstruction-era attempt to integrate blacks and Native Americans.

23 Edward W. Said, *Orientalism* (New York: Vintage Books, 1979), 2. E. M. Collingham refers to the "creation of an 'affective wall' which distanced the British body from India." See E. M. Collingham, *Imperial Bodies: The Physical Experience of the Raj, C. 1800–1947* (Oxford: Polity, 2001), 7.

24 Quoted in Collingham, *Imperial Bodies*, 2.

25 Frantz Fanon, *Black Skin, White Masks,* translated by Charles Lam Markmann (New York: Grove Weidenfield, 1967), 63.

26 Arano Yasunori, *Kinsei Nihon to Higashi Ajia* (Modern Japan and East Asia) (Tokyo: Tokyo daigaku shuppankai, 1988); and Ronald P. Toby, *State and Diplomacy in Early Modern Japan: Asia and the Development of the Tokugawa Bakufu* (Stanford, Calif.: Stanford University Press, 1984).

27 Brett L. Walker, *The Conquest of Ainu Lands: Ecology and Culture in Japanese Expansion, 1590–1800* (Berkeley: University of California Press, 2001); George H. Kerr, *Okinawa: The History of an Island People* (Rutland, Vt.: Charles E. Tuttle, 2000).

28 Kenneth B. Pyle reviews this literature in his *The Making of Modern Japan* (Lexington, Mass.: D. C. Heath, 1996), 71–74.

29 For example, Carol Gluck, *Japan's Modern Myths: Ideology in the Late Meiji Period* (Princeton, N.J.: Princeton University Press, 1985); Byron K. Marshall, *Learning to Be Modern: Japanese Political Discourse on Education* (Boulder, Colo.: Westview, 1994); Sheldon Garon, *Molding Japanese Minds: The State in Everyday Life* (Princeton, N.J.: Princeton University Press, 1997); Takashi Fujitani, *Splendid Monarchy: Power and Pageantry in Modern Japan* (Berkeley: University of California Press, 1996); and Tessa Morris-Suzuki, *Re-inventing Japan: Time, Space, and Nation* (New York: M. E. Sharpe, 1998).

30 General Yamagata Aritomo as prime minister articulated this process in the Diet in its opening session in 1890 when he explained: "The independence and security of the nation depend first upon the protection of the line of sovereignty (*shukensen*) and then the line of advantage (*riekisen*). . . . If we wish to maintain the independence among the powers of the world at the present time, it is not enough to guard only the

line of sovereignty; we must also defend the line of advantage." Quoted in Pyle, *The Making of Modern Japan*, 135.

31 Pak Yŏngje calls Japan's Korean invasion a "product" (*sanmul*) of its Meiji Restoration in his "Kŭndae ilbon ŭi Hanguk insik" (Modern Japanese Perceptions of Korea), in *Ilche ŭi taehan ch'imnyak chŏngch'aeksa yŏn'gu* (Studies on Japanese Imperial Invasion Policy toward Korea), edited by Cho Hangnein, 7–37 (Seoul: Hyŏnumsa, 1996). Yi Kwangnae considers this history in the context of Japan's "Asia syndrome," namely, Fukuzawa Yukichi's "abandon Asia theory" (*datsuaron*) against Japan's "Greater East Asia co-prosperity sphere" in his "Ilbon ŭi 'Asia chuŭi' sok eso ŭi Hanguk insik" (Korea in the Context of Japan's "Asianism"), in *Hanil yangguk ŭi sangho insik* (Shared Perceptions of Korea and Japan), edited by Chŏng Ch'anyong (Seoul: Kukhak charyowŏn, 1998). See also Pak Kyŏnsik, *Nihon teikokushugi no Chōsen shihai* (Japan's Imperial Control over Korea) (Tokyo: Aoki shoten, 1993); and Ch'a Kibyŏk, "Ilbon chegukchuŭi singmin chŏngch'aek ŭi hyŏngsŏng paegyŏng kwa kŭ chŏn'gae" (The Development and Formation of Imperial Japan's Colonial Strategy), in *Ilche ŭi Han'guk singmin t'ongch'i* (Japanese Colonial Administration in Korea), edited by Ch'a Kibyŏk, 12–44 (Seoul: Chongumsa, 1985). Unno Fukuju, *Kankoku heigoshi no kenkyū* (Research on the History of Korean Annexation) (Tokyo: Iwanami shoten, 2000); Hilary Conroy, *The Japanese Seizure of Korea, 1868–1910: A Study of Realism and Idealism in International Relations* (Philadelphia: University of Pennsylvania Press, 1960); and Peter Duus, *The Abacus and the Sword: The Japanese Penetration of Korea, 1895–1910* (Berkeley: University of California Press, 1995).

32 Chŏng Okcha, "Sinsa yuramdan ko" (Considerations of the Gentry-Officials Touring Group), *Yŏksa hakpo* 27 (1965): 105–42.

33 Fukuzawa Yukichi, "Chōsen no mondai" (The Korea Problem), in *Fukuzawa zenshū*, vol. 8, edited by Jiji shinbōsha, 591–93 (Tokyo: Kokumin toshi, 1926). Yi Kwangnae argues that Fukuzawa desired to promote Asian development up until the 1884 coup attempt, after which he advanced his "abandon Asia" discourse (*datsuaron*). See his "Ilbon ŭi Asia chuŭi sok esŏ ŭi Hanguk insik," 208–9.

34 Hirano Yoshitarō, *Ōi Kentarō* (Tokyo: Yoshikawa kōbunkan, 1965), 232–33.

35 Young Ick Lew, "Yüan Shih-k'ai's Residency and the Korean Enlightenment Movement (1885–94)," *Journal of Korean Studies* 5 (1984): 63.

See also C. I. Eugene Kim and Kim Hankyo, *Korea and the Politics of Imperialism, 1876–1910* (Berkeley: University of California Press, 1968), 64–65.

36 Kirk W. Larsen, *Tradition, Treaties, and Trade: Qing Imperialism and Chosŏn Korea, 1850–1910* (Cambridge, Mass.: Harvard University Asia Center, 2008), 161–62.

37 Angus Hamilton, *Korea* (New York: Charles Scribner's Sons, 1904), 25–26.

38 Howard K. Beale, *Theodore Roosevelt and the Rise of American World Power* (Baltimore: Johns Hopkins, 1969), 319. See also Fred H. Harrington, *God, Mammon, and the Japanese* (Madison: University of Wisconsin Press, 1966). For Allen's correspondence as head of the United States Legation to Korea see Scott S. Burnett, ed. *Korean-American Relations: Documents Pertaining to the Far Eastern Diplomacy of the United States*, vol. 3: *The Period of Diminishing Influence, 1896–1905* (Honolulu: University of Hawai'i Press, 1989), 155–93.

39 "An Important Talk on Annexation," *The Japan Times* (August 30, 1910).

40 James B. Palais, *Politics and Policy in Traditional Korea* (Cambridge, Mass.: Harvard University Press, 1975), 272. In a later effort Palais argues that it was the inflexibility of the social and political structures that prevented the Korean peninsula from later enacting necessary reforms, namely, "maladministration, internecine bureaucratic factionalism, unfair taxation, the concentration of wealth, the evasion of responsibility, and the deterioration of national defense." *Confucian Statecraft and Korean Institutions: Yu Hyŏngwŏn and the Late Chosŏn Dynasty* (Seattle: University of Washington Press, 1996), 1004.

41 Martina Deuchler, *Confucian Gentlemen and Barbarian Envoys: The Opening of Korea, 1875–1885* (Seattle: University of Washington Press, 1977), 222–23.

42 Shin Yong-ha, *Modern Korean History and Nationalism*, translated by N. M. Pankaj (Seoul: Jimoondang, 2000) 139–40; Vipan Chandra, *Imperialism, Resistance, and Reform in Late Nineteenth-Century Korea: Enlightenment and the Independence Club* (Berkeley: University of California Press, 1988), 215.

43 Yi T'ae-jin, *Tōdaisei ni katatta Kankokushi* (Narrating Korean History to Tokyo University Students), translated by Torikumi Yutaka (Tokyo: Akashi shoten, 2006). See also Yi T'ae-jin, *The Dynamics of Confucian-*

ism and Modernization in Korean History (Ithaca, N.Y.: East Asia Program, Cornell University, 2007), especially part 3.

44 This understanding predated the 1868 Meiji Restoration. See Donald Keene, *The Japanese Discovery of Europe, 1720–1830* (Stanford, Calif.: Stanford University Press, 1952), 176–204; and Bob Tadashi Wakabayashi, *Anti-Foreignism and Western Learning in Early Modern Japan: The New Theses of 1825* (Cambridge, Mass.: Harvard University Press, 1991).

45 Eric Hobsbawm, *The Age of Empire, 1875–1914* (New York: Vintage Books, 1987).

46 For examples of Tokugawa-era Japanese seeing Koreans as foreigners, see Ronald P. Toby, "Carnival of the Aliens: Korean Embassies in Edo-Period Art and Popular Culture," *Monumenta Nipponica* 41, no. 4 (1986): 415–56; and Ikeuchi Satoshi, *Kinsei Nihon to Chōsen hyōryūmin* (Modern Japan and Korean castaways) (Tokyo: Sanseisha, 1998).

47 One of the more comprehensive efforts on Japan's colonial policy is Ōe Shinobu, Asada Kyōji, Mitani Taichirō, Gotō Ken'ichi, Kobayashi Hideo, Takasaki Sōji, Wakabayashi Masatake, and Kawamura Minato's eight-volume edited set titled *Kindai Nihon to shokuminchi* (Modern Japan and Its Colonies) (Tokyo: Iwanami shoten, 1993). For Japan's language policy, see Yasuda Toshiaki, *Teikoku Nihon no gengo hensei* (Imperial Japan's Linguistic Formation) (Yokohama: Seori shobō, 1997); and Yi Yŏ, *Nihon tōchishita Chōsen no genron tōseishi* (Korean Speech Regulation History under Japanese Administration) (Tokyo: Shinsansha, 2002). For Japan's education policy, see Kim Puja, *Shokuminchiki Chōsen no kyōiku to jendaa* (Korean Education and Gender during Colonial Rule) (Yokohama: Seori shobō, 2005).

48 The French example has produced the most interesting studies on assimilation history. See Raymond F. Betts, *Assimilation and Association in French Colonial Theory, 1890–1914* (New York: Columbia University Press, 1961); and Eugen Weber, *Peasants into Frenchmen: The Modernization of Rural France, 1870–1914* (Stanford, Calif.: Stanford University Press, 1976). Oguma Eiji considers the French influence on Japan in his "Sabetsu soku byōdō: Nihon shokuminchi tōchi shisō no Furansu jinshu shakaigaku no eikyō" (The Influence of French Racial Sociology on Japanese Colonial Administrative Thought), *Rekishigaku kenkyū* 662 (1994): 16–31.

49 See Gi-Wook Shin and Michael Robinson's fine introduction to their edited volume *Colonial Modernity in Korea* (Cambridge, Mass.: Harvard University Press, 1999), 1–18.

50 Students of Taiwanese colonial history have been more active on this issue. See Leo T. S. Ching, *Becoming "Japanese": Colonial Taiwan and the Politics of Identity Formation* (Berkeley: University of California Press, 2001); and Chen Peifeng, *"Dōka": No dōshō imu* ("Assimilation": Shared Bed, Different Dreams) (Tokyo: Sangensha, 2001). For the Korean case, see Komagome Takeshi, *Shokuminchi teikoku Nihon no bunka seiji* (Colonial Imperial Japan's Culture Rule) (Tokyo: Iwanami shoten, 1996); and Ch'oe Sŏg'yŏng, *Ilche ŭi tonghwa ideollogi ŭi ch'angch'ul* (A Framework for Imperial Japanese Assimilation Ideology) (Seoul: Sŏgyŏng munhwasa, 1997). Oguma Eiji examines Japanese colonial boundaries in his *"Nihonjin" no kyōkai* (The Boundaries of the "Japanese") (Tokyo: Shin'yōsha, 2002).

51 This caution was particularly evident in the wake of Korea's 1919 March First Independence Movement. Frank P. Baldwin Jr., "The March First Movement: Korean Challenge and Japanese Response" (Ph.D. diss., Columbia University, 1969); Nagata Akifumi, *Nihon no Chōsen tōchi to kokusai kankei: Chōsen dokuritsu undō to Amerika, 1910–1922* (Korea Rule and International Relations: Korean Independence Movement and the United States, 1910–1922) (Tokyo: Heibonsha, 2005); and Dae-yeol Ku, *Korea Under Colonialism: The March First Movement and Anglo Japanese Relations* (Seoul: Seoul Computer Press for Royal Asiatic Society, 1985).

52 Dong Wonmo, "Japanese Colonial Policy and Practice in Korea, 1905–1945: A Study in Assimilation" (Ph.D. diss., Georgetown University, 1969); Dong Wonmo, "Assimilation and Social Mobilization in Korea," in *Korea under Japanese Rule*, edited by Andrew C. Nahm, 146–82 (Kalamazoo: Center for Korean Studies, Western Michigan University, 1973). Nagata Akifumi examines Japanese colonial policy up until the March First Movement in his *Nihon no Chōsen tōchi to kokusai kankei*.

53 See Duus, *The Abacus and the Sword*, chap. 11.

54 The major works in English are Michael Edson Robinson, *Cultural Nationalism in Colonial Korea, 1920–1925* (Seattle: University of Washington Press, 1988); Kenneth M. Wells, *New God, New Nation: Protestants and Self-Reconstruction Nationalism in Korea, 1896–1937* (Honolulu: University of Hawai'i Press, 1990); and Shin, *Ethnic Nationalism in Korea*.

1   WESTERN ASSIMILATION PRACTICES

1   Hobsbawm, *The Age of Empire*, 59.

2   Kume Kunitake, *Tokumei zenken taishi Bei-ō kairan jikki* (A True Account of the Special Embassy's Tour of America and Europe), ed. Tanaka Akira, vol. 2 (Tokyo: Iwanami shoten, 1996), 22–23.

3   Ibid., vol. 3, 22.

4   Raymond Betts, *France and Decolonization, 1900–1960*, translated by William Glanville Brown (New York: St. Martin's Press, 1991), 5.

5   Hobsbawm, *The Age of Empire*, 56.

6   Quoted in Woodruff D. Smith, *The German Colonial Empire* (Chapel Hill: University of North Carolina Press, 1978), 13.

7   Quoted in Winfried Baumgart, *Imperialism: The Idea and Reality of British and French Colonial Expansion 1880–1914* (Oxford: Oxford University Press, 1982), 57.

8   Kume, *Tokumei zenken taishi Bei-ō kairan jikki*, vol. 1, 10–11.

9   Jean-Jacques Rousseau, *The Social Contract and Discourses*, translated by G. D. H. Cole (London: Everyman's Library, 1973), 181.

10 Betts, *Assimilation and Association in French Colonial Theory*, chap. 2.

11 For discussion on Le Bon, see ibid., 64–69. The Korean author Yi Kwangsu challenged Le Bon's thinking in his essay "Minjok kaejoron" (A Discourse on Racial Renovation) by contending that racial characteristics were more flexible than Le Bon's ideas allowed. Yi's point was that Koreans must develop racially before choosing assimilation or self-rule. *Yi Kwangsu chŏnjip*, vol. 17 (Seoul: Samjungdang, 1971), 187.

12 Stephen Jay Gould, *The Mismeasure of Man* (New York: W. W. Norton, 1996).

13 Betts, *Assimilation and Association in French Colonial Theory*, 116. Advocates of scientific colonialism such as Fredrick Ratzel and Bernhard Dernberg voiced similar ideas. Woodruff D. Smith, *The Ideological Origins of Nazi Imperialism* (New York: Oxford University Press, 1986), 147–52.

14 Raymond L. Buell, *The Native Problem in Africa*, vol. 1 (New York: Macmillan, 1928), 946. At the time, of the 1.2 million people in Senegal, 22,700 were granted native citizen status, a higher percentage than in other areas of French West Africa. Buell attributes this to "historical accident": their citizenship was granted at a time of relaxed regulations (ibid., 925, 947). For the Vietnam example see Thomas Ennis,

French Policy and Development in Indochina (Chicago: University of Chicago Press, 1936); Joseph Buttinger, *Vietnam: A Dragon Embattled*, vol. 1: *From Colonialism to the Vietminh* (New York: Frederick A. Praeger, 1967); David G. Marr, *Vietnamese Anti-Colonialism, 1885–1925* (Berkeley: University of California Press, 1971), and *Vietnamese Tradition on Trial, 1920–1945* (Berkeley: University of California Press, 1981); and Hue-Tam Ho Tai, *Radicalism and the Origins of the Vietnamese Revolution* (Cambridge, Mass.: Harvard University Press, 1996).

15   Marr, *Vietnamese Anti-Colonialism*, 46.

16   Between 1865 and 1913, only 1,557 Muslim Algerians were granted French citizenship. Vincent Confer, *France and Algeria: The Problem of Civil and Political Reform, 1870–1920* (New York: Syracuse University Press, 1966), 27.

17   David Prochaska, *Making Algeria French: Colonialism in Bône, 1870–1920* (Cambridge: Cambridge University Press, 1990). Prochaska argues that the French liberalized their nationalization policies toward the European residents to build demographic defenses against Algerians (152–53).

18   Ibid., 234–35.

19   John Ruedy, *Modern Algeria: The Origins and Development of a Nation* (Bloomington: Indiana University, 1992), 89.

20   Ibid., 112.

21   Confer, *France and Algeria*, 96–97.

22   Ruedy, *Modern Algeria*, 130.

23   For Emir Khaled, see ibid., 129–31.

24   M. B. Hocker, *Legal Pluralism: An Introduction to Colonial and Neo-Colonial Laws* (Oxford: Clarendon Press, 1975), 212.

25   Marr, *Vietnamese Tradition on Trial*, 46.

26   Tai, *Radicalism and the Origins of the Vietnamese Revolution*, 40–43.

27   Ibid., 45.

28   Ibid., 156.

29   Weber, *Peasants into Frenchmen*, 1.

30   James, *The Rise and Fall of the British Empire*, 220–21.

31   Thomas Babington Macaulay, "Minute recorded in the General Department by Thomas Babington Macaulay, Law Member of the Governor-general's Council (February 2, 1835)," reprinted in *The Great Indian Education Debate: Documents Relating to the Orientalist-Anglicist Con-*

troversy, 1781–1843, edited by Lynn Zastoupil and Martin Moir, 161–73 (Surrey, U.K.: Curzon Press, 1999), 171.

32 Charles Trevelyan, "On the Education of the People of India (1838)" reprinted in *The Great Indian Education Debate,* ed. Zastoupil and Moir, 298–99, 302.

33 H. H. Wilson, "Letter to the *Asiatic Journal* concerning the 'Education of the Natives of India' (December 5, 1835)," reprinted in *The Great Indian Education Debate,* ed. Zastoupil and Moir, 217.

34 James, *The Rise and Fall of the British Empire,* 192; Byron Farwell, *Queen Victoria's Little Wars* (New York: W. W. Norton, 1972), chaps. 8–11.

35 Prosser Gifford, "Indirect Rule: Touchstone or Tombstone for Colonial Policy," in *Britain and Germany in Africa,* ed. Gifford and Louis, 351–91 (New Haven, Conn.: Yale University Press, 1967), 351.

36 From *The Last Will and Testament of Cecil John Rhodes* in Fage, "British and German Colonial Rule," in *Britain and Germany in Africa,* ed. Gifford and Louis, 351.

37 See Hechter, *Internal Colonialism.*

38 Donald J. Withrington, "Education and Society in the Eighteenth Century," in *Scotland in the Age of Improvement,* edited by N. T. Phillipson and Rosalind Mitchison, 169–99 (Edinburgh: Edinburgh University Press, 1996).

39 Charles D. Hazen, *Alsace-Lorraine under German Rule* (New York: Henry Holt, 1917).

40 For discussion on the German Constitution's "dictatorship paragraph," see Dan Silverman, *Reluctant Union: Alsace-Lorraine and Imperial Germany, 1871–1918* (University Park: Pennsylvania State University Press, 1972), 76.

41 Quoted in K. Tsianina Lomawaima, *They Called It Prairie Light: The Story of Chilocco Indian School* (Lincoln: University of Nebraska Press, 1994), 5.

42 Grace Elizabeth Hale, *Making Whiteness: The Culture of Segregation in the South, 1890–1940* (New York: Vintage Books, 1998).

43 See Linda Colley, *Britons: Forging a Nation, 1707–1837* (New Haven, Conn.: Yale University Press, 1992), 1.

44 At this time the Welsh Prince Llywelyn the Great wrote to King Philip Augustus of France to acknowledge receipt of "your letters, impressed by your golden seal in witness of the alliance of the kingdom of the

French and the principality of North Wales." "Llywelyn Fawr to Philip Augustus," reproduced in *Letters from Wales*, edited by Joan Abse (Bridgend, Wales: Poetry Wales Press, 2000), 16.

45 Robert Clyde, *From Rebel to Hero: The Image of the Highlander, 1745–1830* (East Lothian, Scotland: Tuckwell Press, 1998). The "forty-five" (1745) rebellion was the last of a series of Jacobite attempts to push the English out of Scotland, the others coming in 1708, 1715, and 1719. See J. D. Mackie, *A History of Scotland* (Middlesex, U.K.: Penguin Books, 1964), 274–81.

46 Colley, *Britons*, 19.

47 Theobald McKenna, "A Memoire on Some Questions Respecting the Projected Great Britain and Ireland," reprinted in *The Catholic Question in Ireland, 1762–1829*, vol. 4, edited by Nicholas Lee (Bristol, U.K.: Thoemmes Press, 2000; Tokyo: Edition Synapse, 2000), 5. This document was originally published in 1805.

48 Silverman, *Reluctant Union*, 10, 30.

49 Thio Eunice, *British Policy in the Malay Peninsula, 1880–1910* (Singapore: University of Malaya Press, 1969), xviii.

50 D. K. Fieldhouse, *The Colonial Empires: A Comparative Survey from the Eighteenth Century* (New York: Dell, 1966), 207–9.

51 Ibid.

52 Scotland, for example, claimed education institutions superior to England.

53 Natorp quoted in Karl A. Schleunes, *Schooling and Society: The Politics of Education in Prussia and Bavaria* (Oxford: Berg, 1989), 50, 78.

54 Victor Cousin, "Report on the State of Public Instruction in Prussia," reprinted in *Reports on European Education*, edited by Edward H. Reisner (New York: McGraw Hill, 1930), 130–31.

55 "A French View of the Prussians," *The Nation* (March 30, 1871). The magazine claimed that war might have been avoided had his remarks been read before the war.

56 Roger Brubaker, *Citizenship and Nationhood in France and Germany* (Cambridge: Cambridge University Press, 1992), 15.

57 Weber, *Peasants into Frenchmen*, 332–36.

58 Ruedy, *Modern Algeria*, 103. Alexis de Tocqueville quoted in ibid., 104. European parents also refused to allow their children to study alongside the "semi-civilized natives," and the Muslim families refused to allow their children to be taught by "infidel teachers" (ibid., 103).

59 Ngō Viñh Long, *Before the Revolution: The Vietnamese Peasants under the French* (New York: Columbia University Press, 1991), 73.

60 Marr, *Vietnamese Tradition on Trial*, 34.

61 Tai, *Radicalism and the Origins of the Vietnamese Revolution*, 34.

62 Marr, *Vietnamese Tradition on Trial*, 148.

63 Tai, *Radicalism and the Origins of the Vietnamese Revolution*, 35.

64 Long, *Before the Revolution*, 74.

65 Marr, *Vietnamese Tradition on Trial*, 35.

66 Coleman Phillipson, *Alsace-Lorraine: Past, Present, and Future* (New York: E. P. Dutton, 1918), 48–49.

67 Hazen, *Alsace-Lorraine Under German Rule*, 166–69.

68 The German administration initially permitted education in the French language. Silverman, *Reluctant Union*, 76–81.

69 "What shall we do with the Indians?" *The Nation* (October 31, 1867).

70 A report from the 1888 Lake Mohawk Conference estimated the "cost of educating the Indian [to be] a fraction of the cost of fighting" him. Francis Paul Prucha, *American Indian Policy in Crisis: Christian Reformers and the Indian: 1865–1900* (Norman: University of Oklahoma Press, 1976), 293. *The Nation* priced this at $70,000 per head in its article "What shall we do with the Indians?"

71 Prucha, *American Indian Policy in Crisis*, 288.

72 Pratt quoted in Lomawaima, *They Called It Prairie Light*, 3, 4. The number of such institutions reached twenty-four in 1899, where 6,263 students received instruction. By the 1930s these schools accommodated 29 percent of all Native American children. See ibid., 10.

73 "What shall we do with the Negro?" *The Nation* (November 12, 1868).

74 Robert Selph Henry, *The Story of Reconstruction* (1938; New York: Konecky & Konecky, 1999), 431–43.

75 Morgan quoted in Michael C. Coleman, *American Indian Children at School, 1850–1930* (Jackson: University Press of Mississippi, 1993), 42.

76 One such person was Prime Minister Hara Takashi in his 1919 opinion paper discussed in chap. 4.

77 Fanon, *Black Skin White Masks*, 60.

78 Morag Bell, Robin A. Butlin, and Michael Hefferman describe geographers at this time as "midwives of European imperialism," and the teaching of geography as "little more than a thinly disguised form of racial and imperial propaganda." See their "Introduction: Geography and Imperialism, 1820–1940," in *Geography and Imperialism, 1820–*

1940, edited by Morag Bell, Robin A. Butlin, and Michael Hefferman (Manchester: Manchester University Press, 1995), 4.

79 H. V. Morton, *In Search of Scotland* (New York: Dodd, Mead, 1935), 8, 9.

80 Andrew Simmons, ed., *Burt's Letters from the North of Scotland* (Edinburgh: Birlinn Limited, 1998), 3. The Tweed River runs along part of the English-Scottish border.

81 Hale, *Making Whiteness*, 284.

82 "Archbishop Beckham to Edward I," in *Letters from Wales*, edited by Joan Abse, 27.

83 Ronald Takaki, *A Different Mirror: A History of Multicultural America* (Boston: Back Bay Books, 1993), 26–27, 39–41.

84 Quoted in Prucha, *American Indian Policy in Crisis*, 293.

85 Syed Hussein Alatas, *The Myth of the Lazy Native: A Study of the Image of the Malays, Filipinos, and Javanese from the Sixteenth to the Twentieth Century and Its Function in the Ideology of Colonial Capitalism* (London: Frank Cass, 1977), 2.

86 Colley, *Britons*, 117. Colley notes increases in the Scots entering into "well-defined areas of British life" from the late eighteenth century. Wilkes was elected Lord Mayor of London in 1774 (ibid., 113).

87 Hale, *Making Whiteness*, 16–21, 284.

88 This sexual boundary was artificial, established to control interracial marriage. Ann L. Stoler, "Rethinking Colonial Categories: European Communities and the Boundaries of Rule," *Comparative Studies in Society and History* 31, no. 1 (1989): 134–61; and Renisa Mawani, "'The Iniquitous Practice of Women': Prostitution and the Making of White Spaces in British Columbia, 1898–1905," in *Working through Whiteness: International Perspectives*, edited by Cynthia Levine-Rasky, 43–68 (Albany: State University of New York, 2002). For a discussion on Japanese *kansai* (Korean wife), see Ichi Kisha (pseudonym), *Chōsen nyōbō no kenkyū* (A Study on Korean Wives), *Chōsen oyobi Manshū* (July 1912): 24–25.

89 Elizabeth Friedman, *Colonization and After: An Algerian Jewish Community* (South Hadley, Mass.: Bergin & Garvey, 1988).

90 Northern European migrants to the United States proved the exception. Charlotte Erickson, *Invisible Immigrants: The Adaptation of English and Scottish Immigrants in Nineteenth-Century America* (Ithaca, N.Y.: Cornell University Press, 1972).

91 Glanmor Williams, *Religion, Language, and Nationality in Wales* (Cardiff: University of Wales, 1979), 4, 24.

92 Gareth E. Jones, *Modern Wales: A Concise History* (Cambridge: Cambridge University Press, 1995), 4; and Prys Morgan, "From a Death to a View: The Hunt for the Welsh Past in the Romantic Period," in *The Invention of Tradition*, edited by Eric Hobsbawm and Terence Ranger, 43–100 (Cambridge: Cambridge University Press, 1992).

93 D. George Boyce, *Nationalism in Ireland* (London: Routledge, 1995), 197.

94 Ibid., 228.

95 Pierre Bourdieu uses the label "colonial traditionalism" for "ways of behavior that appear unchanged were endowed with a very different meaning and function." Amal Vinogradov, "French Colonialism as Reflected in the Male-Female Interactions in Morocco," *Transitions of the New York Academy of Sciences* 36, no. 2 (February 1974): 194–95.

96 Hugh Trevor-Roper, "The Invention of Tradition: The Highland Tradition of Scotland," in *The Invention of Tradition*, ed. Hobsbawm and Ranger, 14–42.

97 The most vicious attack on the Welsh language was the *Reports on the Commissioners of Inquiry into the State of Education in Wales*, better known in Wales as "Brad y Llyfrau Gleision" (Treachery of the Blue Books). Gwyneth Tyson Roberts, "'Under the Hatches': English Parliamentary Commissioners' View of the People and Language of Mid-Nineteenth Century Wales," in *The Expansion of the English Race: Race, Ethnicity, and Cultural History*, edited by Bill Schwarz, 171–97 (London: Routledge, 1996), 182–89, and *The Language of the Blue Books: The "Perfect Instrument of Empire"* (Cardiff: University of Wales Press, 1998).

98 D. George Boyce, *Nationalism in Ireland*, 254. Tom Garvin attributes the Irish lack of a social revolution to the people's Anglicization in his "The Anatomy of a Nationalist Revolution: Ireland, 1888–1928," *Comparative Studies in Society and History* 28 (1986): 468–501.

99 The *Cherokee Phoenix* is recognized as the first Native American newspaper. James E. Murphy and Sharon M. Murphy, *Let My People Know: American Indian Journalism* (Norman: University of Oklahoma Press, 1987), 16.

100 Lewis quoted in R. A. Houston, *Scottish Literacy and the Scottish Identity: Illiteracy and Society in Scotland and Northern England, 1600–1800* (Cambridge: Cambridge University Press, 1985), 10.

101 Aled G. Jones, *Press, Politics, and Society: A History of Journalism in Wales* (Cardiff: University of Wales Press, 1993), 186.

102 Kamari Jayawardena, *The White Women's Other Burden: Western Women and South Asia During British Rule* (New York: Routledge, 1995), 180–81.

103 Charles-Robert Ageron, *Modern Algeria: A History from 1830 to the Present*, translated by Michael Brett (London: Hurst, 1991), 93–94.

104 Silverman, *Reluctant Union*, 188–89.

105 For the Egyptian "1919 National Revolution," see Huda Shaarawi, *Harem Years: The Memoirs of an Egyptian Feminist (1879–1924)*, translated by Margot Badran (London: Virago, 1986); and Marius Deeb, "The 1919 Popular Uprising: A Genesis of Egyptian Nationalism," *Canadian Review of Studies in Nationalism* 1, no. 1 (Fall 1973): 106–19.

106 Denis Judd, *Empire: The British Imperial Experience from 1765 to the Present* (London: Basic Books, 1996), 258–72.

107 A. Adu Boahen, ed., *General History of Africa: Africa under Colonial Domination, 1880–1935* (London: James Currey, 1990), 140–41. The Vietnamese reaction is mentioned briefly in Tai, *Radicalism and the Origins of the Vietnamese Revolution*, 68. For Korea's independence movement see Baldwin, "The March First Movement: Korean Challenge and Japanese Response"; Ku, *Korea Under Colonialism*; and Nagata, *Nihon no Chōsen tōchi to kokusai kankei*. For the Chinese "May Fourth Movement" see Chow Tse-tsung, *The May Fourth Movement: Intellectual Revolution in Modern China* (Stanford, Calif.: Stanford University Press, 1960).

108 For Vietnamese figures see Buttinger, *Vietnam: A Dragon Embattled*, 96; for Algeria's contribution see Confer, *France and Algeria*, 96–97; for British Empire numbers see Judd, *Empire*, 245–46; for Welsh participation see John Davies, *A History of Wales* (London: Penguin Books, 1993), 515–16.

109 "Home Rule for Wales," *North Wales Times*, March 15, 1919, and June 14, 1919.

110 James, *The Rise and Fall of the British Empire*, 383.

2 JAPAN'S DEVELOPMENT OF INTERNAL AND PERIPHERAL ASSIMILATION

1 Akira Iriye, *Pacific Estrangement: Japanese and American Expansion* (Cambridge, Mass.: Harvard University Press, 1972), 35. Nakae Chōmin's *A Discourse by Three Drunkards on Government* (trans.

Nobuko Tsukui [New York: Weatherhill, 1984]) provides an excellent read of pre-Sino-Japanese War expansionist thinking among Japanese.

2 Mark R. Peattie, "The Japanese Colonial Empire, 1895–1945," in *Cambridge History of Japan*, edited by Peter Duus, vol. 6, 217–70 (Cambridge: Cambridge University Press, 1988), 224.

3 Ōe Shinobu, "Higashi Ajia shinkyū teikoku Nihon" (Old and New Imperial Japan in East Asia), in *Kindai Nihon to shokuminchi* (Modern Japan and Its Colonies), edited by Ōe Shinobu et al., 6–16.

4 For example, Sawada Yōtarō, *Okinawa to Ainu: Nihon no minzoku mondai* (Okinawa and the Ainu: Japan's Ethnic Problem) (Tokyo: Shinsensha, 1996); David L. Howell, "Ainu Ethnicity and the Boundaries of the Early Modern Japanese State," *Past and Present* 142 (February 1994): 75–87; Walker, *The Conquest of Ainu Lands*; Alan S. Christy, "The Making of Imperial Subjects in Okinawa," in *Foundations of Colonial Modernity in East Asia*, edited by Tami Barlow, 141–70 (Durham, N.C.: Duke University Press, 1997); and Morris-Suzuki, *Re-Inventing Japan*.

5 Honda Toshiaki's ideas are found in his *Seiki monogatari* (Tales of the West) as described in Donald Keene, *The Japanese Discovery of Europe*, 115–19; Aizawa Seishisai, as described in Wakabayashi, *Anti-Foreignism and Western Learning in Early Modern Japan*; and Yoshida Shōin's *Yushuroku* (Record of Confinement), as described in David M. Earl, *Emperor and Nation in Japan: Political Thinkers of the Tokugawa Period* (Seattle: University of Washington Press, 1964), 173.

6 Mark R. Peattie, "Introduction," in *The Japanese Colonial Empire*, ed. Myers and Peattie, 7.

7 Ibid.

8 Conrad Totman, "Ethnicity in the Meiji Restoration: An Interpretive Essay," *Monumenta Nipponica*, 37, no. 3 (Spring 1984): 269–87.

9 Tessa Morris-Suzuki writes that the Tokugawa *bakufu* instructed Ryukyu officials to look Chinese, when they traveled from Satsuma to Edo, to give the impression of foreignness. Morris-Suzuki, *Re-Inventing Japan*, 19.

10 Takekoshi Yosaburō, *Shin Nihonshi* (A New History of Japan), quoted in Yun Kūnja, *Nihon kokuminron: Kindai Nihon to aidenchichi* (Discourse on the Japanese Nation: Modern Japan and Identity) (Tokyo: Chikuma shobō, 1977), 3–4.

11 The Meiji Restoration as a process is a topic that has received much attention. See Gluck, *Japan's Modern Myths*; Fujitani, *Splendid Monar-*

chy; Garon, *Molding Japanese Minds*; and Michael Lewis, *Becoming Apart: National Power and Local Politics in Toyama, 1868–1945* (Cambridge, Mass.: Harvard University Press, 2000).

12 Marlene Mayo, "The Western Education of Kume Kunitake, 1871–76," *Monumenta Nipponica* 28, no. 1 (Spring 1973): 43.

13 Kume, *Tokumei zenken taishi Bei-ō kairan jikki*, vol. 1, 215. Translation taken from Kume Kunitake, *The Iwakura Embassy, 1871–73, a True Account of the Ambassador Extraordinary Plenipotentiary's Journey of Observations Through the United States and Europe: The United States of America*, 5 vols., ed. Graham Healey and Chūshichi Tsuzuki (Chiba: The Japan Documents, 2002), 219. See also Mayo, "The Western Education of Kume Kunitake," 43. Kume made these observations while in Washington, D.C. Kido Takayoshi, another tour participant, made a similar reflection when he entered into his diary that the black militia unit he observed was "almost equal to that of a white battalion on the battlefield." Kido Takayoshi, *The Diary of Kido Takayoshi*, vol. 2, *1871–1874*, translated by Sidney Devere Brown and Akiko Hirota (Tokyo: University of Tokyo Press, 1985), 167.

14 Kume, *Tokumei zenken taishi Bei-ō kairan jikki*, vol. 2, 114. Translation taken from Kume, *The Iwakura Embassy*, vol. 2, 109–10. For the tour's experiences in England see Andrew Cobbing, "Britain (1): Early Meiji Encounters," in *The Iwakura Mission in America and Europe: A New Assessment*, edited by Ian Nish (Surrey, U.K.: Japan Library, 1988).

15 Kume, *The Iwakura Embassy*, vol. 2: 57–58.

16 Ibid., 89–90.

17 Richard Sims, "France," in *The Iwakura Mission in America and Europe*, ed. Nish, 74.

18 Stefan Tanaka, *Japan's Orient: Rendering Pasts into History* (Berkeley: University of California Press, 1993), 71–75.

19 Ulrich Wattenberg, "Germany: An Encounter Between Two Emerging Countries," in *The Iwakura Mission in America and Europe*, ed. Nish, 117–18. For commentary on German influence on Japan, see Kenneth B. Pyle, "Advantages of Followership: German Economics and Japanese Bureaucrats, 1890–1925," *Journal of Japanese Studies* 1 (Fall 1974): 127–64.

20 Discussion between Bismarck and Japanese members of the Iwakura Mission taken from Kume, *The Iwakura Embassy*, vol. 3, trans. Andrew Cobbing, 323–25.

21 Ōkubo Toshimichi, "Reasons for Opposing the Korean Expedition," in

Sources of Japanese Tradition, vol. 2, edited by Ryusaku Tsunoda, Wm. Theodore De Bary, and Donald Keene, 151–55 (New York: Columbia University Press, 1958).

22   James L. Huffman, *Creating a Public: People and Press in Meiji Japan* (Honolulu: University of Hawai'i Press, 1997), 57–58.

23   See John H. Sagers, *Origins of Japanese Wealth and Power: Reconciling Confucianism and Capitalism, 1830–1885* (New York: Palgrave Macmillan, 2006), for a discussion on Tokugawa-era contributions to Meiji-era economic development.

24   Maruyama Masao, *Studies in the Intellectual History of Tokugawa Japan*, translated by Mikiso Hane (Tokyo: University of Tokyo Press, 1974), 323–28.

25   Fukuzawa Yukichi quoted from his *Bunmeiron no gaiyaku* (Outline on a Theory of Civilization), in Maruyama, *Studies in the Intellectual History*, 331.

26   Quoted in Kuwabara Takeo, *Japan and Western Civilization: Essays on Comparative Culture*, edited by Katō Hidetoshi, translated by Patricia Murray (Tokyo: Tokyo University Press, 1983), 135.

27   E. Patricia Tsurumi, *Factory Girls: Women in the Thread Mills of Meiji Japan* (Princeton, N.J.: Princeton University Press, 1990), 27. Nitobe Inazō wrote on the frustration he felt over his not being able to understand the Tokyo dialect after he arrived from his hometown in present-day Morioka Prefecture. Nitobe Inazō, *Nitobe Inazō zenshū* (The Complete Works of Nitobe Inazō), edited by Yanaihara Tetsuō vol. 19, 621–22 (Tokyo: Kyōbunkan, 1983–87).

28   Quoted in Lewis, *Becoming Apart*, 1.

29   Iwakura Tomomi quoted in Igarashi Akio, *Meiji ishin no shisō* (Ideology of the Meiji Restoration) (Yokohama: Seori shobō, 1996), 145.

30   Iwakura Tomomi, *Iwakura ko jikki* (An Authentic Biography of Prince Iwakura), vol. 2, edited by Tada Kōmon (Tokyo: Hara shobō, 1968), 929.

31   Fukuzawa Yukichi, *An Outline on a Theory of Civilization*, translated by David A. Dilworth (Tokyo: Sophia University, 1973), 23.

32   Garon, *Molding Japanese Minds*. A third important institution was universal military conscription.

33   Quoted in Mark Lincicome, *Principles, Praxis, and the Politics of Educational Reform in Meiji Japan* (Honolulu: University of Hawai'i, 1995), 2. Somehow these "scoundrels" managed to produce one of the more literate societies of its time. Herbert Passin estimates that all male members,

and half of women members, of the samurai class were literate. Herbert Passin, *Society and Education in Japan* (Tokyo: Kodansha International, 1982), 57. Robert P. Dore compares favorably Japanese literacy levels at this time to those in European countries in his *Education in Tokugawa Japan*, Michigan Classics in Japanese Studies, no. 8 (Ann Arbor: Center for Japanese Studies, University of Michigan Press, 1984), 291.

34 Iwakura, *Iwakura no jikki*, vol. 2, 931–32, 937–98.

35 Meiji bunka shiryōsho kangyōkai, ed., *Meiji bunka shiryōsho: dai 8 kan, kyōikuhen* (Meiji Culture Materials Collection: no. 8, Education Edition) (Tokyo: Kaimeitō, 1961), 23.

36 Quoted in Shiro Amioka, "Changes in Education Ideals and Objectives (from Selected Documents, Tokugawa Era to the Meiji Period)," in *The Modernizers: Overseas Students, Foreign Employers, and Meiji Japan*, edited by Adrath W. Burks (Boulder: Westview Press, 1985), 344. See also Marshall, *Learning to be Modern*, chap. 3.

37 Mori Arinori, "Wakayamaken Jinjō Shihangakko" (Wakayama Prefecture Jinjo Shihan school) (November 15, 1887), translated in Ivan P. Hall, *Mori Arinori* (Cambridge: Harvard University Press, 1973), 398.

38 For Japan's early media history see Albert A. Altman, "The Press," in *Japan in Transition: From Tokugawa to Meiji*, edited by Marius B. Jansen and Gilbert Rozman, 231–47 (Princeton, N.J.: Princeton University Press, 1986); and Nishida Taketoshi, *Meiji jidai no shinbun to zasshi* (Meiji-Era Newspapers and Magazines) (Tokyo: Shibundō, 1961); and Huffman, *Creating a Public*, 19–21.

39 Suzuki Kenji, *Nashonarizumu to media* (Nationalism and the Media) (Tokyo: Iwanami shoten, 1997), 228, 236.

40 Huffman, *Creating a Public*, 2.

41 Thongchai Winichakul, *Siam Mapped: A History of the Geo-Body of a Nation* (Honolulu: University of Hawai'i Press, 1994).

42 George B. Sansom, *The Western World and Japan: A Study in the Interaction of European and Asiatic Cultures* (Tokyo: Charles E. Tuttle, 1977), 385–86.

43 Altman, "The Press," 245–46.

44 Huffman, *Creating a Public*, 66.

45 Gluck, *Japan's Modern Myths*, 232–33, writes that the Osaka *Asahi* grew from 50,000 copies in 1890 to 250,000 by 1913, and to 800,000 by 1923. She further notes that between 1905 and 1913 only the Germans published more than the Japanese (12). Andrew Gordon examined Tsuk-

ishima, a working-class island in Tokyo, to find that by 1919, 80 percent of all households subscribed to at least one newspaper, and 19 percent to multiple newspapers. Andrew Gordon, *Labor and Imperial Democracy in Prewar Japan* (Berkeley: University of California Press, 1991), 19.

46   Huffman, *Creating a Public*, 57–58.

47   Nishida, *Meiji jidai no shinbun to zasshi*, 92.

48   Ibid., 145.

49   Huffman, *Creating a Public*, 204–14.

50   See Michael Lewis's account of the role of the press in Toyama Prefecture in his *Becoming Apart*, chap. 5. Regarding Manchuria see Louise Young, *Japan's Total Empire: Manchuria and the Culture of Wartime Imperialism* (Berkeley: University of California Press, 1998).

51   See evidence of this in Lewis, *Becoming Apart*, chap. 4.

52   Gluck, *Japan's Modern Myths*, 9–10.

53   Kerr, *Okinawa*, 156–69.

54   The Perry mission is one such example. William Heine, an artist employed by the mission, left detailed descriptions of the group's experiences with the Ryukyu people in his *With Perry to Japan: A Memoir by William Heine*, translated by Frederic Tractmann (Honolulu: University of Hawai'i Press, 1990).

55   Inoue Kaoru, *Inoue segai den* (The Biography of Inoue Kaoru), edited by Inoue Kaoruka deni hensankai (Tokyo: Hakubunkan, 1910). Marlene Mayo writes that fifty-four shipwrecked Ryukyu sailors were massacred. Marlene Mayo, "The Korean Crisis of 1873 and Early Meiji Foreign Policy," *Journal of Asian Studies* 31, no. 4 (August 1973): 819. Koji Taira argues the invasion to have been unnecessary as the Chinese and Ryukyu governments had amicably resolved the incident according to diplomatic protocol. It did not concern Japan. See Koji Taira, "Troubled National Identity: The Ryukyuans/Okinawans," in *Japanese Minorities: The Illusion of Homogeneity*, edited by Michael Weiner (London: Routledge, 1997), 155.

56   For Ulysses S. Grant's role as arbitrator, see Edwin Pak-wah Leung, "Li Hung-chang and the Liu-ch'iu (Ryukyu) Controversy, 1871–1881," in *Li Hung-chang and China's Early Modernization*, edited by Samuel C. Chu and Kwang-Ching Liu, 162–75 (New York: M. E. Sharpe, 1994); Michael H. Hunt, *The Making of a Special Relationship: The United States and China to 1914* (New York: Columbia University Press, 1983), 118–25; and Kerr, *Okinawa*, 381–92.

57 Walker, *The Conquest of Ainu Lands*, 227. Honda Toshiaki advanced the idea of Ezo control in his 1798 *Secret Plan of Government* (Keisei Hisaku); see Keene, *The Japanese Discovery of Europe*, 175–204. Aizawa Seishisai petitioned the Tokugawa government to establish control over Ezo in his 1825 *New Theses* (Shinron). For an English translation and commentary on this text, see Wakabayashi, *Anti-Foreignism and Western Learning.*

58 Agreement was reached in the Shimoda Treaty that Russia and Japan signed on February 7, 1855. George A. Lensen, *The Russian Push Toward Japan: Russo-Japanese Relations, 1697–1875* (Princeton, N.J.: Princeton University Press, 1959), 327.

59 Howell, "Ainu Ethnicity and the Boundaries," 91.

60 For information on Tokyo Kaitakushi karigakkō, see Kariya Yūichi, "Kaitakushi kagakkō ni okeru Ainu kyōiku" (Ainu Education at the Temporary Developments School), in *Meiji ishin no chiiki to minshū*, edited by Meiji ishin shinshi gakkai, 157–76 (Tokyo: Yoshikawa Kōbunka, 1996). Kuroda Kiyotaka headed the mission sent to negotiate the 1876 Kanghwa Treaty that "opened" Korea to Japanese trade.

61 Ibid., 166.

62 Richard Siddle, *Race, Resistance, and the Ainu of Japan* (New York: Routledge, 1996), 94.

63 Noah McCormack discusses Japanese migration to Hokkaido, particularly that of the outcast *Burakumin*, in his "*Buraku* Emigration in the Meiji Era—Other Ways to Become 'Japanese,'" *East Asian Studies* 23 (2002): 87–108.

64 Fred C. C. Peng, "Education: An Agent of Social Change in Ainu Community Life," in *The Ainu: The Past and the Present*, edited by Fred C. C. Peng and Peter Geiser, 185–87 (Hiroshima: Bunka Publishing Company, 1977). Ainu children were also made to start school one year later than their *wajin* (Japanese) counterparts because of perceived emotional and intellectual differences that Japanese argued existed between the two peoples. See Siddle, *Race, Resistance, and the Ainu of Japan*, 72.

65 Asano Makoto, *Okinawa-ken no kyōikushi* (The History of Education in Okinawa Prefecture) (Kyoto: Shibunkaku shuppan, 1991), 169.

66 See Kinjō Shigeaki, "Kōminka kyōiku no shūchaku eki" (The Terminal Station of Imperialization Education), in *Okinawa tennōsei e no gyakko* edited by Akisaki Moriteru and Kawamitsu Shin'ichi, 104–13 (Okinawa:

The Retrogradation of the Emperor System) (Tokyo: Shakai hyōronsha, 1988), 114–15.

67 Hugh Clarke, "The Great Dialect Debate: The State and Language Policy in Okinawa," in *Society and State in Interwar Japan*, edited by Elise K. Tipton, 193–217 (London: Routledge, 1997).

68 Ogawa Masahito describes the royal visits to the Ainu Schools in his "Kotan e no 'gyōkō'/'gyōkei' to Ainu kyōiku" (A Study of the Royal Visits to Kotan Village with Consideration of Ainu Education Policy), *Kyōikushi gakkai kiyō* 34 (October 1991): 50–65.

69 Iwakura, *Iwakura ko jikki*, vol. 2, 566–68.

70 *Nihongi: Chronicles of Japan from the Earliest Times to A.D. 697*, translated by W. G. Aston (Tokyo: Charles E. Tuttle, 1972), 146.

71 Taira, "Troubled National Identity," 151. Hideyoshi also requested assistance from the Philippines and Korea.

72 Kerr, *Okinawa*, 45–50. Kerr writes that the "tale of Tametomo" took form in 1609, just after Satsuma invaded the islands (46).

73 The four great kings of the Ryukyu Islands were Shunten, Shō En, Shō Nei, and Shō Tai. Tametomo descended from the Minamoto family founded by Emperor Seiwa (r. 858–876). See Kerr, *Okinawa*, 452.

74 Ibid., 453.

75 Quoted in Siddle, *Race, Resistance, and the Ainu of Japan*, 88.

76 Quoted in Peng, "Education," 201.

77 Siddle, *Race, Resistance, and the Ainu of Japan*, 103.

78 This petition also noted the "struggle for survival" that the Ainu would face if given the same rights as Japanese. Ibid., 117–18.

79 Ibid., 111–12.

80 Asano, *Okinawa-ken no kyōikushi*, 141.

81 Ibid., 135.

82 Sawada, *Okinawa to Ainu*, 56.

83 Christy, "The Making of Imperial Subjects in Okinawa," 143.

84 Mochiki Kanjin, "Ryukyu no onna fūzoku" (Customs of Ryukyu Women), *Fujin kōron* (January 1917): 12–33.

85 Iha Fuyū, *Ko-Ryukyo* (Old Ryukyu) (Tokyo: Gansoji, 1922). This work was first published in 1911. Iha notes in his preface that his stimulation for researching his people's history and culture came from a comment made to him by his principal while in the fifth grade, who told him that providing the "Rikijin" (a derogatory term for the Ryukuan) with higher education does not serve the state well (ibid., 14). See also Tomiyama

Ichirō, "The Critical Limits of the National Community: The Ryukyuan Subject," *Social Science Japan Journal* 1, no. 2 (1998): 171.

86 Iha, *Ko-Ryukyu*, 103–14. This section was left out of the book's 1942 edition.

87 Ibid., 120–29, 138.

88 Ibid., 106.

89 The former Crown Prince, Shō Ten, had held the hereditary seat in Japan's Privy Council. Kerr, *Okinawa*, 428. By contrast, the first Ainu to enter the Diet did so almost a full century later, in 1994.

90 Myers and Peattie, eds. "The Japanese Colonial Empire," 224.

91 Fredrick R. Dickinson, *War and National Reinvention: Japan in the Great War, 1914–1919* (Cambridge, Mass.: Harvard University Asia Center, 1999), 87. Japan also considered invading Fujien Province at the onset of World War I. Ibid., 76. For a survey of the Japanese military's role in Japan's expansion see Stewart Lone, *Army, Empire, and Politics in Meiji Japan: The Three Careers of General Katsura Tarō* (New York: St. Martin's Press, 2000).

92 Edward I-te Chen, "Japan's Decision to Annex Taiwan: A Study of Itō-Mutsu Diplomacy, 1894–95," *Journal of Asian Studies* 37, no 1 (November 1977): 61–72.

93 Quoted in Kenneth Pyle, *The New Generation in Meiji Japan: Problems of Cultural Identity, 1885–1895* (Stanford, Calif.: Stanford University Press, 1969), 179.

94 Ibid., 4.

95 Takekoshi Yosaburō, *Japanese Rule over Formosa*, translated by George Braithwaite (London: Longmans, Green, 1907), vii.

96 Montague Kirkwood's ideas are found in his "Shokuminchi seido" (Colonial Policy), in Itō Hirobumi's *Hisho ruisan: Taiwan shiryō* (Classified Collection of Private Documents, Taiwan Materials), edited by Itō Hirobumi and Hirazuka Atsushi, Meiji hyakunenshi sōshi (Meiji Centennial History Collection), vol. 127 (Tokyo: Hara shobō, 1970), and "Taiwan seido Tennō no daiken oyobi gikai ni kan suru ikensho" (An Opinion Paper on the Supreme Authority of the Emperor and the Imperial Diet in Taiwan), ibid., 108–48. Edward I-te Chen also considers Itō's secret papers in his "The Attempt to Integrate the Empire: Legal Perspectives," in *The Japanese Colonial Empire*, ed. Myers and Peattie, 249–50.

97 Michel Lubon, "Ryōtō oyobi Taiwan tōchi ni kan suru kōgi" (A Dis-

cussion on the Administration of the Liaotung Peninsula and Taiwan), in *Hisho ruisan*, ed. Itō and Hirazuka, 399–409.

98 William L. Neumann, *America Encounters Japan: From Perry to MacArthur* (Baltimore: Johns Hopkins Press, 1963), 85.

99 H. W. Denison, "Taiwan oyobi sono tsuizoku shima jumin no genji no kokumin bungen narabi ni Nihonkoku to no shōrai no kankei" (The Present Social Standing of Residents in Taiwan and Neighboring Islands and Their Future Relations with Japan), in *Hisho ruisan*, ed. Itō and Hirazuka, 226–33. His views appear to contradict United States immigration policy at the time that encouraged foreign migration and granted citizenship to Europeans.

100 Mary Elizabeth Berry verifies this—Hideyoshi did send letters to the island and demanded tribute. She concludes, however, that "he was not prepared to elicit with [this] anything more than threatening letters." Mary Elizabeth Berry, *Hideyoshi* (Cambridge, Mass.: Harvard East Asian Monographs, 1982), 212–13.

101 Fujizaki Sainosuke, *Taiwan no hanzoku* (Tribes of Taiwan) (Tokyo: Kokushikan gyokai, 1930), 521–23.

102 Nitobe Inazō, "Japanese Colonization," in *Nitobe Inazō zenshū*, vol. 23, 113–14. First published in *Asian Review*, January 1920.

103 Fujizaki, *Taiwan no hanzoku*, 531.

104 Gotō Shinpei, "The Administration of Formosa (Taiwan)," in *Fifty Years of New Japan*, edited by Okuma Shigenobu and Marcus B. Huish, 530–53 (London: Smith, Elder, 1909), 533.

105 The Tokyo *Asahi shinbun* carried a translation of this document's text on June 1, 1895, and continued to report on the movement for two weeks.

106 Takekoshi Yosaburō calculated that by 1907 "almost 150,000 head-hunting aborigines" had killed off 1,900 Japanese. Takekoshi, *Japanese Rule in Formosa*, 230.

107 Fukuzawa Yukichi, "Taiwan eien no hoshin" (Long-Term Plans for Taiwan), reprinted in *Fukuzawa zenshū*, edited by Jiji shinbōsha, vol. 4, 424. This article originally appeared in the *Seiji Gaikō* (January 8, 1896).

108 Fukuzawa Yukichi, "Taiwan zengo no hōshin" (A Carefully Thought Out Plan for Taiwan), *Fukuzawa zenshū*, ed. Jiji shinbōsha, vol. 4, 602.

109 Takeyoshi Yosaburō describes this policy in his *Japanese Rule in Formosa*, 214.

110 Tsurumi Yūsuke, *Gotō Shinpei*, vol. 1 (Tokyo: Sanshūsha, 1937), 403, 432.

111 Gotō's ideas on this subject particularly resemble those put forth by Friedrich Ratzel. See Smith, *The Ideological Origins of Nazi Imperialism*, 144–52.

112 See Kitaoka Shin'ichi, *Gotō Shinpei: Gaikō to vijon* (Gotō Shinpei: Diplomacy and Vision) (Tokyo: Chūō Kōronsha, 1988), 40.

113 Edward I-te Chen, "Gotō Shinpei, Japan's Colonial Administrator in Taiwan: A Critical Reexamination," *American Asian Review* 13 (Spring 1995): 55.

114 Ibid., 40–44. Chen mentions that on some occasions Japanese police opened fire on those who surrendered. Gotō is also credited with curtailing the island's opium addiction and curbing its general hygiene problems.

115 Fujizaki, *Taiwan no hanzoku*, 857. Recall that the term *buiku* was also used to describe Ainu policy in Tokugawa Japan. For more recent discussion on Japan's assimilation policy in Taiwan, see Ching's *Becoming "Japanese."*

116 Chung Chin-han, *Nihon shokuminchika ni okeru Taiwan kyōikushi* (The History of Taiwanese Education under Japanese Colonialism) (Tokyo: Taga shuppan, 1993), 69–70. E. Patricia Tsurumi, *Japanese Colonial Education in Taiwan, 1895–1945* (Cambridge: Harvard University Press, 1977), provides the most comprehensive work in the English language on Japan's colonial education policy in Taiwan. See also her "Colonial Education in Korea and Taiwan," in *The Japanese Colonial Empire, 1845–1945*, edited by Ramon H. Myers and Mark R. Peattie, 275–311 (Princeton, N.J.: Princeton University Press, 1987).

117 See Tsurumi, *Japanese Colonial Education in Taiwan*, 134–35.

118 Chung, *Nihon shokuminchika ni okeru Taiwan kyōikushi*, 328–31. In Korea the Japanese were able to educate 39.4 percent of school-age children by 1942. See Dong, "Assimilation and Social Mobilization in Korea," 169. Both figures were dwarfed by the 96 percent rate that Japan realized domestically by 1906, over a comparable four-decade time frame. Gluck, *Japan's Modern Myths*, 163.

119 Kim Minsu provides this figure to illustrate Japan's limited success (27 percent) in Korea in his, "Nittei no taikan shinryaku to gengo seisaku" (Imperial Japan's Invasion of Korea and Its Linguistic Policy), *Han* 2, no. 5 (1973): 96–97.

120 Another indication of this education's low level was the extent to which the Japanese avoided it. In 1940, Japanese enrollment in Taiwanese

schools peaked at 396 students. See Tsurumi, *Japanese Colonial Education in Taiwan*, 110. The establishment of Taihoku National University in 1928 marginally benefited the Taiwanese student as the school admitted far more Japanese students (in 1944, 270 as compared to 85 Taiwanese students) (254).

121 Ibid., 215.

122 William Kirk, "Social Change in Formosa," *Sociology and Social Research* 26 (1941–42): 19–20.

123 Tour members did not necessarily cooperate upon their return. Mōna Ludao, who took part in the 1911 tour, later led a major rebellion against Japanese rule in 1933 that left 137 Japanese dead. See Takenaka Nobuko, *Shokuminchi Taiwan no Nihon josei seikatsushi* (The History of Japanese Women's Lifestyles in the Taiwan Colony) (Tokyo: Tabata shoten, 1995), 143.

124 "Formosa Aborigines in Tokyo," *Japan Times*, August 16, 1897. Fujizaki offers brief notes on five of these tours in his *Taiwan no hanzoku*, 874–75. This commentary on the childlike behavior of Taiwanese on trains reminds us of the reaction by U.S. Commodore Matthew Perry's crew upon witnessing the "ludicrous" spectacle of a "dignified mandarin (samurai) whirling around" on the toy train—built to "hardly carry a child of six years of age"—that they presented the Japanese in 1854. See Commodore M. C. Perry, *Narrative of the Expedition to the China Seas and Japan, 1852–1854* (1856; Mineola, N.Y.: Dover, 2000), 357–58.

125 Ayako Hotta-Lister, *The Japan-British Exhibition of 1910: Gateway to the Island Empire of the East* (Surry, U.K.: Japan Library, 1999), 224.

126 "Tokyo Peace Exhibit," *Tourist* 10, no. 2 (March 1922): 23–36. Timothy Mitchell's discussion on "representation"—"everything collected and arranged to stand for something, to represent progress and history, human industry and empire, everything set up, and the whole set-up always evoking somehow some larger truth"—is relevant here. Timothy Mitchell, *Colonizing Egypt* (Berkeley: University of California Press, 1991), 6.

127 Takenaka, *Shokuminchi Taiwan no Nihon josei seikatsushi*, 146.

128 Quoted from *Taiwan kyōkaihō* (November 1898) in ibid., 49.

129 Harry Lamley, "Assimilation Efforts in Colonial Taiwan: The Fate of the 1914 Movement," *Monumenta Serica* 29 (1970–71): 496–520.

130 Edward I-te Chen, "Japanese Colonialism in Korea and Formosa: A Comparison of the Systems of Political Control," *Harvard Journal of*

Asiatic Studies 30 (1970): 134, 147. The Korean police force did, however, outnumber its Taiwanese counterpart 23,000 to 8,600.

131 These formed the three discourses introduced by Nakae Chōmin in his *A Discourse by Three Drunkards on Government*. Edward I-te Chen describes the military's desire to annex Korea after the Sino-Japanese War in his "Japan's Decision to Annex Taiwan."

3   FORMING KOREAN ASSIMILATION POLICY

1   The August 25 issue of the *San Francisco Chronicle* reported that the Japanese minister of the interior warned the major Japanese newspapers against reporting unauthorized news regarding annexation.

2   Ebina Danjō, "Chōsenjin wa Nihon ni dōka shiuru ka" (Can the Korean Be Assimilated into Japan?), *Tokyo Asahi shinbun* (August 25, 1910).

3   Ukita Kazutami, "Kankoku heigō no kōka ikan" (What Are the Effects of Korean Annexation?), *Taiyō* (October 1, 1910). Marius B. Jansen offers biographical information on Ukita in his "Japanese Imperialism: Late Meiji Perspectives," in *The Japanese Colonial Empire*, ed. Myers and Peattie (61–79), 73. Nitobe Inazō offered a similar comparison in December 1919 by writing "to an English student of colonization it will be highly interesting to watch the development of Korea to a Wales or— to an Ireland." Nitobe Inazō, "Japanese Colonization," *Nitobe Inazō zenshū*, vol. 23, 120.

4   Hayashi's comments were included in a longer article titled "Heigō go no Chōsen tōchi mondai" (Korean Administration Issues Following Annexation), *Taiyō* (October 1, 1910): 77–78.

5   Kita Sadakichi, "Kankoku no heigō to kokushi" (National History and Korean Annexation) (Tokyo: Sanseido, 1910); "Chōsen minzoku to wa nan zoya" (What Is the Korean Race), *Minzoku to rekishi* (June 1919): 1–13; and "Nissen ryōminzoku dōgenron" (The Same Origin Theory of the Korean and Japanese Races), *Minzoku to rekishi* (January 1921): 3–39. See also Duus, *The Abacas and the Sword*, 415–17.

6   "Annexation of Korea and Its Practical Effects," *Taiyō* (November 1, 1910): 2–3.

7   Shiratori Kurakichi, "Nihon wa hatashite Chōsen wo kanka shiubekika" (Can Japan Inspire Korea?), *Kyōiku jiron* (September 15, 1910): 6–11. Shiratori, who authored books on the history and geography of both Korea and Manchuria, was a member of Tokyo Imperial University's

history department from 1904 to 1925. See Stefan Tanaka, *Japan's Orient*, 24–25.

8   "Heigō go no Chōsen tōchi mondai," 82. Takekoshi admitted here that at first he was not very supportive of annexation. He now advised the Japanese to move the capital of the colony from Keijō to Heijō (P'yŏngyang) to prepare for Japan's next colonial adventure, Manchuria.

9   "Chōsenjin no dōkaryoku" (Korean Assimilation Capacity), *Chōsen oyobi Manchū* (November 1911): 10, 13.

10   "Nihonjin to Nihon shinmin to no kubetsu" (The Distinction between a Japanese National and a Japanese Subject), *Keijō nippō* (September 13, 1910). The government-general tied a vernacular newspaper, the *Maeil sinbo* (Daily Times), and an English newspaper *The Seoul Press*, to this Japanese language newspaper. The content of the newspapers overlapped, but they also had their own agendas based on their primary readership.

11   "Chōsenjin dōkaron to meishi" (Korean Assimilation and Celebrities), *Chōsen oyobi Manshū* (November 1911): 2–8.

12   Yamashita Nankai, "Jiji no shōrai zenshin dōka seisaku" (A Policy of Gradual Assimilation for Future Self-Rule), *Chōsen shinbun* (September 22, 1910).

13   For a systematic study on Western colonial discourse, see David Spurr, *The Rhetoric of Empire: Colonial Discourse in Journalism, Travel Writing, and Imperial Administration* (Durham, N.C.: Duke University Press, 1993).

14   Quoted in Toby, "Carnival of the Aliens," 424. See also Nakao Hiroshi, "Chōsen shisetsu no mita Edo to hitobito ni utsutta tsūshinshi" (What the Korean Embassies Saw in Edo and What They Left to the People), in *Chōsen tsūshinshi to Nihonjin* (The History of Korean Embassies), edited by Yi Wŏnsik et al., 102–31 (Tokyo: Gakuseisha, 1996), 121–22.

15   Kate Wildman Nakai, *Shogunal Politics: Arai Hakuseki and the Premises of Tokugawa Rule* (Cambridge, Mass.: Harvard University Press, 1988), 334–35.

16   Ronald P. Toby, *State and Diplomacy in Early Modern Japan*, 41–42. The Korean government granted the Japanese one visit to Seoul in 1629 (ibid., 38). James B Lewis also treats pre-Meiji Japan-Korea relations in his *Frontier Contact Between Chosŏn Korea and Tokugawa Japan* (London: Routledge, 2003).

17   Hatada Takashi, *Nihonjin no Chōsenkan* (Japanese Views of the Korean People) (Tokyo: Keisō shobō, 1969), 12–17. Hatada himself dissemi-

nated images of the Korean as an ancient and backward people in his colonial-era writing. See, for example, his "Chōsen no hōken seido ni kan suru oboe gaki" (Notes on Korea's Feudal System), *Rekishi to chiri* 9 (1935): 45–50.

18   The pictures described here are posted on the Tokyo Keizai University Library Web page at http://mdat.ff.tku.ac.jo/korea (accessed May 14, 2008). I am indebted to Kenneth Robinson for introducing this site to me. Katō Kiyomasa led the Japanese invasion of Korea in 1592. Palais, *Confucian Statecraft and Korean Institutions*, 79.

19   Alexis Dudden summarizes foreign views of Korea around the time of the 1907 Hague Peace Conference in her *Japanese Colonization of Korea: Discourse and Power* (Honolulu: University of Hawai'i Press. 2005), chap. 1.

20   Nitobe Inazō, "Primitive Life and Presiding Death in Korea," in *Nitobe Inazō zenshū*, ed. Yanaihara, vol. 12, 327–28.

21   Duus, *The Abacus and the Sword*, chap. 11.

22   Yamaji Aizan quoted in Seung-Mi Han, "Korea through Japanese Eyes: An Analysis of Late Meiji Travelogues on Korea," *Asia Cultural Studies* 24 (March 1998): 61. In the eyes of the colonizer, laziness was a characteristic of all colonized peoples, as Syed Hussein Alatas informs us in his *The Myth of the Lazy Native*, passim.

23   Nanba Kasui, "Chōsen inshō ki" (A Record of Korean Impressions), *Chōsen oyobi Manshū* (February 1912): 65–68.

24   "Chōsen ryōko ni tai suru ippan chūi" (General Cautions regarding Travel in Korea), *Tsūrisuto* (July 1919): 21–23.

25   Seika Ayaka, "Chōsen yori" (From Korea), *Chōsen oyobi Manshū* (August 1912): 70–72. See also Sonia Ryang, "Japanese Travelers' Accounts of Korea," *East Asian History* 13/14 (1997): 138–41, for other images.

26   Both studies appeared in Kubo Takeshi, "Chōsenjin no jinshu kaibō-gakuteki kenkyū" (Research on the Korean Racial Anatomy), *Chōsen igakkai zasshi* 22 (July 1918): 52–86, 146–53. His research was also published in *Chōsen oyobi Manshū*, giving him a larger reader audience.

27   Sŏul taehakkyo ŭikkwa taehak, *Sŏul taehakkyo ŭikkwa taehaksa* (The History of the College of Medicine, Seoul National University) (Seoul: Sŏul taehakkyo ŭikkwa taehak, 1978), 46–49.

28   Nakajima Motojirō, "Chōsen fujin no kotsuban gaikei keizokusu ni oite" (On the Outer Diameter Measurements of the Korean Women's Pelvic Bone), *Chōsen igakkai zasshi* (January 1913): 125–26.

29 Toriga Ramon, *Chōsen e iku hito ni* (To People Going to Korea) (Osaka: Hakuaisha joseikappan, 1914).

30 Hara Sōchiro, *Chōsen no tabi* (A Korean Trip) (Tokyo: Iwamatsudō Shoten, 1917), 69–70.

31 Toriga, *Chōsen e iku hito ni*, 19–21.

32 Quoted in Duus, *The Abacus and the Sword*, 398.

33 See Hildi Kang, *Under the Black Umbrella: Voices from Colonial Korea* (Ithaca, N.Y.: Cornell University Press, 2001), 51–52. This probably was not the case for schools in Keijō. From the 1920s, the *Tong'a Ilbo* frequently reported that schools here never had enough seats to accommodate all who wished to attend.

34 Pak Sunmi, *Chōsen josei no chi no kaiyū: Shokuminchi bunka shihai to Nihon ryūgaku* (Korean Women Journeys of Knowledge: Colonial Cultural Control and Overseas Studies in Japan) (Tokyo: Yamakawa shuppansha, 2005), 28. For information on the Kim brothers, see Carter J. Eckert, *Offspring of Empire* (Seattle: University of Washington Press, 1991).

35 Terauchi Masatake, *Terauchi Masatake monjo*, Reel 32 (Terauchi Masatake papers) (Japanese Diet Library), 74–85. Terauchi offered a similar opinion after he had assumed the position of governor general saying that "people in Korea today are not quite ready for noble learning yet. We must therefore place the emphasis on giving common education on matters familiar to them to make the people capable of performing their allotted work well." Quoted in Abe Hiroshi, "Higher Learning in Korea under Japanese Rule: Keijō Imperial University and the 'People's University' Movement," *Developmental Economics* 9, no. 2 (June 1971): 175.

36 "Gappōgo no Chōsenjin kyōiku" (Korean Education after Annexation), *Kyōikukai* (November 1910): 1–3.

37 "Sirŏp kyoyuk e ch'wihaya" (Concerning Practical Education), *Maeil sinbo* (September 29, 1910). This Korean newspaper's Japanese sister newspaper complemented this opinion by arguing that the Japanese must train the Korean people in economic development, public finance, and military service to enable them to walk alongside the Japanese in global activity. "Chōsenjin kyōiku no konpon'gi" (Fundamental Principles of Korean Education), *Keijō nippō* (September 8, 1910).

38 Mitsuchi Chūzō, "Chōsenjin no kyōiku" (Korean Education), *Kyōikukai* (December 1910): 23–26.

39 Horio Mine, "Shinkokumin no kyōiku" (Education for the New Nationals), *Kyōiku jiron* (September 5, 1910): 13–15.

40 Korean language study among Japanese progressed as Japanese presence onto the Korean peninsula intensified. See Yamada Kanto, *Shokuminchi Chōsen ni okeru Chōsengo shorei seisaku: Chōsengo wo mananda Nihonjin* (Japan's Korean Encouragement Policies in Colonial Korea: Japanese Who Learned the Korean Language) (Tokyo: Fuji shuppan, 2004), chap. 1, for the historical overview of Korean language study by Japanese.

41 The two articles, titled "Needs of Greater Japan" and "School Textbooks for Chosen," appeared in the *Seoul Press* on September 8, 1910. The *Seoul Press* was founded in 1906 as the *Seoul Times* to provide a pro-Japanese voice to counter Ernest Bethell's *Korean Daily News*'s generally anti-Japanese tone. Resident General Itō Hirobumi's former secretary and *Japan Times* editor, Jimoto Motosata, served as the newspaper's first editor. The newspaper published its last issue in May 1937. Andrei Lankov, "The Dawn of Modern Korea: The Seoul Times," *Korea Times* (August 21, 2005).

42 *Seoul Press* (November 26, 1910). We find a similar statement in the government-general's report to commemorate the twenty-fifth anniversary of Japanese rule, which informed its readers that Korean students require only one and a half months to master classroom terms in Japanese. Chōsen government-general, *Thriving Chōsen: A Survey of Twenty-five Years' Administration* (Keijō: Chōsen government-general, 1935), 16.

43 Yamada, *Shokuminchi Chōsen ni okeru Chōsengo shorei seisaku*, 48–49.

44 Ibid., 86, 174.

45 "Yŏja kyoyuk ŭi kŏmmu" (The Urgency of Women's Education), *Maeil sinbo*, September 22, 1910. Kim Puja's *Shokuminchiki Chōsen no kyōiku to jendaa* presents an interesting discussion on female education during this period.

46 Quoted in Chōsen government-general, *Thriving Chosen*, 9–10.

47 Education Ordinance quoted in Chōsen government-general, *Results of Three Years' Administration of Chosen* (Keijō: Chōsen government-general, 1914), 52.

48 See Moon-Jong Hong, "Japanese Colonial Education Policy in Korea" (Ph.D. diss., Harvard University, 1992), appendix, 13.

49 Chōsen government-general, *Chōsen sōtokufu shisei nenpō* (Chōsen government-general administration annual), vol. 4 (Keijō: Chōsen government-general, 1914), 292.

50   For the content of textbooks used by Koreans during this initial period of Japanese rule, see Yi Sukcha, *Kyōkasho ni egakareta Chōsen to Nihon* (Japan and Korea in Textbooks) (Tokyo: Horupu shuppan, 1985), esp. 275–99.

51   E. Patricia Tsurumi, "Colonial Education in Korea and Taiwan," in *The Japanese Colonial Empire*, ed. Myers and Peattie, 300.

52   Dong Wonmo calculated that the government-general per capita spending for education was lower for the Korean than the Japanese student throughout the period of colonial rule. By 1942 the Japanese administration expenditures averaged close to 4 times more (22.86 to 82.57 yen) for the Japanese student's education. This trend was also seen in classroom size. While almost even in 1912 (27.9 Koreans to 31.7 Japanese), by 1942 Korean classrooms had just over twice as many students (73.1) as Japanese classrooms (35.9). Dong Wonmo, "Japanese Colonial Policy and Practice in Korea, 385.

53   Quoted in Byron K. Marshall, *Learning to be Modern*, 40.

54   For example, the *Kyŏngnam ilbo* lasted until 1915, when it went out of business. For a review of newspapers in Korea over this period, see Michael E. Robinson, "Colonial Publication Policy and the Korean Nationalist Movement," in *The Japanese Colonial Empire*, ed. Myers and Peattie, 312–46. Robinson does note that the Japanese administration allowed for a small number of religious and youth publications to publish during this period (324).

55   *Korean Daily News* and *Taehan maeil sinbo*. Suyo Yŏkusa Yŏn'guhŏe, ed., *Singminji Chosŏn kwa Maeil sinbo* (The *Maeil sinbo* and Colonial Korea) (Seoul: Sinsŏwan, 2003); Kim and Kim, *Korea and the Politics of Imperialism, 1876–1910*, 181–82; and Andre Schmid, *Korea Between Empires, 1895–1919* (New York: Columbia University Press, 2002), 166–67.

56   Hwang Minho, "Ch'ongnon: 1910 yŏndae Chosŏn ch'ongdokbu ŭi ŏllon chŏngch'aekgwa *Maeil sinbo*" (Introduction: The 1910s Government-General's Press Policy and the *Maeil sinbo*). In *Singminji Chosŏn kwa Maeil sinbo*, edited by Suyo Yŏkusa Yŏn'guhŏe, 11–31 (Seoul: Sinsŏgwan, 2003), 19.

57   The newspaper's excessive use of Chinese characters could have in part accounted for the newspaper's low sales, especially after the government-general allowed rival Korean newspapers publication rights from 1920. In 1930, for example, the *Maeil sinbo* sold 23,000 issues daily, far less than the *Chosŏn ilbo* and the *Tong'a ilbo*. See Robinson, "Colonial

Publication Policy and the Korean Nationalist Movement," 325–26, for a discussion on sales figures. For an early history of the newspaper, see Hwang Minho, "Ch'ongnon," 11–31.

58 "Sinmun kwa munmyŏng" (The Newspaper and Civilization), *Maeil sinbo* (February 19, 1911).

59 "Sin sasang ŭi chuip" (Infusion of New Thought), *Maeil sinbo* (August 31, 1910).

60 "Kaehyŏk ŭi sidae" (A Revolutionary Era), *Maeil sinbo* (September 7, 1910). The newspaper occasionally reinforced this idea of innovation and reform in a column titled "World History" in which it introduced its readers to such events as the Church of England reforms, the thirty-year war, and great discoveries of the sixteenth century.

61 "Tonghwa ŭi chuŭi (The Meaning of Assimilation), *Maeil sinbo* (August 30, 1910). Although the article was clearly written from a colonizer perspective (and perhaps even translated from Japanese) the authors appealed to their Korean audience by stressing the need for "we" (*a*) Koreans working with the Japanese (*Ilbon'in*).

62 "Taeu e kwanhan sa" (Regarding the Matter of Treatment), *Maeil sinbo* (September 9, 1910). Koreans had referred to Japanese as *wae* or *waein* from ancient times. The word *yŏbo* could be the Japanese parroting a shortened form of the Korean greeting *yŏbo seyŏ* (hello), or an intimate address commonly used by spouses (dear or honey). Either way, the Korean people interpreted the Japanese use of the word as derogatory, and rather comical if the user added the Japanese honorific ending *san* (that is, y*obo-san*, or Hey you, sir/madam). Nakajima Atsushi illustrated this confrontation over the word's use in his "Junsa no iru fūkei" (The Scenery Where the Police Are). In one scene, a Japanese girl offers her seat to an elderly Korean gentleman who becomes upset by her calling him y*obo-san*:

> Japanese girl: "But didn't I call you 'Yobo-san?'"
> Korean man: "It doesn't matter either way, this yobo thing."
> Japanese girl: "I didn't say 'Yobo,' I said 'Yobo-san.'"
> Another Japanese passenger: "Yobo-san, the seat is empty. She offered you the seat politely so why are you angry?"

(From *"Gaichi" no Nihongo bungakusen, 3: Chōsen* [Japanese Literature in the Empire, 3: Korea], ed. Kurokawa Sō [Tokyo: Shinjuku shobō, 1996], 76–77.)

63 "Tonghwa ŭi pangbŏp" (Assimilation Techniques), *Maeil sinbo* (September 14, 1910).

64 "Kugŏ yŏn'gu ŭi p'iryo" (The Necessity of National Language Research), *Maeil sinbo* (February 23, 1911).

65 "Wisaeng kwa susin" (Hygiene and Ethics), *Maeil sinbo* (October 7, 1910). See also Todd A. Henry, "Sanitizing Empire: Japanese Articulation of Korean Otherness and the Construction of Early Colonial Seoul, 1905–1919," *Journal of Asian Studies* 64, no. 3 (August 2005): 639–76.

66 Korean marriage arrangements, as in most traditional societies, were determined by the families through a matchmaker. Often these arrangements were made when the future bride and groom were still young. Impoverished families sent their girls as "child brides" (*minmyŏnŭri*) to their husband-to-be's house to be raised by their future mother-in-law. See Laurel Kendall, *Getting Married in Korea: Of Gender, Morality, and Modernity* (Berkeley: University of California Press, 1996), 62.

67 "P'ungsŏl kwa chohon" (Rumor and Early Marriage), *Maeil sinbo* (October 16, 1910). The newspaper again addressed women problems in April 1911. Here it argued early marriage to be a product of Korean society's disregard for human rights. In the second half of this two-part editorial on people trafficking, the *Maeil sinbo* addressed the issue of selling girls into prostitution. See "Inmul ŭi aksŭp" (The Terrible Custom of People Trafficking), *Maeil sinbo* (October 26–27, 1911).

68 For the Kabo Reform Edicts, see Peter H. Lee, ed., *Sourcebook of Korean Literature*, vol. 2 (New York: Columbia University Press, 1996), 382–84. For discussion on early marriage, see Kendall, *Getting Married in Korea*, 62–63.

69 At least one Korean recalls using the grounds of the shrine as a picnic site; the vistas it provided were the best Seoul had to offer. See Kang, *Under the Black Umbrella*, 114.

70 As described in the *Maeil sinbo* (July 25 and 30, 1912). Sunjong ascended the Korean imperial throne as emperor in 1907 when his father, Kojong, was ordered by Resident General Itō Hirobumi to abdicate. At the time of annexation, the Japanese administration demoted him to king. The *Seoul Press* referred to him as "prince."

71 *Seoul Press* (October 16 and 21, 1910). The October 23 issue published a complete list of the tour's participants. C. I. Eugene Kim and Han-Kyo Kim describe Min Chŏngsik as a former high government official who organized and led an opposition group of 500 people following the

signing of the Protectorate Treaty in 1905. See their *Korea and the Politics of Imperialism*, 197–98.

72   Information on the tour taken from the *Kyŏngnam ilbo* (October 29 and November 5, 1910). The *Maeil sinbo* and the *Seoul Press* also gave the tour considerable coverage.

73   "Kwijok chegong ŭi Tokyo kwangwang ŭl hahan" (Celebrating the Aristocratic Tour's Sightseeing in Tokyo), *Maeil sinbo* (October 20, 1910).

74   "Chōsen kizoku no shaon" (The Gratitude of Korean Aristocrats), *Tokyo Asahi shinbun* (November 3, 1910). The Korean imperial audiences were reported in the November 5, 1910, edition.

75   *Maeil sinbo* (October 29, 1910).

76   The *Maeil sinbo* reported the parade route after the fact, on November 6, 1910.

77   As witnessed by the plot to assassinate Governor General Terauchi that it fabricated in December 1910. Japanese police arrested more than 600, tried 105, and eventually sentenced five Koreans to long-term prison terms following their retrial. Eckert et al., *Korea Old and New*, 261. Pak Kyŏnsik's illustration of rising crime over this initial decade presents another measure of Korean dissatisfaction with Japan's presence, although not necessarily the extent of Korean patriotism, as Pak suggests. Pak, *Nihon teikokushugi no Chōsen shihai*, 168–69.

4   POST-MARCH FIRST POLICY REFORM AND ASSIMILATION

1   Dickinson, *War and National Reinvention*, 200, 229. See also Lewis, *Becoming Apart*, 131–41.

2   Between 1918 and 1924 Korean rice exports to Japan doubled from 2.2 million to 4.6 million *sŏk*. Takashi Hatada, *A History of Korea*, translated by Warren W. Smith and Benjamin H. Hazzard (Santa Barbara, Calif.: Clio Press, 1969), 117.

3   Yun Ch'iho notes his interview with the Osaka *Mainichi shinbun* on why he refused to participate in the March First Movement in his *Yun Ch'iho ilgi*, vol. 7 (March 2, 1919).

4   Quoted in Ku, *Korea Under Colonialism*, 138. See also Nagata, *Nihon no Chōsen kankei to kokusai kankei*, chapter 7, for a review of the U.S. response to Japan's handling of the Korean independence movement.

5   Japan was to receive a permanent seat on the council of the League of

Nations. Norris criticized the United States for not coming to Korea's assistance in 1904. See his statements in 66th Congress, 1st sess., *Congressional Record* 58 (October 13, 1919): 6616, 6626. See similar commentary by Georgia's Thomas E. Watson in Senate records, "Valor Medal for Root—National Arts Club Will Honor Head of Mission to Russia," 67th Congress, 2nd sess., *Congressional Record* 62 (March 21, 1920): 4182–86.

6 Great Britain Parliament, House of Commons, *The Parliamentary Debates*, Official Reports, July 7, 1919 (London: H.M.S.O., 1919): 1007–1008. Harmsworth was responding to an inquiry as to whether the British government "was prepared to take any steps to help secure justice and good government for [the Korean] people."

7 Osborne's report is found in House records, 66th Congress, 3rd sess., *Congressional Record* 60 (December 23, 1920): 707–28. The Japanese did not want the tour to visit Korea in the first place. While in China the group read newspaper reports of cholera outbreaks in Korea, as well as of plans by Korean agitators to do something desperate after their arrival in Korea. Tour members interpreted these reports as attempts by the Japanese to scare them. Once the tour arrived in Korea, the colonial government sheltered them from the Korean people.

8 "Chōsen no tōchi to dōka" (Korean Administration and Assimilation), *Nihon oyobi Nihonjin* (October 1, 1919): 1.

9 Aoyagi Tsunatarō, *Shin Chōsen* (New Korea) (Tokyo: Yūken hansho, 1925), 60–74. For Aoyagi's views in his 1923 book *Chōsen tōchiron* (On Korean Administration), see Mark Peattie, "Japanese Attitudes toward Colonialism," in *The Japanese Colonial Empire*, ed. Myers and Peattie, 109–10.

10 Iwasa Zentarō, "Chōsen tōchi ikensho" (An Opinion on Korean Administration), in *Saitō Makoto monjo* (Official Papers of Saitō Makoto), vol. 15, March 1, 1928 (Seoul: Koryŏ sŏrim, 1990), 31–44.

11 Akagi Kameichi, "Taisen shigi: Dōka seisaku wo haisu" (A Personal Submission concerning Korea: Doing Away with Assimilation Policy), *Nihon oyobi Nihonjin* (February 1 and 15, 1920).

12 Hosoi Hajime's six-part article appeared in *Nihon oyobi Nihonjin* between October 1 and December 15, 1920, under the title "Chōsen no tōchi" (Korean Administration).

13 Ibid. (October 1, 1920), 35.

14 Ibid., 37.

15   Ibid. (October 15, 1920), 24.

16   Ibid., 27–28.

17   Yanaihara was purged in 1937 over his lectures on, among other points, the compatibility of nationalism with pacifism. Kevin M. Doak, "Colonialism and Ethnic Nationalism in the Political Thought of Yanaihara Tadao (1893–1961)," *East Asian History* 10 (1995): 92.

18   Jung-Sun N. Han, "An Imperial Path to Modernity: Yoshino Sakuzō and the Making of a New Liberal Projection in Japan, 1905–1937" (Ph.D. diss., University of Washington, 2003), 37.

19   Yoshino Sakuzō, "Shina-Chōsen no hannichi to waga kokumin no hansei" (Anti-Japanese [feeling] in China and Korea and Our People's Reflection about It), *Fujin kōron* (August 1919): 21.

20   Yoshino Sakuzō, "Chōsenjin no kidai no sangeki ni tsuite no hansei" (Reflecting on the Korean People's Remarkable Tragedy), *Fujin kōron* (July 1921): 3–4.

21   Yanaihara Tadao, "Chōsen tōchi no hōshin" (A Plan for Korean Administration), *Chūō Kōron* 41 (June 1926): 35–46. In a 1937 publication titled *Minzoku to kokka* (Nation and State), Yanaihara proposed that a prosperous relationship would have the Japanese and Koreans sharing their cultural strong points to form an entity that was "not the same as the current Korean or Japanese nation but rather . . . something which embraces both." Quoted in Susan C. Townsend, *Yanaihara Tadao and Japanese Colonial Policy: Redeeming Empire* (Surrey, U.K.: Curzon Press, 2000), 238.

22   Yanaihara Tadao, *Yanaihara Tadao zenshū*, vol. 1 (Tokyo: Iwanami shoten, 1963–65), 465–71.

23   Yanaihara Tadao, "Shōnaru kanjō to dainaru kanjō" (Small and Big Emotions), in *Yanaihara Tadao zenshū*, vol. 23, 342. Illustrative of this thinking was his belief that the Korean people should be allowed a local assembly, rather than be granted a seat in Japan's national assembly. Ibid., vol. 1, 292–93. See also Peattie, "Japanese Attitudes Toward Colonialism," 114–18.

24   "Chōsen no sōjō to sōtoku seiji no kaizen" (The Korean Disturbances and Government-General Administration Reforms), *Chōsen kōron* (April 1919): 2–6.

25   Kita Sadakichi, "Toshin Senman ryokō nisshi" (Travels through Korea and Manchuria), *Minzoku to rekishi* (January 1921): 271–82.

26　Kurosaka Katsumi, "Chōsen no rekishiteki kansatsu" (Historical Observations of Korea) *Chōsen* (August 1921): 48–68.

27　Hozumi Shigetō, "Chōsen wo tōtte" (Passing through Korea), *Chūō Kōron* (January 1926): 14–18.

28　Ibid. (February 1926): 54–55.

29　"Chōsen ni okeru eisei ni kan suru meishin" (Superstitions over Health Matters in Korea), *Chōsen* (October 1927): 108–23.

30　Zenshū Eisuke, "Chōsen no hanzai sūko" (Korean Crime Tendencies), *Chōsen* (June 1928): 43–59.

31　Sasagawa Rinfū, "Chōsen sozoro aruki" (A Stroll around Korea), *Chūō Kōron* (August 1926): 79–94.

32　Governor General Hasegawa Yoshimichi outlined a similar set of reform measures before leaving office in August 1919. "Sōjō zengosaku shaken" (A Personal Opinion of Better Strategy after the Disturbances), *Saitō Makoto monjo*, vol. 1, 77–227. See Richard Devine's English translation and commentary in his "Japanese Rule in Korea after the March First Uprising: Governor General Hasegawa's Recommendations," *Monumenta Nipponica* 52, no. 4 (Winter 1997): 523–40.

33　Hara Takashi, "Taiwan mondai futa an" (Two Proposals for the Taiwan Problem), in *Hisho ruisan*, ed. Itō et al., 32–34.

34　Hara Takashi, *Hara Takashi nikki* (Hara Takashi's Diaries), edited by Hara Keiichirō, vol. 4, May 31, 1911 (Tokyo: Kan'gensha, 1950), 276.

35　Hara Takashi, "Chōsen sōtokufu kansei ni oki: Hara sori daijin no dan" (Discussion with Prime Minister Hara Regarding Revisions in the Korean Government-General Organization), in *Saitō Makoto monjo*, vol. 2 (1918), 6.

36　In his September 24, 1918, letter of resignation, Hasegawa noted that the rice riots forced him to delay his request to resign. His letter to Prime Minister Terauchi appears in *Terauchi Masatake monjo*, September 23, 1918.

37　Hara Takashi, "Chōsen tōchi shaken" (A Personal Opinion on Korean Administration), in *Saitō Makoto kankei monjo*, reel 104 (1919), Japanese Diet Library, 1998.

38　Hara changed this legislation to allow for a civilian governor general a week later. However, army generals dominated this post until Japan's retreat from the peninsula in 1945. See Dong, "Japanese Colonial Policy in Korea," 248–49.

39 Quoted in Donald N. Clark, *Living Dangerously in Korea: The Western Experience, 1900–1950* (Norwalk, Conn.: EastBridge, 2003), 63.

40 Saitō Makoto, "A Message from the Imperial Government to the American People: Home Rule in Korea," *The Independent* (January 31, 1920): 167–69. Andre Schmid notes this as one of a number of articles penned by Japanese officials that appeared in foreign presses. See his *Korea Between Empires*, 163.

41 Yamada, *Shokuminchi Chōsen ni okeru Chōsengo shorei seisaku*, 37.

42 Hanguk Charyo yǒnguso, ed., *Chosǒn t'ongji Charyo* (Materials on Korean Administration), vol. 5 (Seoul: Hanguk Charyo yǒnguso, 1996), 809–14. See also Baldwin, "The March First Movement," 191–93.

43 Ibid., 192.

44 "Chōsen chiho no hensen wo kataru" (Transitions in Korea's Local System), in *Kenkyū shūsei: Chōsen kindai shiryō* (Research Compilations: Modern Korean Historical Materials), edited by Kondō Ken'ichi, vol. 2 (Tokyo: Yūhōkyōkai Chōsen shiryō kenkyūkai, 1958), 76–77.

45 Saitō Makoto, "Chōsen tōchi ni tsuite" (Concerning Korean Administration), in *Saitō Makoto monjo*, vol. 2 (January 1921), 424.

46 Saitō Makoto, "Chōsen no tōchi" (Korean Administration), *Chōsen* (January 1921): 3–7. The term *culture* was a buzzword frequently heard in the homeland, as well. Sugimori Kōjirō contrasted it with *militarism* in his definition of the purpose of *culturalism*—freeing the people from the sufferings of narrow-minded patriotism. Sugimori Kōjirō, "Gendai keimō undō no ichi hyōgō" (The Slogan of the Contemporary Enlightenment Movement), which appeared in "Bunka seisaku no kenkyū" (The Study of Culture Lifestyle), *Fujin kōron* (June 1922): 33. Komagame Takeshi contends that *bunka* (culture) replaced *bunmei* (civilization) in textbooks with little apparent change in meaning in his *Shokuminchi keikoku Nihon no bunka tōchi*, 203.

47 Saitō Makoto, "Kaisei chihō seido shikō isshūnen ni saishite" (One Year of Reform in the Local System), *Chōsen* (October 1921): 1–3.

48 Mizuno Rentarō's report was appended to Saitō Makoto, "Dōchiji kaigi ni sai shite" (On the Prefectural Governor's Meeting), *Chōsen* (June 1922): 4–5.

49 This letter is found in Kim Sangman, ed., *Tong'a ilbo sa* (The History of the *Tong'a ilbo*), vol. 1 (Seoul: Tong'a ilbo sa, 1975), 151–52.

50 For the text of the reforms see "Chōsen shisei no kaizen" (Reforms in Korean Administration), *Saitō Makoto monjo*, vol. 1, 73–141.

51 Moon-Jong Hong summarizes these ordinances in his "Japanese Colonial Education Policy in Korea," 139–48.

52 This report, "Chōsen kyōiku reian" (Education Ordinance Proposal), can be found in *Saitō Makoto kankei monjo*, reel 77 (November 21, 1921).

53 Chōsen government-general, *Thriving Chōsen*, 13.

54 Shibata Zensaburō, "Chihō seido no kaisei to kyōiku shisetsu ni tsuite" (Reform of the Regional System and Education Facilities), *Chōsen* (October 1921): 80.

55 Marshall, *Learning to be Modern*, 93–94.

56 Akaike Manjirō, "Chōsen kyōikukai no shin shimei" (The True Mission of the Korean Education Association), *Chōsen kyōiku* (April 1923): 5–7.

57 Sawayanagi Seitarō, "Kyōgaku mondai" (The Problem of Integrated Education), *Chōsen kyōiku* (March 1922): 61–67.

58 Homi K. Bhabha, *The Location of Culture* (London: Routledge, 1994).

59 Kamada Eikichi, "Naisen kyōgaku ni tsuite" (Concerning Japanese-Korean Integrated Education), *Chōsen kyōiku* (March 1922): 75–79.

60 *Chōsen* (January 1925): 143–47.

61 Chōsen government-general, *Chōsen sōtokufu tōkei nenpō* (Chōsen Government-General Annual Book of Statistics) (Keijō: Chōsen government-general, 1930), 614–38. Statistics of Japanese studying in Korean public common schools were 1929 figures.

62 Kang, *Under the Black Umbrella*, 52–54.

63 Takasaki Sōji, *Shokuminchi Chōsen no Nihonjin* (Japanese of Colonial Korea) (Tokyo: Iwanami shoten, 2002), 171–72.

64 Chōsen government-general, "Gakkō kyōren jisshi ketteian" (Proposal Regarding the Implementation of School Military Training), *Saitō Makoto monjo*, vol. 5 (1925), 318.

65 Frequently Korean students alone were punished after their altercations with Japanese students. The most serious incident resulted in the 1929 Kwangju student demonstrations.

66 See Peter Hyun's experiences in Japantown as told in his *Man Sei! The Making of a Korean American* (Honolulu: University of Hawai'i Press, 1986), 63–65.

67 Hashiya Hiroshi, "Shokuminchi toshi" (Colonial City), in *Kindai Nihon no kiseki: toshi to minshū* (The Locus of Modern Japan: The City and the Masses), edited by Narita Ryūichi, 215–36 (Tokyo: Yoshikawa Hiroshi bunkan, 1993). Alain Delissen's presentation, "Seoul, Summer 1925: The Social Space and the 'Natural' Event," given at

Harvard University's Korea Institute (October 31, 2002) also addressed this topic.

68 Quoted in Kawamura Minato, *Sōru toshi monogatari: rekishi, bungaku, to fūkei* (The Story of Seoul: History, Literature, and Landscape) (Tokyo: Heibonsha, 2000), 106.

69 Nanba Kasui, "Chōsen inshōki" (A Record of Impressions of Korea), *Chōsen oyobi Manshū* (February 1912): 66.

70 Yi, *Kyōiku ni okareta Chōsen to Nihon*, 352–66.

71 Yi Hyŏnsin, ed., *Han'guk kyoyuk charyo chipsŏng* (Korean Education Materials Collection) (Sŏngnam: Han'guk chŏngsin munhwa yŏngu won, 1991), vol. 4, 680–81.

72 Yi, *Kyōkasho ni egakareta Chōsen to Nihon*, 352–66.

73 Robert T. Oliver, *Syngman Rhee: The Man Behind the Myth* (New York: Dodd Mead, 1954), 134. For details of their wedding, see Yi Pangja, *The World Is One: Princess Yi Pangja's Autobiography*, translated by Kim Suhkyu (Seoul: Taewon Publishing Company, 1973).

74 Ibid., 72. One rumor was that these wedding arrangements drove Kojong to suicide. See Chong-sik Lee, *The Politics of Korean Nationalism* (Berkeley: University of California Press, 1963), 108.

75 Yi, *The World Is One*, 60, 95, 108–9.

76 Saitō, "Chōsen tōchi ni tsuite," *Saitō Makoto monjo* vol. 1, 3.

77 Ellen Salem, "Women Surviving: Palace Life in Seoul after the Annexation," in *Virtues in Conflict: Tradition and the Korean Woman Today*, edited by Sandra Mattielli, 67–98 (Seoul: Royal Asiatic Society, 1977).

78 *Tokyo Asahi shinbun* (April 28, 1926).

79 Saitō Makoto, "Ri ōdenka wo itami tatematsurite" (Offering Grievances for Prince Yi), *Chōsen* (June 1926): 2.

80 *Japan Times* (June 10, 1926).

81 I consider in greater depth the significance of Sunjong's death and funeral in Japan's colonial history in "The 1920 Colonial Reforms and the June 10 (1926) Movement: A Korean Search for Ethnic Space," in *Colonial Rule and Social Change in Korea, 1910–1945*, edited by Clark Sorensen and Yong-Chool Ha (Seattle: Publications of the Center for Korea Studies, University of Washington Press, forthcoming).

82 Saitō Makoto, "Chōsen shisei no kaizen" (Reform in Korean Administration), *Saitō Makoto monjo*, vol. 2, 100.

83 See Itō Fujitarō, "Zaigai Senjin no sōtokufu kankō" (Chōsen Governmnet-General Tours for Expatriate Koreans), *Chōsen* (February 1921): 131–42.

84 In 1924, the Political Study Club (Yŏnjŏnghoe), organized by *Tonga ilbo* owner Kim Sŏngsu, also considered the idea. See Robinson, *Cultural Nationalism in Colonial Korea*, 143.

85 "Chōsen ni tai suru sanseiken jisshi ni kan suru seigansho" (A Petition regarding the Effectuation of Political Participation Rights in Korea), *Saitō Makoto kankei monjo*, reel 76 (February 1929).

86 Chōsen government-general, Keimu kyoku toshoka. "Ri denka no shikyo ni saishi 'shinbunshi wo tōshite mitaru' Chōsenjin no shisō keikō" (Tendencies in the Korean's Thought "as Seen through Newspapers" at the Time of the Death of the Yi Highness) (Keijō: Chōsen government-general Secret Report, 1926); and Chōsen government-general, "Dokuritsu undō ni okeru minzoku undō no kōgai" (A Summary of the People's Movement from the Cessation of the Independence Movement), *Saitō Makoto kankei monjo*, reel 97, January 1927.

87 Robinson, *Cultural Nationalism in Colonial Korea*, 158. See also his "Colonial Publication Policy," 312–47, and "Broadcasting in Korea, 1924–1937: Colonial Modernity and Cultural Hegemony," in *Japan's Competing Modernities: Issues in Culture and Democracy, 1900–1930*, edited by Sharon A. Minichiello, 358–78 (Honolulu: University of Hawai'i Press, 1998).

88 Baldwin, "The March First Movement," 211.

89 Mizuno Rentarō, "Chōsen ni okeru genron no jiyū-osan no seiji" (Freedom of Speech in Korea: Politics of the Mountain), in *Mizuno Rentarō kaisōroku, kankei bunsho* (Memoirs and Official Papers of Mizuno Rentarō), edited by Nishio Rintarō (Tokyo: Yamagawa shuppansha, 1999), 52.

5   RADICAL ASSIMILATION UNDER WARTIME CONDITIONS

1 Robinson, "Colonial Publication Policy," 327, 339. From May 1926 publications exported to the Korean Peninsula from Japan also were subjected to Korea's publication regulations (ibid., 336).

2 Yamada, *Shokuminchi Chōsen ni okeru Chōsengo shōrei seisaku*, 144.

3 Nakanishi Inosuke predicted that Ugaki's administration would be remembered as "industrial rule" in his "Saikin no Chōsen wo kataru" (Regarding Contemporary Korea), *Tōyō* (October 1933): 137. Bruce Cumings argues this industrial push to be a colonial legacy of Japanese

rule in his "Colonial Formations and Deformations: Korea, Taiwan, and Vietnam," in *Decolonization: Perceptions from Now and Then*, edited by Prasenjit Duara, 278–98 (London: Routledge, 2004).

4   Ugaki Kazunari, "Chōsen tōchi no taidō" (The Great Road of Korean Administration), *Chūō Kōron* (January 1934): 85–87.

5   Ugaki Kazunari, "Chōsen no shōrai" (Korea's Future), *Ugaki Kazunari monjo* (Japanese National Diet Library). Ugaki gave this speech on September 11, 1934.

6   Ugaki, "Chōsen tōchi no taidō," 80.

7   Nakanishi, "Saikin no Chōsen wo kataru," 143.

8   Takahashi Kamekichi, "Chōsen wa umarefukeru" (Korea Is Reborn), *Kaizō* (April 1935): 47–63.

9   Takebe Kin'ichi, "Kōmin kyōiku no hitsuyō" (The Necessity of Civic Education), *Bunkyō no Chōsen* (January 1931): 2–3.

10   Nakamura Sei, "Waga kō no kōmin kunren shisetsu" (The Facilities for Civic Training at Our School), *Bunkyō no Chōsen* (April 1933): 125.

11   Kamatsuka Tamotsu, "Kōmin kyōiku no shin shimei wo akirakani shi: Chōsen no kōminka yōmoku no seishin ni oyobu" (Clarifying the New Mission of Civic Education: Concerning the Principal Items of the Spirit of Korea's Civic Education) *Kōmin kyōiku* (July 1935): 27–28.

12   Nakamura, "Waga kō no kōmin kunren shisetsu," 126–27.

13   Chōsen government-general, "Chōsen sōtokufu jikyoku taisaku chōsakai shimon'an sankōsho" (A Relevance Report for the Korean Government-General Investigative Meeting to Devise Counterplan to Meet the Present Situation), in *Ilcheha chibae chŏngch'aek charyojip*, ed. Sin, vol. 15, 5–329.

14   This document can be found in *Ilcheha chibae chŏngch'aek charyojip*, ed. Sin, 331–671. See also Carter J. Eckert, *Offspring of Empire: The Koch'ang Kims and the Colonial Origins of Korean Capitalism, 1876–1945* (Seattle: University of Washington Press, 1991), 235–39.

15   Chōsen government-general, "Chōsen sōtokufu jikyoku taisaku chōsakai shimonan sankōsho," 356. This figure combined Japanese and Korean visitors, one of the few times the two peoples are listed as such even at this late period.

16   Ibid., 382. This chart also showed more Koreans having a limited knowledge of Japanese, from around 818,000 in 1933 to just over 1.2 million in 1937.

17   Ibid., 347–48, 360–62.

18   See note 86, chap. 4.

19   Chosen government-general, "Chōsen sōtokufu jikyoku taisaku chōsakai shimon tōshinan shian," 418–23.

20   Ibid., 417, 421–42.

21   Ibid.

22   Ibid., 459–60.

23   Ibid., 417, 422.

24   At the deliberation meetings Governor General Minami Jirō defined total war as a war that "used all the country's resources, material resources as well as the people's spiritual and economic capabilities." Chōsen government-general, "Chōsen sōtokufu jikyoku taisaku chōsakai kaigiroku" (Transcript of the Meeting on Korean Government-General Investigation Response to the Circumstances of the Times), in *Ilcheha chibae chŏngch'aek charyojip*, ed. Sin, vol. 16, 294.

25   Chosen government-general, "Chōsen sōtokufu jikyoku taisaku chōsakai shimon tōshinan shian," 429.

26   Ibid., 552.

27   Ibid., 560–62.

28   Ibid., 428–29.

29   See, for example, Kitakan Sanjin (probably a pseudonym), who offers this description in his "Chōsen no futei senjin" (Korea's Lawless Koreans), *Chōsen oyobi Manshū* (November 1921): 81–82; and Pak Sanghŭi, "Chōsen seihokujin no tokushitsu" (Unique Characteristics of the Northwestern Korean), in *Chōsen oyobi Chōsen minzoku* (Korea and the Korean Race), edited by Chōsen oyobi Chōsen minzoku, 112–23 (Chōsen shisō tsūshinsha, 1927). I describe these images in "Images of the North in Occupied Korea."

30   Chōsen government-general, "Chōsen sōtokufu jikyoku taisaku chōsakai gijiroku," in *Ilcheha chibae chŏngch'aek charyojip*, ed. Sin, vol. 16, 295, 306.

31   For a list of participants and their affiliations, see ibid., 233–40.

32   Ibid., 322–24.

33   Ibid., 332–34.

34   Ibid., 336–37.

35   "Daiichi bunka kaigi jiroku" (Transcripts of the First Subcommittee, in *Ilcheha chibae chŏngch'aek charyojip*, ed. Sin, vol. 16, 348.

36   Ibid., 354–57.

37   Ibid., 369–70.

38   Chōsen government-general, *Chōsen sōtokufu nenpō* (Chōsen Government-General Statistics Annual) (Keijō: Chōsen government-general, 1944), 200–201. Statistics were for 1942. The government-general separated Koreans and Japanese in other categories such as teachers and criminals.

39   Hong, "Japanese Colonial Education Policy in Korea," Appendix, 15–17.

40   Copies of these textbooks are found in *Han'guk kyoyuk charyo chibsŏng*, ed. Yi. The quoted material is as follows: 1938 textbook from vol. 17, 222, and the 1938 textbook from vol. 17, 254–55.

41   Tanaka Kōzō, "Kokumin gakkōan no seishin to hantō kyōiku" (The Spirit of the National School Proposal and Peninsular Education), *Chōsen no kyōiku kenkyū* (September 1939): 23–28.

42   "'Jihenka no Chōsen wo kataru' zadankai" (A Roundtable Discussion on 'Korea under the Incident'), *Bungei shunjū* (June 1939): 246.

43   Chōsen government-general, "Chōsen tōchi to kōmin rensei no shinten" (Korean Administration and the Advancement of Imperial Training), in *Ilcheha chibae chŏngch'aek charyojip*, ed. Sin, vol. 17, 695.

44   These figures are from Dong, "Japanese Colonial Policy and Practice in Korea," 400.

45   Takahashi Hamakichi, "Gimu kyōiku jisshi no igi" (The Significance of the Implementation of Compulsory Education), *Chōsen* (June 1944): 2–8.

46   *Sin'in'gan*'s cooperation in advising Koreans on their responsibilities is probably what allowed it to survive. It also ran a regular column titled "Sabyŏn ilyŏn'gan ilji" (The Events Over One Year Since the Incident) (September 1938), and listed the names of Koreans who contributed to the imperial battleground, as well as carried the "imperial pledge."

47   Ch'oe Namsŏn, "Naeil ŭi sin kwangmyŏng yŏn" (The New Bright Training of the Future), and Yun Ch'iho, "Naesŏn ŭn tongil unmyŏng" (Japan and Korea's Shared Fate), *Maeil sinbo* (August 15, 1937).

48   Yun Ch'iho was a major figure in the late nineteenth-century reform movements. He was arrested soon after annexation and charged with leading a plot to assassinate Governor General Terauchi Masatake. Ch'oe Namsŏn became known in the 1920s for his work in promoting Korean indigenous history. He also edited the *Sidae Ilbo* (Times Daily).

49   *Maeil sinbo* (January 4, 1938).

50   The January 8, 1938, issue of the *Maeil sinbo* carried this advertisement.

51 Robinson, "Broadcasting in Korea," 359–60.

52 "Chōsen tōchi to kōmin rensei no shinten," vol. 17, ed. Sin, 679–706.

53 Ibid., 691–92.

54 Yun, *Yun Ch'iho ilgi* (July 7, 1940).

55 "Chōsen tōchi to kōmin rensei no shinten," vol. 17, ed. Sin, 701–2.

56 "Rensei suru Chōsen," in *Ilcheha chibae chŏngch'aek charyojip*, vol. 17, ed. Sin, 717–23.

57 Ibid., 722.

58 "Chōsen no seinen rensei" (Korean Youth Training), in *Ilcheha chibae chŏngch'aek charyojip*, vol. 17, ed. Sin, 725–26.

59 The first eight training centers had been established in 1928, primarily for Japanese youth. Ibid., 727.

60 Ibid., 728–35.

61 Ibid., 697.

62 Ibid., 697–98. A later pamphlet, "Shiganhei yori chōhei e" (From Volunteer to Conscription Army), stated that the Japanese ability to "enlist a draft system at this time is the result of the thirty-three-plus years of efforts made by governor generals and prime ministers." Ibid., 711.

63 Ibid., 712.

64 Ibid., 703.

65 Miyata Setsuko, Kim Yŏngjŭl, and Yang Taeho, in *Sōshi kaimei* (Name Changes) (Tokyo: Akashi shoten, 1994), review Korean and Japanese attitudes to name changing policies.

66 See Kang, *Under the Black Umbrella*, 114.

67 Hyŏn Yŏngsŏp, *Chōsenjin no susumu beki michi* (The Path That the Korean Must Take) (Keijō: Ryokki renmei, 1940), 2–3.

68 Mitarai Tatsuo, "Atarashii Chōsen shimei" (The New Korean Mission), *Chōsen* (October 1940): 5–7.

69 "Chōsen sōtokufu jikyoku chōsakai gijiroku" (Record of the Proceedings of the Korean Government-General Investigation on Strategy for the Present Circumstances), in *Ilcheha chibae chŏngch'aek charyochip*, ed. Sin, vol. 16, 307–9.

70 "Chōsen tōchi no kako to genzai" (Korean Administration Past and Present), in *Ilcheha chibae chŏngch'aek charyojip*, ed. Sin, vol. 17, 665–78.

71 "'Jihenka no Chōsen wo kataru' zadankai," 246–64.

72 Ibid., 250. We will examine Hyŏn's writing in chap. 6.

73 Ibid., 251–56.

74 Ibid., 245–47.

75   Ibid., 247.

76   Ibid., 247–48.

77   Ibid., 250, 253, 254.

78   Ibid., 254.

79   Ibid., 261–62.

80   Kajiyama Toshiyuki, "The Clan Records," in *The Clan Records: Five Stories of Korea*, translated by Yoshiko Dykstra (Honolulu: University of Hawai'i Press, 1995), 12.

81   Ibid., 58.

82   Utsumi Aiko, "Korean 'Imperial Soldiers': Remembering Colonialism and Crimes against Allied POWs," in *Perilous Memories: The Asian-Pacific Wars*, edited by T. Fujitani, Geoffrey White, and Lisa Yoneyama, 199–217 (Durham, N.C.: Duke University Press, 2001), 208.

83   Higuchi, *Kōgun heishi ni sareta Chōsenjin*, 90.

84   Utsumi, "Korean Imperial Soldiers," 211–13.

85   Yuasa Katsuei, "Kannani" *and* "Document of Flames": *Two Japanese Colonial Novels*, translated by Mark Driscoll (Durham, N.C.: Duke University Press, 2005), 52–53.

86   Ibid., 97.

87   Both stories are retold in Takasaki, *Shokuminchi Chōsen no Nihonjin*, 178.

88   Soon-Won Park, *Colonial Industrialization and Labor in Korea: The Onada Cement Factory* (Cambridge, Mass.: Harvard University Press, 1999), 148.

89   Sin, ed., *Ilcheha chibae chŏngch'aek charyojip*, vol. 17, 688.

90   Ibid., 709.

91   Ibid., 703–4.

92   See also Higuchi, *Kōgun heishi ni sareta Chōsenjin*, 162.

6   KOREAN CRITIQUES OF JAPANESE ASSIMILATION POLICY

1   See Induk Park, *September Monkey* (New York: Harper & Brothers, 1954), chap. 5; and Louise Kim, *My Forty Year Fight for Korea* (Seoul: Chungang University, 1959), chaps. 3 and 4.

2   I consider the question of Korean collaboration in my "Loyal Patriot or Traitorous Collaborator? Reassessing Yun Ch'iho's Colonial Activities in Contemporary Japan-Korea Relations," *Journal of Colonialism and Colonial History* 7, no.3 (December 2006). One other response was pas-

sive resistance, as shown in Gi-Wook Shin, *Peasant Protest and Social Change in Colonial Korea* (Seattle: University of Washington, 1996), chap. 8.

3   Caprio, "Loyal Patriot or Traitorous Collaborator?"

4   Hyun, *Man Sei!*, and Richard E. Kim, *Lost Names: Scenes from a Korean Boyhood* (Berkeley: University of California Press, 1998). Kang's informants recall their March First experiences in her *Under the Black Umbrella*, 17–23.

5   Hyun, *Man Sei!*, 62.

6   For discussion on the Hyŏn lineage see Kyung Moon Hwang, *Beyond Birth: Social Status in the Emergence of Modern Korea* (Cambridge, Mass.: Harvard University Press, 2004), 127–30. For charges of Hyŏn Yŏngsŏp as a Korean collaborator see *Ch'inilp'a 99 in* (2), ed. Panminjok munje yŏn'guso, 66–76.

7   Kim Sangman estimates that at least 29 underground newspapers circulated during the first decade of Japanese rule. See Kim, ed., *Tong'a ilbosa*, 66.

8   Robinson, *Cultural Nationalism in Colonial Korea*, 6.

9   By 1939 *Tong'a ilbo* sales reached 55,977, second to the *Chosŏn ilbo*, which sold 95,939 copies daily. Robinson, "Colonial Publication Policy," 326.

10   Hyung Il Pai offers an interesting survey on Korean state-formation approaches, including the use of Tan'gun, under Japanese colonial rule, in her *Constructing Korean Origins: A Critical Review of Archaeology, Historiography, and Racial Myth in Korean State-Formation Theories* (Cambridge, Mass.: Harvard University Press, 2000).

11   "Sait'o ch'ongdok ege mun hanora" (Questions for Governor General Saitō), *Tong'a ilbo* (April 12, 1924).

12   "Saito ŭi chŏngch'aek" (Saitō's Policies), *Tong'a ilbo* (August 21, 1924). This article is found in *Ilchŏnga Tong'a ilbo apsu sasŏljip*, ed. Yi Tong'uk, 83. Chŏng T'ae'ik reported that her house in Kangwŏn Province was inspected twice annually. One inspector made the house owner eat the worms he found in the ceiling. Kang, *Under the Black Umbrella*, 103–4.

13   "Chosŏn'in ŭi kyoyuk yong'ŏ rŭl ilbon'ŏ ro kangje ham ŭl p'yeji hara (sang)" (Banning the Forced Use of Japanese in Korean Education Terminology, [part 1]), *Tong'a ilbo* (April 12, 1920).

14   Chu Yosŏp, *Chosŏn kyoyuk ŭi kyŏrham* (Deficiencies in Korean Education) (Keijō: Sekai soin, 1930), 1–7.

15   Ibid., 20.

16 Ibid., 23–28. Chu also criticized the decline in the number of Korean school principals (from 43 in 1926 to zero in 1930) and the lack of Korean history in the classroom textbooks. He also attacked the Japanese moral-based curriculum as lacking practical application and warned that "for education to be effective it had to be practical; the Japanese-based education was not." Ibid., 29, 45–56, 60.

17 Yun, *Yun Ch'iho ilgi*, vol. 8 (March 4, 1921).

18 See, for example, the *Yorūzochōhō* (January 25, 1920). The media referred to this invitation and Yŏ's activities as the "Yŏ Unhyŏng jihen" (incident).

19 For Yŏ's visit, see Ku, *Korea Under Colonialism*, 220–1, and Kan Doksun, *Yŏ Unhyŏng hyōden 1: Chōsen san'ichi dokuritsu undō* (A Critical Biography of Yŏ Unhyŏng 1: Korea's March First Independence Movement) (Tokyo: Shinkansha, 2002), chap. 6.

20 Kan Doksun, *Yŏ Unhyŏng hyōden*, 260.

21 Ibid., 289.

22 Yŏ Unhyŏng, "Tonggyŏng cheguk hot'el yŏnsŏl yoji" (Fundamental Points of Yŏ's Speech at the Tokyo Imperial Hotel) in Yŏ Unhyŏng, *Mongyang Yŏ Unhyŏng chŏnjip* (Yŏ Unhyŏng Collection), vol. 1 (Seoul: Hanul, 1991), 32–34.

23 Yŏ Unhyŏng, "Ilbon chŏngch'aek ŭi chuyo insadŭl kwa ŭi hoedam: Ch'ŏksik kukchang Koga Kennozo wa ŭi hoedam" (Discussions with Influential Members of the Japanese Government: A Discussion with Colonial Office Chief Koga Renzō), in *Yŏ Unhyŏng chŏnjip*, vol. 1, 34–36.

24 Herbert B. Bix writes that Tanaka Giichi was fired after being scolded by the emperor for wanting to "hush . . . up" the 1929 assassination of Manchurian warlord Chang Tso-lin in his *Hirohito and the Making of Modern Japan* (New York: HarperCollins, 2000), 217.

25 Yŏ Unhyŏng, "Ilbon chŏngch'aek ŭi chuyo insadul kwa ŭi hoedam: Ilbun ŭi mudan chŏngch'aek kwa Tanaka taechang kwa ŭi hoedam" (Discussions with Influential Members of the Japanese Government: A Discussion with Military Rule Advocate General Tanaka), in *Yŏ Unhyŏng chŏnjip*, vol. 1, 37–38.

26 Yŏ, "Ilbon chŏngch'aek ŭi chuyo insadul kwa ŭi hoedam," 35–36.

27 Yŏ, "Tonggyŏng cheguk hot'el yŏnsŏl," 32.

28 "Sinbom kwa oin ŭi hŭimang (The New Spring and Our Ambitions), *Tong'a ilbo* (April 1, 1920). This editorial can also be found in Kim, ed., *Tong'a ilbosa*, 99–100.

29 See, for example, "Aenan munje ŭi yurae (The Origins of the Irish Problem), *Tong'a ilbo* (April 9, 1920). Yanaihara Tadao found this comparison interesting. See Susan Townsend, "Yanaihara Tadao and the Irish Question: A Comparative Analysis of the Irish and Korean Questions, 1919–36," *Irish Historical Studies* 30, no.118 (November 1998): 195–205.

30 "Ulster in Ireland," *Tong'a ilbo* (September 16, 1924). The newspaper occasionally carried editorials written in English.

31 "Nationalist Activities in the Frontier Districts," *Tong'a ilbo* (October 30, 1924).

32 *Tong'a ilbo* (July 16, 1924).

33 *Tong'a ilbo* (December 4, 1927).

34 "Welcome to the Congressional Party," *Tong'a ilbo* (August 24, 1920).

35 House records, 66th Congress, 3rd sess., *Congressional Record* 60 (December 23, 1920): 707–28. The tour received reports (apparently false) of cholera outbreaks on the peninsula, as well as of rumors that the Koreans would harm the congressmen, from the start of their trip.

36 This letter can be found in Kim, ed., *Tong'a ilbosa*, 151–52.

37 Japanese had been critical of Korean treatment of women from before annexation. In 1906 the lawyer Matsumoto Ginkun wrote that "Korean women are so ignorant, we cannot expect their offspring to be great and ingenious. . . . Can we still wonder why the Coreans are so rapidly degenerating?" Matsumoto Ginkun, "Are the Coreans Bound to Degenerate?" *Taiyō* (July 1, 1906): 8. See also Theodore Jun Yoo, *The Politics of Gender in Colonial Korea: Education, Labor, and Health, 1910–1945* (Berkeley: University of California Press, 2008).

38 Ok Sunch'ŏl, "Chagi haebang ŭl manggak hanŭn Chosŏn sinyŏsŏng" (Forgotten Self-Liberation: Korea's New Woman), *Tong'a ilbo* (October 11–14, 1926). See also Kyeong-Hee Choi, "Neither Colonial nor National: The Making of the 'New Woman' in Pak Wansŏ's 'Mother's Stake 1," in *Colonial Modernity*, ed. Shin and Robinson, 221–47.

39 "Chosŏn yŏja kyoyuk ŭi kyŏlchŏm" (The Weak Elements of Women's Education), *Tong'a ilbo* (September 21, 1929).

40 Paek Pa, "Sowi 'sin yŏsŏng' kwa yangch'ŏ hyŏnmo chuŭi?" (The So-Called New Woman and the Good Wife-Wise Mother Ideology), *Hyŏndae p'yŏngnon* (Contemporary Review) (January 1928): 161–72.

41 Hong Kiwŏn, "Namsŏng ŭi todŏk ŭl non haya namyŏ ŭi pansŏng ŭl yogu ham" (Examining Male Morals and the Demand for Male-Female Reflection), *Tong'a ilbo* (August 14, 1920). See also Chŏng

Saehyŏn, "Han'guk yŏsŏng ŭi sin munhwa undong: yŏndae ch'ogi ŭi yŏsŏng munhwa undong ŭl chungsim ŭro" (The New Cultural Movement for Korean Women: A Consideration of the Women's Cultural Movement of the Early 1920s), *Asea yŏsŏng yŏn'gu* (December 1971).

42 Yi Kiwŏn, "Namsŏng ŭi todŏk ŭl non haya namyŏ ŭi pansŏng ŭl yogu ham" (The Need to Reflect on the Morals of the Male), *Tong'a ilbo* (August 13, 1920).

43 Anonymous, "Chosŏn minjok ŭi mirae rŭl non ham" (Thoughts on the Future of the Korean People), *Chosŏn ŭi kwang* 1 (1922): 2–14. The second volume of this journal carried an article titled "Chosŏn minjok paltalsa ŭi kaegwan (A Historical Survey of the Korean People's Development), *Chosŏn ŭi kwang* 2 (1922): 1–9. This survey traced Korea's downfall from Silla unification, when a united Korea had to relinquish territory north of the Yalu and Tumen rivers.

44 See Wells, *New God, New Nation*, especially chap. 6.

45 "Chayu charip ŭi ŭiji" (The Will of Freedom and Individual Independence), *Tong'a ilbo* (May 17, 1920). This article is found in Yi Tong'uk, ed., *Ilchŏngha ha Tong'a ilbo apsu sasŏlchip* (A Collection of Confiscated Editorials of the *Tong'a ilbo*) (Seoul: Tong'a ilbo sagan, 1974), 18.

46 The Japanese censors let stand, for example, the *Tong'a ilbo*'s August 17, 1920, headline that carried primarily in Chinese characters "Chosŏn'in ŭi cheich'a tongnip undong" (The Second Korean Independence Movement), allowed perhaps because it appeared at the time the U.S. congressmen arrived.

47 For French collaboration see Peter Davies, *Dangerous Liaisons: Collaboration and World War Two* (Harlon, U.K.: Pearson Longman, 2004). For Chinese collaboration with Japanese, see Timothy Brook, *Collaboration: Japanese Agents and Local Elites in Wartime China* (Cambridge, Mass.: Harvard University Press, 2005).

48 One result is the three-volume *Ch'inilp'a 99 in*. In 2005, a government committee published a list of 3,090 collaborators. Kim Chŏngwŏn, "List of 3,090 Pro-Japanese Collaborators Made Public," *Empas News*, http://news.empas.com/print.tsp/20050829n06308 (accessed May 21, 2008).

49 See Eckert, *Offspring of Empire*, and Park, *Colonial Industrialization and Labor in Korea*.

50 Yun Ch'iho, *Yun Ch'iho ilgi*, vol. 11 (December 8, 1941).

51 Kim Tohyŏng, *Ilche ch'imnyak ch'ogi (1905–1919) ch'inilp'a seryŏk ŭi*

chŏngch'inon yŏn'gu (A Study on the Political Thought of the Pro-Japanese in the Early Period of Japanese Rule [1905–1919]), *Kyemyŏng sahak* 3 (November 1992): 1–63.

52 Han Myŏnggŭn, *Hanmal hanil happangnon yŏngu* (Research on Late Korean Japan-Korea Annexation Theories) (Seoul: Kukhak charyowŏn, 20002), 54.

53 Yumi Moon, "The Populist Contest: The Ilchinhoe Movement and the Japanese Colonization of Korea, 1896–1910" (Ph.D. diss., Harvard University, 2005). See also Vipan Chandra, "An Outline Study of the Ilchinhoe (Advancement Society of Korea)," *Occasional Papers on Korea* 2 (March 1974): 43–72.

54 For example, the November 1925 issue, commemorating the fifteenth anniversary of annexation, contained a series of articles authored by Korean provincial governors.

55 Han Yun, "Dōhō in gekisui" (An Appeal to My Countrymen), *Chōsen* (September 1921): 119–20.

56 Ch'ae Mandal, "Zaisen Naichijin ni tai suru kansō" (Impressions of Japanese Living in Korea), *Chōsen* (September 1921): 121–25.

57 Kim Yŏngsun, "Shina kanken no Senjin appaku mondai ni kan suru konponteki taisaku" (A Fundamental Strategy against Korean Oppression by Chinese Authorities), in *Saitō Makoto monjo*, vol. 15 (April 15, 1928): 93–154.

58 Han Ŭl, "Chōsen tōchi iken" (An Opinion of Korean Administration), *Saitō Makoto monjo*, vol. 15 (January 1929): 169–75.

59 Yi Yŏngson, "Naisen yūwa wa doko e?" (Where Is Japanese-Korean unity), *Jiyū* (May 1937): 90–92.

60 Eckert, *Offspring of Empire*, 241.

61 The document's final version (dated the same as the Counterplan Proposal) is included in Sin, ed., *Ilcheha chibae chŏngch'aek charyojip*, vol. 16, 5–213.

62 Ibid., 359–61.

63 Ibid., 361–62.

64 Ibid., 368. Japan amended this law in 1985 to permit foreign males married to Japanese to be included on the woman's family register.

65 Ibid., 365–67. See also Eckert, *Offspring of Empire*, 240.

66 Sin, ed., *Ilcheha chibae chŏngch'aek charyojip*, vol. 16, 367.

67 Ibid., 364, 413.

68   Ibid., 373.

69   Ibid., 419. Murayama Michio's article "Chōsen no zeisei kaisei" (Korea's Tax Reform), *Chōsen* (February 1940): 16–23, suggests that the Japanese accepted this advice.

70   Ibid., 377–78.

71   Karl Moskowitz, "The Creation of the Oriental Development Company: Japanese Illusions Meet Korean Reality," *Occasional Papers on Korea* 2 (March 1974): 85–87, 93–94.

72   Quoted in Young, *Japan's Total Empire*, 310–11.

73   I consider northern Korean development in my "Images of the North in Occupied Korea," in *Northern Region, Identity, and Culture in Korea,* edited by Sun Joo Kim (Seattle: University of Washington Press, forthcoming).

74   Hyŏn, *Chōsenjin no susumu beki michi*, 18.

75   Ibid., 1–4.

76   Ibid., 4–13.

77   Ibid., 15–17.

78   Ibid., 29.

79   Ibid., 41–43.

80   Ibid., 119–23.

81   Ibid., 143–45, 151–54.

82   Ibid., 57.

83   This would be true unless Hyŏn's Japanese wife chose to be entered onto her husband's Korean register, which was rarely the case.

84   Kim Saryang's award-winning Japanese-language novel *Hikari no naka ni* (Within the Light), published in October 1939, uses names to introduce identity dilemmas that Japan-based Koreans faced. His three characters address identity in different ways: Yamada uses his Japanese name to hide his Korean identity and the shame of his mother's background as mistress; Yamada's English teacher (read in Korean as Nam but in Japanese as Minami) used the ambiguity in the pronunciation of his name to protect his Korean identity (what would the students think?) from exposure; and Yi openly displayed his Korean roots by using his Korean name. *Nihon gendai bungakushū,* vol. 69 (Tokyo: Kōdansha, 1980), 263–79.

85   Fanon, *Black Skin, White Masks*, 93.

86   This was the case with Kim Namhi Wagner, who adopted a Japanese name but had "Chōsenjin" (Korean) stamped in red on a certificate that she was to present to a school principal for employment purposes.

CONCLUSION: EVALUATING PERIPHERAL COLONIZATION

1   Dong, "Assimilation and Social Mobilization in Korea," 178.

2   For example, Richard H. Ritter, "Industrial Education in Korea," *North American Review* (October 1920): 524–30.

3   Eckert, *Offspring of Empire*, chap. 8.

4   Choi, "Another Layer of the Pro-Japanese Literature," 61.

5   For discussion of this potential, see State-War-Navy Coordinating Committee, "Utilization of Koreans in the War Effort (April 23, 1945)," compiled in *Haebang chŏnhusa charyojip*, vol. 1, *Mi kunjŏng chunbi charyo* (Collection of Historical Documents around the Time of Liberation, vol. 1, Materials for Preparation of United States Military Administration), edited by Yi Kilsang, 253–63 (Seoul: Wŏnju munhwasa, 1992).

6   For information on how Korean men entered the Japanese military, see Higuchi, *Kōgun heishi ni sareta Chōsenjin*.

7   Quoted in Haruko Taya Cook and Theodore F. Cook, *Japan at War: An Oral History* (New York: W. W. Norton, 1992), 114.

8   Chung Taekyun, *Kankoku no imeeji: Sengo Nihonjin no rinkokukan* (Korean Images: Japanese Postwar Image of the Country Next Door) (Tokyo: Chūkoshinsho, 1995), 68–69.

9   John P. Prendergast, *The Cromwellian Settlement of Ireland* (1865; London: Constable, 1996).

10 Even when the chance presented itself they shied away from doing so. For example, the *Tokyo keizai shinbun* at the time of annexation presented two separate articles, one titled "Taiwan no tōchi ni tsuite" (Concerning Taiwan Administration), a four-part article that ran from August 15, 1910, to September 15, 1910, and the other "Chōsen tōchi no hōshin" (A Plan for Korean Administration) carried on September 15, 1910. Neither considered these cases in comparative (Taiwan-Korea) terms.

11 Nitobe, "Japanese Colonization," 115.

12 "Japan's Influence in Korea," *Korean Daily News* (September 2, 1904).

13 "Kaehyŏk ŭi sidae" (A Revolutionary Era), *Maeil sinbo* (September 7, 1910).

14 As recorded in an interview by Hildi Kang in her *Under the Black Umbrella*, 56.

15 "Chōsenjin no dōkaryoku" (Korean Assimilation Capacity), *Chōsen oyobi Manshū* (November 1911), 10, 13.

16   Takasaki, *Shokuminchi Chōsen no Nihonjin*, 178.

17   Gregory Henderson estimates that the rate of Korean-Japanese inter-
      marriage was probably lower than that between Koreans and Ameri-
      cans during the U.S. occupation of southern Korea (*Korea: The Politics
      of the Vortex*, 6). His estimates might be low given the number of cou-
      ples who did not register their marriages. See also Aoki Atsuko, "Kikoku
      kigyō ni okeru 'Nihonjin zuma' wo megutte" (Regarding the Repatria-
      tion Operations of "Japanese wives"), in *Kikoku undō to wa nan datta
      no ka*, ed. Takasaki and Pak, 125–29.

18   Sawaō Kyokuhō, "Chōsenkaron" (Koreanization Theory), *Chōsen oyobi
      Manshū* (April 1918): 2–8.

19   Takasaki, *Shokuminchi Chōsen no Nihonjin*, 174.

20   *The Independent* (April 18, 1896).

21   Quoted in Kwan Bong Kim, *The Korea-Japan Treaty Crisis and the
      Instability of the Korean Political System* (New York: Praeger, 1971), 49.

22   Orlando Patterson, *The Ordeals of Integration: Progress and Resentment
      in America's "Racial" Crisis* (New York: Basic Books, 1997), 181.

23   Thomas Sowell, *Race and Culture: A World View* (New York: Basic
      Books, 1994), 113, 175. See also Alastair Bonnet, *Anti-Racism* (London:
      Routledge, 2000), 111–14.

GLOSSARY

aguk　我國
ai　愛
aibu shido　愛撫志度
Aikokubi　愛國日
Aikokufujinkai　愛國婦人会
arappoi　荒っぽい
azayaka　鮮やか
banzai/manse　萬材
binjyaku　瓶弱
bōchō　防諜
bokoku kokoku　母國子國
budan seiji　武断政治
budō　武道
buiku　撫育
bunka seiji　文化政治
Buriten eikoku no shinmin　ブリ
　テン英國の臣民
butsuri　物理
chihō gikai　地方議会
ch'inilp'a　親日派
Ch'ŏndogyo　天道教
chŏng'in　正人
chŏngsa　正事
Chōsen dōhō　朝鮮同胞
Chōsen kōron　朝鮮公論

Chōsen oyobi Manshū
　朝鮮及び満州
Chōsen sangyō ginko
　朝鮮産業銀行
Chōsen sansei shingikai kōseiin
　朝鮮参政審議会構成員
Chōsen seimei hoken
　朝鮮生命保険
Chōsen shimei　朝鮮使命
Chōsen shinbun　朝鮮新聞
Chōsen shōkō kaigisho kaitō
　朝鮮商工会議書会頭
Chōsen sōtokufu hōmu kyoku
　朝鮮総督府法務局
Chōsenjin junsaho
　朝鮮人巡査補
Chosŏn ilbo　朝鮮日報
Chungoe ilbo　中外日報
Chōsenka　朝鮮化
chūjitsu　忠実
chūsūin sangi　中枢院参議
daiichibu keihi　第一部経費
daikichi　大吉
dainibu keihi　第二部経費
dai Nippon teikoku　大日本帝國

269

dō ikkoku   同一國

dōhō kyōdai   同胞兄弟

dōitsu kokumin   同一國民

dojin torishime   土人取り閉め

dōkakai   同化会

dokuritsu no seishin   独立の精神

dōyō dōka   同様同化

Eijin   英人

fu   府

fujoshi   婦女子

fukabun no ryōdo   不可分の領土

fuken seido   府県制度

fuketsu no fujin   不潔の婦人

funa   鮒

furigana   振り仮名

futei senjin   不逞鮮人

futsū gakkō   普通学校

gaichi   外地

gakumu kyokuchō   学務局長

genshiteki   原始的

genzen to sonzai shiteiru   厳然と存在している

goseishi   御聖旨

gyokudenka   王殿下

hai-Nichiha   排日派

hai-Nihonjin   排日本人

hakkō itchū   八絋一宇

han-Shinajin   半支那人

han-shukoku   半主國

hantōjin   半島人

hantōmin zenbu no koe   半島民全部の声

hatake   畑

heigai   弊害

hi no maru   日の丸

hibiki ga warui   響きが悪い

higai   鰉

Hisho ruisan   秘書類纂

honseki   本籍

hontō no Nihonjin   本当の日本人

hyōgen   表現

hyōgikai   評議会

hyōjō undō   表情運動

ichi chihō   一地方

ichi kokumin   一國民

ihaku   威迫

ikensho   意見書

ikka sorotte hyōjungo   一家揃って標準語

Ilchinhoe   一進會

inken   陰険

iltan chŏngsin   一團精神

ishin   維新

isshi dōjin   一視同仁

itsumo hakihaki hyōjungo   いつもハキハキ標準語

Iwakura shisetsu   岩倉使節

jihen   事変

jikyoku/siguk   時局

jinai   仁愛

jinteki shigen   人的資源

jishū dokusai   自習独裁

jishu shugi   自主主義

Jiyū   自由

Jiyūtō   自由党

junbi kyōiku   準備教育

junchi   馴致

kaehyŏk ŭi sidae   改革의時代

kaihai   改廃

kaihatsu   開発

kakugo   覚悟

kakusei no kan naki   隔世の感なき

kaikoku　開國

kaitakushi kagakkō　開拓使仮
　学校

kamishibai　紙芝居

kangeki　感激

karyūbyō　花柳病

katei kyōiku　家庭教育

katte ni suru　勝手にする

kazoku seishin　家族精神

kazokushugi　家族主義

keiji konjo　継兒根性

Keijō nippo　京城日報

keimusōchō　警務總長

keishi　継子

keizai konjō　根性

kenpeitai　憲兵隊

ki ga nagaku shidō　気が長く
　指導

Kimi ga yo　君が代

kisha　記者

kōbo　鴻謨

kokugo　國語

kōkoku shinmin　皇國臣民

kokumin　國民

kokumin gakkō　國民学校

kokumin keizairyoku　國民経
　済力

kōmin kyōiku　公民教育

kyōikuteki dōki　民教育的動機

kokumin seishinryoku　國民精
　神力

Kokumin shinbun　国民新聞

kokumin sōryoku renmei　國民総
　力連盟

kokusei　國性

kokutai　國体

kōminka　皇民化

kōmin kyōiku　公民教育

kōmin shinminka no kansei　皇民
　臣民化の完成

kōnei　康寧

konpon　根本

kōritsu shōgakkō　公立小学校

kosekihō　戸籍法

kōshūkai　講習会

kosui　湖水

kōtaku　皇澤

kwijok chegong　貴族諸公

kwan'gwangdan ilchi　観光団
　日誌

kyōgaku　共学

kyōgikai　協議会

Kyōikusha seishin sakkō kinenbi
　教育者精神作興記念日

kyōka　教化

kyōyū　俠勇

Kyŏngnam ilbo　慶南日報

kyōren　教練

kyū dojin　旧土人

Kyushujin　九州人

machi　町

Maiil sinbo　毎日申報

Mansen　満鮮

meichō　明徴

minsekihō　民籍法

minshin　民心

minzoku jiketsu　民族自決

minzoku no haji　民族の恥

mōjū　猛獣

mokhaeng chŏngch'aek　暴行政策

mujō　無情

mukimi　無気味

mura　村

myŏn　面

Naichi enchōshugi no bunka seiji
内地延長主義の文化政治

Naichijin　内地人

Naichi to onaji teido　内地と同
じ程度

Naisen ikka　内鮮一家

Naisen ittai　内鮮一体

Naisen kyōgaku　内鮮共学

Naisenjin isshi dōjin　内鮮人一
視同仁

Naisen yūwa no tame no shisetsu
内鮮融和のための施設

natsukashii　懐かしい

netsubō　熱望

Nihon angya bunshū　日本行脚
文集

Nihon kokumin no hitori　日本
國民の一人

Nihon oyobi Nihonjin　日本及び
日本人

Nikkan ikka/ilhan ilka　日韓一家

ninjō　人情

ninku　忍苦

ninyō　認容

Osaka jiken　大阪事件

oseibo　お歳暮

panǒ　反語

raichō　來朝

raikō　來貢

rajio taisō　ラジオ体操

rakuryōchū　楽龍中

Renseibi　錬成日

riekisen　利益線

rippa na katei　立派な家庭

risō　理想

rō kurushii　陋苦しい

ryōkai　了解

ryōsai kenbo　良妻賢母

Ryukyu shinpō　琉球新報

sabishii　寂しい

saigishin　猜疑心

sakoku seisaku　鎖國政策

Sangatsu jiken　三月事件

sangiin　参議院

sangyō seisaku　産業政策

sankin kōtai　参勤交代

sankōsho　参考書

seigyō　聖業

seihei　精兵

Seihokudō　西北道

Seikaidō　西海道

seikatsu no sashin　生活の刷新

Seiki monogatari　西紀物語

seimei　姓名

seimei　生命

seinen tokubetsu rensei　青年特別
錬成

seinentai　青年隊

seiōjin　西欧人

seishinteki jisatsu　精神的自殺

seito　生徒

seiyōjin　西洋人

sekai no Nihon　世界の日本

senmon gakkō　専門学校

senryo　浅慮

shakai dōhō shugi　社会同胞主義

shakaika　社会化

shakai kyōiku　社会教育

shaon　謝恩

shashoku　社稷

shi　市

shidō keihatsu　指導啓発

shigen　資源

shin Chōsen　新朝鮮

shin kizoku　新貴族

shin-Nichiha　親日派

shin no yōkyū　真の要求

shinkaichi　新開地

shinmin　臣民

shinwa　親和

shinyoku　身欲

shinzoku jittaihō　親族実体法

shishitsu　資質

shokuminchi　植民地

shukensen　主権線

Siningan　新人間

sinmin sidae　新民時代

sinsa yulamdan　紳士遊覽團

soboku　素朴

sōchō suru seijō　曾長する性情

sŏdang　書堂

sōgō kokuryokusen　綜合國力戦

sōjō　騒擾

sōryoku undō　総力運動

taida　怠惰

tairikujin　大陸人

taiseishin　大精神

Taishō hōtaibi　大詔奉戴日

taisōka　体操科

Taiwan jimu daijin　台湾事務大臣

Taiwan nichi-nichi　臺灣日々

Taiyō　太陽

tamashii　魂

Tan'gun　檀君

tanshi　短資

teikoku no shinmin　帝國の臣民

tekagen　手加減

Tohokujin　東北人

tōitsu　統一

toko no ma　床の間

Tong'a ilbo　東亜日報

tōyō heiwa　東洋平和

tōyō ikka　東洋一家

tōyōshi　東洋史

tsūkon dōka　通婚同化

Tsūrisuto　ツウリスト

uji　氏

umarefukeru　産まれ耽る

ŭnŏ　隠語

wae　倭

waein　倭人

wakaki Nihon　若き日本

Yamato minzoku　大和民族

yawarakai　柔らかい

yoboka　ヨボ化

yōchi　幼稚

yōhai　遥拝

yoron　世論

yūda no min　遊惰の民

yūgō　融合

yūji　有事

yūka　優化

yūwa　融和

zentai seishin　全体精神

zuii kamoku　随科目

BIBLIOGRAPHY

Abe Hiroshi. "Higher Learning in Korea under Japanese Rule: Keijō Imperial University and the 'People's University' Movement." *Developmental Economics* 9, no. 2 (June 1971): 174–96.

Abse, Joan, ed. *Letters from Wales*. Bridgend, Wales: Poetry Wales Press, 2000.

Ageron, Charles-Robert. *Modern Algeria: A History from 1830 to the Present*. Translated by Michael Brett. London: Hurst, 1991.

Akaki Manjirō. "Chōsen kyōikukai no shin shimei" (The True Mission of the Korean Education Association). *Chōsen kyōiku* (April 1923): 5–7.

Akisaki Moriteru and Kawamitsu Shin'ichi, eds. *Okinawa tennōsei e no gyakkō* (Okinawa: The Retrogradation of the Emperor System). Tokyo: Shakai hyōronsha, 1988.

Alatas, Syed Hussein. *The Myth of the Lazy Native: A Study of the Image of the Malays, Filipinos, and Javanese from the Sixteenth to the Twentieth Century and Its Function in the Ideology of Colonial Capitalism*. London: Frank Cass, 1977.

Altman, Albert A. "The Press." In *Japan in Transition: From Tokugawa to Meiji*, edited by Marius B. Jansen and Gilbert Rozman, 231–47. Princeton, N.J.: Princeton University Press, 1986.

Amioka, Shiro. "Changes in Education Ideals and Objectives (from Selected Documents, Tokugawa Era to the Meiji Period)." In *The Modernizers: Overseas Students, Foreign Employers, and Meiji Japan*, edited by Adrath W. Burks. Boulder, Colo.: Westview, 1985.

Anderson, Benedict. *Imagined Communities: Reflections on the Origin and Spread of Nationalism*. London: Verso, 1991.

Anonymous. "Chosŏn minjok ŭi mirae rŭl non ham" (Thoughts on the Future of the Korean People). *Chosŏn ŭi kwang* 1 (1922): 2–14.

Aoki Atsuko. "Kikoku kigyō ni okeru 'Nihonjin zuma' wo megutte" (Regarding the Repatriation Operations of "Japanese Wives"). In *Kikoku undō to wa nan datta no ka*, edited by Takasaki Sōji and Pak Jonjin, 121–44. Tokyo: Heibonsha, 2005.

Aoyagi Tsunatarō. *Shin Chōsen* (New Korea). Tokyo: Yūken hansho, 1925.

Arano Yasunori. *Kinsei Nihon to Higashi Ajia* (Modern Japan and East Asia). Tokyo: Tokyo daigaku shuppankai, 1988.

Arendt, Hannah, *The Origins of Totalitarianism*. Orlando: Harcourt Brace, 1979.

Asano Makoto. *Okinawa-ken no kyōikushi* (The History of Education in Okinawa Prefecture). Kyoto: Shibunkaku shuppan, 1991.

Baldwin, Frank P., Jr. "The March First Movement: Korean Challenge and Japanese Response." Ph.D. diss., Columbia University, 1969.

Barlow, Tami, ed. *Foundations of Colonial Modernity in East Asia*. Durham, N.C.: Duke University Press, 1997.

Baumgart, Winfried. *Imperialism: The Idea and Reality of British and French Colonial Expansion 1880–1914*. Oxford: Oxford University Press, 1982.

Beale, Howard K. *Theodore Roosevelt and the Rise of American World Power*. Baltimore, Md.: Johns Hopkins University Press, 1969.

Bell, Morag, Robin A. Butlin, and Michael Hefferman. "Introduction: Geography and Imperialism, 1820–1940." In *Geography and Imperialism, 1820–1940*, edited by Morag Bell, Robin A. Butlin, and Michael Hefferman. Manchester, U.K.: Manchester University Press, 1995.

———, eds. *Geography and Imperialism, 1820–1940*. Manchester, U.K.: Manchester University Press, 1995.

Berry, Mary Elizabeth. *Hideyoshi*. Cambridge, Mass.: Harvard East Asian Monographs, 1982.

Betts, Raymond F. *Assimilation and Association in French Colonial Theory, 1890–1914*. New York: Columbia University Press, 1961.

———. *France and Decolonization, 1900–1960*. Translated by William Glanville Brown. New York: St. Martin's Press, 1991.

Bhabha, Homi K. *The Location of Culture*. London: Routledge, 1994.

Bix, Herbert B. *Hirohito and the Making of Modern Japan*. New York: Harper Collins, 2000.

Boahen, A. Adu, ed. *General History of Africa: Africa under Colonial Domination, 1880–1935*. London: James Currey, 1990.

Bonnet, Alastair. *Anti-Racism*. London: Routledge, 2000.

Boyce, D. George. *Nationalism in Ireland*. London: Routledge, 1995.

Brook, Timothy. *Collaboration: Japanese Agents and Local Elites in Wartime China*. Cambridge, Mass.: Harvard University Press, 2005.

Brubaker, Roger. *Citizenship and Nationhood in France and Germany*. Cambridge: Cambridge University Press, 1992.

Buell, Raymond L. *The Native Problem in Africa*. 2 vols. New York: Macmillan, 1928.

Burks, Adrath W., ed. *The Modernizers: Overseas Students, Foreign Employers, and Meiji Japan*. Boulder, Colo.: Westview.

Burnett, Scott S., ed. *Korean-American Relations: Documents Pertaining to the Far Eastern Diplomacy of the United States*, vol. 3: *The Period of Diminishing Influence, 1896–1905*. Honolulu: University of Hawai'i Press, 1989.

Buttinger, Joseph. *Vietnam: A Dragon Embattled*, vol. 1: *From Colonialism to the Vietminh*. New York: Frederick A. Praeger, 1967.

Callan, Eamonn. "The Ethics of Assimilation." *Ethics* 115 (April 2005): 471–500.

Caprio, Mark E. "Loyal Patriot or Traitorous Collaborator? Reassessing Yun Ch'iho's Colonial Activities in Contemporary Japan-Korea Relations." *Journal of Colonialism and Colonial History* 7, no. 3 (e-jornal, December 2006).

———. "Images of the North in Occupied Korea, 1905–1945." In *Northern Region, Identity, and Culture in Korea*, edited by Sun Joo Kim. Seattle: University of Washington Press, forthcoming.

———. "The 1920 Colonial Reforms and the June 10 (1926) Movement: A Korean Search for Ethnic Space." In *Colonial Rule and Social Change in Korea, 1910–1945*, edited by Clark Sorensen and Yong-Chool Ha. Seattle: Publications of the Center for Korea Studies, University of Washington Press, forthcoming.

Ch'a Kibyŏk, ed. *Ilche ŭi Han'guk singmin t'ongch'i: Singmin t'ongch'i ŭi chŏn'gae, sahoe kyŏngjejŏk pyŏnhwa, minjok undong* (Japanese Colonial Administration in Korea: Colonial Development, Social Economic Change, and Ethnic Demonstrations). Seoul: Chŏngŭmsa, 1985.

———. "Ilbon chegukchuŭi singmin chŏngch'aek ŭi hyŏngsŏng paegyŏng kwa kŭ chŏn'gae" (The Development and Formation of Imperial Japan's Colonial Strategy). In *Ilche ŭi Han'guk singmin t'ongch'i*, edited by Ch'a Kibyŏk, 12–44. Seoul: Chŏngŭmsa, 1985.

Chandra, Vipan. "An Outline Study of the Ilchin-hoe (Advancement Society of Korea)." *Occasional Papers on Korea* 2 (March 1974): 43–72.

———. *Imperialism, Resistance, and Reform in Late Nineteenth-Century Korea: Enlightenment and the Independent Club*. Berkeley: Institute of East Asian Studies, University of California Press, 1988.

Chatterjee, Partha. *Nationalist Thought and the Colonial World: A Derivative Discourse*. Minneapolis: University of Minnesota Press, 1986.

———. *The Nation and Its Fragments: Colonial and Postcolonial Histories*. Princeton, N.J.: Princeton University Press, 1993.

Chen, Edward I-te. "Japanese Colonialism in Korea and Formosa: A Comparison of the Systems of Political Control." *Harvard Journal of Asiatic Studies* 30 (1970): 126–58.

——. "Japan's Decision to Annex Taiwan: A Study of Itō-Mutsu Diplomacy, 1894–95." *Journal of Asian Studies* 37, no. 1 (November 1977): 61–72.

——. "The Attempt to Integrate the Empire: Legal Perspectives." In *The Japanese Colonial Empire, 1895–1945*, edited by Ramon H. Myers and Mark R. Peattie, 240–74. Princeton, N.J.: Princeton University Press, 1987.

——. "Gotō Shinpei, Japan's Colonial Administrator in Taiwan: A Critical Reexamination." *American Asian Review* 13 (Spring 1995): 25–59.

Chen Peifeng. "*Dōka" no dōshō imu* ("Assimilation": Shared Bed, Different Dream). Tokyo: Sangensha, 2001.

Ching, Leo T. S. *Becoming "Japanese": Colonial Taiwan and the Politics of Identity Formation*. Berkeley: University of California Press, 2001.

Cho Hangnein, ed. *Ilche ŭi taehan ch'imnyak chŏngch'aeksa yŏn'gu* (Studies on Japanese Imperial Invasion Policy toward Korea). Seoul: Hyŏnŭmsa, 1996.

Cho Pyŏngsang. "Shiganhei wo ko ni mochite" (My Son the Volunteer Soldier). *Chōsen* (March 1940): 61–63.

Ch'oe Sŏg'yŏng. *Ilche ŭi tonghwa ideollogi ŭi ch'angch'ul* (A Framework for Imperial Japanese Assimilation Ideology). Seoul: Sŏgyŏng munhwasa, 1997.

Choi Kyeong-Hee. "Another Layer of the Pro-Japanese Literature: Ch'oe Chŏnghŭi's 'The Wild Chrysanthemum.'" *Poetica* 52 (1999): 61–87.

——. "Neither Colonial nor National: The Making of the 'New Women' in Pak Wansŏ's 'Mother's Stake 1." In *Colonial Modernity in Korea*, edited by Gi-Wook Shin and Michael Robinson, 221–47. Cambridge, Mass.: Harvard University Press, 1999.

Chŏng Ch'anyong, ed. *Hanil yangguk ŭi sangho insik* (Shared Perceptions of Korea and Japan). Seoul: Kukhak charyowŏn, 1998.

Chŏng Okcha. "Sinsa yuramdan ko" (Considerations of the Gentleman Touring Corps). *Yŏksa hakpo* 27 (1965): 105–42.

Chŏng Saehyŏn. "Han'guk yŏsŏng ŭi sin munhwa undong: 1920 yŏndae ch'ogi ŭi yŏsŏng munhwa undong ŭl chungsim ŭro" (The New Cultural Movement for Korean Women: A Consideration of the Women's Cultural Movement of the Early 1920s). *Asea yŏsŏng yŏn'gu* (December 1971): 331–57.

Chōsen government-general. *Chōsen sōtokufu tokei nenpō* (Government-General Annual Book of Statistics). Keijō: Chōsen government-general, 1910–1944.

——. *Chōsen sōtokufu shisei nenpō* (Chōsen Government-General Administration Annual). Keijō: Chōsen government-general, 1914.

————. *Results of Three Years' Administration of Chosen*. Keijō: Government-general, 1914.

————. Keimu kyoku toshoka. "Ri denka no shikyo ni saishi 'shinbunshi wo tōshite mitaru' Chōsenjin no shisō keikō" (Tendencies in the Korean's Thought 'as Seen through Newspapers' at the Time of the Death of the Yi Highness). Keijō: Chōsen government-general Secret Report, 1926.

————. *Thriving Chōsen: A Survey of Twenty-five Years' Administration*. Keijō: Chōsen government-general, 1935.

Chow Tse-tsung, *The May Fourth Movement: Intellectual Revolution in Modern China*. Stanford, Calif.: Stanford University Press, 1960.

Christy, Alan S. "The Making of Imperial Subjects in Okinawa." In *Foundations of Colonial Modernity in East Asia*, edited by Tami Barlow, 141–70. Durham, N.C.: Duke University Press, 1997.

Chu, Samuel C., and Kwang-Ching Liu. *Li Hung-chang and China's Early Modernization*. New York: M. E. Sharpe, 1994.

Chu Yosŏp. *Chosŏn kyoyuk ŭi kyŏrham* (Deficiencies in Korean Education). Keijō: Sekai soin, 1930.

Chung Chin-han. *Nihon shokuminchika shita ni okeru Taiwan kyōikushi* (The History of Taiwanese Education under Japanese Colonialism). Tokyo: Taga shuppan, 1993.

Chung Taekyun. *Kankoku no imeeji: Sengo Nihonjin no rinkokukan* (Korean Images: Japanese Postwar Image of the Country Next Door). Tokyo: Enūōkōronsha, 1995.

Clark, Donald N. *Living Dangerously in Korea: The Western Experience, 1900–1950*. Norwalk, Conn.: EastBridge, 2003.

Clarke, Hugh. "The Great Dialect Debate: The State and Language Policy in Okinawa." In *Society and State in Interwar Japan*, edited by Elise K. Tipton, 193–217. London: Routledge, 1997.

Clyde, Robert. *From Rebel to Hero: The Image of the Highlander, 1745–1830*. East Lothian, Scotland: Tuckwell Press, 1998.

Cobbing, Andrew. "Britain (1): Early Meiji Encounters." In *The Iwakura Mission in America and Europe: A New Assessment*, edited by Ian Nish, 36–53. Surrey, U.K.: Japan Library, 1988.

Coleman, Michael C. *American Indian Children at School, 1850–1930*. Jackson: University Press of Mississippi, 1993.

Colley, Linda. *Britons: Forging a Nation 1707–1837*. New Haven, Conn.: Yale University Press, 1992.

Collingham, E. M. *Imperial Bodies: The Physical Experience of the Raj, C. 1800–1947*. Oxford: Polity Press, 2001.

Confer, Vincent. *France and Algeria: The Problem of Civil and Political Reform, 1870–1920*. New York: Syracuse University Press, 1966.

Conroy, Hilary. *The Japanese Seizure of Korea, 1868–1910: A Study of Realism and Idealism in International Relations*. Philadelphia: University of Pennsylvania Press, 1960.

Cook, Haruko Taya, and Theodore F. Cook. *Japan at War: An Oral History*. New York: W. W. Norton, 1992.

Cousin, Victor. "Report on the State of Public Instruction in Prussia." In *Reports on European Education*, edited by Edward H. Reisner, 115–240. New York: McGraw Hill, 1930.

Cumings, Bruce. *The Origins of the Korean War: Liberation and the Emergence of Separate Regimes, 1945–1947*. Princeton, N.J.: Princeton University Press, 1981.

——. *Korea's Place in the Sun: A History*. New York: W. W. Norton, 1997.

——. "Colonial Formations and Deformations: Korea, Taiwan, and Vietnam." In *Decolonization: Perceptions from Now and Then*, edited by Prasenjit Duara, 278–98. London: Routledge, 2004.

Davies, John. *A History of Wales*. London: Penguin Books, 1993.

Davies, Peter. *Dangerous Liaisons: Collaboration and World War Two*. Harlon, U.K.: Pearson Longman, 2004.

De Ceuster, Koen. "The Nation Exorcised: The Historiography of Collaboration in South Korea." *Korea Studies* 25, no. 2 (2001): 207–42.

Deeb, Marius. "The 1919 Popular Uprising: A Genesis of Egyptian Nationalism." *Canadian Review of Studies in Nationalism* 1, no. 1 (Fall 1973): 106–19.

Delissen, Alain. "Seoul, Summer 1925: The Social Space and the 'Natural' Event." Paper presented at Harvard University's Korea Institute, October 31, 2002.

Denison, H. W. "Taiwan oyobi sono tsuizoku shima jumin no genji no kokumin bungen narabi ni Nihonkoku to no shōrai no kankei" (The Present Social Standing of Residents in Taiwan and Neighboring Islands and Their Future Relations with Japan). In *Hisho ruisan*, edited by Itō Hirobumi and Hirazuka Atsushi, 226–33. Tokyo: Hara shobō, 1970.

Deuchler, Martina. *Confucian Gentlemen and Barbarian Envoys: The Opening of Korea, 1875–1885*. Seattle: University of Washington Press, 1977.

Devine, Richard. "Japanese Rule in Korea after the March First Uprising: Governor General Hasegawa's Recommendations." *Monumenta Nipponica* 52, no. 4 (Winter 1997): 523–40.

Dickinson, Fredrick R. *War and National Reinvention: Japan in the Great War, 1914–1919*. Cambridge, Mass.: Harvard University Asia Center, 1999.

Doak, Kevin M. "Colonialism and Ethnic Nationalism in the Political Thought of Yanaihara Tadao (1893–1961)." *East Asian History* 10 (December 1995): 79–98.

Dong Wonmo. "Japanese Colonial Policy and Practice in Korea, 1905–1945: A Study in Assimilation." Ph.D. diss., Georgetown University, 1969.

———. "Assimilation and Social Mobilization in Korea." In *Korea Under Japanese Rule*, edited by Andrew C. Nahm, 146–82. Kalamazoo: Center for Korean Studies, Western Michigan University, 1973.

Dore, Robert P. *Education in Tokugawa Japan*. Michigan Classics in Japanese Studies, no. 8. Ann Arbor: Center for Japanese Studies, University of Michigan Press, 1984.

Duara, Prasenjit, ed. *Decolonization: Perceptions from Now and Then*. London: Routledge, 2004.

Dudden, Alexis. *Japanese Colonization of Korea: Discourse and Power*. Honolulu: University of Hawai'i Press, 2005.

Duus, Peter, ed. *Cambridge History of Japan*, vol. 6, 217–70. Cambridge: Cambridge University Press, 1988.

———. *The Abacus and the Sword: The Japanese Penetration of Korea, 1895–1910*. Berkeley: University of California Press, 1995.

Earl, David M. *Emperor and Nation in Japan: Political Thinkers of the Tokugawa Period*. Seattle: University of Washington Press, 1964.

Eckert, Carter J. *Offspring of Empire: The Koch'ang Kims and the Colonial Origins of Korean Capitalism, 1876–1945*. Seattle: University of Washington Press, 1991.

Eckert, Carter J., Ki-Baik Lee, Young Ick Lew, Michael Robinson, and Edward W. Wagner. *Korea Old and New: A History*. Seoul: Ilchokak and Cambridge, Mass.: Harvard University Press, 1990.

Eguchi Keiichi. *Nihon teikokushugishi kenkyū* (Research in the History of Japanese Imperialism). Tokyo: Aoki shoten, 1998.

Erickson, Charlotte. *Invisible Immigrants: The Adaptation of English and Scottish Immigrants in Nineteenth-Century America*. Ithaca, N.Y.: Cornell University Press, 1972.

Eunice, Thio. *British Policy in the Malay Peninsula, 1880–1910*. Singapore: University of Malaya Press, 1969.

Fage, John D. "British and German Colonial Rule: A Synthesis and Summary." In *Britain and Germany in Africa: Imperial Rivalry and Colonial Rule*, edited by Prosser Gifford and William Roger Louis, 691–706. New Haven, Conn.: Yale University Press, 1967.

Fanon, Frantz. *Black Skin, White Masks*. Translated by Charles Lam Markmann. New York: Grove Weidenfield, 1967.

Farwell, Byron. *Queen Victoria's Little Wars*. New York: W. W. Norton, 1972.

Fieldhouse, D. K. *The Colonial Empires: A Comparative Survey from the Eighteenth Century*. New York: Dell, 1966.

Friedman, Elizabeth. *Colonization and After: An Algerian Jewish Community*. South Hadley, Mass.: Bergin & Garvey, 1988.

Fujitani, Takashi. *Splendid Monarchy: Power and Pageantry in Modern Japan*. Berkeley: University of California Press, 1996.

Fujizaki Sainosuke. *Taiwan no hanzoku* (Tribes of Taiwan). Tokyo: Kokushikan gyokai, 1930.

Fukuzawa Yukichi. *Fukuzawa zenshū*, edited by Jiji shinbōsha. 10 vols. Tokyo: Kokumin tosho, 1926.

———. *An Outline on a Theory of Civilization*. Translated by David A. Dilworth. Tokyo: Sophia University, 1973.

"Gappōgo no Chōsenjin kyōiku" (Korean Education after Annexation). *Kyōikukai* (November 1910): 1–3.

Garon, Sheldon. *Molding Japanese Minds: The State in Everyday Life*. Princeton, N.J.: Princeton University Press, 1997.

Garvin, Tom. "The Anatomy of a Nationalist Revolution: Ireland, 1888–1928." *Comparative Studies in Society and History* 28, no. 3 (1986): 468–501.

Gifford, Prosser. "Indirect Rule: Touchstone or Tombstone for Colonial Policy." In *Britain and Germany in Africa: Imperial Rivalry and Colonial Rule*, edited by Prosser Gifford and William Roger Louis, 351–91. New Haven, Conn.: Yale University Press, 1967.

Gifford, Prosser, and William Roger Louis, eds. *Britain and Germany in Africa: Imperial Rivalry and Colonial Rule*. New Haven, Conn.: Yale University Press, 1967.

Gluck, Carol. *Japan's Modern Myths: Ideology in the Late Meiji Period*. Princeton, N.J.: Princeton University Press, 1985.

Gordon, Andrew. *Labor and Imperial Democracy in Prewar Japan*. Berkeley: University of California Press, 1991.

Gotō Shinpei. "The Administration of Formosa (Taiwan)." In *Fifty Years of New Japan*, edited by Okuma Shigenobu and Marcus B. Huish, 530–53. London: Smith, Elder, 1909.

Gould, Stephen Jay. *The Mismeasure of Man*. New York: W. W. Norton, 1996.

Hale, Grace Elizabeth. *Making Whiteness: The Culture of Segregation in the South, 1890–1940*. New York: Vintage Books, 1998.

Hall, Ivan P. *Mori Arinori*. Cambridge, Mass.: Harvard University Press, 1973.

Hamilton, Agnus. *Korea*. New York: Charles Scribner's Sons, 1904.

Han, Jung-Sun N. "An Imperial Path to Modernity: Yoshino Sakuzō and the Making of a New Liberal Projection in Japan, 1905–1937." Ph.D. diss., University of Washington, 2003.

Han Myŏnggŭn. *Hanmal hanil happangnon yŏn'gu* (Research on Late Korean Japan-Korea Annexation Theories). Seoul: Kukhak charyowŏn, 2002.

Han, Seung-Mi. "Korea through Japanese Eyes: An Analysis of Late Meiji Travelogues on Korea." *Asia Cultural Studies* 24 (March 1998): 49–72.

Hanguk charyo yŏnguso, ed. *Chosŏn t'ongji charyo* (Materials on Korean Administration). Seoul: Hanguk charyo yŏnguso, 1996.

Hara Sōichiro. *Chōsen no tabi* (A Korean Trip). Tokyo: Iwamatsudō Shoten, 1917.

Hara Takashi. *Hara Takashi nikki* (Hara Takashi's Diaries). 8 vols. Edited by Hara Keiichirō. Tokyo: Kan'gensha, 1950.

———. "Taiwan mondai futa an" (Two Proposals for the Taiwan Problem). In *Hisho ruisan,* edited by Itō Hirabumi and Hirazuka Atsushi, 32–34. Tokyo: Hara shobō, 1970.

Harrington, Fred H. *God, Mammon, and the Japanese.* Madison: University of Wisconsin Press, 1966.

Hashiya Hiroshi. "Shokuminchi toshi" (Colonial City). In *Kindai Nihon no kiseki: Toshi to minshū* (The Locus of Modern Japan: The City and the Masses), edited by Narita Ryūichi, 215–36. Tokyo: Yoshikawa Hiroshi bunkan, 1993.

Hatada Takashi. "Chōsen no hōken seido ni kan suru oboe gaki" (Notes on Korea's Feudal System). *Rekishi to chiri* 9 (1935): 45–50.

———. *A History of Korea.* Translated by Warren W. Smith and Benjamin H. Hazzard. Santa Barbara, Calif.: Clio Press, 1969.

———. *Nihonjin no Chōsenkan* (Japanese Views of the Korean People). Tokyo: Keisō shobō, 1969.

Hazen, Charles D. *Alsace-Lorraine under German Rule.* New York: Henry Holt, 1917.

Hechter, Michael. *Internal Colonialism: The Celtic Fringe in British National Development, 1536–1966.* Berkeley: University of California Press, 1975.

Heine, William. *With Perry to Japan: A Memoir by William Heine.* Translated by Frederic Tractmann. Honolulu: University of Hawai'i Press, 1990.

Henderson, Gregory. *Korea: The Politics of the Vortex.* Cambridge, Mass.: Harvard University Press, 1968.

Henry, Robert Selph. *The Story of Reconstruction.* 1938. New York: Konecky & Konecky, 1999.

Henry, Todd A. "Sanitizing Empire: Japanese Articulation of Korean Otherness and the Construction of Early Colonial Seoul, 1905–1919." *Journal of Asian Studies* 64, no. 3 (August 2005): 639–76.

Higuchi Yūichi. *Kōgun heishi ni sareta Chōsenjin* (Koreans Enlisted in the Imperial Army). Tokyo: Hyōronsha, 1992.

Hirano Yoshitarō. *Ōi Kentarō*. Tokyo: Yoshikawa kōbunkan, 1965.

Hobsbawm, Eric. *The Age of Empire, 1875–1914*. New York: Vintage Books, 1987.

Hobsbawm, Eric, and Terence Ranger, eds. *The Invention of Tradition*. Cambridge: Cambridge University Press, 1992.

Hocker, M. B. *Legal Pluralism: An Introduction to Colonial and Neo-Colonial Laws*. Oxford: Clarendon Press, 1975.

Hong, Moon-Jong. "Japanese Colonial Education Policy in Korea." Ph.D. diss., Harvard University, 1992.

Horio Mine. "Shinkokumin no kyōiku" (Education for the New Nationals). *Kyōiku jiron* (September 5, 1910): 13–15.

Hotta-Lister, Ayako. *The Japan-British Exhibition of 1910: Gateway to the Island Empire of the East*. Surry, U.K.: Japan Library, 1999.

Houston, R. A. *Scottish Literacy and the Scottish Identity: Illiteracy and Society in Scotland and Northern England, 1600–1800*. Cambridge: Cambridge University Press, 1985.

Howell, David L. "Ainu Ethnicity and the Boundaries of the Early Modern Japanese State." *Past and Present* 142 (February 1994): 75–87.

Huffman, James L. *Creating a Public: People and Press in Meiji Japan*. Honolulu: University of Hawai'i Press, 1997.

Hunt, Michael H. *The Making of a Special Relationship: The United States and China to 1914*. New York: Columbia University Press, 1983.

Hwang, Kyung Moon. *Beyond Birth: Social Status in the Emergence of Modern Korea*. Cambridge, Mass.: Harvard University Press, 2004.

Hwang Minho. "Ch'ongnon: 1910 nyŏngdae Chosŏn ch'ongdokpu ŭi ŏllon chŏngch'aek gwa *Maeil sinbo*" (Introduction: The 1910s Government-General's Press Policy and the *Maeil sinbo*). In *Singminji Chosŏn kwa Maeil sinbo*, edited by Suyo Yŏksa Yŏngu Hoe, 11–31. Seoul: Sinsŏwan, 2003.

Hyŏn Yŏngsŏp. *Chōsenjin no susumu beki michi* (The Path That the Korean Must Take). Keijō: Ryokki renmei, 1940.

Hyun, Peter. *Man Sei! The Making of a Korean American*. Honolulu: University of Hawai'i Press, 1986.

Igarashi Akio. *Meiji ishin no shisō* (Ideology of the Meiji Restoration). Yokohama: Seori shobō, 1996.

Iha Fuyū. *Ko-Ryukyu* (Old Ryukyu). Tokyo: Gansoji, 1922.

Ikeuchi Satoshi. *Kinsei Nihon to Chōsen hyōryūmin* (Modern Japan and Korean Castaways). Tokyo: Sanseisha, 1998.

Inoue Kaoru. *Inoue segai den* (The Biography of Inoue Kaoru). Edited by Inoue Kaoruka deni hensankai. Tokyo: Hakubunkan, 1910.

Iriye, Akira. *Pacific Estrangement: Japanese and American Expansion.* Cambridge, Mass.: Harvard University Press, 1972.

Itō Hirobumi and Hirazuka Atsushi, eds. *Hisho ruisan: Taiwan shiryō* (Classified Collection of Private Documents: Taiwan Materials). Meiji hyakunenshi sōshi (Meiji Centennial History Collection), vol. 127. Tokyo: Hara shobō, 1970.

Itō Sei, Kamai Shōichirō, Nakamura Mitsuo, Hirano Ken, Yamamoto Kenkichi, eds. *Nihon gendai bungaku zenshū* (Collection of Contemporary Japanese Literature). 213 volumes. Tokyo: Kōdansha, 1980.

Iwakura Tomomi. *Iwakura ko jikki* (An Authentic History of Prince Iwakura). Edited by Tada Kōmon. 2 vols. Tokyo: Hara shobō, 1968.

James, Lawrence. *The Rise and Fall of the British Empire.* London: Little Brown, 1994.

Jansen, Marius B. "Japanese Imperialism: Late Meiji Perspectives." In *The Japanese Colonial Empire, 1895–1945,* edited by Ramon H. Myers and Mark R. Peattie, 61–79. Princeton, N.J.: Princeton University Press, 1984.

Jansen, Marius B., and Gilbert Rozman, eds. *Japan in Transition: From Tokugawa to Meiji.* Princeton, N.J.: Princeton University Press, 1986.

Jayawardena, Kamari. *The White Women's Other Burden: Western Women and South Asia During British Rule.* New York: Routledge, 1995.

"'Jihenka no Chōsen wo kataru' zadankai" (A Roundtable Discussion on 'Korea under the Incident'). *Bungei shunjū* 64 (June 1939): 246–64.

Jones, Aled G. *Press, Politics, and Society: A History of Journalism in Wales.* Cardiff: University of Wales Press, 1993.

Jones, Gareth E. *Modern Wales: A Concise History.* Cambridge: Cambridge University Press, 1995.

Judd, Denis. *Empire: The British Imperial Experience from 1765 to the Present.* London: Basic Books, 1996.

Kajiyama, Toshiyuki. *The Clan Records: Five Stories of Korea.* Translated by Yoshiko Dykstra. Honolulu: University of Hawai'i Press, 1995.

Kamada Eikichi. "Naisen kyōgaku ni tsuite" (Concerning Japanese-Korean Integrated Education). *Chōsen kyōiku* (March 1922): 75–79.

Kamatsuka Tamotsu. "Kōmin kyōiku no shin shimei wo akiraka ni shi: Chōsen no kōminka yōmoku no seishin ni oyobu" (Clarifying the New Mission of Civic Education: Concerning the Principle Items of the Spirit of Korea's Civic Education). *Kōmin kyōiku* (July 1935): 27–38.

Kan Doksun. *Yŏ Unhyŏng hyōden 1: Chōsen sanichi dokuritsu undō* (A Critical Biography of Yŏ Unhyŏng 1: Korea's March First Independence Movement). Tokyo: Shinkansha, 2002.

Kang, Hildi. *Under the Black Umbrella: Voices from Colonial Korea*. Ithaca, N.Y.: Cornell University Press, 2001.

Kariya Yūichi. "Kaitakushi kagakkō ni okeru Ainu kyōiku" (Ainu Education at the Temporary Developments School). In *Meiji ishin no chiiki to minshū* (Regions and Peoples in the Meiji Restoration), edited by Meiji ishin shinshi gakkai, 157–76. Tokyo: Yoshikawa kōbunkan, 1996.

Kawamura Minato. *Sōru toshi monogatari: Rekishi, bungaku, to fūkei* (The Story of Seoul: History, Literature, and Landscape). Tokyo: Heibonsha, 2000.

Keene, Donald. *The Japanese Discovery of Europe, 1720–1830*. Stanford, Calif.: Stanford University Press, 1952.

Kendall, Laurel. *Getting Married in Korea: Of Gender, Morality, and Modernity*. Berkeley: University of California Press, 1996.

Kerr, George H. *Okinawa: The History of an Island People*. Rutland, Vt.: Charles E. Tuttle, 2000.

Kido Takayoshi. *The Diary of Kido Takayoshi*, vol. 2: *1871–1874*. Translated by Sidney Devere Brown and Akiko Hirota. Tokyo: University of Tokyo Press, 1985.

Kim, C. I. Eugene, and Kim Hankyo. *Korea and the Politics of Imperialism, 1876–1910*. Berkeley: University of California Press, 1968.

Kim Chŏng-won. "List of 3,090 Pro-Japanese Collaborators Made Public." *Empas News*, http://news.empas.com/print.tsp/20050829n06308 (accessed May 21, 2008).

Kim Kwan Bong. *The Korea-Japan Treaty Crisis and the Instability of the Korean Political System*. New York: Praeger, 1971.

Kim Minsu. "Nittei no taikan shinryaku to gengo seisaku" (Imperial Japan's Invasion of Korea and Its Linguistic Policy). *Han* 2, no. 5 (1973): 81–102.

Kim Puja. *Shokuminchiki Chōsen no kyōiku to jendaa* (Korean Education and Gender during Colonial Rule). Yokohama: Seori shobō, 2005.

Kim, Richard E. *Lost Names: Scenes from a Korean Boyhood*. Berkeley: University of California Press, 1998.

Kim Sangman, ed. *Tong'a ilbosa* (The History of the *Tong'a ilbo*). 2 vols. Seoul: Tong'a ilbosa, 1975.

Kim Saryang. "Hikari no naka ni" (Within the Light). In *Nihon gendai bungakushū*, vol. 69. Tokyo: Kōdansha, 1980, 263–79.

Kim Tohyŏng. *Ilche ch'imnyak ch'ogi (1905–1919) ch'inilp'a seryŏk ŭi chŏngch'inon yŏn'gu* (A Study on the Political Thought of the Pro-Japanese in the Early Period of Japanese Rule [1905–1919]). *Kyemyŏng sahak* 3 (November 1992): 1–63.

Kim Yŏlchin, ed. *Panminja tae kongp'an'gi* (A Record of the Great Trial of Treason). Vol. 1. Seoul: Hanp'ung ch'ulp'ansa, 1986.

Kinjō Shigeaki. "Kōminka kyōiku no shūchaku eki" (The Terminal Station of Imperialization Education). In *Okinawa tennōsei e no gyakko* (Okinawa: The Retrogradation of the Emperor System), edited by Akisaki Moriteru and Kawamitsu Shin'ichi, 104–13. Tokyo: Shakai hyōronsha, 1988.

Kirk, William. "Social Change in Formosa." *Sociology and Social Research* 26 (1941–42): 10–26.

Kirkwood, Montague. "Shokuminchi seido" (Colonial Policy). In *Hisho ruisan*, edited by Itō Hirobumi and Hirazuka Atsushi, 79–107. Tokyo: Hara shobō, 1970.

———. "Taiwan seido Tennō no daiken oyobi gikai ni kan suru ikensho" (An Opinion Paper on the Supreme Authority of the Emperor and the Imperial Diet in Taiwan). In *Hisho ruisan*, edited by Itō Hirobumi and Hirazuka Atsushi, 108–48. Tokyo: Hara shobō, 1970.

Kita Sadakichi. "Kankoku no heigō to kokushi" (Natural History and Korean Annexation). Tokyo: Sanseidō, 1910.

———. "Chōsen minzoku to wa nan zoya" (What Is the Korean Race). *Minzoku to rekishi* (June 1919): 1–13.

———. "Nissen ryōminzoku dōgenron" (The Same Origin Theory of the Korean and Japanese Races). *Minzoku to rekishi* (January 1921): 3–39.

———. "Toshin Senman ryokō nisshi" (Travels through Korea and Manchuria). *Minzoku to rekishi* (January 1921): 271–82.

Kitaoka Shin'ichi. *Gotō Shinpei: Gaikō to vijon* (Gotō Shinpei: Diplomacy and Vision). Tokyo: Chūō Kōronsha, 1988.

Komagome Takeshi. *Shokuminchi teikoku Nihon no bunka seiji* (Colonial Imperial Japan's Culture Rule). Tokyo: Iwanami shoten, 1996.

Kondō Ken'ichi, ed. *Kenkyū shūsei: Chōsen kindai shiryō* (Research Compilations: Modern Korean Historical Materials). 4 vols. Tokyo: Yūhōkyōkai Chōsen shiryō kenkyūkai, 1958.

Ku, Dae-yeol. *Korea under Colonialism: The March First Movement and Anglo Japanese Relations*. Seoul: Seoul Computer Press, 1985.

Kubo Takeshi. "Chōsenjin no jinshu kaibōgakuteki kenkyū" (Research on the Korean Racial Anatomy). *Chōsen igakkai zasshi* 22 (July 1918): 52–86, 146–53.

Kume Kunitake. *Tokumei zenken taishi Bei-ō kairan jikki* (A True Account of the Special Embassy's Tour of America and Europe). Edited by Tanaka Akira. 5 vols. Tokyo: Iwanami shoten, 1996.

———. *The Iwakura Embassy, 1871–73, a True Account of the Ambassador Extraordinary Plenipotentiary's Journey of Observations Through the United States and Europe.* 5 vols. Edited by Graham Healey and Chūshichi Tsuzuki. Chiba: The Japan Documents, 2002.

Kurokawa Sō, ed. *"Gaichi" no Nihongo bungakusen, 3: Chōsen* (Japanese Literature from the Empire, 3: Korea). Tokyo: Shinjuku shobō, 1996.

Kuwabara Takeo. *Japan and Western Civilization: Essays on Comparative Culture.* Edited by Katō Hidetoshi, translated by Patricia Murray. Tokyo: Tokyo University Press, 1983.

Lamley, Harry. "Assimilation Efforts in Colonial Taiwan: The Fate of the 1914 Movement." *Monumenta Serica* 29 (1970–71): 496–520.

Larsen, Kirk W. *Tradition, Treaties, and Trade: Qing Imperialism and Chosŏn Korea, 1850–1910.* Cambridge, Mass: Harvard University Asia Center, 2008.

Lee, Chong-sik. *The Politics of Korean Nationalism.* Berkeley: University of California Press, 1963.

Lee, Peter H., ed. *Sourcebook of Korean Literature.* 2 vols. New York: Columbia University Press, 1996.

Lehning, James R. *Peasant and French: Cultural Contact in Rural France during the Nineteenth Century.* Cambridge: Cambridge University Press, 1995.

Lensen, George A. *The Russian Push toward Japan: Russo-Japanese Relations, 1697–1875.* Princeton, N.J.: Princeton University Press, 1959.

Leung, Edwin Pak-wah. "Li Hung-chang and the Liu-ch'iu (Ryukyu) Controversy, 1871–1881." In *Li Hung-chang and China's Early Modernization*, edited by Samuel C. Chu and Kwang-Ching Liu, 162–75. New York: M. E. Sharpe, 1994.

Levine-Rasky, Cynthia, ed. *Working through Whiteness: International Perspectives.* Albany: State University of New York, 2002.

Lew, Young Ick. "Yüan Shih-k'ai's Residency and the Korean Enlightenment Movement (1885–94)." *Journal of Korean Studies* 5 (1984): 63–107.

Lewis, James B. *Frontier Contact Between Chosŏn Korea and Tokugawa Japan.* London: Routledge, 2003.

Lewis, Michael. *Becoming Apart: National Power and Local Politics in Toyama, 1868–1945.* Cambridge, Mass.: Harvard University Press, 2000.

Lincicome, Mark. *Principles, Praxis, and the Politics of Educational Reform in Meiji Japan.* Honolulu: University of Hawai'i Press, 1995.

Lomawaima, K. Tsianina. *They Called It Prairie Light: The Story of Chilocco Indian School.* Lincoln: University of Nebraska Press, 1994.

Lone, Stewart. *Army, Empire and Politics in Meiji Japan: The Three Centers of General Katsura Tarō.* New York: St. Martin's Press, 2000.

Long, Ngô Viñh. *Before the Revolution: The Vietnamese Peasants Under the French.* New York: Columbia University Press, 1991.

Lubon, Michel. "Ryōtō oyobi Taiwan tōchi ni kan suru kōgi" (A Discussion on the Administration of the Liaotung Peninsula and Taiwan). In *Hisho ruisan*, edited by Itō Hirobumi and Hirazuka Atshushi, 399–409. Tokyo: Hara shobō, 1970.

Macaulay, Thomas Babington. "Minute Recorded in the General Department by Thomas Babington Macaulay, Law Member of the Governor-general's Council (February 2, 1835)." In *The Great Indian Education Debate: Documents Relating to the Orientalist-Anglicist Controversy, 1781–1843*, edited by Lynn Zastoupil and Martin Moir, 161–73. Surrey, U.K.: Curzon Press, 1999.

Mackie, J. D. *A History of Scotland*. Middlesex, U.K.: Penguin Books, 1964.

Marr, David G. *Vietnamese Anti-Colonialism, 1885–1925*. Berkeley: University of California Press, 1971.

———. *Vietnamese Tradition on Trial, 1920–1945*. Berkeley: University of California Press, 1981.

Marshall, Byron K. *Learning to Be Modern: Japanese Political Discourse on Education*. Boulder, Colo.: Westview, 1994.

Maruyama Masao. *Studies in the Intellectual History of Tokugawa Japan*. Translated by Mikiso Hane. Tokyo: University of Tokyo Press, 1974.

Mattielli, Sandra, ed. *Virtues in Conflict: Tradition and the Korean Woman Today*. Seoul: Royal Asiatic Society, 1977.

Mawani, Renisa. "'The Iniquitous Practice of Women': Prostitution and the Making of White Spaces in British Columbia, 1898–1905." In *Working through Whiteness: International Perspectives*, edited by Cynthia Levine-Rasky, 43–68. Albany: State University of New York, 2002.

Mayo, Marlene. "The Western Education of Kume Kunitake, 1871–76." *Monumenta Nipponica* 28 (Spring 1973): 3–67.

———. "The Korean Crisis of 1873 and Early Meiji Foreign Policy." *Journal of Asian Studies* 31, no. 4 (August 1973): 793–819.

McCormack, Noah. "*Buraku* Emigration in the Meiji Era—Other Ways to Become 'Japanese.'" *East Asian Studies* 23 (2002): 87–108.

McKenna, Theobald. "A Memoire on Some questions Respecting the Projected Great Britain and Ireland." In *The Catholic Question in Ireland, 1762–1829*, edited by Nicholas Lee . Bristol, U.K.: Thoemmes Press; Tokyo: Edition Synapse, 2000.

Meiji bunka shiryōsho kangyōkai, ed. *Meiji bunka shiryōsho: Dai 8 kan, kyōikuhen* (Meiji Culture Materials Collection: no. 8, education edition). Tokyo: Kaimeitō, 1961.

Meiji ishin shinshigakkai, ed. *Meiji ishin no chiiki to minshū* (Regions and the Masses of the Meiji Restoration). Tokyo: Yoshikawa kōbunkan, 1996.

Minichiella, Sharon A., ed. *Japan's Competing Modernities: Issues in Culture and Democracy, 1900–1930*. Honolulu: University of Hawai'i Press, 1998.

Mitchell, Timothy. *Colonizing Egypt*. Berkeley: University of California Press, 1988.

Mitsuchi Chūzō. "Chōsenjin no kyōiku" (Korean Education). *Kyōikukai* (December 1910): 23–26.

Miyata Setsuko, Kim Yŏngdal, and Yang Taeho. *Sōshi kaimei* (Name Changes). Tokyo: Akashi shoten, 1994.

Mizuno Rentarō. *Mizuno Rentarō kaisōroku, kankei bunsho* (Memoirs and Official Papers of Mizuno Rentarō). Edited by Nishio Rintarō. Tokyo: Yamagawa shuppansha, 1999.

Mochiki Kanjin. "Ryukyu no onna fūzoku" (Customs of Ryukyu Women). *Fujin kōrōn* (January 1917): 12–33.

Moon, Yumi. "The Populist Contest: The Ilchinhoe Movement and the Japanese Colonization of Korea, 1896–1910." Ph.D. diss., Harvard University, 2005.

Morgan, Prys. "From a Death to a View: The Hunt for the Welsh Past in the Romantic Period." In *The Invention of Tradition*, edited by Eric Hobsbawm and Terence Ranger, 43–100. Cambridge: Cambridge University Press, 1992.

Morris-Suzuki, Tessa. *Re-inventing Japan: Time, Space, and Nation*. New York: M. E. Sharpe, 1998.

Morton, H. V. *In Search of Scotland*. New York: Dodd, Mead, 1935.

Moskowitz, Karl. "The Creation of the Oriental Development Company: Japanese Illusions Meet Korean Reality." *Occasional Papers on Korea* 2 (March 1974): 73–121.

Murphy, James E., and Sharon M. Murphy. *Let My People Know: American Indian Journalism*. Norman: University of Oklahoma Press, 1987.

Myers, Ramon H., and Mark R. Peattie, eds. *The Japanese Colonial Empire, 1895–1945*. Princeton, N.J.: Princeton University Press, 1984.

Nagata Akifumi. *Nihon no Chōsen tōchi to kokusai kankei: Chōsen dokuritsu undō to Amerika, 1910–1922* (Korea Rule and International Relations: Korean Independence Movement and the United States, 1910–1922). Tokyo: Heibonsha, 2005.

Nahm, Andrew C., ed. *Korea under Japanese Rule*. Kalamazoo: Center for Korean Studies, Western Michigan University, 1973.

Nakae, Chōmin. *A Discourse by Three Drunkards on Government*. Translated by Nobuko Tsukui. New York: Weatherhill, 1984.

Nakai, Kate Wildman. *Shogunal Politics: Arai Hakuseki and the Premises of Tokugawa Rule*. Cambridge, Mass.: Harvard University Press, 1988.

Nakajima Atsushi. "Junsa no iru fūkei" (The Scenery Where the Police Are). In *"Gaichi" no Nihongo bungakusen 3: Chōsen*, edited by Kurokawa Sō, 75–86. Tokyo: Shinjuku shobō, 1996.

Nakajima Motojirō. "Chōsen fujin no kotsuban gaikei keizokusu ni oite" (On the Outer Diameter Measurements of the Korean Women's Pelvic Bone). *Chōsen igakkai zasshi* (January 1913): 125–26.

Nakamura Sei. "Waga kō no kōmin kunren shisetsu" (The Facilities for Civic Training at Out School). *Bunkyō no Chōsen* (April 1933): 124–46.

Nakanishi Inosuke. "Saikin no Chōsen wo kataru" (Regarding Contemporary Korea). *Tōyō* (October 1933): 137–44.

Nakao Hiroshi. "Chōsen shisetsu no mita Edo to hitobito ni utsutta tsūshinshi" (What the Korean Embassies Saw in Edo and What They Left to the People). In *Chōsen tsūshinshi to Nihonjin* (History of the Korean Embassies), edited by Yi Wŏnsik et al., 102–31. Tokyo: Gakuseisha, 1996.

Narita Ryūchi, ed. *Kindai Nihon no kiseki: Tōshi to minshū* (The Locus of Modern Japan: The City and the Masses). Tokyo: Yoshikawa Hiroshi bunkan, 1993.

Neumann, William L. *America Encounters Japan: From Perry to MacArthur.* Baltimore: Johns Hopkins University Press, 1963.

Nihongi: Chronicles of Japan from the Earliest Times to A.D. 697. Translated by W. G. Aston. Tokyo: Charles E. Tuttle, 1972.

Nish, Ian, ed. *The Iwakura Mission in America and Europe: A New Assessment.* Surrey, U.K.: Japan Library, 1988.

Nishida Taketoshi. *Meiji jidai no shinbun to zasshi* (Meiji Era Newspapers and Magazines). Tokyo: Shibundō, 1961.

Nitobe Inazō. *Nitobe Inazō zenshū* (The Complete Works of Nitobe Inazō). 24 vols. Edited by Yanaihara Tadao. Tokyo: Kyōbunkan, 1983–87.

Ōe Shinobu. "Higashi Ajia shinkyū teikoku Nihon" (Old and New Imperial Japan in East Asia). In *Kindai Nihon to shokuminchi* (Modern Japan and Its Colonies), edited by Ōe Shinobu et al., 6–16. Tokyo: Iwanami shoten, 1993.

Ōe Shinobu, Asada Kyōji, Mitani Taichirō, Gotō Ken'ichi, Kobayashi Hideo, Takasaki Sōji, Wakabayashi Masatake, and Kawamura Minato, eds. *Kindai Nihon to shokuminchi* (Modern Japan and Its Colonies). Tokyo: Iwanami shoten, 1993.

Ogawa Masahito. "Kotan e no 'gyōkō'/'gyōkei' to Ainu kyōiku" (A Study of the Royal Visits to Kotan Village with Consideration of Ainu Education Policy). *Kyōiku shi gakkai kiyō* 34 (October 1991): 50–65.

Oguma Eiji. "Sabetsu soku byodō: Nihon shokuminchi tōchi shisō no Furansu jinshu shakaigaku no eikyō" (The Influence of French Racial Sociology on Japanese Colonial Administrative Thought). *Rekishigaku kenkyū* 662 (1994): 16–31.

———. *"Nihonjin" no kyōkai* (The Boundaries of the "Japanese"). Tokyo: Shin'yōsha, 2002.

Ōkubo Toshimichi, "Reasons for Opposing the Korean Expedition," in *Sources of*

Japanese Tradition, vol. 2, edited by Ryusaku Tsunoda, Wm. Theodore De Bary, and Donald Keene, 151–55. New York: Columbia University Press, 1958.

Okuma Shigenobu and Marcus B. Huish, eds. *Fifty Years of New Japan*. London: Smith, Elder, 1909.

Oliver, Robert T. *Syngman Rhee: The Man behind the Myth*. New York: Dodd Mead, 1954.

Oxaal, Ivar, Tony Barnett, and David Booth, eds. *Beyond the Sociology of Development: Economy and Society in Latin America and Africa*. London: Routledge & Kegan Paul, 1975.

Paek Pa. "Sowi 'sin yŏsŏng' kwa yangch'ŏ hyŏnmo chuŭi?" (The So-Called New Woman and the Good Wife-Wise Mother Ideology). *Hyŏndae p'yŏngnon* (Contemporary Review) (January 1928): 161–72.

Pai, Hyung Il. *Constructing Korean Origins: A Critical Review of Archeology, Historiography, and Racial Myth in Korean State-Formation Theories*. Cambridge, Mass.: Harvard University Press, 2000.

Pak Kyŏnsik. *Nihon teikokushugi no Chōsen shihai* (Japan's Imperial Control over Korea). Tokyo: Aoki shoten, 1993.

Pak Sanghŭi. "Chōsen seihokujin no tokushitsu" (Unique Characteristics of the Northwestern Korean). In *Chōsen oyobi Chōsen minzoku* (Korea and the Korean Race), edited by Chōsen oyobi Chōsen minzoku, 112–23. Chōsen shisō tsūshinsha, 1927.

Pak Sunmi. *Chōsen josei no chi no kaiyū: Shokuminchi bunka shihai to Nihon ryūgaku* (Korean Women Journeys of Knowledge: Colonial Cultural Control and Japanese Overseas Students). Tokyo: Yamakawa shuppansha, 2005.

Pak Yŏngje. "Kŭndae ilbon ŭi Hanguk insik" (Modern Japanese Perceptions of Korea). In *Ilche ŭi taehan ch'imnyak chŏngch'aeksa yŏn'gu* (Studies on Japanese Imperial Invasion Policy toward Korea), edited by Cho Hangnein, 7–37. Seoul: Hyŏnumsa, 1996.

Palais, James B. *Politics and Policy in Traditional Korea*. Cambridge: Harvard University Press, 19751.

———. *Confucian Statecraft and Korean Institutions: Yu Hyŏngwŏn and the Late Chosŏn Dynasty*. Seattle: University of Washington Press, 1996.

Panminjok munje yŏn'guso, ed. *Ch'inilp'a 99 in* (99 Members of the Pro-Japanese Group). 1993; Seoul: Tosŏ ch'ulgwan tol pegge, 2002.

Park, Induk. *September Monkey*. New York: Harper & Brothers, 1954.

Park, Soon-Won. *Colonial Industrialization and Labor in Korea: The Onada Cement Factory*. Cambridge, Mass.: Harvard University Press, 1999.

Passin, Herbert. *Society and Education in Japan*. Tokyo: Kodansha International, 1982.

Patterson, Orlando. *The Ordeals of Integration: Progress and Resentment in America's "Racial" Crisis*. New York: Basic Books, 1997.

Peattie, Mark R. "Introduction." In *The Japanese Colonial Empire, 1895–1945*, edited by Ramon H. Myers and Mark R. Peattie, 3–52. Princeton, N.J.: Princeton University Press, 1987.

———. "Japanese Attitudes toward Colonialism." In *The Japanese Colonial Empire, 1895–1945*, edited by Ramon H. Myers and Mark R. Peattie, 80–127. Princeton, N.J.: Princeton University Press, 1987.

———. "The Japanese Colonial Empire, 1895–1945." In *Cambridge History of Japan*, vol. 6, edited by Peter Duus. 217–70. Cambridge: Cambridge University Press, 1988.

Peng, Fred C. C. "Education: An Agent of Social Change in Ainu Community Life." *The Ainu: The Past and the Present*, edited by Fred C. C. Peng and Peter Geiser, 178–206. Hiroshima: Bunka, 1977.

Peng, Fred C. C., and Peter Geiser, eds. *The Ainu: The Past and the Present*. Hiroshima: Bunka, 1977.

Perry, Commodore M. C. *Narrative of the Expedition to the China Seas and Japan, 1852–1854*. 1856; Mineola, N.Y.: Dover, 2000.

Phillipson, Coleman. *Alsace-Lorraine: Past, Present, and Future*. New York: E. P. Dutton, 1918.

Phillipson, N. T., and Rosalind Mitchison. *Scotland in the Age of Improvement*. Edinburgh: Edinburgh University Press, 1996.

Prendergast, John P. *The Cromwellian Settlement of Ireland*. 1865; London: Constable, 1996.

Prochaska, David. *Making Algeria French: Colonialism in Béne, 1870–1920*. Cambridge: Cambridge University Press, 1990.

Prucha, Francis Paul. *American Indian Policy in Crisis: Christian Reformers and the Indian: 1865–1900*. Norman: University of Oklahoma Press, 1976.

Pyle, Kenneth B. *The New Generation in Meiji Japan: Problems of Cultural Identity, 1885–1895*. Stanford, Calif.: Stanford University Press, 1969.

———. "Advantages of Followership: German Economics and Japanese Bureaucrats, 1890–1925." *Journal of Japanese Studies* 1 (Fall 1974): 127–64.

———. *The Making of Modern Japan*. Lexington, Mass.: D.C. Heath, 1996.

Ritter, Richard H. "Industrial Education in Korea," *North American Review* (October 1920): 524–30.

Roberts, Gwyneth Tyson. "'Under the Hatches': English Parliamentary Commissioners' View of the People and Language of Mid-Nineteenth Century Wales."

In *The Expansion of the English Race: Race, Ethnicity, and Cultural History*, edited by Bill Schwarz, 171–97. London: Routledge, 1996.

———. *The Language of the Blue Books: The "Perfect Instrument of Empire."* Cardiff: University of Wales Press, 1998.

Robinson, Michael Edson. "Colonial Publication Policy and the Korean Nationalist Movement." In *The Japanese Colonial Empire, 1895–1945*, edited by Ramon H. Myers and Mark R. Peattie, 312–46. Princeton, N.J.: Princeton University Press, 1987.

———. *Cultural Nationalism in Colonial Korea, 1920–1925*. Seattle: University of Washington Press, 1988.

———. "Broadcasting in Korea, 1924–1937: Colonial Modernity and Cultural Hegemony." In *Japan's Competing Modernities: Issues in Culture and Democracy, 1900–1930*, edited by Sharon A. Minichiello, 358–78. Honolulu: University of Hawai'i Press, 1998.

Rousseau, Jean-Jacques. *The Social Contract and Discourses*. Translated by G. D. H. Cole. London: Everyman's Library, 1973.

Ruedy, John. *Modern Algeria: The Origins and Development of a Nation*. Bloomington: Indiana University Press, 1992.

Ryang, Sonia. "Japanese Travelers' Accounts of Korea." *East Asian History* 13/14 (1997): 133–52.

Sagers, John H. *Origins of Japanese Wealth and Power: Reconciling Confucianism and Capitalism, 1830–1885*. New York: Palgrave Macmillan, 2006.

Said, Edward W. *Orientalism*. New York: Vintage Books, 1979.

Saitō Makoto. *Saitō Makoto monjo* (Official Papers of Saitō Makoto). 17 vols. Seoul: Koryŏ sŏrim, 1990.

———. *Saitō Makoto kankei monjo* (Official Papers Regarding Saitō Makoto). Tokyo: Japanese National Diet Library (microfilm), 1998.

———. "A Message from the Imperial Government to the American People: Home Rule in Korea." *The Independent* (January 31, 1920): 167–69.

Salem, Ellen. "Women Surviving: Palace Life in Seoul after the Annexation." In *Virtues in Conflict: Tradition and the Korean Woman Today*, edited by Sandra Mattielli, 67–98. Seoul: Royal Asiatic Society, 1977.

Sansom, George B. *The Western World and Japan: A Study in the Interaction of European and Asiatic Cultures*. Tokyo: Charles E. Tuttle, 1977.

Sasagawa Rinbū. "Chōsen sozoro aruki" (A Stroll around Korea). *Chūō kōron* (August 1926): 79–94.

Sawada Yōtarō. *Okinawa to Ainu: Nihon no minzoku mondai* (Okinawa and the Ainu: Japan's Ethnic Problem). Tokyo: Shinsensha, 1996.

Sawayanagi Seitarō. "Kyōgaku mondai" (The Problem of Integrated Education). *Chōsen kyōiku* (March 1922): 61–67.

Schleunes, Karl A. *Schooling and Society: The Politics of Education in Prussia and Bavaria.* Oxford: Berg, 1989.

Schmid, Andre. *Korea Between Empires, 1895–1919.* New York: Columbia University Press, 2002.

Schwarz, Bill, ed. *The Expansion of the English Race: Race, Ethnicity, and Cultural History.* London: Routledge, 1996.

Shaarawi, Huda. *Harem Years: The Memoirs of an Egyptian Feminist (1879–1924).* Translated by Margot Badran. London: Virago, 1986.

Shin, Gi-Wook. *Peasant Protest and Social Change in Colonial Korea.* Seattle: University of Washington Press, 1996.

———. *Ethnic Nationalism in Korea: Genealogy, Politics, and Legacy.* Stanford, Calif.: Stanford University Press, 2006.

Shin, Gi-Wook, and Michael Robinson. *Colonial Modernity in Korea.* Cambridge, Mass.: Harvard University Press, 1999.

———. "Introduction: Rethinking Colonial Korea." In *Colonial Modernities,* edited by Gi-wook Shin and Michael Robinson, 1–20. Cambridge, Mass.: Harvard University Press, 1999.

Shin, Yong-ha. *Modern Korean History and Nationalism.* Translated by N. M. Pankaj. Seoul: Jimoondang, 2000.

Shiratori Kurakichi. "Nihon wa hatashite Chōsen wo kanka shiubekika" (Can Japan Inspire Korea?). *Kyōiku jiron* (September 15, 1910): 6–11.

Siddle, Richard. *Race, Resistance, and the Ainu of Japan.* New York: Routledge, 1996.

Silverman, Dan. *Reluctant Union: Alsace-Lorraine and Imperial Germany, 1871–1918.* University Park: Pennsylvania State University Press, 1972.

Simmons, Andrew, ed. *Burt's Letters from the North of Scotland.* Edinburgh: Birlinn Limited, 1998.

Sims, Richard. "France." In *The Iwakura Mission in America and Europe: A New Assessment,* edited by Ian Nish, 69–85. Surrey, U.K.: Japan Library, 1988.

Sin Chubaek, ed. *Ilcheha chibae chŏngch'aek charyojip* (Compilation of Materials on Control Policy under Imperial Japan). 17 vols. Seoul: Koryŏ sŏrim, 1993.

Smith, Woodruff D. *The German Colonial Empire.* Chapel Hill: University of North Carolina Press, 1978.

———. *The Ideological Origins of Nazi Imperialism.* New York: Oxford University Press, 1986.

Sŏul taehakkyo ŭikkwa taehak. *Sŏul taehakkyo ŭikkwa taehaksa* (The History of the

College of Medicine, Seoul National University). Seoul: Sŏul taehakkyo ŭikkwataehak, 1978.

Sowell, Thomas. *Race and Culture: A World View*. New York: Basic Books, 1994.

Spurr, David. *The Rhetoric of Empire: Colonial Discourse in Journalism, Travel Writing, and Imperial Administration*. Durham, N.C.: Duke University Press, 1993.

State-War-Navy Coordinating Committee. "Utilization of Koreans in the War Effort (April 23, 1945)." Compiled in *Haebang chŏnhusa charyojip, I: Mi kunjŏng chunbi charyo* (Collection of Historical Documents around the Time of Liberation, I: Materials for Preparation of United States Military Administration), edited by Yi Kilsang, 253–63. Seoul: Wonjumunhwasa, 1992.

Stoler, Ann L. "Rethinking Colonial Categories: European Communities and the Boundaries of Rule." *Comparative Studies in Society and History* 31, no. 1 (1989): 134–61.

Suyo Yŏksa Yŏn'guhoe, ed. *Singminji Chosŏn kwa Maeil sinbo* (The *Maeil sinbo* and Colonial Korea). Seoul: Sinsŏwŏn, 2003.

Suzuki Kenji. *Nashonarizumu to media* (Nationalism and the Media). Tokyo: Iwanami shoten, 1997.

Tai, Hue-Tam Ho. *Radicalism and the Origins of the Vietnamese Revolution*. Cambridge, Mass.: Harvard University Press, 1996.

Taira, Koji. "Troubled National Identity: The Ryukyuans/Okinawans." In *Japanese Minorities: The Illusion of Homogeneity*, edited by Michael Weiner, 140–77. London: Routledge, 1997.

Takahashi Kamekichi. "Chōsen wa umarefukeru" (Korea Is Reborn). *Kaizō* (April 1935): 47–63.

Takaki, Ronald. *A Different Mirror: A History of Multicultural America*. Boston: Back Bay Books, 1993.

Takasaki Sōji. *Shokuminchi Chōsen no Nihonjin* (Japanese of Colonial Korea). Tokyo: Iwanami shoten, 2002.

Takasaki Sōji and Pak Jonjin, eds. *Kikoku undō to wa nan datta no ka* (What Was the Repatriation Movement?). Tokyo: Heibonsha, 2005.

Takebe Kin'ichi. "Kōmin kyōiku no hitsuyō" (The Necessity of Civic Education). *Bunkyō no Chōsen* (January 1931): 1–3.

Takekoshi, Yosaburō *Japanese Rule over Formosa*. Translation by George Braithwaite. London: Longmans, Green, 1907.

Takenaka Nobuko. *Shokuminchi Taiwan no Nihon josei seikatsushi* (The History of Japanese Women's Lifestyles in the Taiwan Colony). Tokyo: Tabata shoten, 1995.

Tanaka Kōzō. "Kokumin gakkōan no seishin to hantō kyōiku" (The Spirit of the

National School Proposal and Peninsular Education). *Chōsen no kyōiku kenkyū* (September 1939): 23–28.

Tanaka, Stefan. *Japan's Orient: Rendering Pasts into History*. Berkeley: University of California Press, 1993.

Terauchi Masatake. *Terauchi Masatake monjo* (The Official Papers of Terauchi Masatake). Tokyo: Japanese National Diet Library (microfilm).

Thongchai Winichakul. *Siam Mapped: A History of the Geo-Body of a Nation*. Honolulu: University of Hawai'i Press, 1994.

Tipton, Elise K., ed. *Society and State in Interwar Japan*. London: Routledge, 1997.

Toby, Ronald P. *State and Diplomacy in Early Modern Japan: Asia and the Development of the Tokugawa Bakufu*. Stanford, Calif.: Stanford University Press, 1984.

———. "Carnival of the Aliens: Korean Embassies in Edo-Period Art and Popular Culture." *Monumenta Nipponica* 41, no. 4 (1986): 415–56.

Tomiyama, Ichirō. "The Critical Limits of the National Community: The Ryukyuan Subject." *Social Science Japan Journal* 1, no. 2 (1998): 165–79.

Toriga Ramon. *Chōsen e iku hito ni* (To People Going to Korea). Osaka: Hakuaisha joseikappan, 1914.

Totman, Conrad. "Ethnicity in the Meiji Restoration: An Interpretive Essay." *Monumenta Nipponica* 37, no. 3 (Spring 1984): 269–87.

Townsend, Susan. "Yanaihara Tadao and the Irish Question: A Comparative Analysis of the Irish and Korean Questions, 1919–36." *Irish Historical Studies* 30, no. 118 (November 1998): 195–205.

———. *Yanaihara Tadao and Japanese Colonial Policy: Redeeming Empire*. Surrey, U.K.: Curzon Press, 2000.

Trevelyan, Charles. "On the Education of the People of India (1838)." In *The Great Indian Education Debate: Documents Relating to the Orientalist-Anglicist Controversy, 1781–1843*, edited by Lynn Zastoupil and Martin Moir, 281–303. Surrey, U.K.: Curzon Press, 1999.

Trevor-Roper, Hugh. "The Invention of Tradition: The Highland Tradition of Scotland." In *The Invention of Tradition*, edited by Eric Hobsbawm and Terrance Ranger, 14–42. Cambridge: Cambridge University Press, 1992.

Tsunoda, Ryusaku, Wm. Theodore De Bary, and Donald Keene, eds. *Sources of Japanese Tradition*. 2 vols. New York: Columbia University Press, 1958.

Tsurumi, E. Patricia. *Japanese Colonial Education in Taiwan, 1895–1945*. Cambridge, Mass.: Harvard University Press, 1977.

———. "Colonial Education in Korea and Taiwan." In *The Japanese Colonial Empire, 1895–1945*, edited by Ramon H. Myers and Mark R. Peattie, 275–311. Princeton, N.J.: Princeton University Press, 1987.

———. *Factory Girls: Women in the Thread Mills of Meiji Japan*. Princeton, N.J.: Princeton University Press, 1990.

Tsurumi Yūsuke. *Gotō Shinpei*. 2 vols. Tokyo: Sanshūsha, 1937.

Ugaki Kazunari. "Chōsen no shōrai" (Korea's Future). *Ugaki Kazunari Kankei monjo* (Official Papers regarding Ugaki Kazunari). Tokyo: Japanese National Diet Library (microfilm), 1995.

———. "Chōsen tōchi no taidō" (The Great Road of Korean Administration). *Chūō kōron* (January 1934): 85–87.

Unno Fukuju. *Kankoku heigoshi no kenkyū* (Research on the History of Korean Annexation). Tokyo: Iwanami shoten, 2000.

———. *Itō Hirobumi to Kankoku heigō* (Itō Hirobumi and the Annexation of Korea). Tokyo: Aoki shoten, 2004.

Utsumi Aiko. "Korean 'Imperial Soldiers': Remembering Colonialism and Crimes against Allied POWs." In *Perilous Memories: The Asian-Pacific Wars*, edited by T. Fujitani, Geoffrey White, and Lisa Yoneyama, 199–217. Durham, N.C.: Duke University Press, 2001.

Vinogradov, Amal. "French Colonialism as Reflected in the Male-Female Interactions in Morocco." *Transitions of the New York Academy of Sciences* 36, no. 2 (February 1974): 192–99.

Wakabayashi, Bob Tadashi. *Anti-Foreignism and Western Learning in Early Modern Japan: The New Theses of 1825*. Cambridge, Mass.: Harvard University Press, 1991.

Walker, Brett L. *The Conquest of Ainu Lands: Ecology and Culture in Japanese Expansion, 1590–1800*. Berkeley: University of California Press, 2001.

Wattenberg, Ulrich. "Germany: An Encounter Between Two Emerging Countries." In *The Iwakura Mission in America and Europe: A New Assessment*, edited by Ian Nish, 109–22. Surrey, U.K.: Japan Library, 1988.

Weber, Eugen. *Peasants into Frenchmen: The Modernization of Rural France, 1870–1914*. Stanford, Calif.: Stanford University Press, 1976.

Weiner, Michael, ed. *Japanese Minorities: The Illusion of Homogeneity*. London: Routledge, 1997.

Wells, Kenneth M. *New God, New Nation: Protestants and Self-Reconstruction Nationalism in Korea, 1896–1937*. Honolulu: University of Hawai'i Press, 1990.

Williams, Glanmor. *Religion, Language, and Nationality in Wales*. Cardiff: University of Wales Press, 1979.

Wilson, H. H. "Letter to the *Asiatic Journal* concerning the 'Education of the Natives of India' (December 5, 1835)." In *The Great Indian Education Debate: Documents Relating to the Orientalist-Anglicist Controversy, 1781–1843*, edited by Lynn Zastoupil and Martin Moir, 205–24. Surrey, U.K.: Curzon Press, 1999.

Withrington, Donald J. "Education and Society in the Eighteenth Century." In *Scotland in the Age of Improvement*, edited by N. T. Phillipson and Rosalind Mitchison, 169–99. Edinburgh: Edinburgh University Press, 1996.

Wolpe, Harold. "The Theory of Internal Colonialism: The South African Case." In *Beyond the Sociology of Development: Economy and Society in Latin America and Africa*, edited by Ivar Oxaal, Tony Barnett, and David Booth, 229–52. London: Routledge & Kegan Paul, 1975.

Yamada Kanto. *Shokuminchi Chōsen ni okeru Chōsengo shorei seisaku: Chōsengo wo mananda Nihonjin* (Japan's Korean Encouragement Policies in Colonial Korea: Japanese Who Learned the Korean Language). Tokyo: Fuji shuppan, 2004.

Yanaihara Tadao. *Yanaihara Tadao Zenshū* (The Complete Works of Yanaihara Tadao). 29 vols. Edited by Yanaihara Tadao. Tokyo: Iwanami shoten, 1963–65.

Yasuda Toshiaki. *Teikoku Nihon no gengo hensei* (Imperial Japan's Linguistic Formation). Yokohama: Seori shobo, 1997.

Yi Hyŏnsin, ed. *Han'guk kyoyuk charyo chipsŏng* (Korean Education Materials Collection). Sŏngnam: Han'guk chŏngsin munhwa yŏngu won, 1991.

Yi Kilsang, ed. *Haebang chŏnhusa charyojip, I: Mi kunjŏng chunbi charyo* (Collection of Historical Documents around the Time of Liberation, I: Materials for Preparation of United States Military Administration). Seoul: Wŏnju munhwasa, 1992.

Yi Kwangnae. "Ilbon ŭi 'Asia chuŭi' sok eso ŭi Hanguk insik" (Korea in the Context of Japan's Asianism). In *Hanil yangguk ŭi sangho insik* (Shared Perceptions of Korea and Japan), edited by Chŏng Ch'anyong, 203–22. Seoul: Kukhak charyowŏn, 1998.

Yi Kwangsu. *Yi Kwangsu chŏnjip* (Yi Kwangsu's Collected Works), edited by Cho Yuhan et al. Vol. 17. Seoul: Samjungdang 1971.

Yi Pangja. *The World Is One: Princess Yi Pangja's Autobiography.* Translated by Kim Suhkyu. Seoul: Taewon, 1973.

Yi Sukcha. *Kyōkasho ni egakareta Chōsen to Nihon* (Japan and Korea in Textbooks). Tokyo: Horupu shuppan, 1985.

Yi T'ae-jin. *Tōdaisei ni katatta Kankokushi* (Narrating Korean History to Tokyo University Students). Translated by Torikumi Yutaka. Tokyo: Akashi shoten, 2006.

———. *The Dynamics of Confucianism and Modernization in Korean History.* Ithaca, N.Y.: East Asia Program, Cornell University, 2007.

Yi Tong'uk. *Ilchŏngha Tong'a ilbo apsu sasŏljip* (A Collection of Confiscated Editorials of the *Tong'a ilbo*). Seoul: Tong'a ilbo sagan, 1974.

Yi Wŏnsik et al., eds. *Chōsen tsūshinshi to Nihonjin* (History of the Korean Embassies). Tokyo: Gakuseisha, 1996.

Yi Yŏ. *Nihon tōchika Chōsen no genron tōseishi* (Korean Speech Regulation History under Japanese Administration). Tokyo: Shinsansha, 2002.

Yi Yŏngsun. "Naisen yūwa wa doko e?" (Where Is Japanese-Korean Unity?). *Jiyū* (May 1937): 90–92.

Yim, Louise. *My Forty Year Fight for Korea*. Seoul: Chungang University, 1959.

Yŏ Unhyŏng. "Tonggyŏng cheguk hot'el yŏnsŏl yoji" (Fundamental Points of Yŏ's Speech at the Tokyo Imperial Hotel). In Yŏ Unhyŏng, *Mongyong Yŏ Unhyŏng chŏnjip* (Yŏ Unhyŏng Collection, 3 vols., edited by Mongyong Yŏ Unhyŏng chŏnjip Sŏnsaeng Chŏnjip Palgan Wiwŏnhoe. Seoul: Tosŏ ch'ulp'an, 1991.

Yoo, Theodore Jun. *The Politics of Gender in Colonial Korea: Education, Labor, and Health, 1910–1945*. Berkeley: University of California Press, 2008.

Yoshino Sakuzō. "Shina-Chōsen no hannichi to waga kokumin no hansei" (Anti-Japanese [Feeling] in China and Korea and Our People's Reflection about It). *Fujin kōron* (August 1919): 20–26.

———. "Chōsenjin no kidai no zangeki ni tsuite no hansei" (Reflecting on the Korean People's Remarkable Tragedy). *Fujin kōron* (July 1921): 1–4.

Young, Louise. *Japan's Total Empire: Manchuria and the Culture of Wartime Imperialism*. Berkeley: University of California Press, 1998.

Yuasa Katsuei. "Kannani" *and* "Document of Flames": *Two Japanese Colonial Novels*. Translated by Mark Driscoll. Durham, N.C.: Duke University Press, 2005.

Yun Ch'iho. *Yun Ch'iho ilgi* (Yun Ch'iho Diaries). Seoul: Kuksa p'yŏnch'an wiwŏnhoe, 1986.

Yun Kŭnja. *Nihon kokuminron: Kindai Nihon to aidenchichi* (Discourse on the Japanese Nation: Modern Japan and Identity). Tokyo: Chikuma shobō, 1977.

Zastoupil, Lynn, and Martin Moir, eds. *The Great Indian Education Debate: Documents Relating to the Orientalist-Anglicist Controversy, 1781–1843*. Surrey, U.K.: Curzon Press, 1999.

Zureik, Elia T. *The Palestinians in Israel: A Study of Internal Colonialism*. London: Routledge & Kegan Paul, 1979.

NEWSPAPERS AND MAGAZINES

Chōsen

Chōsen kōron

Chōsen oyobi Manshū

Chōsen shinbun

Kyōngnam ilbo

The Independent

Japan Times
Keijō nippō
Korea Daily News
Korea Times
Maeil sinbo
Nihon oyobi Nihonjin
North Wales Times
San Francisco Chronicle
Seoul Press
Siningan
Taiwan kyōkaiho
Taiwan nichi-nichi
Taiyō
The Nation
Tokyo Asahi shinbun
Tokyo keizai shinbun
Tsūrisuto
Yorōzuchōhō

INDEX

Abe Kazunari, 163

Age of Empire, 33

Akagi Kameichi, 116–18, 119

Akashi Genjirō, 85

Algeria/Algerians: annexation of, 16, 32, 216n22; assimilation policy and, 23–24, 222n14; reaction to colonization, 24–26, 45; education policies toward, 35; French images of, 42; as example for Japan, 53, 68, 116, 123, 200; war of liberation, 210

Alsace: as example for Japan, 16, 21, 74, 82, 123; as peripheral colony, 16, 216n22; and Algeria 24; Prussian administration of, 29, 32, 36; reaction to colonization, 45; postwar, 210

Amaterasu Ōmikami, 83

American Civil War, 21, 30, 32

An Ch'angman, 175

Anarchism, 193

Anderson, Benedict, 8

Anglo-Japanese Treaty, 72

Annexation of Korea, 3–5, 18, 89, 212; U.S. policy toward, 15, 113; justifications for, 16, 53, 54, 124, 125; cautions over, 74; treaty of, 82, 101; remembering, 85, 134, 136; Rescript of, 126; Korean support for, 134, 136, 185, 194, 196; *Naisen ittai* and, 151–52; compared with English annexation of Ireland, 179; and Yamagata Aritomo, 205

Aoyagi Tsunatarō, 114–15

Arab-Israelis, 7

Arai Hakuseki, 86

Arakawa Gorō, 91

Arano Yasunori, 13

Arendt, Hannah, 7, 9–10

Aristocratic tour, 106–7

Asahi Kunio, 84

Assimilation: views of colonized, 3–5, 6, 12; in Korea, 6, 17, 18, 82–84, 85, 95–97, 99; philosophy of, 7–8, 10, 42; Great Britain and, 7, 22, 26–29, 44, 47, 202–3, 209; and internal colonization, 9, 10; and peripheral colonization, 10, 211; in Ezo, 14, 53, 62–63, 69; Japan and, 16, 18, 50, 82, 92; Korean views on, 18, 172–74, 185–96, 198, 221n11; Iwakura Mission and, 21, 51–52; history of, 21–22; French and, 22, 31, 35–36, 47, 210, 219n48; arguments against, 23,